Bilingual Figurative Language

Bilingual Figurative Language Processing is a timely book that provides a much-needed bilingual perspective to the broad field of figurative language. This is the first book of its kind to address how bilinguals acquire, store, and process figurative language, such as idiomatic expressions (e.g., *kick the bucket*), metaphors (e.g., *lawyers are sharks*), and irony, and how these tropes might interact in real time across the bilingual's two languages. This volume offers the reader and the bilingual student an overview of the major strands of research, both theoretical and empirical, currently being undertaken in this field of inquiry. At the same time, *Bilingual Figurative Language Processing* provides readers and under-graduate and graduate students with the opportunity to acquire hands-on experience in the development of psycholinguistic experiments in bilingual figurative language. Each chapter includes a section on suggested student research projects. Selected chapters provide detailed procedures on how to design and develop psycholinguistic experiments.

ROBERTO R. HEREDIA, PHD, is professor of psychology in the Department of Psychology and Communication at Texas A&M Inter-national University. He served as chair of the Department of Behavioral Sciences for two years. He is currently the director and principal investigator of a multimillion-dollar grant from the U.S. Department of Education. He has published on bilingual memory, bilingual lexical representation, and bilingual nonliteral language processing. He is coauthor of *Bilingual Sentence Processing; An Introduction to Bilingualism: Principles and Processes*, first edition; and *Foundations of Bilingual Memory*; and he was guest editor for *Experimental Psychology*.

ANNA B. CIEŚLICKA, PHD, is associate professor of psychology in the Department of Psychology and Communication at Texas A&M International University. Her recent publications in *Brain and Language* and the *Journal of Psycholinguistic Research* explore hemispheric differ-ences in the course of bilingual figurative language processing and factors affecting bilingual lexical access, such as language dominance, context, and salience. Dr. Cieślicka is the recipient and principal inves-tigator of a National Science Foundation Major Research Instrumenta-tion research grant to establish the Cognitive Neuroscience Laboratory to study the neurophysiology of bilingual language processing. She is also coeditor of *Methods in Bilingual Reading Comprehension Research*.

Bilingual Figurative Language Processing

Edited by

Roberto R. Heredia
Texas A&M International University

Anna B. Cieślicka
Texas A&M International University

CAMBRIDGE
UNIVERSITY PRESS

CAMBRIDGE
UNIVERSITY PRESS

32 Avenue of the Americas, New York, NY 10013-2473, USA

Cambridge University Press is part of the University of Cambridge.

It furthers the University's mission by disseminating knowledge in the pursuit of education, learning, and research at the highest international levels of excellence.

www.cambridge.org
Information on this title: www.cambridge.org/9781107609501

© Cambridge University Press 2015

First published 2015

Printed in Great Britain by Clays Ltd, St Ives plc

A catalog record for this publication is available from the British Library.

Library of Congress Cataloging in Publication Data
Bilingual figurative language processing / edited by Roberto Heredia, Texas A&M International University; Anna B. Cieslicka, Texas A&M International University.
    p. cm
ISBN 978-1-107-02954-5 (Hardback) – ISBN 978-1-107-60950-1 (Paperback)
1. Language and languages–Study and teaching.   2. Phraseology–Study and teaching.   3. Vocabulary–Study and teaching.   4. Figures of speech.
5. Idioms.   6. Metaphor.   7. Education, Bilingual.   8. Psycholinguistics.
I. Heredia, Roberto R., 1964– editor.   II. Cieslicka, Anna B.   III. Title.
P53.6123.B55 2015
808'.032–dc23   2014035118

ISBN 978-1-107-02954-5 Hardback
ISBN 978-1-107-60950-1 Paperback

Para mamá, papá, y mi hija con mucho cariño
Esperanza Ramírez, Eliseo Heredia, y Andrea T. Heredia

Roberto R. Heredia

Moim najukochańszym Rodzicom, Tamarze i Jerzemu Cieślickim

Anna B. Cieślicka

Contents

SECTION I   Theoretical Implications

SECTION II   Methodological Approaches

SECTION III   Figurative Language Processing

Contributors

ELIF ARICA AKKÖK Linguistics Department, Ankara University, Turkey

OLGA BLANCO-CARRIÓN Departamento de Filologías Inglesa y Alemana, Universidad de Córdoba, Spain

FRANK BOERS School of Linguistics and Applied Language Studies, Victoria University of Wellington, New Zealand

ANDREA BOWES Department of Psychology, St. Thomas University, New Brunswick, Canada

KATARZYNA BROMBEREK-DYZMAN Department of Pragmatics of English, Adam Mickiewicz University, Poznań, Poland

CRISTINA CACCIARI Dipartimento di Scienze Biomediche, Metaboliche e Neuroscienze, Modena, Italy

ANNA B. CIEŚLICKA Department of Psychology and Communication, Texas A&M International University, Laredo, Texas, United States

GEORGIE COLUMBUS Department of Psychology, McGill University, Montreal, Canada

CLAUDIA FELSER University of Potsdam, Potsdam Research Institute for Multilingualism, Germany

OMAR GARCÍA Department of Psychology and Communication, Texas A&M International University, Laredo, Texas, United States

ZAINAB GHAREEB-ALI Department of Language and Linguistics, University of Essex, Colchester, United Kingdom

ROBERTO R. HEREDIA Department of Psychology and Communication, Texas A&M International University, Laredo, Texas, United States

ALBERT KATZ Department of Psychology, University of Western Ontario, London, Canada

ISTVAN KECSKES Department of Educational Theory and Practice, University at Albany, State University of New York (SUNY), Albany, New York, United States

ZOLTÁN KÖVECSES Department of American Studies, Eötvös Loránd University, Hungary

MAYA LIBBEN Department of Psychology, McGill University, Montreal, Canada

JOHN I. LIONTAS Department of Secondary Education, University of South Florida, Lakeland, Florida, United States

BELEM G. LÓPEZ Department of Psychology, Texas A&M University, College Station, Texas, United States

FRANCISCO E. MARTÍNEZ Department of Psychology, Texas A&M University, College Station, Texas, United States

JULIE MERCIER Department of Psychology, McGill University, Montreal, Canada

MÓNICA E. MUÑOZ Department of Psychology and Communication, Texas A&M International University, Laredo, Texas, United States

ESZTER NUCZ Corvinus University of Budapest, Hungary

SILKE PAULMANN Department of Psychology, University of Essex, Colchester, United Kingdom

RÉKA SZABÓ Research Institute for Linguistics, Hungarian Academy of Sciences, Hungary

VERONIKA SZELID Szent Margit Gimnázium, Hungary

DEBRA TITONE Department of Psychology, McGill University, Montreal, Canada

JYOTSNA VAID Department of Psychology, Texas A&M University, College Station, Texas, United States

STUART WEBB School of Linguistics and Applied Language Studies, Victoria University of Wellington, New Zealand

VERONICA WHITFORD Department of Psychology, McGill University, Montreal, Canada

Acknowledgments

Our *Thank you!* to the many people who helped us directly and indirectly in the completion of this book. First, we thank Cambridge University Press for catching the vision of this unique work on *nonliteral language in the bilingual mind*. Also, we would like to express our gratitude to the contributors, our friends and colleagues, who were extremely cooperative in meeting our deadlines and graciously incorporated some of our sometimes "interesting" suggestions into their chapters. I, Roberto, dedicate this volume to my family: Esperanza Ramírez (mi mamá), Eliseo Heredia (¡un gran tipo mi Viejo!), mi chilpayatl Tonantzin Cihuacóatl, my beloved Michelle, mis adoradas hermanas y querido hermano, mis sobrinos y sobrinas (¡que son muchos!), Fiona, Mocha, and Ceci, *mi gallinita de los huevos de oro!* I am grateful to my students (Wualú A. Altamira, Valeria González, Jacklyn Orr, and Nelsa Liendo), my dear friends and colleagues (Dan Mott, Peter Haruna, Bonnie Rudolph, Mónica Muñoz, Jeffrey M. Brown), and my co-author Anula!

I, Anna, would like to dedicate this volume to my beloved parents, Jerzy and Tamara Cieśliccy, and my very dear sister Iwona Sobolewska, whose love, support, and pride in my work have been a rock in this journey through life and a motivation to never stop pursuing my dreams. *Moi Kochani, odległość nie ma znaczenia- jesteście tu ze mną każdego dnia, far away and yet so close!* I thank my dear friends and colleagues at Texas A&M International University, Bonnie Rudolph, Mónica Muñoz, William Manger II, and Robe, my co-author, for making me feel welcome here in Laredo, which has become my second home. Our wonderful students at TAMIU are a never-ending source of inspiration and motivation and have immensely contributed to the idea of this volume, so they deserve heartfelt thanks for their intellectual curiosity and for stimulating us to ask new research questions. My academic journey started in Poland, at the School of English, Adam Mickiewicz University, where my research ideas first developed and matured through discussions with friends and colleagues. They are too many to name, so I will simply say *dziękuję Wam wszystkim* and you all know who you are. Last, but not least, I need to thank my cats, Kacper, Bambi, Daktyl, Chmurka, and Pisia, whose purring and warm presence on, at, under, and behind my desk have made long hours spent at the computer a pleasurable experience.

The writing of this book was in part supported by grant P031M105048 from the U.S. Department of Education, Promoting Postbaccalaureate Opportunities for Hispanic Americans Program (Title V Part B). Finally, we wish to acknowledge all our past and present undergraduate and graduate students, our colleagues and friends, too numerous to name, and our wonderful families – related, extended throughout the world (in Poland and Mexico). It is their love and support that always motivates and encourages us. *Con mucho cariño para todos ustedes! Z najserdeczniejszymi podziękowaniami dla Was wszystkich! With gratitude and thanks to all of you!*

Con el cariño de siempre,
Roberto R. Heredia and
Anna B. Cieślicka

Foreword

Writing a foreword to a book on two of the most complex topics of the research on language processing – figurative language and bilingualism – is quite an endeavor, especially when the volume provides an up-to-date, comprehensive theoretical and experimental treatment of the topic. It is not by accident that in a foreword to a book on idiomatic expressions of some decades ago (Cacciari & Tabossi, 1993) Phil Johnson-Laird used the comprehension of idiomatic expressions in another language as an example of the complexity and elusiveness of nonliteral language: "We have the ability to speak in riddles. These riddles are neither constructed nor interpreted in the normal way. Yet we use them so readily that we are usually unaware of their special character – unless we have the misfortune not to be a native speaker. We call these special riddles idioms" (Johnson-Laird, 1993).

According to the philosopher John Searle (1979), American English native speakers adopt the following adagio in everyday conversations, *Speak idiomatically unless there is some special reason not to.* That this indeed is the case is confirmed by simple frequency counts estimating that figurative expressions, notably idioms, are as frequent as words (Jackendoff, 1995) and by the common observation that the presence of an idiom often remains unnoticed by native speakers. Searle's claim parallels what Sinclair (1991) called the *Idiom Principle* (see Kecskes, this volume), according to which subjects use formulaic language as much as possible to increase communicative efficiency, at the same time reducing the cognitive load on receivers (see, for example, Siyanova-Chanturia & Martinez, 2014).

However, non-native use of nonliteral expressions (especially in late second language [L2] learners) seems to defy Searle and Sinclair's assumption. In fact, even advanced L2 users are known to have difficulties with nonliteral language, such that using and comprehending figurative language effortlessly constitute a test of how fluent and native-like an L2 speaker is or thinks he or she is. Understanding and moreover producing idiomatic expressions in L2 is a challenge even for proficient L2 speakers, and it seems even more challenging than understating metaphors in L2. Why is it so? Idiomatic expressions, unlike metaphors, belong to the vast family of multiword expressions that are conventional, over-learned literal and nonliteral sequences of words whose representations are stored in semantic, long-term memory. One may argue that by definition idiomatic expressions reflect cultural motives and habits, pieces of local history, and so forth that are grounded in tradition and culture underlying a specific language. According to the *Oxford Dictionary*, 5th ed., one of the meanings of the word *idiom* is *form of expression peculiar to a language*. One possibility is that proficient L2 speakers would be reluctant to use idioms not because of lexico-semantic limitations, but because they ignore the cultural background that motivated the appearance of a specific idiom in a language and/or its contextual appropriateness. However, lack of etymological/cultural awareness may not be the entire story, given that also many native speakers ignore the cultural origin of idioms they still commonly use. A more appealing alternative is that, beyond linguistic etymology, idiomatic expressions may reflect the conceptual metaphors we live by, as argued by *Conceptual Metaphor* theorists (e.g., Gibbs, 1994; Lakoff & Johnson, 1980). They argued that the mapping between an idiom and its meaning is motivated by pre-existing metaphorical connections between conceptual templates and images. Hence, regardless of specific language-based wording, idiomatic expressions would put into words a conceptual apparatus that in principle should not be language-specific but grounded in experiential, sensory domains (although some conceptual metaphors may be more salient in one language than in another). Whether this is indeed the case is still controversial, and evidence has accumulated showing that "instead of serving as a linguistic window onto conceptual structure, idiomatic expressions may mirror the content put into them. And just like mirrors, they might be mistaken for windows" (Keysar & Bly, 1999).

It is undeniable that so far idiom processing models have been built on evidence gathered from first language (L1) speakers. Even though the first hypotheses on idiom comprehension date back to the 1970s, we still are far from having a unified account of idiom processing in L1, and still little is known on idiom (and more generally on nonliteral language) processing in L2. This may in part reflect the fact that idioms form a rather heterogeneous family that differs on a number of characteristics that include frequency, predictability, ambiguity, literal plausibility, affective valence, semantic transparency, and decomposability, to name only some. Explaining how individuals who form the community of L2 speakers produce and comprehend idiomatic expressions constitutes a real challenge that may importantly contribute also to L1 idiom processing models. This is one of the reasons why this is an important book that further contributes to showing that figurative language is not a peripheral phenomenon that language theories may ignore, as it was believed in the early 1990s. Another, and perhaps the most important, reason why this volume is indeed an impressive achievement and a major contribution to the field, is that it uniquely fills a crucial gap. In fact, so far the complex links between bilingualism and figurative language processing were totally ignored by important books and textbooks on figurative language comprehension and production, and also by recent important handbooks on language and cognition in bilinguals.

What we know now for sure is that idioms are good candidates for revealing the repertoire of strategies for making sense of linguistic expressions in L1 as well as in L2. In L2, this repertoire encompasses several different strategies that go from assuming that any incomprehensible expressions one runs across in discourse may be an idiom to the presence of *idiom-prone* lexemes (e.g., *take*, *put*, *get* in English) that we probabilistically associate to nonliteral expressions, from looking at whether an idiom string with similar wording exists in L1 to computing the semantic interpretation of the string trying to infer the potential nonliteral meaning (a hardly successful strategy with many idioms). Another thing that we know for sure is that during L1 online idiom processing at least part of the constituent word meanings are activated. In fact, idioms are not semantically empty strings, as posited by early models of idiom comprehension. This raises a number of interesting questions concerning idiom processing in both L1 and L2. For instance, due to a general between-language transfer mechanism, well known in the bilingualism literature, both comprehension and production of L2 idioms are modulated by the degree of idiom similarity to their L1 translation equivalents (see the *Parasitic Hypothesis*, Cieślicka, this volume). This does not necessarily lead to improvements in the capacity of L2 learners to understand idioms and/or use them appropriately, because cross-language similarities may cause interference and misunderstanding. Whether transfer from L1 to L2 reflects pure retrieval of stored units from semantic memory or is mediated by words and conceptual structures is still an open issue, as is the issue of whether subjects differentially use compositional versus direct retrieval strategies in comprehending idioms in their L1 and L2. In fact, L2 speakers, unlike L1 speakers, may be more inclined to process idioms, and in general multiword units, analytically/compositionally rather than globally. They would activate the literal meaning of idiom constituent words because they did not recognize at all the presence of an idiom in a sentence, or they did it to a lesser extent and not as easily and early on as L1 speakers. But this is indeed a "double-edged sword" (Boers & Webb, this volume), because idiom semantic transparency is often illusory when one does not know the conventionalized idiom meaning. Indeed, we are often able to trace back the motivation for an idiomatic meaning based on the constituent word meanings and the rhetorical structure underlying the idiom string because we already know what the idiom means. This was already noted years ago by Reagan (1987), who claimed that, when faced with idioms (and in general with multiword units, I would add), we should distinguish between *breaking down* meaning into parts and *building up* meaning from parts.

Intuition as well as experimental evidence suggests that L2 knowledge (proficiency) affects the comprehension of literal and nonliteral language. Interestingly, some processing differences seem to exist among different types of nonliteral expressions, in that proficient bilinguals seem to understand metaphors and irony (but not idioms) not dissimilarly from monolinguals, although in general at a slower pace. That metaphorical meanings may be easier to grasp than conventionalized idiomatic meanings may not be surprising if one considers that metaphors are assertions of categorization similar to those conveyed by literal language (Glucksberg, 2001). In fact, metaphors are used not simply to call the reader's attention to superficial similarity between concepts, but rather to label categories that have no conventional names of their own. Some of the contributors to this book highlighted that still more experimental work with online experimental paradigms and L2 participants with similar characteristics (e.g., proficiency, language exposure, and context) is needed to obtain a more thorough understanding of nonliteral processing in L2. Notwithstanding this prudential stance, the chapters collected in this book show that some of the mysteries that characterize figurative language have started to be unveiled. The endeavor is not an easy one, if it is true that, as Donald Davidson (1978) argued years ago for metaphors, figurative language *is the dreamwork of language and, like all dreamwork, its interpretation reflects as much on the interpreter as on the originator. The interpretation of dreams requires collaboration between a dreamer and a waker ... So too understanding a metaphor is as much a creative endeavor as making a metaphor, and as little guided by the rules.*

Cristina Cacciari

REFERENCES

Cacciari, C., & Tabossi, P. (1993). *Idioms: Processing, structure and interpretation.* Hillsdale, NJ: Erlbaum.

Davidson, D. (1978). What metaphors mean. In S. Sacks (Ed.), *On metaphor* (pp. 29–46). Chicago, IL: The University of Chicago Press.

Gibbs, W.R. (1994). *The poetics of mind: Figurative thought, language and understanding.* Cambridge, UK: Cambridge University Press.

Glucksberg, S. (2001). *Understanding figurative language.* New York: Oxford University Press.

Jackendoff, R. (1995). The boundaries of the lexicon. In M. Everaert, E. van der Linden, A. Schenk, & R. Schreuder (Eds.), *Idioms: Structural and psychological perspectives* (pp. 133–166). Hillsdale, NJ: Erlbaum.

Johnson-Laird, P.N. (1993). Foreword. In C. Cacciari & P. Tabossi (Eds.), *Idioms: Processing, structure and interpretation* (pp. vii–x). Hillsdale, NJ: Erlbaum.

Keysar, B., & Bly, B. (1999). Swimming against the current: Do idioms reflect conceptual structure? *Journal of Pragmatics, 38,* 1559–1578.

Lakoff, G., & Johnson, M. (1980). *Metaphors we live by.* Chicago, IL: The University of Chicago Press.

Reagan, R.T. (1987). The syntax of English idioms: Can the dog be put on? *Journal of Psycholinguistic Research, 16,* 417–441.

Searle, J.R. (1979). *Expression and meaning: Studies in the theory of speech acts.* Cambridge, UK: Cambridge University Press.

Sinclair, J. (1991). *Corpus, concordance, collocation.* Oxford, UK: Oxford University Press.

Siyanova-Chanturia, A., & Martinez, R. (2014). The Idiom Principle revisited. *Applied Linguistics, 1,* 1–22. doi:10.1093/applin/amt054.

Preface

The presentation of a volume on *bilingual figurative language processing* is timely and provides a much-needed bilingual perspective in the broad field of figurative language. *Bilingual Figurative Language Processing* is the first book of its kind to address how bilinguals acquire, store, and process figurative language, such as idiomatic expressions (e.g., *kick the bucket*), metaphors (e.g., *lawyers are sharks*), and irony, and how these tropes might interact in real time across the bilingual's two languages.

It is our hope that this book contributes to the development and establishment of *bilingual figurative language* as a subfield of bilingual sentence processing and fills a significant gap in the literature on bilingual language processing and thought. *Bilingual Figurative Language Processing* offers the reader and the bilingual student an overview of the major strands of research, both theoretical and empirical, currently being undertaken in this field of enquiry. At the same time, *Bilingual Figurative Language Processing* provides readers and undergraduate/graduate students with the opportunity to acquire *hands-on* experience in the development of psycholinguistic experiments in bilingual figurative language. Each chapter is composed of a *Suggested Student Research Projects* section. Selected chapters include detailed procedures on how to design and develop psycholinguistic experiments using sample scripts from experiment builder software (e.g., E-Prime, PsyScope).

Bilingual Figurative Language Processing is divided into four main sections. The first section (Chapters 1–3) focuses on the theoretical underpinnings of figurative language processing and bilingualism. After a compelling argument of the embodiment of language, namely, that language comprehension is inextricably tied to a relationship between bodily experiences and language, Katz and Bowes (Chapter 1) underscore the limited literature on bilingual nonliteral language processing and bilingual language embodiment in particular. They go on to ask whether bilinguals who learned their two languages simultaneously might evoke similar embodied structures, as opposed to late bilinguals (who learned their second language later in life), who might elicit dissimilar embodied structures. One possibility, of course, is that it would depend on the type of conceptual metaphor. Conceptual metaphors such as LIFE IS A JOURNEY, that are more likely to be universal, might be understood similarly across the different types of bilinguals (see, for example, Kövecses et al., this volume). However, as accurately put by Katz and Bowes, "the future in this domain [i.e., bilingualism and language embodiment] is at our fingertips, all we have to do now is grasp it" (p. 17). In the second chapter, Kecskes hypothesizes whether the *idiom principle* that drives word selection in monolinguals is impaired in the bilingual's second language (L2; see also Siyanova-Chanturia & Martinez, 2014). Accordingly, users of a language (typically the first language) have access to a large number of semi-preconstructed phrases or chunks that they may use during the communicative process to ease cognitive load and processing effort. Kecskes concludes that the idiom principle does indeed affect the use of any language of bilinguals or multilinguals. However, L2 factors such as language proficiency and willingness to use certain formulas affect the functioning of the idiom principle. In the third chapter, Vaid et al. examine metaphoric processing by bilingual speakers and conclude that, like findings in the monolingual literature, nonliteral activation is obligatory. Moreover, Vaid et al.'s contribution goes on to examine the relationship between figurative language, humor processing, and creativity.

Section II (Chapters 4–5) critically discusses some of the methodologies employed for studying the ongoing psychological processes taking place as bilinguals comprehend/process figurative language. Heredia and Muñoz (Chapter 3) examine the online comprehension of metaphoric reference, where a metaphoric description (e.g., *creampuff*) makes a reference to an antecedent describing a *cowardly boxer*. Using a cross-modal priming task and measuring meaning activation (i.e., nonliteral vs. literal) for a metaphoric referential description across critical locations throughout a sentence, Heredia and Muñoz show contrasting figurative language processing differences between highly proficient bilinguals immersed in a linguistic environment in which the L2 is dominant, and bilinguals in a "purely" bilingual community. García et al. (Chapter 5) critically review some of the classic behavioral reading paradigms such as *rapid serial visual presentation, visual moving windows*, and other newly developed techniques, such as the *maze task*, as well as eye-tracking. García et al. further elaborate on the *cross-modal lexical priming task* (CMLP), and *event-related potentials*, and make a clear distinction between *offline* (e.g., rating, interpretation) and *online* (e.g., CMLP, eye tracking) tasks and the mental/linguistic processes involved in/tapped by these tasks.

Section III (Chapters 6–9) focuses on language processing and provides a general overview of some of the existing models of bilingual figurative language processing. Titone et al. (Chapter 6) provide an excellent overview of what is currently known about bilingual idiom processing. They specifically introduce the *Constraint-Based Processing Model of L2*, which hypothesizes that, during idiom comprehension, bilinguals, like monolinguals, simultaneously make use of all the available information (e.g., idiom familiarity or predictability), resulting both from direct retrieval and compositional analysis of idiomatic expressions. Cieślicka (Chapter 7) further elaborates on bilingual figurative language comprehension and shows how a bilingual idiom-processing model that relies on the literal analysis of L2 idioms (i.e., *Literal Salience Model*) accounts for the acquisition and processing of idiomatic expressions by foreign language learners. In addition to reviewing a range of factors (e.g., cross-linguistic similarity, literal plausibility, predictability) influencing idiom processing, Cieślicka discusses some of the classic theories of L2 lexical acquisition (e.g., *Parasitic Hypothesis* of vocabulary development). Using *event-related potentials*, Paulmann et al. (Chapter 8) investigate phrasal verbs in monolinguals and bilinguals. Phrasal verbs (e.g., *run into*), like idiomatic expressions, are ambiguous and can be understood literally (e.g., *to go inside: He ran into the building*) or figuratively (e.g., *to meet someone: He ran into his old friend*). Paulmann et al.'s results reveal that comprehension of phrasal verbs is not necessarily problematic for proficient L2 learners of English. Their overarching conclusion is that non-native but proficient speakers of English use processing strategies similar to those of native speakers when comprehending phrasal verbs. In Chapter 9, Bromberek-Dyzman provides an excellent review of irony processing research and offers evidence showing that it is not so much the literal/nonliteral language distinction that determines irony processing patterns in L1 and L2, but rather its affective meaning.

The fourth and final section focuses on cross-linguistic perspectives and pedagogical issues, such as how best to acquire figurative competency. Liontas (Chapter 10) investigates the effects of different tasks and idiom subtypes on the comprehension and production of L2 idioms by adult foreign language learners. More importantly, the chapter identifies essential research questions that need to be addressed by L2 idiom scholars in order to develop the most appropriate instructional interventions and make the process of L2 idiom learning more efficient. Kövecses et al. (Chapter 11) further expand on the concept of language embodiment. Using a corpus-linguistic and *cognitive linguistics approach*,

Kövecses et al.'s goal in this chapter is to investigate how the emotion of *anger* is conceptualized across American English, Spanish, Turkish, and Hungarian. Kövecses et al.'s overall conclusion is that in all four languages considered in their study, people have remarkably similar cultural models of anger. In addition, Kövecses et al. propose a novel measure of metaphorical salience that allows capturing how conceptual metaphors are used to comprehend different target domains. The major components of this measure are token frequency, type frequency, the number of mappings, and the scope of the source domain. In the last chapter, Boers and Webb explore the dimension of semantic transparency of idioms and its usefulness in L2 teaching. While capitalizing on L2 learners' propensity to interpret idiomatic expressions literally has been favored by L2 materials writers, the authors caution against applying this pedagogical technique indiscriminately, without first considering learners' intuitions and their L1 cultural background. Based on their study, Boers and Webb show how judgments of semantic transparency can be divergent for native speaker teachers, on the one hand, and L2 learners on another.

We would be remiss if we failed to mention that our intense interest in *bilingual figurative language processing* is in large part due to our fascination with the way the human mind in general, and the bilingual mind in particular, works. Language is at the core of human experience, thus exploring the architecture of the mental lexicon provides us with a unique insight into how the mind organizes the linguistic universe. Despite the inherently ambiguous nature of figurative expressions, they are understood effortlessly by language users, given their pervasiveness in everyday communication. Exploring the mechanisms that lie at the core of figurative language acquisition, storage, and processing might hence enrich the scientific understanding of how the human mind works.

Finally, rather than trying to provide a set of definitive answers, this volume aims at stimulating a critical discussion and inspiring further research into the mechanisms underlying bilingual figurative language processing. As Honeck and Hoffman (1980, p. 3) aptly put it, "Research on figurative language is fun. It leads one to find all sorts of intriguing phenomena." It is hoped that the current volume indeed provides the bilingual student, teacher, and researcher with much fun and inspiration to further explore the fascinating intricacies of the bilingual mind.

Roberto R. Heredia
Anna B. Cieślicka

REFERENCES

Honeck, R.P., & Hoffman, R.R. (Eds.). (1980). *Cognition and figurative language*. Hillsdale, NJ: Lawrence Erlbaum Associates.

Siyanova-Chanturia, A., & Martinez, R. (2014). The idiom principle revisited. *Applied Linguistics*, 1–22. doi:10.1093/applin/amt054.

Section I

Theoretical Implications

1   Embodiment in Metaphor and (Not?) in Bilingual Language

Albert Katz[1] and Andrea Bowes[2]
[1]University of Western Ontario; [2]St. Thomas University

ABSTRACT

In this chapter we look at the role that sensory motor activation plays in the understanding of figurative and bilingual language. The chapter is divided into three basic parts. First we examine what is known about the evolution of human language, with reference to figurative and bilingual language activities, emphasizing the emerging conceptualization that sensory-motor brain areas have played a vital role. In the next section we examine how this emerging conceptualization that language might be embodied has been translated into our understanding of online comprehension tasks in general and, increasingly, in grounding our understanding of figurative language. The last section examines how the notion of embodied cognition has been viewed in our understanding of bilingual language, noting the near absence of a relevant literature. We conclude by indicating some aspects of the archival bilingual processing literature that could benefit from taking an embodied perspective.

Keywords: bilingual embodiment, embodied cognition, figurative language, language evolution, metaphor processing

The classic approach in both the study of bilingualism and of figurative language has taken an amodal computational perspective. From this perspective, these models have been based on the assumption that the basic representational aspects of language are tied to symbols, which themselves are not tied to direct experience with the environments in which they have developed and in which they are expressed. In contrast, starting about a decade or so ago, an alternative approach has emerged in which language comprehension is directly and inextricably tied to a relationship between bodily experiences and language. In this chapter we will engage in a form of *science fiction* in which we examine what modern biological psychology, cognitive science, and cognitive neuroscience suggest about the embodiment of language in general, the inroads that embodied cognition has made into our understanding of figurative

3

language, and the seeming lack of the same in our understanding of bilingual cognition. We end by suggesting some possible ways to look at questions relevant to the bilingual experience from an embodied perspective.

The Evolution of the Modern Human Brain and Human Language Abilities

The human brain has evolved considerably over the 5 to 6 million years since we diverged into the lineages that led to our species, *Homo sapiens*, and to that of the modern-day chimp (our closest living relative). Anthropologists (e.g., Walker & Shipman, 1996), linguists (e.g., Bickerton, 1990) and psychologists (e.g., Pinker, 1994) alike have examined the fossil and artifact record as a means of understanding the evolution of language, often taken as the most important precursor to the development of culture. The emphasis has been largely on the emergence of grammar and here, implicitly or explicitly adopted the classic amodal approach to cognition.

Interestingly, the discussion of language has taken place in intellectual silos, with, for instance, little cross talk between those interested in bilingualism and those interested in metaphor or irony. Even though the basic research questions asked by inhabitants of each silo appear to be similar, they differ in important ways. Researchers in both camps, for instance, are interested in the nature of the underlying meaning representation and the processes that work on that representation. However, in one case the question is framed as the distinction between the literal and nonliteral or between metaphors as expressions versus metaphors as conceptual structures and, in the other, as whether bilingual language users share the same basic structures as monolingual users, or whether language activation in one language automatically activates meaning in the other. With respect to generalizability, scholars from both silos argue for the importance of linguistic flexibility, but in one case the emphasis is on whether being bilingual creates expertise that enhances domain-general cognitive control (and hence facilitated performance on tasks ostensibly unrelated to language use *per se*) and, in the other, the notion that metaphor is a tool that can be used to think creatively. Here we take the position that insight from the metaphor literature, especially from recent examinations of embodiment in metaphor, might provide insights into the other silo and provide unexplored avenues for future research into bilingualism. Theories of embodied cognition posit that just as physical acts (e.g., combing one's hair) or emotions (e.g., feeling happy) are tied to sensory-emotive-motor neural systems, these systems are involved even when one is not doing the acts or feeling the emotions but is merely thinking, reading, or hearing about them.

The Evolution of the Lingual Brain

A *standard* version of language evolution has held that the growth of language abilities over time was somewhat discontinuous and especially was associated with two important cultural changes, both associated with corresponding increases in brain size (see Bickerton, 1990; Lieberman, 1991). From this perspective, the first of these evolutionary crossroads started approximately 1.8 million years ago with the emergence of *Homo erectus*, the first hominid to spread out of Africa, and with a brain size that would put it within the low-end of variability that is found in modern humans. Bickerton has speculated, as did Walker and Shipman (1996), that *Homo erectus* might have developed what he calls *protolanguage*. Protolanguage, Bickerton argues, is nonsyntactic with the form, *Me Tarzan, Jane run*. Presumably comprehension would be very context-dependent so that to understand the utterance one would have to be aware of the situation in which it is being produced. The evidence Bickerton employs to bolster his speculation is that protolanguage speech in modern humans can be found under special situations, such as with the creation of pidgin languages or with adults deprived of language as children during a critical period of development. Walker and Shipman employ anthropological evidence, such as evidence of coordinated hunting activities, to support the notion that *Homo erectus* had protolanguage.

The second phase is associated with the emergence of *true* grammatical language, which they claim is coincident with the emergence of our species. By about 200,000 years ago *Homo sapiens* had the anatomical structure to support language production, especially modification to the vocal tract. Somewhere between 50,000 to 25,000 years ago, there was an explosion in human symbolic expression available in the physical record, with symbolic representations involving carvings, beads, fanciful imaginative creatures, and well-known cave paintings. It is argued that by that time in our evolutionary history those humans had developed syntactic-based language, had the cognitive abilities to communicate nonliterally, and demonstrated symbolic activities. From this perspective, by that time humans had the flexibility to talk and conceptualize free of the immediate context. Presumably, we would now be able to go beyond stating *Me Tarzan, Jane run* to talk about the *when, where, how* and often in the nonliteral manner characteristic of modern language (for instance describing, *I will run toward Jane tomorrow* or *I, Tarzan, saw Jane run away from danger* or *Jane, I am no good for you and if you had any sense you'd run as far away from me as you can*, or maybe even *Jane you should know I have had a run of good luck in hunting this past season and would make for a passably good mate*).

In recent years, this two-stage version of language evolution has been challenged by novel advances in the neurosciences and in comparative animal studies. Two important characteristics of this challenge are that more emphasis is given to the continuity of language evolution and, second, to grounding our understanding of language evolution with *embodied cognition*. One such independent line of inquiry into understanding the unique cognitive and linguistic characteristics of the human brain is based on cataloging the conceptual abilities of monkeys and apes, including those of our nearest living relative, the chimpanzee. In essence, this line of research has attempted to find evidence that nonhuman animals possess some cognitive capabilities important for language (and, by implication, that these functions were available for evolutionary selection and adaptation in a distant shared ancestor). Among such characteristics would be the ability to imitate the actions of conspecifics or behaviors that provide evidence for *Theory of Mind* (ToM), or beliefs about the mental states with which one is interacting. Premack (2004) indicates that nonhuman primates possess a set of pragmatic communicative functions. The suggestion that nonhuman primates may share some of these abilities suggests that some components of nonliteral speech are not dependent on the emergence of so-called true or syntax-based language. The ability to represent the mental states of interlocutors is especially important with the use (and understanding) of nonliteral language because what one expresses literally with such language often will not correspond with what one is intending. One could expect the same argument should be advanced in bilingual communication, given the increased possibility of miscommunication when one is talking in one's second language (L2) or to a bilingual person in his or her L2.

With respect to brain locus of ToM, there is emerging evidence in the literature of the involvement of many neural systems. Evidence from people with autism (who perform poorly on ToM tasks) and from studies of nonhuman primates implicates subcortical circuits (in the amygdala) as being the core or central to a ToM system, with secondary systems in the frontal lobe (that subserve executive functioning), areas of the right temporal-parietal cortex important for visuospatial processing, and language-related regions of the left hemisphere (Siegel & Varley, 2002). A viable possibility is that ToM involves a simulation in which motor or emotion facial cues exhibited by an interlocutor evoke analogous areas in one's own brain. As will be discussed shortly, there is evidence that ToM

plays a role in metaphor processing even when people are not in interactive communication (Bowes, 2013).

A second line of evidence can be found in the study of human and
nonhuman genomes. Fisher and Marcus (2005) review some of these
data. Genomic sequencing "yields a catalogue of almost every sequence
differences that distinguishes a human from a chimpanzee" (p. 10), our
closest living hominid relative. Using these data and those derived from
within-species diversity in human populations, one can sometimes make
inferences about which allele represents the state that was present in the
common ancestor shared by humans and chimps. Examining people
with language disorders provides a strategy in identifying specific genes
to examine in more depth. For instance, there is evidence that children
affected with a FOXP2 gene mutation have problems with speech
articulation, even for those with normal nonverbal intelligence. Modeling
data estimates that the gene was subject to evolutionary selection about
200,000 years ago, about the time that modern humans emerged,
although some estimates push back that date considerably earlier (see
Newbury, Fisher, & Monaco, 2010). As Fisher and Marcus state, ". . . a
compelling hypothesis is that earlier forms of the gene were important for
shaping cortical and subcortical sensory-motor networks; circuits which
were subsequently recruited on more than one occasion, to sub-serve
learning and production of complex combinatorial sequences of movements" (p. 17). The FOXP2 gene is known to encode a transcription
factor that regulates the expression of other genes, including a gene on
Chromosome 7, the CNTNAP2 gene, which has been shown to be
associated with a range of disorders, including autism. Interestingly,
the gene is also associated with personality dimensions, such as openness
to experience (Newbury et al., 2010).

A third line of evidence comes from scientists who use brain imaging
technology on modern humans to make inferences about our hominid
ancestors. For instance, Stout, Toth, Schick, and Chaminade (2008)
employed *positron emission tomography* (PET) scans to examine modern
expert stone tool makers using the older *Oldowan* and the later *Ache lean*
techniques found in the archeological record from roughly 2.6 million to
about 250,000 years ago. For the more sophisticated stone tool creation,
an increasing engagement of neural circuits was found with visuomotor
coordination and hierarchical action organization. There is an overlap
with neural circuits found with language, "strongly suggesting that these
behaviors share a foundation in more general human capacities for
complex, goal-directed action and are likely to have evolved in a mutually
reinforcing way" (p. 1947). Interestingly, some of this circuitry is in the
right hemisphere homologue of Broca's area and the authors note further

that the right hemisphere "plays an important role in language processing particularly with respect to large scale phenomena such as metaphor, figurative language, connotative meaning, prosody and discourse comprehension" (p. 1947). This is not to suggest that metaphor was being employed in the early Stone Age but rather than the incipient capabilities were available for evolutionary adaptation even in nonhuman hominid species.

All these quite disparate lines of evidence point to a relation between language and motor activities. Fogassi and Ferrari (2012) review the available evidence from an evolutionary perspective. Work with monkeys has demonstrated that neurons in the premotor cortex (Brodmann's area, F5) are activated during goal-related activities and conclude that all "these studies strongly demonstrate that the main role of the motor cortex is coding goals" (p. 310). A major discovery has been the identification of mirror neurons in F5 and in the inferior parietal lobe. Mirror neurons discharge both when the monkey performs a given activity and, importantly, when it observes the same or similar activity performed by another monkey or by a human experimenter. Some research has shown that these neurons discharge even when only listening to the sound produced by that activity. Imaging techniques have shown the presence of mirror neurons in humans, including areas 44 and 45 in the inferior frontal gyrus, which in the left hemisphere corresponds to Broca's area. As Fogassi and Ferrari (2012) stated,

Summing up, in monkey premotor cortex there are several features that can pre-adapt this cortical sector for the evolution of a sophisticated communicative system. The core of these features consists in encoding the production and perception of both oro-facial and forelimb gestures in the same cortical area. This double control, once integrated with vocalization, would have constituted the basis for a communicative system with an increased complexity and efficiency, and a higher level of flexibility in transferring information to conspecifics (p. 322).

They go on to state, "... there is much evidence that language and gestures share a common motor code, thus supporting several theories proposing that at cortical level some of the properties and organization of the motor system have been exploited within the vocal domain" (p. 325). And they claim further

Both the order of a motor series and the organization of natural action sequence can be coded by cortical single neurons. The premotor-parietal motor system plus the prefrontal cortex can provide a substrate for sequential organization and hierarchical combination of motor elements. We posit that such an organization has been exploited in other domains including some aspects of the syntactic structure of language (p. 326).

In summary, these disparate lines of research suggest an important link between motor brain areas and language that have a cognitive basis that go beyond that necessary to produce the motor sequences found in speech. In a subsequent section, we will examine behavioral data that indicates an important embodied element in language comprehension.

The Evolution of the Bilingual Brain

The discussion of language evolution is almost completely mute on the bilingual capacity of the human brain. This is not surprising if we assume that the brain evolved as a flexible multipurpose language machine capable of picking up whatever language was employed in a given linguistic community, as is the standard linguistic assumption. The speculations that have emerged come from anthropologists and ecological psychologists, who consider the adaptive value of being multilingual.

A basic assumption is that for much of our evolutionary history humans lived in fairly small communities, relatively separated from other human communities. Several adaptive functions have been suggested. Dyson (1979) argues that linguistic diversity evolved as a mechanism to improve the survival of humans during critical times in our history when population numbers fell so dangerously low that our survival as species was in doubt. He argues that the prevalence of different languages in different groups provides increased linguistic or related cognitive opportunities for innovation, necessary for increasing our odds for survival when and if the environment changed. One could argue that Dyson's hypothesis regarding *linguistic diversity* could be expanded to consider the adaptive advantages to being bilingual. Consistent with the evolutionary proposal, there is recent evidence for the cognitive advantages in being bilingual, both for children and in old age (e.g., see Adesope, Lavin, Thompson, & Ungerleider, 2010; Bialystok, Craik, & Luk, 2012, for reviews).

Extending Dyson's hypothesis to include bilingual language abilities does not, however, address a basic evolutionary question. If large-scale cultural contact was not the norm in our evolutionary history, as is believed by evolutionary anthropologists (see Hagen, 2008), what would be the *evolutionary* advantages for having multilingual abilities for communities that did not interact frequently? Most of the (admittedly limited) speculations on this question revolve around the age-related differences in learning one language (i.e., the so-called native language or L1) and an L2, and the importance played by the fact that interactions between groups were somewhat infrequent. One evolutionary school of thought argues that imperfections in L2 use when two groups met could serve to signal to both groups that each is dealing with outsiders, marking them as potential threats and, paradoxically, as people with whom one can mate, being sufficiently genetically distant (see Schumann, 2013). Signals of either sort would be adaptive.

Hagen (2008) places the emphasis in bilingual language evolution not on the speech characteristics of late learners of L2, but on the adaptive advantages that are implicit in the ease when L2 is learned early and the difficulty when learned later in age. Basically, the argument suggests that is what is important for the survival of the species must be learned early in life. Thus, just as having the ability to walk almost immediately after birth is important for survival for horses and many other species, the ability to comprehend and use language plays an equally important role in our success as a species. From this perspective, learning to walk for a horse when he or she is 3 years old would be maladaptive and could well lead to species extinction, just as learning to use and comprehend language only later in life would be maladaptive. Schumann (2013) claims the force behind early L1 (or L1 and L2) is an interactional instinct theory, which holds that humans have evolved biological processes "which allow children to attach to, affiliate and bond with caregivers" (p. 205). These processes include the ability to detect and learn patterns of sounds, words, and larger language units.

An impediment in learning L2 later in life is the lack of the necessary culturally rich environmental support found with early learning of L1. Recognizing that L2 learning is more difficult for adults than for children, Schumann (2013) describes general strategies found in numerous cultures employed to overcome limitations in adult L2 learning. These strategies all include one or the other of the following: simplifying the learning task (e.g., having people only learn a single L2 shared by a number of different linguistic communities, such as is often the case with English today), creating a more simple version of L2, leaving L2 learning to a specialized group of people in the culture, and providing specialized training.

Thus, there is a general agreement that early in life one can easily learn both L1 and L2 but that L2 learning is difficult in later life. Taking this perspective, Hagan (2008) bases his evolutionary perspective for the adaptive value of early L2 learning on the following evidence. First, he notes that early L2 learning occurs rapidly, seemingly effortlessly, without formal training and is found as such universally. This, he argues, is not true of other complex tasks we must learn as humans. Second, based on examination of pathological studies (such as recovery rates in aphasia for traumatic events that occur at different times in one's life), brain mapping studies, and other biologically based evidence, he sees the

Critical Period Hypothesis proposed by Lennenberg (1967) as an argument that we evolved to be multilingual but that adaptive advantages for such disappear fairly early in one's life. Thus, Hagen argues that our evolution as a species to be lingual and multilingual is parasitic on processes for which the child's (but not the adult's) brain is specialized. Finally, based on anthropological evidence, Hagen speculates that violence between different human communities (with different languages) was a hallmark of our evolutionary history when two communities met. The integration of young captives (and nubile females) would be a benefit to the conquering group. No such advantage would be seen for use of conquered older males and females, who would be massacred. Hirschfield (2008), while accepting much of Hagen's perspective, argues that Hagen ignores an important point, namely that the evidence for early learning of an L2 occurs without a noticeable cost to L1 learning. This characteristic, he argues, would be adaptive in environments in which different cultural/linguistic groups co-exist in a mutually supportive environment. In such environments, when communities came into contact, there would be a peaceful movement of nubile women between cultural and linguistic communities, providing an adaptive advantage for their children to be fluent in the languages of both their mother and father.

The biological basis for a discontinuity between L1 and L2 later-life learning is a given in much of the bilingual language literature, much of it now disputed by recent cognitive neuroscience research (see reviews by Abutalebi & Chang-Smith, 2013; Faust, Ben-Artzi, & Vardi, 2012; Petitto, Berens, Kovelman, Dubins, Jasińska, & Shalinsky, 2012; but see Heredia & Cieślicka, 2013, for conceptual and methodological issues). As Abutalebi and Chang-Smith put it, "... The long-held assumption that L1 and L2 are necessarily represented in different brain regions or even in different hemispheres in bilinguals is not confirmed by neuroimaging studies. On the contrary, there is ample evidence that the L1 and L2 are processed by the same neural structures" (p. 7). Second, there is ever-increasing evidence that an important factor in the interpretation of bilingual data is the proficiency one has in L2, independent of the age at which the L2 was acquired. Third, both behavioral data and imaging data indicate similarities in learning one or two languages within the first few years of birth, although recent work (Hoff, Core, Place, Rumiche, Senor, & Parra, 2012) indicates that learning two language simultaneously does not progress at the same rate for both languages, although the rate of learning two languages falls within the normal range observed in learning one language.

Taken together then, the evidence presented above suggests that evolutionary discontinuities proposed both for the evolution of language in general or for learning L1 and L2, based on a strong version of the critical learning hypothesis, have been undercut by recent scientific evidence. On the one hand, there is evidence for the importance of embodied language comprehension in language processing in general and, on the other, that bilinguals and monolinguals employ the same brain structures in processing, although it is understood that L2 users may be less expert in doing so. There is a marked lacuna in the archival literature discussing embodiment and bilingual language.

Embodied Cognition, with Relevance to Nonliteral Language

In the earlier section, we discussed how brain structures originally evolved for handling sensory and motor activities that have been coopted in the evolution of language, most notably in the production of rapid coordinated motor movements, such as needed for production of speech. But notably the argument has developed further that these neural structures work online during language usage to motivate our understanding of what is being said. *Embodied cognition* holds that language processing should be viewed in the context of relations between the mind and the body. As noted above, the assumption is that thinking about an action or an emotion activates neural networks that are used in producing the action or experiencing the emotion. Thus, for instance, on reading a sentence such as *the boy kicked the soccer ball,* the neural structures involved in performing the action of kicking would be activated, whereas other structures, for instance those involved in performing the action of throwing, would not be aroused, although conversely, they would be if the sentence had read *the boy threw the baseball.* Similarly, reading about a specific emotion would activate select neural systems associated with that feeling and not with other feelings. This general premise has gained much support over the last decade. For instance, it has been shown repeatedly that the same sensory-motor regions of the brain are activated when people process an object or the name of the object (e.g., Martin, 2007) and, conversely, that embodied information, such as emotional or motoric, is activated during sentence processing (e.g., Gibbs, 2006). Moreover, it has even been found that patients diagnosed with one or another disorder in producing learned motor activities (apraxia) are impaired also in comprehending action words (Buxbaum & Saffran, 2002).

A central corollary of this position is that the semantics or meaning of an action or emotion plays an important role online during language comprehension. An increasingly large literature supports this corollary.

For example, over several studies Zwaan and colleagues have shown that orientation, visual clarity, and shape information all are simulated during reading tasks in which such information is linguistically manipulated (e.g., see Engelen, Bouwmeester, de Bruin, & Zwaan, 2011; Zwaan & Pecher, 2012).

Much of the supporting evidence is based on two basic types of tasks. In one, the critical data are the differences between mismatch and matched information. For instance, consider a task where you have to indicate comprehension of sentences such as *the boy threw the ball* versus *the boy kicked the ball* and responses are motoric, either an arm or a leg movement. In the first sentence, an arm movement would be a matched situation and a leg movement a mismatch, and the reverse would be true for the second sentence. If the embodied information is aroused during comprehension, one would expect an interaction between word knowledge and the associated motor system. That is, responses should be more rapid in the match conditions. In the second type of task, one attempts to block the putative sensory or motor system. For instance, if one posits that emotion is based in part on sensory motor information, then performance should be hindered by, for instance, preventing a participant from smiling when reading happy or humorous sentences.

There is by now a wealth of evidence supporting embodied contributions to language comprehension. Supporting evidence includes finding compatibility between physical motor movements and motor actions described in sentences (see Zwaan & Taylor, 2006). Importantly, the linkage extends to grammatical effects. For instance, in one study, participants were asked to rotate a knob in a given direction while reading stories that implied rotating motions in the same or different direction. A grammatical manipulation had the stories suggest the motion had been performed in the past, was being performed, or will be performed in the future. Motor resonance (e.g., superior performance when the physical rotation and that implied in the story were in the same direction) was found for stories that described the action as having occurred in the past or was current, a finding the authors took to show that resonance was based on the linguistic focus on the execution of the motion and not on its preparation.

A related line of research has shown compatibility effects for the direction of an actual gesture and one implied linguistically. For instance, Masson, Bub, and Warren (2008) trained participants to make a hand action in response to a visual cue while listening to a sentence. Sentences referred to manipulable objects that were either related or unrelated to the cued action. Related actions pertained either to the function of the object or to its volumetric properties (e.g., shape).

Masson et al. demonstrated compatibility wherein both functional and volumetric responses were facilitated when a match occurred between the movement and the action implied in the sentence and interpret their findings as showing that motor representations play a role in constructing sentence meaning.

In summary, there is now a large literature showing that perceptual and action simulations occur when processing language. It should be noted that virtually all this evidence occurs when concrete language is involved. Importantly for the generalizability of an embodiment view of language, there is now a growing literature that analogous effects can be found with abstract language, such as those involving the description of emotion or time (see review by Pecher, Boot, & van Dantzig, 2011). For instance, Havas, Glenberg, Gutowski, Lucarelli, and Davidson (2010) have shown effects with emotions comparable with those described above for motor activity, such as the finding that one processes pleasant sentences more rapidly when smiling and unpleasant sentences more rapidly when not smiling. Moreover, when facial muscles responsible for frowning are (temporarily) paralyzed, participants are slowed when reading sad or angry statements. Presumably one cannot easily simulate those negative emotions when frowning is eliminated. Analogous findings that necessitate an embodiment explanation can be found with reading texts that describe time and compatible motor activity (assuming future events are further from one's body or a left/past to right/future time line).

It should be noted that the abstract concepts under discussion are those often described metaphorically and were the basis of the analyses presented by Lakoff and Johnson in their classic work, *Metaphors We Live By* (1980) and their basic argument that abstract and literal concepts alike are understood by a metaphoric conceptual structure grounded in concrete embodied experiences. Although there are fewer studies in this tradition that have examined metaphor explicitly, those that have been done are consistent with an embodiment explanation. Santana and de Vega (2011) have shown that people are faster at processing sentences describing a metaphorical action when performing a motor action that matched the direction suggested by the sentence, compared to a motor action that was mismatched. Gibbs (2013) has shown in a series of studies that metaphorical phrase reading time is faster when the metaphorical phrases matched either actual motor movements or imagined motor movements.

Bowes (2013) has added a new methodology for examining embodiment. Unlike the match-mismatch or the inhibitory paradigms described above, she looked at generalization effects. Her basic argument is that if a basic embodied mechanism is important in comprehension, then the effects of that embodiment should generalize to performance on a later, seemingly unrelated task. Moreover, she argues that the use of metaphor plays a basic social role in creating intimacy between interlocutors and would be embodied in how one expresses him- or herself, and how the interlocutor uses ToM to make sense of that expression. Over a series of studies she had participants read metaphors (or literal counterparts). In some studies the metaphors or their counterparts were read one at a time without any discourse context and in some cases within a longer discourse context. Once finished reading metaphors or their literal counterparts, participants completed an ostensibly unrelated task, namely identifying emotions from pictures of eyes. In fact, this task is commonly employed for examining ToM abilities.

Bowes provides evidence for her first premise (that social effects are engendered in the mere act of reading metaphor) by analyzing the discourse context that people produce for those metaphors or literal counterparts. Of more direct interest to the thesis of this chapter, the facilitation in identifying emotions in others when processing metaphors (relative to literal counterparts) is consistent with the evidence, presented earlier, that comprehending language is based on simulations of embodied information. In this case the language was metaphoric, the simulation was of social factors evoked by metaphors, and as shown by Bowes, the simulation has an emotional component that generalizes to a basic communicative function, namely monitoring whether the emotional force of the metaphor is understood.

Embodied Language and Bilingualism

Unlike research on language processing in general, or on nonliteral language specifically, the literature on embodiment in bilingual populations is virtually absent. This lacuna is to us a surprising and somewhat discouraging illustration of what we see as the silos that exist between the different aspects of language processing. In this last section of the chapter we wish to finish on an optimistic note by outlining a scattering (and noncomprehensive) list of opportunities for research into bilingualism that is made available by taking an embodied perspective. In each case, we envision the utility of studies that employ the techniques described above for showing the embodied aspects of language, addressing questions, or framing them somewhat differently, than has hitherto been the case in the bilingual research literature. For instance, do people who learn two languages concurrently early in life evoke the same embodied structures, whereas late L2 learners do not unless they become very skilled in L2? Can the differential expression of L1 and L2, sometimes seen in bilingual aphasia and recovery, be tied to problems in apraxia and individual differences in strength of embodiment of the two languages? How do cultural factors interact with the degree to which different motoric or emotional neural networks are aroused during L1 and L2 learning, or in subsequent language comprehension? As examples we consider in more detail a few possibilities.

Multiple Languages and Identifying the Underlying Conceptual Structure

A central question in much of the modern research into the processing of language by bilinguals focuses on what is shared across languages and how bilinguals may capitalize on this shared information. For instance, Dijkstra, Van Jaarsveld, and Ten Brinke (1998) tested Dutch/English bilinguals' lexical performance on *cognates* (words that share the same form and meaning across languages) and *noncognates* (with no overlap of form and meaning). They posited that if lexical and semantic representations are shared across languages, cognates should have a privileged role in the bilingual mind, as evidenced by faster reaction times compared to noncognates. When required to make a lexical decision (e.g., deciding if a letter string they were reading was a word in either language), participants showed significantly faster reaction times to cognates than noncognates. Since Dijkstra et al.'s findings, other studies have shown the impact one language can have on the other. The current consensus is that the bilinguals' languages are not neatly compartmentalized and they cannot help but use information from both languages. Naturally, this line of research has proven valuable and will almost certainly continue. What an embodied perspective provides is a new way of conceptualizing what information is shared and what is nonshared at the conceptual level, not just at the lexical or phonological level. That is, from an embodied perspective one can ask and test whether bilinguals understand basic concepts such as space, time, or color in the same ways in their different languages or relative to monolingual counterparts.

A long-standing hypothesis found in the literature is that language determines (or, in a milder form, encourages) specific forms of thought, such as conceptualizations of time and space. Until very recently, the consensus was that there was no support at all for the strong version of the hypothesis and very little for the milder form. In a review of this literature 15 years ago, Katz (1998) pointed out the limited and variable nature of the support for the hypothesis, but unlike the received wisdom of the day, he did note that one can find some supportive evidence in selected domains, such as those that obtain with the plural marking of a noun and on transitive reasoning about spatial location. Since that time, Boroditsky (2011) has provided much additional and stronger support for the notion that language shapes thought, especially for domains of space and time, although it should be noted that some of the findings are still controversial (e.g., Tse & Altarriba, 2008). In addition, using a variant of the match-mismatch paradigm, Blom and Semin (2013) have shown that differences in conceptualizing the temporal distribution of events are moderated by movements. In line with the concept, *left is associated with earlier times, and right is associated with later times*, Blom and Semin demonstrated that performing left hand–arm movements while thinking about a past event increases the perceived temporal distance to the event, whereas performing right-hand movements decreases the perceived distance to the event. Thus the perceived age of an event is dependent in part on hand–arm movements, again implicating an embodied explanation of time perception. A demonstration that color perception is tied to sensory-perceptual factors has been shown with Japanese English bilinguals by Athanasopoulos, Damjanovic, Krajciova, and Sasaki (2011). We see the use of techniques, such as the match-mismatch paradigms described by Santana and de Vega (2011), as a useful tool to better understand how bilinguals conceptualize the basic concepts in the world and as an additional way to see which aspects of different languages are shared and which are not shared.

Differences between L1 and L2

Above we made the argument for a greater neural commonality between L1 and L2 than has been the case traditionally, especially when expertise in L2 is high. Nonetheless, there are some behavioral differences that often occur when L2 is learned later in life, such as with emotional reactions to words. There is a literature that has indicated emotional reactions to L1 words are stronger than to L2 words, although admittedly the literature is somewhat scattered and inconclusive (e.g., Altarriba, 2014; Heredia & Cieślicka, 2014). Recent work, however, suggests that while behavioral measures were similar for reacting to emotional words in L1 and L2, skin conductance measures showed that native L1 users reacted more strongly to negative and taboo words (Eilola & Havelka, 2010). In an even more recent review, Pavlenko (2012) argues that L1 advantages can be found in increased automaticity of affective processing in L1 and heightened electrodermal reactivity to emotion-laden words as measured by electrical conductivity of the skin. She concludes that the data "suggest that in some bilingual speakers respective languages may be differently embodied" (p. 405).

A test of this notion can be done employing techniques described above for studying emotion and embodiment. For example, one can ask participants to judge words in L1 and L2 on a neutral dimension, such as about physical properties of the referent or on a dimension that calls upon the emotion evoked (e.g., *happy-sad*) while electromyographic activity is measured. An embodied perspective would predict that increased electromyographic activity would be found when emotion is being evoked. Based on the emotional embodied literature one would expect emotion-specific activity. Judgments about objects that typically evoke joy should be associated with activation of the zygomaticus and orbicularis oculi muscles, whereas judgments about objects that elicit disgust should be associated by activation of the levator muscle (see Niedenthal, Winkielman, Mondillon, & Vermeulen, 2009). As extended to bilingual populations, one would expect that these activation patterns should be greater when the judgments were done in L1 than when done in L2. A causal link could be determined by manipulating in a follow-up study the ability of participants to move their faces freely. That is, one could ask half the participants to perform the task as above but have the other half hold a pen in their mouth while performing the judgment tasks. The expectation would be that preventing one from simulating the emotion should reduce the degree to which the object is rated as joyful or disgusting overall and should eliminate completely the differences in performances in L1 and L2. (Some of these proposed effects might depend on proficiency in L2.)

Code Switching and Embodied Cognition

Code switching is a phenomenon in which bilingual participants switch between L1 and L2 as a function of the audience with whom they are interacting. Generally, code switching increases as both interlocutors possess increased proficiency in both languages (Grosjean, 1997). Thus, for instance, a bilingual person speaking to a monolingual person will speak in the same language as the monolingual, even if that is his or her L2, whereas code switching is much more prevalent when both are fluent in both L1 and L2. Indeed, one can argue that a person using L2 with a monolingual interlocutor has to inhibit L1, even if a more apt way of expressing a point can be found in L1. In a more general sense, one can argue that the degree to which L1 and L2 are aroused, even in noncommunicative contexts, depends on social contexts that differ in the degree to which one's bilingual status is made salient.

Embodied effects might be demonstrated in code switching. In experimental tasks, for instance, one could employ a variant of the studies using cognates and noncognates similar to the Dijkstra et al.'s (1998) study described above. Specifically, one can ask participants to make lexical decisions to determine whether a letter string is or is not a word in L1 or in L2. Arguably, when having to decide whether a letter string is a word in either L1 or L2, one's status as being bilingual is activated to a greater extent than when doing the same task solely in one language. The degree of embodiment in these experimental conditions can be inferred by using a novel response task (for this literature), wherein the lexical decision is made by moving a lever either toward oneself or away from oneself. Movements toward oneself would be a motion consistent with affirming oneself and should lead to faster correct responses than the same decision made when the lever is moved away from oneself. Such an effect should not be observed if the response lever were to be pushed left or right.

Another extension would be to examine embodiment for cues as to when code switching is taking place. A recent paper by Greer (2013) is illustrative. As Greer points out, "one important aspect of word searching in face-to-face communication is its relation to embodied action-gestures, gaze, posture, proximity and other associated multimodal features of interaction" (p. 101). Studying Japanese/English bilinguals, he examined the use of such devices. Bringing the notion of the role(s) played by embodiment under laboratory control may be more difficult. One possibility might be to apply a modification of a technique used by Hussey and Katz (2009) for the study of metaphor use. To examine for gender effects, participants in Internet communication were led to believe they were in communication with another student who was the same or opposite gender. In fact, the interlocutor was a confederate of the experimenters trained to use either literal or metaphoric language; half of the participants communicated with a person of the opposite gender than what they had been told. This design permitted disentanglement of beliefs about gender and the effects of language actually used in communication. Using this type of design, but in face-to-face communication, one can manipulate the likelihood that code switching would occur by training a highly proficient bilingual confederate to demonstrate differing levels of L2 competency. That is, the research participant could be led to believe that the interlocutor was monolingual in what is the participant's L2, was only partially bilingual in the participant's L1, or was completely fluent in both L1 and L2. A design conceptually similar to this was conducted by Grosjean (1997). In this study, L1 French-L2 English bilinguals were presented French stories that contained English code-switches and were told that that they were taking part in experiment in which their retelling of the story would be used by another person who would pass on their retelling. Grojean manipulated to whom the participant believed he or she was telling the story (e.g., in one case the "other" person was referred to as a recent arrival from France with difficulties in speaking English, whereas another person was described as a person from France who has lived in the United States for many years and was fluently bilingual). Grosjean measured the number of L2 syllables used, the number of L1 syllables used, and the number of hesitations. He found, as he had predicted, that the amount of code switching increased as the person believed he or she was talking to a fluent bilingual. In the envisioned study, the same measures as used by Grosjean (1997) could be used again, but now the story would be told in eye-to-eye contact with the interlocutor and the frequency of changes found with Grojean's measures now tied directly to the frequency with which these changes were accompanied by indices of embodiment, such as gestures, or direct gazes.

Mental Imagery

As reviewed above, evidence for embodiment can be found, on the one hand, with concrete concepts and motor or sensory tasks and, on the other, with more abstract concepts and tasks that measured, for instance, emotional reactions. These data may merely suggest that embodiment is multi-dimensional, involving many body states. An alternative is that concrete concepts and language and abstract concepts and language are grounded in two quite different experiences, sensory-motor on the one hand and linguistic experiences with greater emotional than motoric embodiment on the other. This alternative is in fact the basis of what one can characterize as an early version of embodiment: the *Dual Code Theory* posited by Alan Paivio (1971; see the explicit extension to bilingualism in Paivio, 1986, 2014).

There are some intriguing studies suggesting that predictions arising from or consistent with this theory are worth pursuing. For instance, Scorolli, Binkofski, Buccino, Nicoletti, Riggio, and Borghi (2011) had participants read sentences that included those that were verb-noun compatible (both being abstract or both being concrete) and those that were noncompatible (e.g., abstract verb with a concrete noun). They found faster reading times for sentences with the compatible verb-noun pairings, a finding consistent with the notion of separable embodied sources for concrete and abstract knowledge.

A more recent study by Jared, Poh, and Paivio (2013) explicitly tested a more nuanced notion of sensory embodiment drawn from Paivio's

(2014) theorizing, namely the notion that learning two languages in separate contexts can result in different referential sensory images for the same concept. In this task with Mandarin and English bilinguals, participants were asked to name in L1 and L2 pictures that were biased toward Chinese representation or American representation or were non-biased. Consistent with an embodiment explanation, culturally biased pictures were named more rapidly in the culturally congruent language than incongruent language. Fruitful avenues of bilingual research are envisioned by manipulating the variables described by Paivio so long ago, namely stimulus type (pictures, concrete and abstract words), instructional set (use imagery or neutral), or individual difference indices of habitual imagery use.

Summary and Conclusions

In this short review we have presented an argument, currently gaining increasing prominence in the cognitive neurosciences, that language is embodied and that online usage and understanding of language is tightly correlated with brain structures evolved and used for motor, sensory, and perceptual activities. We have drawn a broad picture and have not delved into some of the subtleties in the embodiment literature: Does embodied circuitry come into play in the earliest phases of language comprehension or as a slightly later interaction of information from semantic and sensory-motor systems?

Most of the direct experimental evidence for embodiment is based on unilingual populations and with literal language. There is a growing literature on embodiment in nonliteral language comprehension. There is almost no such literature with bilingual populations, although one can discern the beginnings of such a literature as just emerging. It is hoped that this chapter will hasten the hatching of considering implications of embodiment for understanding the acquisition, use, and representation of multiple languages by an individual.

What we have not dealt with are issues found throughout this book: How do bilingual individuals process and understand nonliteral language? From an embodied perspective one cannot simply assume that because a given individual has experienced the same physical environment that the same neural systems will be aroused in the same way, and consequently embodied reactions to nonliteral language will be the same whether tested in L1 or L2. We have described above some cases where that simple view cannot be the case. For instance, in the section on mental imagery above, Jared et al. (2013) have shown that the cultural context in which a language was learned influences performance. In other sections we have described how late L2 learners might not be as embodied as early L2 learners or that common motor-sensory circuits might emerge in both L1 and L2 as a function of expertise in the second language. For at least a decade, some scholars have considered the cultural aspect of metaphor use and in many ways have anticipated the neuroscience discussed here (e.g., see Kövecses, 2000; Yu, 2003). An intriguing possibility is that different neural circuitry, tied to sensorymotor and emotional circuitry, will be engaged for bilinguals considering abstract metaphoric description of emotions.

In conclusion, we list here only a few of the ways that embodiment can be useful in reconsidering questions of interest to bilingual researchers. As noted earlier, we have presented a sampling of testable possibilities for examining embodiment from a bilingual perspective. The list we present is not meant as comprehensive and can easily be increased. Some additions could be, for example, as a means of understanding bilingual aphasia (and its relationship to apraxia), the role played by experience in acquiring L2 and differences in use of embodiment to facilitate comprehension, or, although not discussed here in any detail, how embodied cognition plays a role in language production. If the reader will forgive us a metaphor: *The future in this domain is at our fingertips, all we have to do now is grasp it.*

List of Keywords

Amodal, Archeological record, Brain mapping, Brodmann's area F5, CNTNAP2, Cognates, Conceptual structures, Context-dependent, Critical Period Hypothesis, Culturally congruent, Domain-general cognitive control, Dual Code Theory, Dyson's Hypothesis, Embodied cognition, Evolutionary perspective, Figurative language, Fossil record, FOXP2, Interactional instinct theory, Language evolution, Language production, Lexical decision task, Linguistic diversity, Literal, Match-mismatch paradigms, Meaning representation, Metaphor, Mirror neurons, Oldowan, Pidgin languages, Positron emission tomography (PET), Proficiency, Protolanguage, Stone Age, Symbolic expressions, Syntax-based language, Theory of Mind (ToM), Visuomotor coordination, Visuospatial processing

Thought Questions

1. How are concepts such as *love* or *jealousy* embodied? Which *neural structures* would be involved? How might this be demonstrated scientifically?

2. Do people who speak different languages (monolinguals) understand the world differently (e.g., have different conceptualizations of time or space)? What about fluent bilinguals? Do they adopt one view of time or space? Do their conceptualizations change (even if only slightly) when talking in one or the other language?

3. What can an embodied perspective bring to the teaching of a second language?

4. Do men and women differ in how they embody emotional concepts? If so, what are the implications for male-female communication, couples therapy, and the like?

Suggested Student Research Projects

1. Do right- and left-handers view the abstract concepts *good* and *bad* in the same way? From an embodiment perspective, one could argue that the hand in which you are most proficient is considered the *good* or better hand. If so right-handers might see *good* as being represented on the right and *bad* on the left, whereas left-handers might see it represented in the opposite manner (*left is good, right is bad*). Construct a study to test this hypothesis using Casanto (2009) in the suggested readings as a guide for your experiment.

2. Is emotion embodied? Existing emotional states may match or mismatch emotions conveyed in language. Thus, to the extent that experiencing or simulating the emotion is a necessary component of deep comprehension, then being in the appropriate state should help to understand the language. Manipulating facial configurations reliably induces the state (or at least makes it easier to enter the state) typical of the configuration. This can be done by asking participants to hold a pen using only their teeth, which induces smiling and brightens the mood, or they hold the pen using only the lips, which induces a frown or pout. While holding the pen, students should have the participants silently read and judge sentence chosen to be viewed typically as *happy*, *sad*, and *angry*. Time to read each sentence should be measured. If emotion is embodied, one would predict an interaction between the pen position and the valence of the sentences on the time to make the judgment. Participants should be faster to read and judge sentences describing a pleasant state of affairs (e.g., *Your lover chases you playfully around your bedroom*) when holding the pen in the teeth (*smiling*) than when holding the pen in the lips (*frowning*). The opposite should be found for sentences describing an unpleasant situation (see Glenberg et al., (2009) in the suggested readings).

Related Internet Sites

Embodiment Resources: www.embodiment.org.uk
Society for the Scientific Study of Embodiment: www.ssse.org

Suggested Further Readings

Barsalou, L.W. (2008). Grounded cognition. *Annual Review of Psychology, 59,* 617–645.
Casanto, D. (2009). Embodiment of abstract concepts: Good and bad in right- and left-handers. *Journal of Experimental Psychology: General, 138,* 351–367.
Glenberg, A., Webster, B., Mouilso, E., Havas, D., & Lindman, L. (2009). Gender, emotion, and the embodiment of language comprehension. *Emotion Review, 1,* 151–161.
Lakoff, G., & Johnson, M. (1999). *Philosophy in the flesh: The embodied mind and its challenge to western thought.* New York, NY: Basic Books.
Meteyard, L., Cuadrado, S., Bahrami, B., & Vigliocco, G. (2012). Coming of age: A review of embodiment and the neuroscience of semantics. *Cortex, 48,* 788–804.

REFERENCES

Abutalebi, J., & Chang-Smith, M. (2012). Second language representation in the brain. *The encyclopedia of applied linguistics.* Hoboken, NJ: Wiley Online Library.
Adescope, O., Lavin, T., Thompson, T., & Ungerleider, C. (2010). A systematic review and meta-analysis of the cognitive correlates of bilingualism. *Review of Educational Research, 80,* 207–245.
Altarriba, J. (2014). Emotion, memory, and bilingualism. In R.R. Heredia & J. Altarriba (Eds.), *Foundations of bilingual memory* (pp. 11–39). New York: Springer
Athanasopolus, P., Damjanovic, L., Krajciova, A., & Sasaki, M. (2011). Representation of color concepts in bilingual cognition: The case of Japanese blues. *Bilingualism: Language and Cognition, 14,* 9–17.
Bialystok, E., Craik, F., & Luk, G. (2012). Bilingualism: Consequences for mind and brain. *Trends in Cognitive Sciences, 16,* 240–250.
Bickerton, D. (1990). *Language and species.* Chicago: University of Chicago Press.
Blom, S., & Semin, G. (2013). Moving events in time: Time-referent hand-arm movements influence perceived temporal distance to past events. *Journal of Experimental Psychology: General, 142,* 319–322.
Boroditsky, L. (2011). How language shapes thought. *Scientific American, 304,* 62–65.
Bowes, A. (2013). *The social life of metaphor* [Unpublished doctoral dissertation]. University of Western Ontario.

Buxbaum, L., & Saffran, E. (2002). Knowledge of object manipulation and object function: Dissociations in apraxic and nonapraxic subjects. *Brain and Language, 82,* 179–199.

Dijkstra, T., Van Jaarsveld, H., & Ten Brinke, S. (1998). Interlingual homograph recognition: Effects of task demands and language intermixing. *Bilingualism: Language and Cognition, 1,* 51–66.

Dyson, F. (1979). *Disturbing the universe.* New York: Harper and Row.

Eilola, T., & Havelka, J. (2010). Behavioral and physiological responses to the emotional and taboo Stroop tasks in native and non-native speakers of English. *International Journal of Bilingualism, 15,* 353–369.

Engelen, J., Bouwmeester, S., de Bruin, A., & Zwaan, R. (2011). Perceptual simulation in developing language comprehension. *Journal of Experimental Child Psychology, 110,* 659–675.

Faust, M., Ben-Artzi, E., & Vardi, N. (2012). Semantic processing in native and second language: Evidence from hemispheric differences in fine and coarse semantic coding. *Brain and Language, 123,* 228–233.

Fisher, S., & Marcus, G. (2005). The eloquent ape: Genes, brains and the evolution of language. *Nature Reviews Genetics, 7,* 9–20

Fogassi, L., & Ferrari, P. (2012). Cortical motor organization, mirror neurons, and embodied language: An evolutionary perspective. *Biolinguistics, 6,* 308–337.

Gibbs, R. (2006). *Embodiment and cognitive science.* Cambridge,UK: Cambridge University Press.

  (2013). Walking the walk while thinking about the talk: Embodied interpretation of metaphorical narratives. *Journal of Psycholinguistic Research, 42,* 363–378.

Greer, T. (2013). Word search sequences in bilingual interaction: Codeswitching and embodied orientation toward shifting participant constellations. *Journal of Pragmatics, 57,* 100–117.

Grosjean, F. (1997). Processing mixed language: Issues, findings and models. In A. de Groot & J. Kroll (Eds.), *Trends in bilingualism: Psycholinguistic perspectives* (pp. 225–254). Mahwah, NJ: Erlbaum.

Hagen, L. (2008). The bilingual brain: Human evolution and second language acquisition. *Evolutionary Psychology, 6,* 43–67.

Havas, D., Glenberg, A., Gutowski, K., Lucarelli, M., & Davidson, R. (2010). Cosmetic use of botulinum toxin-A affects processing of emotional language. *Psychological Science, 21,* 895–900.

Heredia, R.R., & Cieślicka, A.B. (2014). Bilingual memory storage: Compound-coordinate and derivatives. In R.R. Heredia & J. Altarriba (Eds.), *Foundations of bilingual memory* (pp. 11–39). New York: Springer.

Hirschfield, L. (2008). The bilingual brain revisited: A commentary on Hagen (2008). *Evolutionary Psychology, 6,* 182–185.

Hoff, E., Core, C., Place, S., Rumiche, R., Senor, M., & Parra, M. (2012). Dual language exposure and early bilingual development. *Journal of Child Language, 39,* 1–27.

Hussey, K., & Katz, A. (2009). Perception of the use of metaphor by an interlocutor in discourse. *Metaphor and Symbol, 24,* 203–236.

Jared, D., Poh, R., & Paivio, A. (2013). L1 and L2 picture naming in Mandarin-English bilinguals: A test of bilingual dual coding theory. *Bilingualism: Language and Cognition, 16,* 383–396.

Katz, A. (1998). Figurative language and figurative thought: A review. In A. Katz, C. Cacciari, R. Gibbs, & M. Turner (Eds.), *Figurative language and thought* (pp. 3–43). Oxford, UK: Oxford University Press.

Kövecses, Z. (2000). *Metaphor and emotion: Language, culture and body in human feeling.* Cambridge, UK: Cambridge University Press.

Lakoff, G., & Johnson, M. (1980). *Metaphors we live by.* Chicago: Chicago University Press.

Lennenberg, E.H. (1967). *Biological foundations of language.* New York: Wiley.

Lieberman, P. (1991). *Uniquely human: The evolution of speech, thought and selfless behavior.* Cambridge, MA: Harvard University Press.

Martin, A. (2007). The representation of object concepts in the brain. *Annual Review of Psychology 58,* 25–45.

Masson, M., Bub, D., & Warren, C. (2008). Kicking calculators: Contribution of embodied representations to sentence comprehension. *Journal of Memory and Language, 59,* 256–265.

Newbury, D., Fisher, S., & Monaco, A. (2010). Recent advances in the genetics of language impairment. *Genome Medicine, 2, 6.* doi:10.1186/gm127

Niedenthal, P., Winkielman, P., Mondillon, L., & Vermeulen, N. (2009). Embodiment of emotion concepts. *Journal of Personality and Social Psychology, 96,* 1120–1136.

Paivio, A. (1971). *Imagery and verbal processes.* New York: Holt, Rinehart and Winston.

(1986). *Mental representations: A dual coding approach.* Oxford: Oxford University Press.

(2014). Bilingual dual coding theory and memory. In R.R. Heredia & J. Altarriba (Eds.), *Foundations of bilingual memory* (pp. 41–62). New York: Springer.

Pavlenko, A. (2012). Affective processing in bilingual speakers: Disembodied cognition? *International Journal of Psychology, 47,* 405–428.

Pecher, D., Boot, I., & van Dantzig, S. (2011). Abstract concepts: Sensory-motor grounding, metaphors and beyond. *The Psychology of Learning and Motivation, 54,* 217–248.

Petitto, L., Berens, M., Kovelman, I., Dubins, M., Jasińska, K., & Shalinsky, M. (2012). Functional near-infra red spectroscopy (fNIRS): A promising functional imaging technique for the study of brain and language. *Brain and Language, 121,* 130–143.

Pinker, S. (1994). *The language instinct.* New York: W. Morrow and Co.

Premack, D. (2004). Is language the key to human intelligence? *Science, 303,* 318–320.

Santana, E., & de Vega, M. (2011). Metaphors are embodied, and so are their literal counterparts. *Frontiers in Cognition, 2, 90.* doi:103389/fpsyg.2011.00090

Schuman, J. (2013). Societal responses to adult difficulties in L2 acquisition: Toward an evolutionary perspective on language acquisition. *Language Learning, 63,* 190–209.

Scorolli, C., Binkofski, F., Buccino, G., Nicoletti, R., Riggio, L., & Borghi, A. (2011). Abstract and concrete sentences, embodiment and languages. *Frontiers in Psychology*, *2*, 1–11.

Siegel, M., & Varley, R. (2002). Neural systems involved in theory of mind. *Nature Reviews. Neuroscience*, *3*, 463–471.

Stout, D., Toth, N., Schick, K., & Chaminade, T. (2008). Neural correlates of early Stone Age toolmaking: Technology, language and cognition in human evolution. *Philosophical Transactions of the Royal Society B*, *363*, 1939–1949.

Tse, C.-S., & Altarriba, J. (2008). Evidence against linguistic relativity in Chinese and English: A case study of spatial and temporal metaphors. *Journal of Cognition and Culture*, *8*, 335–357.

Walker, A., & Shipman, P. (1996). *The wisdom of the bones*. New York: Knopf.

Yu, N. (2003). Metaphor, body, and culture: The Chinese understanding of gallbladder and courage. *Metaphor and Symbol*, *18*, 13–31.

Zwaan, R., & Pecher, D. (2012). Revisiting mental simulation in language comprehension: Six replication attempts. *PLoS ONE*, *7*, 12.

Zwaan, R., & Taylor, L. (2006). Seeing, acting, understanding: Motor resonance in language comprehension. *Journal of Experimental Psychology: General*, *135*, 1–11.

2   Is the Idiom Principle Blocked in Bilingual L2 Production?

Istvan Kecskes
University at Albany, State University of New York

ABSTRACT

This paper hypothesizes that the *idiom principle* (Sinclair, 1991) that drives word selection in monolinguals may be blocked in the second language (L2) of bilinguals and the *open choice principle* governs instead. In order to investigate the validity of this hypothesis a small corpus of non-native speaker – non-native speaker (*lingua franca*) communication is examined and compared to a similar study (Kecskes, 2007) where the bilingual speakers used their L2 (English). Based on the two studies we can conclude that the idiom principle is the most salient guiding mechanism in any language production. But it results in less formulaic language use in L2 than in the first language(L1) of bilinguals. This claim basically concurs with the findings of other studies (cf. Bolander, 1989; Pawley & Syder, 1983; Warga, 2008; Weinert, 1995), which also talked about the limited use of formulaic language in L2.

Keywords: idiom principle, bilingual idiom processing, formulaic language, psychological salience, second language idiom processing, lingua franca

Based on the findings of some studies that argued that even advanced second language (L2) users have difficulty with formulaic language (Ellis, Simpson-Vlach, & Carson, 2008; Kecskes, 2007; Prodromou 2008; Warga, 2005), this paper hypothesizes that the *idiom principle* (Sinclair, 1991) that drives word selection in monolinguals may be blocked in the L2 of bilinguals and the *open choice principle* governs instead. In order to investigate the validity of this hypothesis, a small corpus of non-native speaker – non-native speaker (*lingua franca*) communication is examined where the bilingual speakers use their L2 (English).

Before analyzing bilingual speech production, there is a need to discuss utterance production in general and discuss why formulaic language has a special role in both production and comprehension. In some recent publications (Kecskes, 2012, 2013), I argued that a speaker's utterance is the result of the interplay of salience and recipient design. While fitting words into actual situational contexts, speakers are driven not only by the intent (*conscious*) that the hearer recognize what is meant as intended by the speaker (*cooperation*), but also by speaker individual salience that affects production subconsciously (*egocentrism*). The interplay of these social (cooperation) and individual (egocentrism) factors shapes the communicative process.

In order to succeed, speakers must correctly express intended illocutionary acts by using appropriate words and make their attempt in an adequate context. Speakers relate propositional contents to the world (actual situational context; audience) with the intention of establishing a correspondence between words and things from a certain direction of fit. A speaker's utterance is a full proposition that is the result of the speaker's intention, which is a private reaction to a communicative situation. A speaker's intention is expressed in lexical items whose selection is affected not only by recipient design but also by the speaker's egocentrism governed by salience. Salience, which operates subconsciously and automatically, may affect word selection and utterance formation just like recipient design.

Salience affecting language production is motivated by both private and collective elements. What is salient for a speaker is based on the prior experience of the individual. However, the mechanism according to which salience works is also affected by universal elements and forces that language users share with others. One such phenomenon is *the economy principle in language use*. Human beings want to achieve as much as possible with the least possible effort both in production and comprehension. In the *Relevance Theory* (Sperber & Wilson, 1995), *economy* has been used with two functions: first, to explain how cognitive processes are linked to utterance interpretation (processing efforts must be balanced by cognitive effects), and second, to explain how communication may be successful (inferences complete the under-specified content of the utterance to obtain its intended meaning). In other words, economy is a property of the cognitive system devoted to utterance interpretation. It is also required in order to ensure successful communication, by the computational devices, which are combined with linguistic decoding to yield the intended meaning of an utterance.

There is psycholinguistic evidence that fixed expressions and formulas have an important economizing role in speech production (cf. Miller & Weinert, 1998; Wray, 2002). Sinclair's (1991) idiom principle says that the use of prefabricated chunks may "... illustrate a natural tendency to economy of effort" (p. 110). This means that in communication we want to achieve more cognitive effects with less processing effort. Formulaic expressions ease the processing overload not only because they are *ready-made* and do not require any *putting together* by the speaker/hearer, but also because their salient meanings are easily accessible in online production and processing.

Wray (2002) said that by favoring formulaic units, speakers are able to reduce both their own processing – the larger the units, the fewer the operations needed to construct the message – and also the processing load of the hearer. She argued that there are major benefits to the speaker in ensuring that the hearer does not have to engage in too much processing. She also proposed that both parties are to some extent obliged to find ways of minimizing their processing, because the grammar of human language is too complex for human memory to cope with all the time (Wray, 2002, p. 15). Thus Wray converged with Sinclair's proposal (1991) that the formulaic option, which he calls the idiom principle, is the *default processing strategy*. Analytic processing, the *open choice principle* in Sinclair's terminology, is invoked only when the idiom principle fails.

This is the main point in this paper. *Because it is the default processing strategy, the formulaic option (i.e., idiom principle) is expected to be most salient in language production.* It means that the speaker is expected to come up primarily with utterances that contain ready-made, formulaic expression(s) if possible and plausible. If it is not, the *open choice principle* steps in. This looks like a logical mechanism in monolingual language production where participants can rely on the mutual understanding of formulaic expressions that are motivated by common ground, conventions, commonalities, norms, common beliefs, and mutual knowledge. But is that also the case in bilingual speakers when they use their L2? Does their mind prewired for the idiom principle work with the required circumstances (partly) missing? No matter which of their languages they use, bilingual speakers, to some extent, miss common ground, conventions, communalities, norms, and other elements. In order for us to answer these questions, we first need to look at how the idiom principle works in monolingual language production.

Formulaic Units

By *formulaic language* we usually mean multiword collocations that are stored and retrieved holistically rather than being generated *de novo* with each use. Collocations, fixed semantic units, frozen metaphors, phrasal verbs, speech formulas, idioms, and situation-bound utterances can all be considered as examples of formulaic language (Howarth, 1998; Kecskes, 2000; Wray, 1999, 2002, 2005). These word strings occurring together tend to convey holistic meanings that are either more than the sum of the individual parts, or else diverge significantly from a literal, or word-for-word meaning and operate as a single semantic unit (Gairns & Redman, 1986, p. 35).

Formulaic language is the heart and soul of native-like language use. In intercultural communication, the type of communication in which bilinguals usually participate most frequently, one of the major issues is to decide how exactly we expect interlocutors to use the common language, the lingua franca. Is it enough for the participants just to use the common language as a system of linguistics signs (sticking mainly to the literal meanings of lexical units) with possible meanings that are disambiguated and negotiated in the process of interaction, or do we expect that the interlocutors stick to the rules of the game and speak similarly to the native speakers of that language (i.e., rely on both prefabricated chunks and *ad-hoc* generated elements and combine them in a creative way)?

In monolingual production there is hardly any doubt about the salience of the idiom principle. Coulmas (1981, p. 1) argued that much of what is actually said in everyday conversation is by no means unique. "Rather, a great deal of communicative activity consists of enacting routines making use of prefabricated linguistic units in a well-known and generally accepted manner." He continued, claiming that "successful co-ordination of social intercourse heavily depends on standardized ways of organizing interpersonal encounters" (p. 3). Howarth (1998) also talked about the fact that native speaker linguistic competence has a large and significant phraseological component. This means that the ability to sound idiomatic (i.e., achieving *nativelike selection*, in the words of Pawley and Syder, 1983) plays a very important role in language production and comprehension. This fact has a profound effect on how we explain intercultural interaction because both figurative and formulaic language is the result of conventionalization and standardization that is supported by regular use of certain lexical units for particular purposes in a speech community. This is usually what non-native speakers have limited access to in the target language.

People using a particular language and belonging to a particular speech community have *preferred ways of saying things* (cf. Kecskes, 2007; Wray, 2002) and *preferred ways of organizing thoughts* (Kecskes, 2007). Preferred ways of saying things are generally reflected in the use of formulaic language and figurative language, while preferred ways of organizing thoughts can be detected through analyzing, for instance, the use of subordinate conjunctions, clauses, and discourse markers. Selecting the right words and expressions and formulating utterances in ways preferred by the native speakers of that language (*nativelike selection*) is more important than syntax. The following example from a sign in an Austrian hotel catering to skiers (Octopus, 1995, p. 144) demonstrates this clearly. The sentence shows absolutely bad word choices but acceptable syntax.

(1) *Not to perambulate the corridors in the hours of repose in the boots of descension.*
    Correctly: *Don't walk in the halls in ski boots at night.*

Psychological Saliency and the Formulaic Continuum

Psychological Saliency of Word Sequences

The importance of formulaic language was noticed in earlier linguistic research. Hymes (1962) pointed out that an immense portion of verbal behavior consists of linguistic routines. Bolinger (1976, p. 2) suggested that "speakers do at least as much remembering as they do putting together." Fillmore (1976, p. 4) also found that "an enormously large amount of natural language is formulaic, automatic and rehearsed, rather than propositional, creative or freely generated." However, with the appearance of huge corpora, understanding formulaic language has become more complicated. Working with large corpora, Altenberg (1998) went so far as to claim that almost 80 percent of our language production can be considered formulaic. Whatever the proportion actually is, one thing is for sure: Speakers in conventional speech situations tend to do more remembering than putting together. *Our everyday conversations are often restricted to short routinized interchanges where we do not always mean what we say.* So a typical conversation between a customer and a store assistant may sound like this:

(2) Conversation between store assistant (A), and customer (B):

A: – *What can I do for you?*
C: – *Thank you, I am just looking.*
A: – *Are you looking for something particular?*
C: – *No, not really.*
A: – *If you need help, just let me know.*

None of the expressions used by the speakers look freely generated. Each of them can be considered a formula that is tied to this particular kind of situation. However, if we consider the following conversation, we may see something different.

(3) Sam (S) and Bob (B) are talking:

S: – *If you want to see me again, you will need to do what I tell you to.*
B: – *OK, my friend.*

Can the underlined expressions be considered formulas? Are they in any way different from the ones in example (2)? There is no doubt that the underlined expressions consist of words that are frequently used together. But are they formulas here? Do they have some kind of psychological saliency as formulas for the speakers? We must be careful with the answer because *frequency is only one of the criteria* by which we can identify formulaic expressions. The problem is that the role of frequency seems to be over-emphasized in present-day linguistics, especially in corpus linguistics. Recent research analyzing written and spoken discourse has established that highly frequent, recurrent sequences of words, variously called lexical bundles, chunks, and multiword expressions, are not only salient but also functionally significant. Cognitive research demonstrated that knowledge of these ready-made expressions is crucial for fluent processing. The recurrent nature of these units is discussed in the relevant literature (Biber, Johansson, Leech, Conrad, & Finegan, 1999; McEnery & Wilson, 1996). Simpson-Vlach and Ellis (2010) confirmed that large stretches of language are adequately described as collocational streams where patterns flow into each other. However, Sinclair's (1991) idiom principle is based primarily on frequency that results in long lists of recurrent word sequences (Biber, Conrad, & Cortes, 2004; Biber et al., 1999), which hardly give any chance to distinguish where we have conventionalized formulas or where we have just frequently occurring word chunks that lack psychological saliency. Biber et al. (1999, p. 990), in their study of *lexical bundles*, defined formulaic language as *sequences of word forms that commonly go together in natural discourse*, irrespective of their structural makeup or idiomaticity, and argued that conversation has a larger amount of lexical bundle types than academic prose. However, there seems to be a clear difference from the perspective of psychological saliency between sequences such as *to tell the truth, as a matter of fact* on the one hand, and *if they could . . .* or *to make it* on the other, although all these expressions are high on any frequency-based list. This is why we need to distinguish between groups of prefabricated expressions that have psychological saliency for speakers of a particular language community and loosely tied, frequently occurring word-sequences (usually consisting of common words) such as *if they want, to do with it, and of the,* and *tell them to.* Simpson-Vlach and Ellis (2010) argued that psycholinguistically salient sequences like *on the other hand, suffice it to say* cohere much more than would be expected by chance. They are *glued together* and thus are measures of association, rather than raw frequency, and are likely more relevant to these formulaic expressions.

L2 studies that are relevant for bilinguals show something different. They emphasize the importance of frequency in processing formulaic language. Ellis et al. (2008) argued that formula processing by non-natives, despite their many years of English as a Second Language (ESL) instruction, was a result of the frequency of the string rather than its coherence. For learners at that stage of development, it is the number of times the string appears in the input that determines fluency. Ellis et al. argued that tuning the system according to frequency of occurrence alone is not enough for nativelike accuracy and efficiency. According to those authors, what is additionally required is tuning the system for coherence–for co-occurrence greater than chance. Ellis et al. (2008) claimed that this is what solves the two puzzles for linguistic theory posed by Pawley and Syder (1983), nativelike selection and nativelike fluency. Native speakers have extracted the underlying co-occurrence information, often implicitly, from usage; non-natives, even advanced ESL learners with more than ten years of English instruction, still have a long way to go in their sampling of language. These learners are starting to recognize and become attuned to more frequent word sequences, but they need help to recognize distinctive formulas.

Why is this issue important for bilinguals? It is because the development of psychological validity/saliency of these expressions in L2 is *a matter of not only frequency and exposure to the language use but also immersion in the culture and the wish of the non-native speaker regardless of whether s/he wants to use them*. Frequent encounters with these expressions for non-native speakers help but are not enough to develop psychological saliency, as the following encounter between a Korean student and a clerk at the registrar's office demonstrates:

(4) Korean student (Lee) and Registrar (Clerk) encounter:

LEE: *Could you sign this document for me, please?*
CLERK: *Come again...?*
LEE: *Why should I come again? I am here now.*

In spite of the distinctive intonation used by the clerk when uttering *come again*, the Korean student processed the expression not as a formula but a freely generated expression with literal meaning. So what really counts is the *measures of association, rather than raw frequency. What creates psychological saliency is the discursive function in a particular context of that expression.* The functional aspect is what makes immersion in the culture important for non-native speakers, because that is where those functions come from.

The difference in developing and using formulaic language in native and non-native speakers raises the questions: Not having "nativelike selection" skills and "nativelike fluency," how much can bilingual speakers stick to the original rules of the game in intercultural interactions when using their L2? How salient is the "idiom principle" in L2 language production of bilinguals?

I will try to answer the question by analyzing natural language data. However, before the analysis we will briefly need to look at the various groups of formulas that will be subject to analysis.

The Formulaic Continuum

Certain language sequences have conventionalized meanings that are used in predictable situations. This functional aspect, however, is different in each type of fixed expression, which justifies the hypothesis of a *continuum* (Kecskes, 2003, 2007) that contains grammatical units (e.g., *be going to*) on the left, fixed semantic units (cf. *as a matter of fact; suffice it to say*) in the middle, and pragmatic expressions (such as situation-bound utterances: *welcome aboard; help yourself*) and idioms (*make ends meet, spill the beans*) on the right. This continuum (see Table 1, below) categorizes only those expressions that are motivated and have some psychological saliency for the speakers of a speech community.

The more we move to the right on the functional continuum, the wider the gap seems to become between compositional meaning and actual situational meaning of expressions. Language development often results in a change of function (i.e., a right-to-left or left-to-right movement of a linguistic unit on the continuum). Lexical items such as *going to* can become grammaticalized, or lexical phrases may lose their compositionality and develop an *institutionalized* function, such as *I'll talk to you later, Have a nice day, Welcome aboard, Be my guest*, and the like. Speech formulas such as *you know, not bad, that's all right* are similar to situation-bound utterances (SBU). The difference between them is that while SBUs are usually tied to particular speech situations, speech formulas can be used anywhere in the communication process where the

Table 1. *Formulaic Continuum*

Grammar Units	Fixed Semantic Units	Phrasal Verbs	Speech Formulas	Situation-bound Utterances	Idioms
going to	*as a matter of fact*	*put up with*	*going shopping*	*welcome aboard*	*kick the bucket*
have to	*suffice it to say*	*get along with*	*not bad you know*	*help yourself*	*spill the beans*

speakers find them appropriate. See, for instance, the difference between *nice to meet you* and *you know* or *have a nice weekend* and *kinda*.

Pilot Study

In 2007 I conducted a cross-sectional survey to investigate how bilingual English lingua franca speakers use formulaic language in order to answer the following question: With no native speakers participating in the language game, how much will the players stick to the original rules of the game? I thought that the best way to answer this question was to focus on formulaic expressions that are the reflections of *nativelikeness* that is best defined as knowing preferred ways of saying things and preferred ways of organizing thoughts in a language (Kecskes, 2007).

Data were collected in spontaneous lingua franca communication. Participants were thirteen adult individuals in two groups with the following first languages: Spanish, Chinese, Polish, Portuguese, Czech, Telugu, Korean, and Russian. All subjects came from the Albany community, had spent a minimum of six months in the United States, and had at least intermediate knowledge of English before arriving. None of them had English as their first language. Both group 1 (7 students) and group 2 (6 students) participated in a 30-minute discussion about the following topics: housing in the area, jobs, and local customs. The conversations were undirected and uncoached. Subjects said what they wanted to say. No native speaker was present. Conversations were recorded and then transcribed, which resulted in a 13,726 word database.

Data analysis focused on the types of formulaic units given in Table 1 above. The questions I sought to answer can be summarized as follows:

1) How does the use of formulas relate to the *ad hoc* generated expressions in the data?
2) What type of fixed expressions did the subjects prefer?
3) What formulas did speakers create on their own?

Findings

The database consists of 13,726 words. Table 2 below shows the number of words that represent the six types of formulaic units that I focused on in the database. Words were counted in each type of formulaic chunk in the transcripts. Following are samples for each unit:

GRAMMATICAL UNITS: *I am going to stay here; you have to do that.*
FIXED SEMANTIC UNITS: *After a while, for the time being, once a month, for a long time.*

Table 2. *Number of Expressions that Represent the Six Types of Formulaic Units*

Grammar Units	Fixed Semantic Units	Phrasal Verbs	Speech Formulas	Situation-bound Utterances	Idioms	Total
102	235	281	250	57	115	1040

PHRASAL VERBS:	*They were worried about me; take care of the kids.*
SPEECH FORMULAS:	*Not bad; that's why; you know; I mean; that's fine.*
SITUATION-BOUND UTTERANCES:	*How are you?; have a nice day; you are all set.*
IDIOMS:	*Give me a ride; that makes sense.*

What is striking is the relatively low occurrence of formulaic expressions in the database. There were 1,040 formulas total used as formulaic expressions out of 13,726 in the corpus, which is only 7.6 percent. Even if we know that this low percentage refers only to one particular database and the results may change significantly if our focus is on other databases, it is still much less than linguists speak about when they address the issue of *formulaicity* in native speaker conversation. Even if our database is very limited and does not let us make generalizations about lingua franca communication, one thing seems to be obvious. *As far as formulaic language use is concerned, there seems to be a significant difference between native speaker communication and lingua franca communication with bi- and multilingual speakers.* Non-native speakers appear to rely on prefabricated expressions in their lingua franca language production to a much smaller extent than native speakers. The question is why this is so. For an answer to the question, we should look at the distribution of formula types in the database displayed in Table 2.

Most frequent occurrences are registered in three groups: fixed semantic units, phrasal verbs, and speech formulas. It is interesting to note that Ortactepe (2012) also found in her study that these three types of formulaic expressions are the ones most used and preferred in non-native speaker language production. However, we have to be careful with speech formulas that constitute a unique group, because if we examine the different types of expressions within the group, we can see that three expressions (*you know*; *I / you mean*; *you're right*) account for 66.8 percent (167 out of 250) of all units counted in this group. The kind of frequency we see in the use of these three expressions is not comparable to any other expressions in the database. This seems to make sense because these particular speech formulas may fulfill a variety of different functions such as *back-channeling* (i.e., cases in which a listener utters short speech formulas such as *right, I see*, or *OK* to signal to the speaker that she follows or agrees with him) or *filling a gap*. They are also used very frequently by native speakers so it is easy for non-native speakers to pick them up.

If we disregard speech formulas for the reason explained above, formulas that occur in higher frequency than any other expressions are fixed semantic units and phrasal verbs. We did not have a native speaker control group, but we can speculate that this might not be so in native speaker communication. It can be hypothesized (based on studies mentioned earlier) that native speakers use the groups of formulas in a relatively balanced way, or at least in their speech production fixed semantic units and phrasal verbs do not show priority to the extent shown in lingua franca communication. How can this preference of fixed semantic units and phrasal verbs by non-native speakers be explained? How does this issue relate to the first observation about the amount of formulas in native speaker communication and lingua franca communication of bilinguals?

As the *think aloud* sessions (in which subjects talked about their own language production) demonstrated, the two issues are interrelated. English lingua franca (ELF) speakers usually avoid the use of formulaic expressions not necessarily because, as they explained, they do not know these phrases, but because they are worried that their interlocutors, who are also non-native speakers, will not understand them properly. They are reluctant to use language that they know or perceive to be figurative or semantically less transparent (see also Philip, 2005). ELF speakers try to come as close to the compositional meaning of expressions as possible because they think that, if there is no figurative and/or metaphorical meaning involved, their partners will process the English words and expressions the way they meant them. Because bilingual speakers come from different sociocultural backgrounds and represent different cultures, *the mutual knowledge they may share is usually restricted to the knowledge of the linguistic code.* Consequently, semantic analyzability seems to play a decisive role in ELF speech production. This assumption is supported by the fact that the most frequently used formulaic expressions are the fixed semantic units and phrasal verbs in which there is semantic transparency to a much greater degree than in idioms, situation-bound utterances, or speech formulas. Of course, one can argue that phrasal verbs may frequently express figurative meaning and function like idioms, such as *I never hang out...* or *they will kick me out of my home...* However, when I found cases like this in the database, I listed the phrasal verb among the category "idioms" rather than "phrasal verbs." So the group of phrasal verbs above contains expressions in which there is usually clear semantic transparency.

Our subjects were more advanced speakers. This is important because there is a difference in formulaic language use between less and more proficient non-native speakers. Based on longitudinal studies, both Howarth (1998) and Ortactepe (2011) came to the conclusion that less proficient learners pick up formulaic expressions and overuse them, while more advanced learners prefer to generate their own sentences rather than resorting to prefabricated units, a process that Howarth (1998, p. 29) refers to as *deliberate creativity*. Formulaic expressions provide non-native speakers with *survival phrases that achieve basic socio-interactional functions* (Wray & Perkins, 2000, p. 23). They have automatic access to prefabricated chunks, and this eases communication especially in the early stages of language learning (cf. Nattinger & DeCarrico, 1992; Wray, 2002). According to Segalowitz and Freed (2004), at later stages of language development, formulaic expressions function as a database for non-native speakers from which "learners abstract recurrent patterns, leading to the mastery of grammatical regularities" (p. 403). Wray (2002) considers this creative tendency of advanced learners as a major problem resulting from "the production of perfectly grammatical utterances that are simply not used by native speakers" (p. 147). This claim is in line with my finding about the language use of lingua franca speakers. Pawley and Syder (1983) referred to this deliberate creativity of relatively advanced L2 learners as a process of overgenerating and producing grammatical, non-idiomatic utterances due to not having accumulated the native repertoire of formulaic expressions as "nativelike competence and fluency demand such idiomaticity" (Ellis, 2003, p. 12).

The danger for lingua franca speakers in the use of formulaic language is that they often pick up these expressions without comprehending the sociocultural load that they carry. This is especially true for situation-bound utterances in which it is usually the figurative meaning that is dominant rather than the literal meaning. In lingua franca communication, if one of the interactants does not know this figurative meaning and processes the utterance literally, misunderstanding may occur, such as in the following conversation between one of my Japanese students and me:

(5) Conversation between professor (Kecskes) and student (Noritaka):

NORITAKA: *Hi Professor Kecskes.*
KECSKES: *Hi Noritaka. How are you? Why don't you sit down?*
NORITAKA: *Because you did not tell me to.*
KECSKES: *OK, I am telling you now.*

Here I used the expression *why don't you sit down* figuratively as a formula, while the Japanese student processed it literally. In order to avoid cases like this, lingua franca speakers stick to literal rather than figurative production. The use of semantically transparent language resulted in fewer misunderstandings and communication breakdowns than expected in my survey. This finding of my study corresponds with House's (2003) observation about the same phenomena.

Another example of this interesting phenomenon in the database is speakers trying to create their own formulas. This phenomenon fully confirms the general priority of the idiom principle as most salient even in bilingual language production. Speakers (let them be mono- or multi-linguals) make an effort to use formulas, without regard for which of their languages they use.

The formulas our subjects created can be split into two categories. In the first category, we can find expressions that are used only once and demonstrate an effort to sound metaphorical. However, this endeavor is usually driven by the first language (L1) of the speaker in which there may be an equivalent expression for the given idea. For instance:

(6) Formulas that demonstrate an effort to sound metaphorical:
    It is almost skips from my thoughts.
    You are not very rich in communication.
    Take a school.

The other category comprises expressions that are created on the spot during the conversations and are picked up by the members of the *ad hoc* speech community. One of the participants creates or coins an expression that is needed in the discussion of a given topic. It becomes a part of the interculture being created (cf. Kecskes, 2013). This unit functions like a *target language formula*, the use of which may be accepted by the participants in the given conversation, as demonstrated by the fact that other participants also pick it up and use it. However, this is just a temporary formula that may be entirely forgotten when the conversation is over. This is a typical example of how intercultures are created. For instance:

(7) Formulas created on the spot or *ad hoc*:
    We connect each other very often.
    Native American (in the sense of native speaker of American English).

Lingua franca speakers frequently coin or create their own ways of expressing themselves effectively, and the mistakes they may make will carry on in their speech, even though the correct form is there for them to imitate. For instance, several participants adopted the phrase *Native Americans* to refer to native speakers of American English. Although in the think-aloud conversation session, the correct expression (*native speaker of American English*) was repeated several times by one of the researchers, the erroneous formula *Native Americans* kept being used by the lingua franca speakers. They even joked about it and said that the use of target language formulas coined by them in their temporary speech community was considered like a "joint venture" and created a special feeling of camaraderie in the group.

Based on this study we can say that with no native speakers participating in the language game, the lingua franca (L2) speakers cannot always keep the original rules of the game. So the "idiom principle" does not seem to be working as it does in L1. Kecskes (2007) argued that actual speech situations in lingua franca communication can be considered open social situations that do not encourage the use of formulaic language. In first language communication we have many more closed social situations defined by the parameters and values taken for granted in them (see Clark 1996, p. 297). The result of these closed social situations is a highly routine procedure. For instance:

(8) Closed social situations:

BAR:	*Two vodka tonics.*
MUSEUM TICKET BOOTH:	*Three adults and one child.*

In closed social situations the participants know their roles. Clark (1996) claimed that the interlocutors' rights, duties, and potential joint purposes are usually quite clear. All they need to establish is the joint purpose for that occasion, which they can do with a routine procedure. The first interlocutor initiates the conversational routine often with a phrasal unit, and the second interlocutor completes it by complying. Use of conversational routines and formulas requires shared background knowledge, of which there is very little in lingua franca communication. Therefore, it is quite clear why lingua franca communicators avoid formulaic language. For them literality plays a powerful role. But does this really mean that the idiom principle works differently when bilinguals use their L1 or L2?

Dataset

I conducted another study to examine what happens to speech production of bilingual speakers when they participate in lingua franca communication. Will the idiom principle really be blocked for them?

Or will their language production still be driven by the salience of the idiom principle, resulting in significant attempts to use formulas rather than freely generated expressions?

I examined the language production of bilingual non-native speakers of English in seven conversations. These conversations were 30-minute recordings of spontaneous speech on topics like health, sports, and living in Albany, for example. The participants were as follows: C1 Japanese and Korean, C2 Korean and Turkish, C3 Korean and Chinese, C4 Japanese and Chinese, C5 Chinese and Korean, C6 Korean and Burmese, C7 African French and Korean. As it can be seen, the participants were mainly Asian speakers with two exceptions. There is a major difference between the research on lingua franca described in the previous project and this one. In the former project I focused on the general use of all types of formulaic expressions in the conversations. In this research my main focus was on the idiom principle and the way bilingual speakers structured certain sequences within the conversations. Two types of production sequences were selected within the 30-minute sessions: "A," how participants introduce themselves (closed social situation), and "B," one new topic introduction from each conversation (open social situation) that was usually the first attempt to change the topic in the conversation. The excerpts I used for analysis can be found in the Appendix.

Salience of Formulaic Expressions

How Do Participants Introduce Themselves?

Out of the seven conversations, we have introductions in four cases (C1, C3, C4, C7). In the other three cases, speakers started in *medias res*, right in the middle. Introduction, which is supposed to be a closed social situation, requires formulaicity in most languages. Our four examples demonstrate that the idiom principle usually works in the L2 if the bilingual speakers are in a well-known closed social situation that exists across cultures. The speakers relied mainly on well-known situation-bound utterances rather than freely generated expressions. For instance:

- *Let me introduce myself first.*
- *So glad to meet you. Let me ask you how long you have been here?*
- *Can I ask your name?*
- *Nice to meet you.*
- *How long have you been here?*

In the other three conversations, there is no direct introduction because the subjects knew each other. But the start of conversation in each case shows an endeavor to use formulaic expressions such as

> *Do you like sports?*
> *What kind of sports?*
> *... Do you think there are many activities in Albany...*
> *... Do you keep yourself healthy?*

It is important to note that our subjects were students with pre-advanced level of English. They were all familiar with the formulas that are used in introduction in the target language.

Introducing a New Topic

New topic introduction is an open social situation. Although the frame is well known, the language that is associated with it is much less formalized than in closed social situations. As the examples below demonstrate, each subject used mainly some *ad hoc* generated way to introduce the topic. However, the idiom principle was still in play because the *ad-hoc*-generated utterance chunks are combined with some formulaic expressions that are relevant to the matter the participants attempted to talk about, as shown in in C3B, C6B, and C7B.

C1B: *Ok it's been three or... three months so far right? Do you like living in Albany? Living in America?*

C2B: *......... And my country ... in my country peoples don't like sport.*

C3B: *So what about here?*

C4B: *So can you please tell me the difficulties in life here?*

C5B: *Another thing I noticed about American food is that ... although its contains a lot of fat or something unhealthy, but there's always options you can choose like low ... low calorie grocery or zero calorie version of diet thing.*

C6B: *And what about ... do you care more about ... food? Since this is like another other foreign country ... so do you take care more about choosing some food?*

C7B: *You say you live in Albany so how is the place where you live? Can you describe the place where you live?*

Comparison of the Bilingual Project with the Lingua Franca Project

It is interesting to compare the numbers in the bilingual project (BP; see Table 3) with those of the lingua franca project (LFP; see Table 4). The similarities are striking, although the subjects were totally different, their language proficiency was also different, and they talked about different topics. In the BP the subjects worked in pairs, while in the LFP there were six to seven subjects in each group. In the bilingual project only five

Table 3. *Number of Formulas That Represent the Five Types of Formulas in the Bilingual Project (BP)*

Fixed Semantic Units	Phrasal Verbs	Speech Formulas	Situation-bound Utterances	Idioms	Total
276	133	227	240	156	1032

Note. Total number of words: 13513; Total number of formulas: 1032; Percentage: 7.63%.

Table 4. *Number of Expressions that Represent the Six Types of Formulaic Units in the Lingua Franca Project (LFP; same as Table 2)*

Grammar Units	Fixed Semantic Units	Phrasal Verbs	Speech Formulas	Situation-bound Utterances	Idioms	Total
102	235	281	250	57	115	1040

Note. Total number of words: 13726; Total number of formulas: 1040; Percentage: 7.57%.

groups of formulas were considered, while in the LFP grammatical formulas were also counted.

Summary and Conclusion

The research revealed some important features of bilingual language use. Based on the presented results we can claim that the idiom principle does not seem to depend on how many languages an individual can speak and on what level. The important thing is that *the economy principle affects the use of any language of bilinguals and multilinguals,* the question only is to what extent. Human beings want to achieve as much as possible with the least possible effort, both in production and comprehension. The best way to do that is to use as many prefabricated chunks of language as possible and combine them with *ad-hoc*-generated utterances in a creative way. So the hypothesis about the idiom principle being blocked in subsequent languages was not supported by this study. However, there is another side of the matter: How can bilinguals cope with the requirements of the idiom principle in their L2? Does the principle operate to full extent as in L1? The results of both studies show that the answer is not exactly. There are several factors not present in L1 but in L2 that affect the functioning of the idiom principle in different degrees. Such factors include language proficiency, willingness to use certain formulas, language fluency of other participants and lack of core common ground. As a result, the actual production of formulaic expressions in the L2 of a bilingual will always be lower than in L1.

As mentioned above, there are several variables in which the two studies differ. However, they show striking similarities in the use of formulaic language in general. The total number of words in both projects is very close: LFP: 13726, BP: 13513, and so are the total number of formulaic expressions: LFP: 1040, BP: 1032. It just cannot be by chance that these numbers are so close. The number of fixed semantic units and speech formulas is also very similar. This refers to the fact that the conclusion of the LFP (Kecskes, 2007) was correct when it emphasized that bilinguals in their L2 when participating in lingua franca communication prefer the use of semantically more transparent language to formulaic language, in order to make sure that they will be understood by all interactants.

Although the general use of formulaic language is very similar in the two studies, there are still differences in the distribution of formulas under the influence of specific variables mentioned above. For instance, there are differences in the use of phrasal verbs and situation-bound utterances. In the bilingual project the subjects used many more situation-bound utterances than in the LFP. However, the use of phrasal expressions shows a different picture. The use of situation-bound utterances is a sign of the L2 language socialization process (cf. Kecskes, 2003; Ortactepe, 2012). The bilingual participants had pre-advanced proficiency in English and overall spent more time in the target language environment than the subjects in the LFP whose proficiency level was intermediate. Besides, the subjects in the BP were students, while in the LFP participants came from the community.

There is also an explanation for the significant difference in that phrasal expressions were used much more frequently by the LFP subjects. As mentioned above, the participants of the lingua franca projects came from the Albany community to improve their English in evening classes conducted by teachers of English to speakers of other languages students. Their syllabus put special emphasis on the use of phrasal verbs in English.

Based on the two studies (LFP and BP) we can conclude that, although the idiom principle affects any language production, it results in less formulaic language use in L2 than in L1 of bilinguals. This claim basically concurs with the findings of other studies (cf. Bolander, 1989; Pawley & Syder, 1983; Warga, 2008; Weinert, 1995) that also argued about the restricted use of formulaic language in L2.

List of Key Words

Chunks, Closed social situation, Collocational streams, Common ground, Compositionality, Conventionalization, Corpus linguistics, Deliberate creativity, Economy principle, Egocentrism, English as a Second Language (ESL), English Lingua Franca (ELF), Figurative meaning, Fixed semantic units, Formulaic language, Formulaicity, Frozen metaphors, Idiomaticity, Idiom principle, Illocutionary acts, Immersion, Language fluency, Lexical bundles, Metaphorical meaning, Multiword expressions, Nativelike competency, Nativelike selection, Open choice principle, Open social situation, Phrasal verbs, Prefabricated expressions, Production, Psychological saliency, Relevance Theory, Semantic analyzability, Semantic transparency, Situation-bound utterances (SBU), Socialization, Socio-cultural load, Standardization, Word selection

Thought Questions

1. Do you think that code-switching would block the idiom principle?
2. Where do you think human languages use more fomulaicity: in written or oral speech?
3. Why is it that bilinguals stick to semantically more transparent language in their L2 but not necessarily in their L1?
4. Do you think that higher proficiency in a language will result in more frequent use of formulaic language?

Suggested Student Research Projects

1. Using the attached appendix find situation-bound utterances (SBU), categorize them by their functions, and try to explain why exactly those SBUs were used in those conversations.
2. According to Table 3, the number of words representing fixed semantic units is 276. Identify as many fixed semantic units as you can in the excerpts provided in the index.

Related Internet Sites

Corpus of Contemporary American English: http://corpus.byu. edu/coca

Corpus of Spoken Language: www.linguistics.ucsb.edu/ research/santa-barbara-corpus

Idiom Dictionary: www.tomisimo.org/idioms

Suggested Readings

Kecskes, I. (2003). *Situation-bound utterances in L1 and L2*. Berlin/New York: Mouton de Gruyter.

Schmitt, N., Dornyei, Z., Adolphs, S., & Durow, V., (2004). Knowledge and acquisition of formulaic sequences: A longitudinal study. In N. Schmitt (Ed.), *Formulaic sequences: Acquisition, processing and use* (pp. 55–86). Amsterdam: John Benjamins Publishing.

Van Lancker Sidtis, D. (2008). Formulaic and novel language in a "dual process" model of language competence: Evidence from surveys, speech samples, and schemata. In R.L. Corrigan, E.A. Moravcsik, H. Ouali, & K.M. Wheatley (Eds.), *Formulaic language: Volume 2. Acquisition, loss, psychological reality, functional applications* (pp. 151–176). Amsterdam: John Benjamins Publishing.

Wray, A. (2002). *Formulaic language and the lexicon*. Cambridge, UK: Cambridge University Press.

REFERENCES

Altenberg, B. (1998). On the phraseology of spoken English: The evidence of recurrent word-combinations. In A.P. Cowie (Ed.), *Phraseology: Theory, analysis, and applications* (pp. 101–122). Oxford, UK: Clarendon Press.

Biber, D., Conrad, S., & Cortes, V. (2004). If you look at . . .: Lexical bundles in university teaching and textbooks. *Applied Linguistics 25*, 371–405.

Biber, D., Johansson, S., Leech, G., Conrad, S., & Finegan, E. (1999). *Longman grammar of spoken and written English*. London: Pearson Education.

Bolander, M. (1989). Prefabs, patterns and rules in interaction? Formulaic speech in adult learners' L2 Swedish. In K. Hyltenstam & L.K. Obler (Eds.), *Bilingualism across the Lifespan: Aspects of acquisition, maturity, and loss* (pp. 73–86). Cambridge, UK: Cambridge University Press.

Bolinger, D. (1976). Meaning and memory. *Forum Linguisticum 1*, 1–14.

Clark, H.H. (1996). *Using language*. Cambridge, UK: Cambridge University Press.

Coulmas, F. (Ed.). (1981). *Conversational routine: Explorations in standardized communication situations and prepatterned speech*. The Hague: Mouton.

Ellis, N.C. (2003). Constructions, chunking, and connectionism: The emergence of second language structure. In C.J. Doughty & M.H. Long (Eds.), *The Handbook of second language acquisition* (pp. 63–103). Malden, MA: Blackwell.

Ellis, N.C., Simpson-Vlach, R., & Carson, M. (2008). Formulaic language in native and second language speakers: Psycholinguistics, corpus linguistics, and TESOL. *TESOL Quarterly 42*, 375–396.

Fillmore, C.J. (1976). The need for frame semantics within linguistics. *Statistical Methods in Linguistics 12*, 5–29.

(1982). Frame semantics. In The Linguistic Society of Korea (Ed.), *Linguistics in the morning calm* (pp. 111–137). Seoul: Hanshin.

Gairns, R., & Stuart, R. (1986). *Working with words: A guide to teaching and learning vocabulary*. Cambridge, UK: Cambridge University Press.

Giora, R. (1997). Understanding figurative and literal language: The graded
    salience hypothesis. *Cognitive Linguistics, 7*, 183–206.
    (2003). *On our mind: Salience, context and figurative language.* Oxford, UK:
    Oxford University Press.
House, J. (2003). Misunderstanding in intercultural university encounters.
    In J. House, G. Kasper, & S. Ross (Eds.), *Misunderstanding in social life:
    Discourse approaches to problematic talk* (pp. 22–56). London: Longman.
Howarth, P. (1998). Phraseology and second language proficiency. *Applied
    Linguistics 19*, 24–44.
Hymes, D.H. (1962). The ethnography of speaking. In T. Gladwin & W.C.
    Sturtevant (Eds.),*Anthropology and human behavior* (pp. 13–53).
    Washington, DC: The Anthropology Society of Washington.
Kecskes, I. (2000). A cognitive-pragmatic approach to situation-bound
    utterances. *Journal of Pragmatics 32*, 605–625.
    (2003). *Situation-bound utterances in L1 and L2.* Berlin/New York: Mouton de
    Gruyter.
    (2007). Formulaic language in English lingua franca. In I. Kecskes &
    Horn, L.R (Eds.), In *Explorations in pragmatics: Linguistic, cognitive and
    intercultural aspects* (pp. 191–219). Berlin/New York: Mouton de Gruyter.
    (2012). Is there anyone out there who really is interested in the speaker?
    Language and Dialogue 2, 283–297.
    (2013). *Intercultural pragmatics.* Oxford, UK: Oxford University Press.
McEnery, T., & Wilson, A. (1996). *Corpus linguistics.* Edinburgh: Edinburgh
    University Press.
Miller, J., & Weinert, R. (1998). *Spontaneous spoken language: Syntax and
    discourse.* Oxford, UK: Clarendon Press.
Nattinger, J.R., & DeCarrico, J.S. (1992). *Lexical phrases and language teaching.*
    New York: Oxford University Press.
Octopus. (1995, October). p. 144.
Ortaçtepe, D. (2012). *The development of conceptual socialization in international
    students: A language socialization perspective on conceptual fluency and social
    identity (advances in pragmatics and discourse analysis).* Cambridge,
    UK: Cambridge Scholars Publishing.
Pawley, A., & Hodgetts S.F. (1983). Two puzzles for linguistic theory: Nativelike
    selection and nativelike fluency. *Language and Communication 5*, 191–226.
Prodromou, L. (2008). *English as a lingua franca: A corpus based analysis.* London:
    Continuum.
Segalowitz, N. & Freed, B.F. (2004). Context, contact, and cognition in oral
    fluency acquisition: Learning Spanish in at home and study abroad contexts.
    Studies in Second Language Acquisition, 26, 173–199.
Simpson-Vlach, R., & Ellis, N.C. (2010). An academic formulas list: New
    methods in phraseology research. *Applied Linguistics 31*, 487–512
Sinclair, J. (1991). *Corpus, concordance, collocation.* Oxford, UK: Oxford
    University Press.
Sperber, D., & Wilson, D. (1995). *Relevance: Communication and cognition*
    (2nd ed.). Oxford: Blackwell.
Warga, M. (2005).'Je serais très merciable': Formulaic vs. creatively produced speech
    in learners' request closings. *Canadian Journal of Applied Linguistics, 8*, 67–94.

Weinert, R. (1995). The role of formulaic language in second language acquisition: A review. *Applied Linguistics, 16*, 180–205.

Wray, A. (1999). Formulaic language in learners and native speakers. *Language Teaching 32*, 213–231.

(2002). *Formulaic language and the lexicon.* Cambridge, UK: Cambridge University Press.

(2005). Idiomaticity in an L2: Linguistic processing as a predictor of success. In B. Briony (Ed.), *IATEFL 2005: Cardiff conference selections* (pp. 53–60). Canterbury: IATEFL.

Wray, A., & Perkins, M.R. (2000). The functions of formulaic language: An integrated model. *Language and Communication 20*, 1–28.

APPENDIX: EXCERPTS

C1: Korean and Japanese

A

– Can I ask your name?
– I'm Tsubasa.
– Tsubasa, ok.
– And your?
– Seungjung, I'm from South Korea.

B

– Ok it's been three or... three months so far right? Do you like living in Albany? Living in America?
– Yes I like..
– What makes you like this life? What is your ... like.. What you like about living in Albany?
– I stay here only 4 month in this semester so I have no time. I go to many place... I went to Boston, Washington DC, of course New York City.

C2: Korean and Turkish

A

– Sports. Do you like the sports?
– I like.
– What kind of sports?
– I like tennis.
– Oh ok.
– And soccer.

– Soccer.

– When I was young I played soccer.

B

– .... And my country ... in my country peoples don't
like sport.

– Oh really.

– I like but ... they like but they haven't time. I see in Albany too
many people like sport. And they run and fitness.

– Yeah.

– They fitness. Too many people play tennis. So I think they
sport. they they keep yourselves healthy.

C3: Korean and Chinese

A

– How long have you been here?

– Oh like a. ... Getting to be ... almost one year.

– One year?

– Yeah, almost one year. But it's like ... ten months. ... since
I've been here.

– Oh it's good.

– Two months to go..

B

– So what about here?

– Well the only experience I got from here was like hanging out with
American college students. And they were like ... I think they were
really fun to hanging out ... inside the house. Having drinks inside
the house not going out... maybe sometimes go out for a drink. ...

C4: Chinese and Japanese

A

– Let me introduce myself first. I'm a visiting scholar from a
Chinese university. Ok. So we are familiar.

– (laughing).

– Because we are neighbors. Actually ... right. So glad to meet
you. Let me ask you how long you have been here?

– Two and a half month.

B

– So can you please tell me the difficulties in life here..
– Ah.
– Or challenges.
– Everything difficult.
– Very. Could you please give me some examples?
– Shopping is difficult.
– Yeah . . . really. . . would you please describe it in detail?
– In [shopright?] . . . we have to put on . . . my good . . . belt . . . on
  the belt . . .

C5: Chinese and Korean

A

– I surely . . . do you think there are many activities in Albany . . .
  are . . .. Do you many activities are in Albany to s. . .. keep
  healthy ?
– Yeah, actually on campus you know there is a gym.
– A gym . . . ah I heard. . . I heard students can swim.

B

– Another thing I noticed about American food is that . . .
  although its contains a lot of fat or something unhealthy, but
  there's always options you can choose like low . . . low calorie
  grocery or zero calorie version of diet thing.
– Right right.
– The diet version you can always choose like. . ..
– Right.
– That's what I select . . . what I choose when I have to eat
  American food.

C6: Korean and Burmese

A

– Ok good. . . . mmmm . . . do you keep yourself healthy?
  So I just want to ask do you exercise on a regular basis? Here in
  Albany?
– Ah no. but sometime I did it. But sometime not. It's not always.
– Not always
– Yeah

B

– And what about ... do you care more about ... food? Since this is like another other foreign country ... so do you take care more about choosing some food?
– Yeah I choose some food
– Oh like what?
– Like ... You know in my country like a ... we always eat rice and soup...
– Oh right, you are from ...
– Burma like ...

C7: African French and Korean

A

– My name is Patrick.
– My name is Emi.
– Emi. Nice to meet you.
– Me too. Nice to meet you.
– It's not very formal. You can answer a few questions in an informal way. Just be relaxed.

B

– You say you live in Albany so how is the place where you live? Can you describe the place where you live?
– What? Sorry.
– I mean the place where you live. You said you live in Albany right?
– Place? What place? Korea.
– Place ... place...
– Ah place... describe in Albany.
– Yeah is it a good place? How is it? How are the houses there? Can you walk out straight and get the first ... do you like the place where you live here in Albany?
– I like living in Albany. Because the Albany is the... especially I [word] almost two months... it's quiet ... nice people ... neighbor...
– Yeah you have nice neighbors.
– Yeah and making [word].

3   Linking the Figurative to the Creative: Bilinguals' Comprehension of Metaphors, Jokes, and Remote Associates

Jyotsna Vaid, Belem G. López, and Francisco E. Martínez
Texas A&M University

ABSTRACT

The research reported here examined how Spanish-English bilinguals interpret novel metaphors, detect humor, and uncover links between distantly related words. Study 1 found that judgments of the literal truth of statements were slowed by literally false metaphoric statements in bilinguals and monolinguals alike. Study 2 found that when deciding whether sentences were jokes or not jokes, bilinguals tended to be more accurate than monolinguals. Study 3 found that bilinguals' success in arriving at solutions to remote associate problems was affected by their prior experience in informal translation (language brokering) and by their Spanish proficiency: Although no group differences were found in English, language brokers performed better than non-brokers on Spanish remote associates. It is suggested that the study of creative language use can inform the study of bilingual figurative language processing and that future research more systematically probe individual differences among bilinguals in creative language processing.

Keywords: bilingualism, language brokering, creativity, joke detection, metaphoric processing

Inquiry into how bilingual speakers perceive, acquire, produce, and interpret figurative language (metaphors, idioms, proverbs, jokes, etc.) opens up potentially new ways of conceptualizing both the varieties of language use and of language users. In particular, the study of figurative language processing brings into the foreground social, affective, and aesthetic dimensions of language use and offers new ways of examining – and complicating – the process of sense-making in which all individuals engage, whether they are single or multiple language users.

Mastery of appropriate use of figurative expressions in a second language (L2) has been acknowledged to be one of the greatest challenges for L2 learners. Not surprisingly, therefore, early empirical investigations of L2 figurative language use have been guided largely by pedagogical concerns surrounding the appropriate use of humor (Schmitz, 2002), idioms (Cooper, 1999), metaphor (Danesi, 1992), and formulaic expressions (Wray, 2003).

Psycholinguistic research on bilingualism has tended to focus mainly on lexical or semantic variables with little consideration given to the complexities of conceptual representations in bilinguals and how they might change and interact with changes in language proficiency or use (Pavlenko, 2000). Experimental studies of figurative language processing in bilinguals have been relatively scarce (but see Bortfeld, 2002; Matlock & Heredia, 2002).

The approach we take to the study of figurative language processing in bilinguals is to frame it as an exploration of creative language use (see Vaid, 2000, 2006). Further, recognizing that *bilingualism* – just like *figurative language* – is not a unitary construct, we consider it important to identify systematic sources of variation *within* bilinguals' linguistic and/or cultural experiences that may differentially influence figurative language processing. Questions that motivate our broader research program are the following: In what ways do bilinguals play with and through language? Does knowing more than one language enhance the capacity to exploit ambiguity in each language and across language boundaries? Is the interpretation and recall of metaphors, proverbs, or idioms tied to the language in which they are initially encountered? What are the processing consequences of cross-language overlap or divergence in the form or content of nonliteral expressions?

We summarize three studies we conducted on figurative language processing in Spanish-English bilingual adults. Although differing in their specific focus, each study was concerned with multiple meaning activation, that is, how ambiguity is identified and exploited by bilinguals within and across their languages. The first study reports findings from two experiments that addressed whether figurative meaning of novel metaphoric expressions is optionally or nonoptionally activated. The second examines whether bilingualism enhances sensitivity to one-line joke texts that play on multiple meanings. The third study examines whether differences among bilinguals in early informal translation experience (i.e., *language brokering*) affects the ability to identify remote associates of words in each language. After presenting each study we conclude by suggesting directions for further research.

Study 1: Are Metaphoric Meanings Obligatorily Accessed by Bilinguals?

The empirical study of figurative language processing in single-language users has been shaped by two differing theoretical positions with respect to the role of figurative language in linguistic expression or conceptualization. An early view, characterized as the *Standard Pragmatic Model*, regards nonliteral forms of language (e.g., metaphors) as essentially stylistic add-ons. According to this model, utterances are initially obligatorily analyzed for their literal meaning and only when a literal meaning is unavailable or otherwise inappropriate contextually is a nonliteral interpretation sought. This view regards figurative meanings as optionally, rather than obligatorily activated. By contrast, the alternative view maintains that figurative meaning is not only not optional, but in fact central to language and to thinking itself (Gibbs, 1994; Katz, Cacciari, Gibbs, & Turner, 1998; Kövecses, 2002).

Among those who hold the view that figurative meaning is central rather than subsidiary, there are different perspectives taken as to how figurative knowledge guides processing. Two models of particular relevance to the present study are of interest, the *Conceptual Metaphor View* and the *Attributive Categorization View*.

The Conceptual Metaphor View claims that linguistic meaning is based on embodied experience (Lakoff & Johnson, 1980; Lakoff & Turner, 1989; see also Katz & Bowes; Kövecses et al., this volume). In this view, embodied experience shapes language and thought and, through conceptual metaphors, meanings of words and phrases are constrained, which allows for the immediate understanding of linguistic expressions (Gibbs, 1994). Thus, embodied experience is the groundwork on which the conceptual metaphor view is built. The Attributive Categorization View, put forth by Glucksberg (2003), argues that metaphors are to be understood as categorical assertions. Glucksberg proposes that most words in metaphors have a dual reference. For example, in *Some lawyers are sharks*, the attributes of *shark* are not limited to cartilaginous fish but extend to other predatory creatures, allowing the interlocutor to understand the phrase as *some lawyers are predatory*. In the embodiment view, by contrast, our understanding of this metaphor might be explained by claiming that the conceptual metaphor PEOPLE ARE ANIMALS (e.g., *a snake in the grass, sheep in wolf's clothing, dirty rat*) underlies the correspondence between lawyers and sharks.

These two models differ in their underlying assumptions about the type of knowledge structures that guide metaphor processing. Whereas the conceptual view holds that conceptual metaphors guide metaphor interpretation, the Attributive Categorization View holds that categories accessed while encountering a metaphor activate other categories that are relevant to the topic. However, both views theorize that metaphor processing may occur without invoking an initial literal interpretation of the metaphor. That is, both models would reject the view that a specific literal interpretation is first sought and has to be judged anomalous before a figurative interpretation is achieved.

A third model proposes a different view than either of the two above models or the standard pragmatic view. For this view, the *Graded Salience Hypothesis* (Giora, 2003), what guides processing is not the literal or nonliteral status of an expression but its relative salience. Salience here refers to the form in which an expression is conventionally represented in the lexicon in the absence of context. Depending on its salience, a given expression may be more commonly interpreted in its nonliteral sense, whereas another expression might be more commonly interpreted in its figurative sense. The salience of an expression may also change with experience and may well differ as a function of one's degree of proficiency in a language (Cieślicka, 2006). Finally, an integrative framework to metaphor comprehension has been recently proposed by Wolff and Gentner (2011). This view makes use of a structural alignment perspective. In this approach, metaphor comprehension is thought to involve an initial symmetric process of finding commonalities and a subsequent phase in which inferences from a familiar base domain are projected to the target domain (Wolff & Gentner, 2011).

A question motivating early studies of metaphor processing was whether nonliteral meanings can be shown to be activated and understood as quickly as literal meanings. In a seminal study, Glucksberg, Gildea, and Bookin (1982) developed an interference measure to determine whether metaphoric meanings are automatically activated when people encounter sentences containing such meanings. In reviewing reaction time studies of metaphor comprehension, Hoffman and Kemper (1987) concluded that the metaphor interference paradigm is "the most finely tuned figurative language comprehension task" (p. 168).

In the metaphor interference paradigm, participants have to decide whether a class-inclusion statement is literally true or false and not simply whether the statement is grammatical or makes sense. Thus, on seeing the statement *Some animals are dogs,* participants are to respond "true," and on seeing the statement *Some weapons are pelicans,* they are to respond "false." The critical items are novel statements that have a metaphorical truth, such as *Some cats are detectives.* Glucksberg and colleagues (1982) argued that, on reaching a certain level of fluency, users of a language obligatorily activate metaphoric meaning if it is available. They hypothesized that when participants are required to make a "false" response based on a statement's literal meaning, reaction times would be longer if that statement has a metaphorical meaning than if it does not have a metaphorical meaning. That is, "true" metaphorical meanings should interfere with making a correct "false" response. Glucksberg et al. (1982) found that participants were in fact slower at responding to statements that are more easily perceived as metaphorical (e.g., *Some cats are detectives*) than to false statements that are not readily perceived as metaphorical (e.g., *Some weapons are pelicans*).

The metaphor interference task has been studied in a number of different populations (Kazmerski, Blasko, & Dessalegn, 2003; Pierce, MacLaren, & Chiappe, 2010; Wolff & Gentner, 2000). The consensus from several studies of metaphor comprehension is that literal meanings do *not* have priority over figurative meanings and that figurative meanings are for the most part activated automatically and early on in processing. This consensus, though, is based predominantly on research with single-language users. The question we posed was whether, among users of two or more languages, a similar pattern would emerge across languages or whether literal meanings would predominate in processing in the bilinguals' less proficient language.

Previous Research on Metaphor Comprehension in Bilinguals

Previous studies of metaphor comprehension in bilinguals have mainly focused on memory for similes, metaphors, or proverbs. Harris and colleagues, for example, compared bilinguals' memory for similes and metaphors in each language and found that bilinguals remember the metaphor phrases as similes (Harris, Tebbe, Leka, Garcia, & Erramouspe, 1999). Nelson (1992) examined recall of metaphors versus non-metaphors using a levels of processing approach. Under the various orienting conditions nonfluent bilinguals translated into English (L1) either the figurative meaning, literal meaning, or a nonspecific instructed translation or merely copied metaphoric statements presented in Spanish (L2). Nelson found that bilinguals' recall was best when they had to translate the metaphor's figurative meaning. Similarly, Vaid and Martínez (2001) examined bilinguals' incidental memory for the language of proverbs using proverbs that underwent different levels of processing in the encoding phase. They found, among other results, that meaning-based prior encoding (i.e., paraphrasing the proverb) lessened the accuracy of recognition of the input language of the proverbs relative to simply copying the proverb. Finally, some work has examined metaphor interpretation in bilingual children as a function of degree of language competence (e.g., Bountrogianni, 1988; Johnson, 1996).

Previous Research on Bilingualism and Cognitive Development

There has been a longstanding tradition within cognitive research on bilingualism to examine linguistic and conceptual repercussions of mastering two symbolic systems (Bialystok, 2004; Lambert, 1977). Vygotsky (1962) speculated about the enhanced linguistic awareness that may ensue from knowing two languages: "[T]he child learns to see his language as one particular system among many, to view its phenomena under more general categories, and this leads to awareness of his linguistic operations" (p. 110). This insight was put to empirical test in Peal and Lambert's (1962) landmark study that established, for the first time, a positive advantage of bilingualism on linguistic and nonverbal functioning.

Since the Peal and Lambert study, several other studies have also shown specific cognitive repercussions associated with knowing two or more languages beyond a certain minimum level of competence, although not all findings show a bilingual advantage. Of relevance to the present research, among the findings ascribed to bilingualism in the cognitive literature is an enhanced awareness of multiple meanings of ambiguous words or sentences (Cummins & Mulcahy, 1978).

The Present Research

Two experiments were conducted. Experiment 1 examined whether a metaphor interference effect is present in English-speaking monolinguals and in two groups of bilinguals tested in English with varying degrees of L2, Spanish in this case, proficiency. Experiment 2 examined whether a metaphor interference effect can be demonstrated in both languages of English-Spanish bilinguals differing in their L2 proficiency.

Experiment 1: Metaphor Interference in English Monolinguals and Bilinguals

This experiment sought to determine the existence of a metaphor interference effect for novel metaphors in English-speaking monolinguals and in two groups of Spanish-English bilinguals varying in their proficiency in Spanish. Participants were tested in English only. If both groups of bilingual participants take longer to reject as literally true metaphorical phrases over the control phrases that also require a false response, it would be concluded that automaticity of metaphorical activation is not contingent on language-familiarity-based factors such as proficiency.

Instead, one could infer that the participants rely predominantly on their underlying conceptual system to understand the phrases. If, on the other hand, proficiency level interacts with interference size, one might infer that non-optional activation of metaphoric meanings occurs only, or to a larger degree, in the bilingual's more dominant language.

A second question of interest concerned the relative size of the metaphor interference effect obtained in bilinguals versus monolinguals. Given that previous research in bilingualism has ascribed an enhanced inclination among bilinguals to process for meaning (see Lambert, 1977), in the present study one would expect bilinguals to show at least as strong an interference effect as monolinguals from the metaphoric meanings of literally false statements and probably greater interference than monolinguals.

Method

Participants

A group of 33 English-speaking monolinguals and 33 Spanish-English speakers at a large university in Texas participated in the experiment for course credit. An additional group of 30 monolingual students were recruited to provide ratings of the stimuli.

Based on their responses on a self-report language background questionnaire, a composite proficiency score was computed for the bilinguals. The average for the English composite proficiency score was 6.51 ($SD = 1.12$), while the average Spanish composite proficiency score was 5.40 ($SD = 1.44$), a statistically significant difference, $t(36) = 3.34$, $p < .01$ between the two groups. A 95 percent confidence interval was constructed for these data. Participants in the study were classified as balanced bilinguals if the difference between their English and Spanish composite comprehension scores lay inside the confidence interval. Similarly, if the difference between their English and Spanish composite scores lay outside the confidence interval, they were classified as more English or Spanish dominant.

Following the above criteria, 14 of the bilinguals were classified as English dominant (none were classified as Spanish dominant) and 19 were classified as equally proficient in both languages. Participants from the two groups did not differ in their relative dominance in English.

Materials

Stimuli were taken directly from Glucksberg et al. (1982, Experiment 3) and included 48 true high typical items, 48 true low typical items, 48 standard false items, 24 true metaphors and 24 scrambled metaphors (see Table 1). In addition, there were 48 practice stimuli.

Table 1. *Sample Stimuli in Metaphor Interference Study for Experiment 1*

Metaphorical Statements	Scrambled Metaphor Statements
Some cats are detectives	Some cats are chains
Some clouds are ice cream	Some clouds are detectives
Some favors are chains	Some favors are rockets
Some feet are wheels	Some feet are spotlights
Some fingers are forks	Some fingers are telescopes
Some hallways are telescopes	Some hallways are wheels

The metaphor and scrambled metaphor items were rated on metaphoricity and found to differ across the two categories, similar to what was reported in Glucksberg et al. (1982).

The true high typical items were statements that are high typical instances of their given category (e.g., *Some flowers are daisies*); the true low typical instances are not typical of their given category (e.g., *Some flowers are gladiolas*), and the standard false items consisted of true items that were re-paired randomly (e.g., *Some flowers are cobras*). The items were displayed on a computer screen under the control of the E-Prime software package.

Design and procedure
Mean reaction time scores of monolinguals and bilinguals were analyzed in separate analyses of variance (ANOVA). The design in the former case was a single-factor repeated measures design with four levels of Sentence Type (True, Standard False, Scrambled Metaphors, Metaphors). For the analysis of the bilinguals' data the design was a 2 (Group: English Dominant Bilinguals vs. Equally Proficient Bilinguals) x 4 (Sentence Type) mixed factorial with repeated measures on the second factor. For each group a repeated measures design was used with four levels of sentence type as the within subjects factor. Participants were instructed to decide whether each presented phrase was literally true or literally false and to indicate their decision by pressing one of two keys using their right index and middle fingers. They were instructed to respond as quickly as possible but to be accurate as well. At the end of the testing session, participants completed a language background questionnaire.

Results
A summary of mean responses per sentence type is provided in Figure 1. Mean RTs for correct responses only were included in the data analysis. Responses less than 150 ms or greater than 4000 ms were considered outliers and were treated as errors.

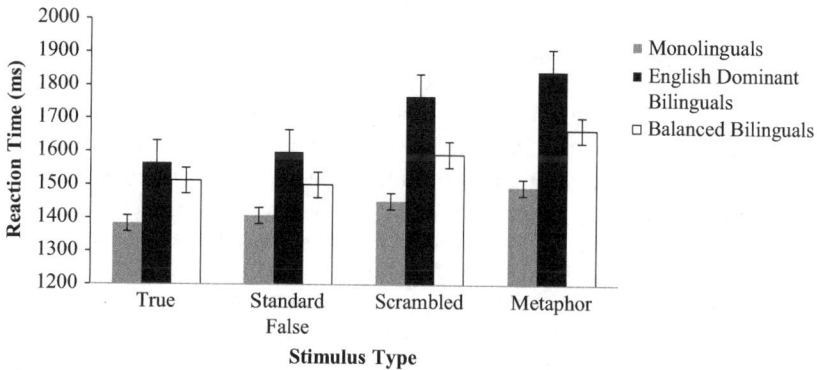

Figure 1. Mean Verification Latencies to English Sentences by Language Group and Sentence Type

Monolinguals

A paired sample t-test was computed to compare responses to True statements according to whether they were high or low in typicality. This comparison serves as a manipulation check to ensure that subjects in the task are processing sentences as they normally do in sentence verification tasks (i.e., faster responding to high typical than low typical). This was indeed the case with the monolingual participants, $t(32) = -9.13$, $p < .01$. The high versus low typicality data were pooled in subsequent analyses.

The mean RT for the four sentence types differed reliably, $F(2, 68) = 9.31$, $p < .01$. Planned comparisons were conducted to test the hypotheses that the average response time for True sentences would differ from that of False sentences and that the average response times of the Metaphor sentences would differ from the average of those other sentences requiring a false response. True sentences were indeed responded to faster than were any other sentence type, $t(160) = -2.99$, and responses to metaphoric statements were slower than any other type of sentence that required a false response, $t(160) = 3.23$. Pairwise comparisons showed that the mean difference between Metaphor sentences and Standard False sentences was significant (*Mean Difference* = 85.68, $p < .01$). The mean difference between the Scrambled and the Metaphor sentences approached significance (*Mean Difference* = 41.2, $p = .069$).

The results from the monolinguals showed that the findings of Glucksberg et al. (1982) were replicated. Monolingual participants in our study activated the nonliteral meanings of the metaphor sentences non-optionally. This supports the view that accessing the nonliteral meanings of sentences need not follow an initial activation and rejection of its literal meaning.

Bilinguals

A paired sample t-test was first computed to compare responses to the High typical ($M = 1433$, $SD = 230$) and Low typical ($M = 1700$, $SD = 264$) True sentences for the English dominant group. This difference was significant, $t(13) = -10.79$, $p < .01$, indicating that the participants in this group were responding as would be expected in a sentence verification task. Therefore, the high/low typicality true data were pooled in subsequent analyses. In the same manner, a paired sample t-test was computed to compare the high typical ($M = 1407$, $SD = 285$) and low typical ($M = 1620$, $SD = 311$) True sentences for the equally proficient group. This analysis also revealed a significant difference between the two sentence types, $t(18) = -10.66$, $p < .01$. These data were also pooled in subsequent analyses.

The reaction time data to correct responses were submitted to a mixed design ANOVA with Bilingual Group (English Dominant vs. Equally Proficient) as the between subjects factor and Sentence Type as the within subjects factor. There was a main effect of Sentence Type, $F(3, 93) = 29.8$, $p < .01$. The Group by Sentence Type interaction approached significance ($p < .058$). As such, responses by Sentence Type were analyzed in separate planned comparisons per group. The planned comparisons were done to determine whether average response time for True sentences was faster than that for Standard False sentences, and whether the average response times for the Metaphor sentences were slower than the average of the Scrambled Metaphor and Standard False sentence types.

Bilingual English–dominant group

The mean responses to the True sentences were indeed faster than those to the False sentences, $t(93) = -5.10$, $p < .01$. Furthermore, the mean responses to the Metaphor sentences were reliably slower than those to any other type of sentence that required a "false" response, $t(93) = 4.48$. The pairwise comparison between Metaphor and Standard False sentences was significant (*Mean Difference* = 38.7, $p < .01$). However, while the difference between the Metaphor and the Scrambled Metaphor conditions was in the expected direction, it failed to reach statistical significance (*Mean Difference* = 74.3, $p = .12$).

Bilingual equally proficient group

The responses to the True sentences were faster than to any of the False sentence types, $t(93) = -2.89$, $p < .01$. Moreover, responses to the Metaphor sentences were reliably slower than to other sentence types requiring a "false" response, $t(93) = 6.45$, $p < .01$. Once again, the pairwise comparison between Metaphor and Standard False sentences was significant (*Mean Difference* = 165, *p* < .01), but the difference between the Metaphor Sentences and the Scrambled Metaphor was not (*Mean Difference* = 73.8, *p* = .12).

Size of metaphor interference effect in bilinguals versus monolinguals Metaphor interference indices were computed by taking the difference between the mean response to Metaphor sentences and the response to the average of the Scrambled and Standard False sentences (both of which also required a "false" response). The size of the index provides an indication of the relative difficulty in rejecting a Metaphor Sentence as false. The Metaphor Interference Index for the monolingual participants in Experiment 1 was 63.42 milliseconds while the corresponding values were 159.31 and 121.54 for the English Dominant and Equally Proficient Bilinguals, respectively. Thus, bilinguals showed nearly twice the amount of interference from metaphoric meaning than monolinguals.

Discussion
Across both experiments a robust metaphor interference effect was found, particularly when bilingual participants were tested only in their more dominant language. That is, for monolinguals and both groups of bilinguals tested in English, responses were slower to metaphoric statements as compared to those to standard false statements, indicating that the metaphoric "truth" of the statement was activated, even though the task did not require participants to do so. From these results, one can conclude that non-optional activation of the figurative meanings of metaphor sentences is not limited to monolinguals. Indeed, the size of the interference effect appears to be greater in bilinguals than monolinguals. Given that bilinguals in this experiment were tested in only one of their languages, it remains to be seen if a comparable effect would be obtained in both languages.

Experiment 2: Metaphor Interference Effect in English-Dominant and Equally Proficient Bilinguals

This experiment investigated whether a metaphor interference effect for novel metaphors is present in both languages of Spanish-English bilinguals and whether its size is affected by the relative language proficiency of participants in Spanish, based on self-reported proficiency.

Method
Participants

A group of 57 English-Spanish bilinguals at a large university in Texas participated in this experiment. The data from nine participants were discarded from any further analyses either because their Spanish composite comprehension score fell below the cut-off point of 4 on a 7-point scale or because their Spanish was more dominant than English. Based on the composite proficiency measure procedure described in Experiment 1, 21 of the participants were judged to be more dominant in English and 27 were equally balanced bilinguals or proficient in Spanish and English. A separate group of English-Spanish bilingual undergraduate students at Texas A&M University provided metaphorical and familiarity ratings for the Spanish translations of the 24 English metaphor sentences.

Materials

The same set of stimuli from the previous experiment were used in the present one. In addition, the stimuli were translated into Spanish (see Table 2). Based on the pretest ratings, the mean metaphoricity and familiarity ratings for the Spanish metaphor sentences were 4.93 and 3.21, respectively. These values are comparable to the metaphoricity and familiarity ratings obtained for the English stimuli in Experiment 1. Participants who provided the metaphorical and familiarity ratings were also asked to back translate the sentences from English to Spanish. This ensured that the most common wording for the Spanish metaphors was maintained. Additionally, the practice items were translated from English to Spanish.

Each participant was given 96 test trials in English and 96 in Spanish. Per language, these consisted of 48 True sentences (24 high and 24 low typicality), 24 Standard False sentences, 12 Metaphors and 12 Scrambled Metaphors. As in the previous experiment, the items in the Metaphor condition were all novel metaphors.

Table 2. *Sample Metaphor Stimuli per Language in Metaphor Interference Study for Experiment 2*

English Metaphors	Spanish Translations
Some hearts are dwellings	Algunos corazones son viviendas
Some ideas are food	Algunas ideas son alimento
Some lies are clothing	Algunas mentiras son artículos de ropa
Some lives are tapestries	Algunas vidas son tapices
Some marriages are sports	Algunos matrimonios son deportes
Some minds are closets	Algunas mentes son gabinetes

Procedure and design

The procedure was identical to that of Experiment 1, except that the items were presented in separate language blocks and language order was counterbalanced. The experiment was a 2 (Group) x 4 (Sentence Type) x 2 (Presentation Language) mixed factorial design with Sentence Type and Presentation Language as within-subjects factors and Bilingual Group as the between-subjects factor.

Results

A summary of the mean correct reaction time responses as a function of Language Presentation, Group, and Sentence Type is presented in Figure 2. Individual paired sample *t*-tests conducted per group determined that the difference in mean response times between the high and low typicality True sentences presented in English (see Figure 2A) and Spanish (see Figure 2B) for each bilingual group were significantly different.

When the language of presentation was English, the English Dominant group responded significantly faster to high typicality True sentences

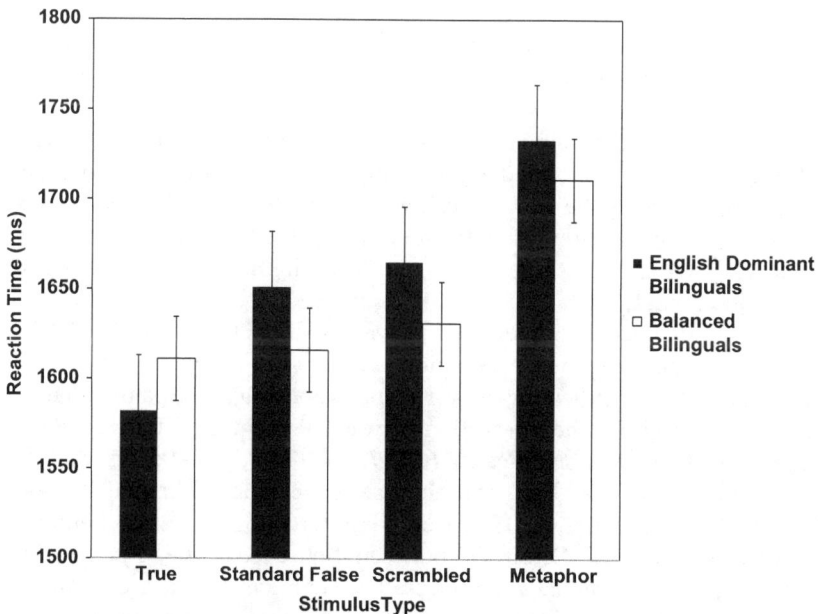

Figure 2A. Mean Verification Latencies to English Sentences by Language Group and Sentence Type

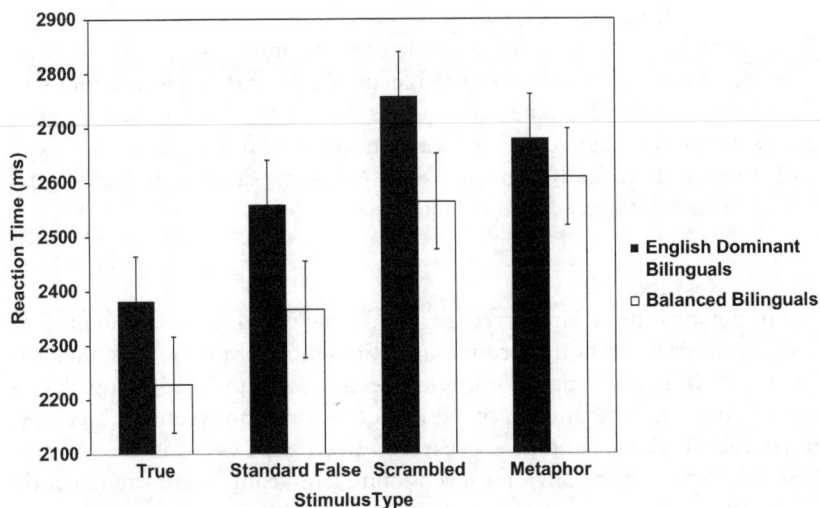

Figure 2B. Mean Verification Latencies to Spanish Sentences by Language Group and Sentence Type

than to the low typicality True sentences. This group also responded faster to the high than the low typicality Spanish True items. The high and low typicality True responses were therefore pooled for subsequent analyses. When the language of presentation was English, the Equally Proficient group responded significantly faster to high typicality True sentences than to the low typicality True sentences. This group also responded significantly faster to the Spanish high typicality versus low typicality sentences. Responses to the True items were pooled for all subsequent analyses.

The main effect for Sentence Type was significant, $F(2, 104) = 10.15$, $p < .01$. Language of Presentation was also significant, $F(1, 47) = 147.31$, $p < .01$, indicating slower responses overall to Spanish than to English sentences. The interaction between Presentation Language and Sentence Type was significant, $F(2, 72) = 3.96$, $p < .05$, as was the interaction between Presentation Language and Bilingual Group, $F(1, 47) = 15.75$, $p < .01$. However, the interactions between Sentence Type and Bilingual Group or between Sentence Type, Presentation Language, and Bilingual Group were not significant. Planned comparison analyses were conducted to determine whether the participants were responding to metaphor sentences reliably slower than any other type of sentence that required a "false" response.

Bilingual English—dominant group

In this group, the reaction times to the metaphor sentences presented in English were *not* reliably slower than to any other type of sentences that required a "false" response, $t(20) = -1.02, p = .32$. Similarly, when the items were presented in Spanish, the responses to the Metaphor sentences were *not* reliably slower than to any other type of sentences that required a "false" response, $t(20) = -.13, p = .9$.

Equally proficient group

Among equally proficient bilinguals, the reaction times from the Metaphor sentences presented in English showed a trend for being slower than to all other false items in English, $t(26) = -1.78, p = .087$. The reaction times from the Metaphor sentences presented in Spanish were significantly slower than those to the other false items in Spanish, $t(26) = -2.73, p = .01$.

Discussion

The results of the second experiment showed that a metaphor interference effect was present but that it emerged as significant only in the more balanced bilingual group. Unexpectedly, performance of the English dominant group in this experiment did not show a reliable metaphor interference effect in either the dominant or the less dominant language. It may be that the fewer number of trials per language block and the elimination of trials on which there were errors led to fewer remaining trials, thereby lowering the sensitivity to detecting an effect of metaphor interference in this group. However, even with the reduced number of trials per language, the equally proficient bilingual group showed a reliable metaphor interference effect in Spanish, although this effect did not reach an acceptable level of statistical significance in English.

To further examine whether the smaller number of trials in Experiment 2 compared to Experiment 1 could have contributed to the reduced metaphor interference effect observed for the bilinguals, an additional group of 17 English-speaking monolinguals were tested on half of the total number of trials as those used in Experiment 1 (see Martínez, 2003). The results showed significantly slower responses to the metaphor sentences than to all other sentences requiring a "false" response. Thus, use of a smaller set of trials did not attenuate the metaphor interference effect.

General Discussion

The metaphor interference effect has been taken as a measure of early automatic activation of metaphoric meaning (Wolff & Gentner, 2000). We examined how this effect would be influenced by language experience (monolingual vs. bilingual) and degree of language proficiency.

Across two experiments, participants made faster true/false judgments based on the literal truth or falsehood of sentences of the form, *Some As are Bs*, where some of these sentences were literally true, and the literally false sentences included metaphorically true ones, literally scrambled, and metaphorically scrambled exemplars.

The finding of slower latencies to respond "false" to the Metaphor sentences as compared to the other two types of false sentences (Standard False and Scrambled Metaphors) was replicated with English monolingual users and in two groups of bilinguals tested in English (Experiment 1). Further, as hypothesized, bilinguals showed a robust interference effect (Experiment 1) relative to that in monolinguals. When tested in English and Spanish (Experiment 2), an effect of metaphor interference emerged as reliable only in the Equally Proficient subgroup and only for one language (Spanish). Our findings provide support for the view that metaphoric meanings can be automatically activated in bilinguals as in monolinguals and in both languages of bilinguals. At the same time, the results showed that bilinguals were generally slower in deciding that statements (whether scrambled or metaphoric) were false. The tendency to be slowed by both true metaphors and scrambled metaphors suggests that bilinguals deliberated over the possible meaning of both metaphoric and metaphor-like statements, which may have resulted in a reduction in the size of the metaphor interference effect in bilinguals, particularly in Experiment 2.

A potential concern is that some metaphors used in the study may either be language specific or may differ in their metaphoricity across languages. That is, because the Spanish stimuli employed in this study were translated from English to Spanish, it is possible that what is seen as metaphorical in English may not always be seen as metaphorical to the same degree in Spanish. Anticipating this issue, we sought to address it empirically by obtaining judgments of metaphoricity from native speakers of each language in Experiment 2 and took steps to ensure that the items used were of comparable rated metaphoricity across languages. Nevertheless, it is possible that there were more subtle language- or culture-specific effects of metaphoricity not tapped by the metaphoricity ratings that affected the pattern of results. To address this issue more fully, future research may need to use metaphoric items generated in Spanish, with English translations. In further research it is also important to examine Spanish-dominant bilinguals, a group that was not included in the present study.

In the second study reported here we turned from an examination of metaphoric meaning to an examination of purposive ambiguity in language play.

Study 2: Is There a Bilingual Advantage in Joke Detection?

Much everyday discourse involves playful uses of language. Joking is a prevalent form of language play. Jokes typically play on listeners' expectations. They set up certain expectations and then subvert them. The expectations that are subverted in verbal humor may either be linguistic (i.e., playing on ambiguity or semantic/syntactic violations) or extralinguistic (i.e., playing on commonly held beliefs in the culture).

Understanding a joke requires the ability to think flexibly and recognize that what one thought the joke text was about turns out to be quite different: The initially favored meaning is replaced by the *punchline* meaning. Lexical ambiguity resolution has been a central topic motivating psycholinguistic research on single-language users as well as with bilinguals (see Altarriba & Gianico, 2003). Nevertheless, very few experimental studies have examined ambiguity processing in a sentential or discourse context, and still fewer have addressed the issue in the context of humor processing (but see Hull, Chen, Vaid, & Martínez, 2005; Vaid, Hull, Heredia, Gerkens, & Martínez, 2003). The present study was a preliminary investigation of joke detection ability in bilinguals and monolinguals.

As noted earlier, several studies have demonstrated that mastery of two or more languages enhances the ability to think more flexibly relative to knowing a single language (Peal & Lambert, 1962). Of particular relevance to the present study, Ianco-Worrall (1972) and Ben-Zeev (1977) found that bilingual children performed better than monolingual counterparts on tasks involving symbol substitution (e.g., calling the sun the moon, and vice versa). Other researchers found that, relative to monolinguals, bilinguals detected significantly more ambiguities in sentences (Cummins & Mulcahy, 1978). These and related studies have led to the view that exposure to two (or more) languages brings about an accelerated awareness of the arbitrary nature of the symbol/referent relationship and promotes a more analytic orientation to language structure. Further, there is evidence for long-term repercussions (in adulthood) of early onset of bilingualism as distinct from late onset of bilingualism. For example, early bilinguals are significantly faster than late bilinguals at judging whether two words are synonyms (Vaid, 1984) and more generally show a greater inclination to process for meaning. Still other studies have found that the cognitive and metalinguistic advantages associated with early bilingualism appear to be linked as well to early experiences in informal translation experience (López & Vaid, 2012; López, Vaid, & Chen, 2012; Vaid, Chen, Rao, & Manzano, 2006; Vaid, Milliken, López, & Rao, 2011).

The present research sought to examine whether a heightened sensitivity to meaning and more analytic orientation to language structure associated with knowing more than one language will affect joke detection ability of fluent bilinguals relative to monolinguals. Simply put, the study examined whether knowing more than one language facilitates joke detection. An additional question of interest in this study was whether individuals would be faster at deciding if something is a joke than if it is not a joke, and whether this in turn will depend on whether the humor is linguistic or extralinguistic in nature.

Method

Participants

Twenty-seven English-speaking monolinguals and 21 English/Spanish bilingual students at a large university in the southwestern region of the United States were recruited for participation in the study. Participants were classified as bilingual if their self-reported understanding of English and Spanish was 4 or higher on a 7-point language proficiency scale; they were classified as monolingual if they had minimal or no knowledge of Spanish (e.g., ratings of 2 or lower).

Materials

A total of 40 one liner English jokes were adapted from stimuli used in Coulson and Kutas (2001). The punchline of the joke occurred at the end in all cases. The joke stimuli were classified into 20 linguistic and 20 extra-linguistic jokes based on consensus ratings from a panel of six judges. Jokes classified as relying on "linguistic" humor involved a play on ambiguity, puns, or semantic or syntactic expectancy violations. Jokes classified as relying on "extralinguistic" humor involved a play on sociocultural knowledge, beliefs, or values. For each joke stimulus, a non-joke counter-part was created by replacing the final word with another word that rendered the sentence plausible but not humorous. In addition to the joke and non-joke stimuli a set of 40 sentences were included as fillers. These were unrelated to either the joke or non-joke items and were not included in the analyses. Sample linguistic, extralinguistic, and filler stimuli are provided below. The joke version is presented first and the final word creating the non-joke counterpart is presented second:

1. *When I asked him how long I should cook the noodles he said at least ten inches/seconds.* [Linguistic humor]
2. *The difference between a good speaker and a bad one is often a nice nap/diction.* [Extralinguistic humor]
3. *After studying all day long, we went over to the coffee shop for some drinks.* [Filler]

The set of joke stimuli were first administered to a group of 13 English speakers who rated the items on familiarity and funniness. Importantly, no significant differences were found in either perceived familiarity or perceived funniness of the linguistic versus extralinguistic jokes.

Procedure

Participants were tested individually in a laboratory setting. Each participant viewed a total of 80 sentences in English randomly displayed one at a time at the center of a computer screen. The sentences included 20 jokes (10 linguistic, 10 extralinguistic), 20 non-jokes, and 40 filler items presented in a random order. Whether a given participant was shown a particular stimulus in joke or non-joke form was counterbalanced across participants. On each trial a fixation stimulus first appeared and was followed by a sentence. Upon seeing the sentence, participants were to read it and decide if it was funny or not. The sentence remained on the screen until the participant responded. Participants were to press a particular response key if the sentence was a joke and a different key to indicate that it was not a joke. Reaction times were recorded in ms from the onset of presentation of the sentence until the response.

Design

The design was a 2 (Sentence Type: Joke vs. Non-Joke) x 2 (Group: Bilingual vs. Monolingual) x 2 (Joke Type: Linguistic vs. Extralinguistic Humor) mixed factorial.

Results

Separate analyses of variance were conducted on the reaction time responses and the accuracy data.

Response Latencies

Mean response latencies for correct responses were analyzed as a function of Group, Sentence Type, and Joke Type. There was a main effect of Sentence Type, $F(1,46) = 15.2$, $p < .0001$, which indicated that responses were faster to classification of items as jokes than as non-jokes (5249 ms vs. 6108 ms, respectively). A main effect of Joke Type was also found, $F(1,46) = 5.25$, $p < .03$, which indicated that responses were faster to extralinguistic than to linguistic joke types (5173 ms vs. 5324 ms, respectively). There were no other significant effects.

Accuracy

There was a marginal effect of Group, $F(1,46) = 3.22$, $p = .079$, which suggested that bilinguals showed higher overall accuracy in joke/non-joke classification than monolinguals (83.3% vs. 77.3%, respectively). A main effect of Sentence Type was also found, $F(1,46) = 28.73$, $p < .0001$, indicating that jokes were classified more accurately than non-jokes (89% vs. 71.6%, respectively). Although there was no main effect of Joke Type ($p = .11$), the interaction of Sentence Type by Joke Type was significant, $F(1,46) = 5.64$, $p < .02$. Follow-up multiple comparisons indicated that while joke classification was more accurate than non-joke classification, this was particularly the case for items in which the humor was linguistic in nature (91.9% vs. 71.5%, respectively, for linguistic jokes vs. non-jokes).

Discussion

Although response latencies on this task were fairly high, when considered alongside accuracy data, we found effects for all three variables of interest. First, it was observed that it takes both bilinguals and monolinguals longer to classify jokes when the humor relies on word play than when the humor does not derive from linguistic elements but rests more on shared extra-linguistic knowledge. Interestingly, slower classification of linguistic than extralinguistic humor was accompanied by better accuracy of detecting linguistic humor. Second, it takes longer for bilinguals and monolinguals alike to decide that something is *not* funny than it does to decide that it is funny. The joke-advantage in response latency was mirrored by a higher accuracy in classification of jokes relative to non-jokes.

Third, although bilinguals were not significantly different from monolinguals in classifying items as funny or not funny, they showed a trend toward being more accurate than monolinguals in joke detection. This would suggest that bilinguals were more careful and thorough in processing the stimuli, which would lead to slower responses but fewer errors in classification. If this interpretation has merit, it could account for the lack of group difference in speed of joke detection. It is also possible, in light of the fairly long response latencies, that any group differences that may have been present were obscured by the fact that it took several seconds simply to read and understand each sentence. In subsequent work it would be important to modify the design by, for example, recording responses from the onset of the final word in the sentence. In a subsequent study we have used such a modified paradigm and found that the overall pattern of results still holds but that there are additional group and language differences of interest related to differences between bilinguals in language brokering status (see Vaid, Chen, Rao, & Manzano, 2006).

In our third study, we directly compared the performance of bilinguals with prior informal translation experience and those without such experience on a task that has been used in creativity research, to examine the repercussions of brokering experience in uncovering relationships between remote associates.

Study 3: Does Language Brokering Experience Influence Performance on a Remote Associates Task?

Language brokering refers to an informal translation practice in which children or adolescents act as linguistic and cultural intermediaries on behalf of family or community members and speakers in the majority community (see Morales & Hanson, 2005, for a review). This practice is highly prevalent in immigrant and/or refugee communities across different regions of the world. Previous research on the impact of language brokering has primarily focused on psychological and sociocultural factors (Donner, Orellana, & Jiménez, 2008; Martínez, McClure, & Eddy, 2009; Umaña-Taylor, 2003). Whereas some studies have reported beneficial effects of language brokering, such as higher standardized test scores (Donner, Orellana, & Li-Grining, 2007) or ethnic identity affirmation (Weisskirch, 2005), others have found heightened stress and accelerated *parentification* (taking on adult support roles) among brokers (Mercado, 2003; Titzmann, 2012). Most studies of language brokering have focused on children or adolescents (but see Esquivel, 2012). Of interest to the present research was whether there are observable long-term cognitive or metalinguistic consequences of prior language brokering experience.

Previous researchers have speculated that the practice of repeatedly moving between two codes may confer greater metalinguistic awareness and cognitive flexibility in bilinguals, as compared to monolinguals (Bialystok, 1988). It would follow that differences among bilinguals in the extent of translating between languages might confer similar effects among brokers as compared to non-brokers. In ongoing work in our laboratory, we have investigated this issue by comparing the metalinguistic and cognitive performance of bilingual adults who had extensive early brokering experience with that of proficient bilinguals without such experience. In a number of different experiments, it was found that the performance of those with prior brokering experience differed significantly from that of proficiency-matched bilinguals without prior brokering experience. The tasks examined in previous experiments have included joke detection (Vaid, Chen, Rao, & Manzano, 2006), phonological awareness (Vaid et al., 2011), phrase interpretation (Vaid et al., 2011), and translation verification speed for literal versus idiomatic translations of expressions (López et al., 2012).

In the present study we sought to examine whether the effects associated with moving between two languages (and two cultural frameworks) may also extend to the domain of creativity, as has been proposed by previous researchers, such as Kharkhurin (2012). Although there is a large body of work that finds an association between bilingualism and creativity, the studies have tended to focus mainly on children or adolescents (see Ricciardelli, 1992, for a review). It is important to examine whether a greater cognitive flexibility, metalinguistic awareness, and ability to generate multiple, original, and varied solutions to problems is something that characterizes bilinguals even in adulthood.

Kharkhurin (2008, cited in Kharkhurin, 2012) found that Russian-English bilingual immigrant adults showed a greater ability than monolinguals to generate multiple solutions to alternate uses of common items, a standard creativity measure. In another study, Cushen and Wiley (2011) examined performance on spatial problems in bilinguals and monolinguals; they found that early bilingual adults showed higher performance on problems that required insight than on non-insight problems; by contrast, monolinguals showed better performance on non-insight than on insight problems. The bilinguals and monolinguals did not differ in their insight problem-solving ability.

Two studies to date have examined bilinguals' performance on the *Remote Associates Test* (Mednick & Mednick, 1967). This is a test in which individuals are presented with a set of three cue words that have no apparent relationship to each other and they have to come up with a fourth word that forms a collocation with each of the three words. Aiello, Jarosz, Cushen, and Wiley (2012) compared the performance of bilinguals from different first language (L1) backgrounds and monolinguals on an English language Remote Associates Test. They found that monolinguals – but not bilinguals – benefitted when instructed to perform the task by going with their *gut feeling*. Moreover, there was a correlation between when bilinguals had acquired English and performance on the test: Bilinguals' performance was better the earlier they had acquired English, suggesting that age of acquisition of the L2 (English) influenced their ability to generate remote associate solutions for English triads.

Hommel, Colzato, Fischer, and Christoffels (2011) compared two groups of bilinguals differing in their L2 proficiency on two measures of creativity: a remote associates test and an alternate uses test. They hypothesized that learning multiple languages to a high level of proficiency leads to a stronger, more selective focusing of cognitive control and that this would predict better performance on the remote associates test than on the alternative uses test, in which less cognitive control would produce more desirable outcomes. The hypothesis was supported: Better performance on the Remote Associates Test was found in the high proficient group, whereas better performance on the alternate uses test was found in the low proficient group.

However, on closer examination of the study design, it becomes apparent that on the Remote Associates Test the two groups were tested only in their L1, and the languages differed across the groups (Dutch for the high proficient group and German for the low proficient group). Thus, it is unclear whether the different performance of the two groups was due to the use of different remote associate stimuli (in different languages). Moreover, the groups were only tested in their L1. It would be important to test them on their L2 as well, especially if one is seeking to make attributions about a differential effect of L2 proficiency on creative task performance.

The present study compared the performance of Spanish-English bilingual adults with or without prior brokering experience on an English and Spanish version of the Remote Associates Test. To our knowledge, no previous study has tested the performance of bilinguals on the Remote Associates Test in both their languages. Moreover, this is the first study to examine whether language brokering experience plays a facilitative role in arriving at the correct solution in a creative problem-solving task.

Method

Participants
Eighty-nine speakers of Spanish and English were recruited from introductory psychology courses for participation in the study for course credit. All were highly proficient in both languages based on their self-ratings on speaking, reading, writing, and general comprehension. Based on their responses on a *Language Brokering Questionnaire* (Vaid, 2008), which asked participants about whether and to what extent they had engaged in informal translation in childhood and adolescence, with whom, in what contexts and for what purposes, participants were subdivided into 43 brokers and 46 non-brokers. Overall English proficiency was not significantly different between brokers ($M = 6.84$) and non-brokers ($M = 6.65$), $t(88) = .44$, $p > .05$; however, brokers ($M = 6.10$) rated their Spanish proficiency higher than non-brokers ($M = 5.68$), $t(88) = 2.10$, $p = .04$.

Table 3. *Sample Stimuli in Remote Associates Experiment*

Spanish Remote Associate Items			Solution	Difficulty
Bailar	Roja	Picosa	SALSA	Easy
Cama	Nuevo	Feroz	LEÓN	Hard
Cejas	Puntas	Corchos	SACA	Easy
Flor	Diente	Piedras	PICA	Hard

English Remote Associate Items			Solution	Difficulty
Wet	Law	Business	SUIT	Hard
Cracker	Fly	Fighter	FIRE	Easy
Fountain	Baking	Pop	SODA	Easy
Marshall	Child	Piano	GRAND	Hard

Materials

A total of 20 *Remote Associate Test* (RAT) problems, including 10 in each language, served as stimuli. The English stimuli were taken from a larger list of RAT stimuli published in Bowden and Jung-Beeman (2003). The Spanish stimuli were developed by the second author and were drawn from a larger pool of 20 stimuli that were pilot tested on a group of Spanish-English speakers and, based on the relative percent of participants who solved the items, were ranked in terms of difficulty (see Table 3). For each language 5 difficult and 5 easy problems were selected.

Procedure

Participants were tested individually in a laboratory setting across two sessions separated by a week. Stimuli were presented in English in one session and in Spanish in the other, with language order counterbalanced across participants in each group. On each trial a set of three unrelated cue words was shown and the participants' task was to think of a fourth word that could form a compound word or common phrase with each of the three words. Practice trials with feedback were given to ensure that participants understood the task.

Each set of three words was presented simultaneously on the screen in a vertical array and remained on the screen for 15 seconds. Then a fixation cross would appear and participants were given about a second in which to write down the fourth word solution. The next trial was then presented. Participants were not given feedback as to whether their responses to the test items were correct. After completing the experiment, participants completed the language background and brokering questionnaire.

Table 4. *Mean Performance (%) on Remote Associates Test by Group, Language, and Item Difficulty*

	Language			
	English		Spanish	
Bilingual Group	Easy	Difficult	Easy	Difficult
Brokers (N = 43)	46.98	7.44	53.95	17.67
Non-Brokers (N = 46)	51.74	10.87	37.83	10.43

Design

The design was a 2 (Language: Spanish vs. English) x 2 (Difficulty: Hard vs. Easy) x 2 (Group Status: Broker vs. Non-Broker) mixed factorial with repeated measures on the first two factors.

Results

A preliminary ANOVA was conducted to determine if the order of language of presentation of the items produced an effect. This was not found, either as a main effect or in interaction with the other factors. The Language Order variable was then removed and an ANOVA was performed on the mean number of correct responses. The mean responses are summarized in Table 4. A main effect was found for Item Difficulty, $F(1,87) = 343.13, p < .0001$: More solutions were generated to easy than to difficult problems.

Although there was no main effect of Group or Language, the interaction of Language and Group was significant, $F(1,87) = 9.58, p = .003$. Followup multiple comparisons revealed that brokers generated a higher percent of correct solutions than non-brokers for the Spanish RAT problems, $t(87) = 3.11, p = .003$. There was no significant difference between brokers and non-brokers for English RAT problems, $t(87) = -1.16$, $p > .05$. Further, brokers performed better on Spanish than English RAT problems, $t(42) = -2.13, p = .04$; non-brokers did better on English RAT problems than Spanish RAT problems, $t(45) = 2.27, p = .03$.

The interaction between Item Difficulty and Broker Status was not significant. There was a significant interaction of Language and Item Difficulty, $F(1,87) = 4.77, p = .03$. Followup tests revealed that, whereas for each language more solutions were generated for easy than for difficult problems, difficult Spanish problems generated more solutions than difficult English RAT problems, $t(88) = -2.03, p = .05$. There was no significant language difference for the easy problems, $t(88) = .95, p > .05$. Finally, the interaction between Language, Item Difficulty, and Group was not significant.

Discussion

A facilitative effect of language brokering was found, particularly for the Spanish remote associate items. Not only did brokers generate significantly more solutions than non-brokers for Spanish remote associate items, they performed better on Spanish than on English items. Non-brokers performed better on English than on Spanish items. The two groups did not differ in their ability to solve English remote associate problems. The pattern of response of the two groups on RAT may in part be attributed to differences in their self-reported proficiency in each language. Brokers and non-brokers did not differ in their self-reported proficiency in English, and they did not differ in their performance on the English RAT. However, on Spanish, brokers reported higher proficiency than non-brokers, particularly for Spanish-speaking ability; brokers also turned out to be better than non-brokers in generating solutions on the Spanish RAT.

Our finding of a positive effect of language brokering on the number of solutions generated on the remote associates task in Spanish is intriguing but should be replicated using a larger set of items and including more items under each difficulty level. Furthermore, difficulty assessment should be based on normative data on RAT performance on each item per language and should be obtained from a large sample of bilinguals, rather than relying on monolingual-generated solutions, as was the case for the English items used in the present study. In followup studies, it will also be important to examine how quickly solutions to remote associate tasks are arrived at in each language, and the types of incorrect solutions that are generated by each group to get insights into how quickly solutions are arrived at and what kinds of distracters impede solution generation.

Summary and Conclusions

With respect to the first question posed at the outset, we may conclude that bilinguals like monolinguals automatically activate metaphoric meanings, and do so for both their languages. Moreover, bilinguals showed a robust metaphor interference effect as compared to that observed in monolinguals, suggesting that they are more inclined to process for meaning (see Lambert, 1977). The design of the metaphor interference study does not allow us to determine whether participants'

slower performance on the metaphor items was because they were activating actual metaphoric meanings or because the meanings of those
items were indeterminate. In future work it would be important to elicit
bilinguals' actual interpretations of the metaphor stimuli. Given that
metaphoric meanings are typically underspecified, one would expect
bilinguals to produce a range of interpretations for figurative expressions,
whether novel or conventional. Nevertheless, our findings of slower
performance on metaphoric expressions relative to standard false
sentences among bilinguals and monolinguals alike supports the view
that figurative meanings are routinely activated, even acknowledging that
the content of the interpretation of figurative expressions may turn out to
vary. Our findings are compatible with those reported on an idiom
meaning interpretation task by Bortfeld (2003) who found that native
and non-native speakers of English presented with common idioms in
English and asked to generate images based on the phrases' literal
meanings reported images that reflected a fusion of the phrases' figurative and literal meanings.

In further research in metaphor interpretation, it would be interesting
to examine if the particular interpretations elicited for metaphoric
expressions in one language carry over to affect the interpretation of
metaphors in the bilinguals' other language, or whether figurative
meanings are tied to the language in which they are more frequently
encountered (Bountrogianni, 1988; Johnson, 1996; Littlemore, 2010).

Our second study showed that joke detection ability is not enhanced in
bilinguals, if by enhanced one means that processing is faster. Bilinguals
were actually not faster than monolinguals at detecting jokes. However,
they tended to be more accurate than monolinguals in classifying statements as humorous or not humorous. Thus, one could interpret the
findings to suggest that bilinguals are more deliberate and thorough in
processing the input before arriving at a decision about its humorous
status. Given that this study tested bilinguals only in one language, in
further work it would be important to extend the scope of investigation to
consider joke detection in both languages of the bilinguals. This would
enable us to determine if bilinguals are more attuned to (linguistic or
cultural) markers of humor in joke texts in one of their languages more
than in the other and whether their facility at detecting joke text cues
depends on their own pattern of use of their languages for joking behavior. Another important area for further research in this domain would be
to examine the processing of interlingual humor, that is, joke texts that
play on bilinguals' knowledge of two languages.

Our third study showed that there is a facilitative effect of prior informal translation experience on bilinguals' ability to identify remote

associates, particularly in Spanish. This *brokering advantage* demonstrates that there are long-term metalinguistic effects of differences among early bilinguals in the ways in which language is used. In further work it would be important to probe further the ways in brokering experience may differentially enhance linguistic and cognitive performance. Differences in the extent to which early bilinguals engage in translation for family members have clear consequences for their performance on a range of tasks, including the task reported here of identifying words that relate in specific collocational ways to other words.

Taken together, these three studies demonstrate that there is much to be gained by probing figurative language processing in speakers of multiple languages and with varied linguistic experiences. One specific direction for future work in this area that would be particularly promising is to extend the study of creative language use to production tasks. Possible contexts in which figurative and creative language production in bilinguals may be fruitfully studied include code-switching in spoken conversations and in text messages, discourse elicitation, and translation or brokering behavior in different actual or virtual social contexts (Valdes, 2003).

Acknowledgments

The research summarized in Study 1 formed the basis of a Master's thesis by Francisco E. Martínez at Texas A&M University (TAMU) and was presented at the 2003 meeting of the Psychonomics Society. Study 2 was supported by an undergraduate research grant to Lindsay Wilkinson and Erin Price by the Glasscock Center for Humanities Research at TAMU. We thank Seana Coulson for providing a list of joke stimuli used in her research, Fabiola Perry for assistance in stimulus classification, and Hsin Chin Chen for assistance in data analysis of Study 2. We are also grateful to Eleazar Montes and Zahira Cortez for assistance in data collection of Study 3. This study is part of a larger, ongoing research project on language brokering. Chaitra Rao, Isabel Manzano, and Kelly Millikan assisted in data collection for the larger project, and initial funding for this project was provided by a seed grant awarded to Jyotsna Vaid and Roberto R. Heredia by the Mexican and Latino/a Research Center at TAMU.

List of Keywords

Alternate uses test, Ambiguity, Attributive Categorization View, Brokering, Class inclusion, Cognitive control, Cognitive flexibility, Conceptual Metaphor View, Embodied experience, Graded Salience Hypothesis,

Interference, Jokes, Language brokering, Literal meaning, Metalinguistic awareness, Metaphor interference effect, Metaphor interference paradigm, Metaphor, Multiple meaning activation, Phonological awareness, Phrase interpretation, Remote Associates Test (RAT), Sentence verification task, Standard Pragmatic Model, Translation verification

Thought Questions

1. In what ways can knowing two or more languages increase the forms that humor can take? Provide examples of bilingual puns or other forms of interlingual humor.
2. How could the study of figurative language production provide insight into bilinguals' creativity?
3. In what ways do bilinguals differ from one another in terms of their language experience (e.g., age of acquisition, fluency in both languages, and everyday language use), and how might those differences influence the way they process figurative language?
4. How might the sociopolitical status of a language (i.e., dominant or minority status) affect the content and style of humor produced by users of that language?

Suggested Student Research Projects

1. Design a study to examine if formulaic expressions (e.g., idioms, proverbs, metaphors) that overlap in content or imagery across the languages of bilinguals are processed faster and/or remembered better than formulaic expressions that are distinct in the two languages. Select a set of four jokes and four cartoons from a media source in one language and another set of eight jokes/cartoons in another language. Identify the implicit cultural knowledge in each item. Then try and come up with an "equivalent" form of the joke/cartoon in the other language. Note down what obstacles you may encounter in attempting to produce an effective translation.

Related Internet Sites

Idiom Connection: www.idiomconnection.com
Idiom Site: www.idiomsite.com
The Literary Link: http://theliterarylink.com/metaphors.html
The Poetics of Robert Frost: www.frostfriends.org/figurative.html

Suggested Readings and Resources

Cardillo, E., Schmidt, G., Kranjec, A., & Chatterjee, A. (2010). Stimulus design is an obstacle course: 560 matched literal and metaphorical sentences for testing neural hypotheses about metaphor. *Behavior Research Methods, 42,* 651–664.

Chiaro, D. (1992). *The language of jokes: Analyzing verbal play.* New York: Routledge.

Haugen, E. (1986). Bilinguals have more fun. *Journal of English Linguistics, 19,* 106–120.

Martínez, R., & Schmitt, N. (2012). A phrasal expressions list. *Applied Linguistics, 22,* 299–320.

Ward, T., Smith, S., & Vaid, J. (Eds.). (1997). *Creative thought: An investigation of conceptual structures and processes.* Washington, DC: American Psychological Association.

REFERENCES

Aiello, D., Jarosz, A.F., Cushen, P.J., & Wiley, J. (2012). Firing the executive: When an analytic approach to problem solving helps and hurts. *The Journal of Problem Solving, 4,* 116–127.

Altarriba, J., & Gianico, J.L. (2003). Lexical ambiguity resolution across languages: A theoretical and empirical review. *Experimental Psychology, 50,* 159–170.

Ben-Zeev, S. (1977). The influence of bilingualism on cognitive strategy and cognitive development. *Child Development, 48,* 1009–1018.

Bialystok, E. (1988). Levels of bilingualism and levels of linguistic awareness. *Developmental Psychology, 24,* 560–567.

(2004). The impact of bilingualism on language and literacy development. In T.K. Bhatia & W.C. Ritchie (Eds.), *The handbook of bilingualism* (pp. 577–601). Oxford: Blackwell.

Bountrogianni, M. (1988). Bilingualism and metaphor comprehension. *European Journal of Psychology of Education, 3,* 53–64.

Bortfeld, H. (2002). What native and non-native speakers' images for idioms tell us about figurative language. In R.R. Heredia & J. Altarriba (Eds.), *Bilingual sentence processing* (pp. 275–295). Amsterdam: Elsevier.

Bowden, E.M., & Jung-Beeman, M. (2003). Normative data for 144 compound remote associate problems. *Behavior Research Methods, Instruments, & Computers, 35,* 634–639.

Cieślicka, A.B. (2006). Literal salience in on-line processing of idiomatic expressions by second language learners. *Second Language Research, 22,* 115–144.

Cooper, T.C. (1999). Processing of idioms by L2 learners of English. *TESOL Quarterly, 33,* 233–262.

Coulson, S., & Kutas, M. (2001). Getting it: Human event-related brain response to jokes in good and poor comprehenders. *Neuroscience Letters, 316,* 71–74.

Cummins, J., & Mulcahy, R. (1978). Orientation to language in Ukrainian-English bilingual children. *Child Development, 49,* 1239–1242.

Cushen, P.J., & Wiley, J. (2011). Aha! Voila! Eureka! Bilingualism and insightful problem solving. *Learning and Individual Differences, 21,* 458–462.

Danesi, M. (1992). Metaphorical competence in second language acquisition and second language teaching: The neglected dimension. In J.E. Alatis (Ed.), *Georgetown University Round Table on Languages and Linguistics: Language, communication, and social meaning* (pp. 489–500). Washington, DC: Georgetown University Press.

Donner, L.M., Orellana, M.F., & Jiménez, R. (2008). It's one of those things that you do to help the family: Language brokering and the development of immigrant adolescents. *Journal of Adolescent Research, 23,* 515–543.

Donner, L.M., Orellana, M.F., & Li-Grining, C. P. (2007). I helped my mom and it helped me. Translating skills of language brokers into improved standardized test scores. *American Journal of Education, 113,* 451–478.

Esquivel, A. (2012). *Language brokering is a dynamic phenomenon: A qualitative study examining the experiences of Latina/o language brokers* [Unpublished senior thesis], Scripps College.

Gibbs, R.W. (1994). *The poetics of mind: Figurative thought, language and understanding.* Cambridge,UK: Cambridge University Press.

Giora, R. (2003). *On our mind: Salience, context, and figurative language.* New York: Oxford University Press.

Glucksberg, S. (2003). The psycholinguistics of metaphor. *Trends in Cognitive Sciences, 7,* 92–96.

Glucksberg, S., Gildea, P., & Bookin, H.B. (1982). On understanding nonliteral speech: Can people ignore metaphors? *Journal of Verbal Learning & Verbal Behavior, 21,* 85–98.

Harris, R.J., Tebbe, M.R., Leka, G.E., Garcia, R.C., & Erramouspc, R. (1999). Monolingual and bilingual memory for English and Spanish metaphors and similes. *Metaphor and Symbol, 14,* 1–16.

Hoffman, R.R., & Kemper, S. (1987). What could reaction-time studies be telling us about metaphor comprehension? *Metaphor and Symbolic Activity, 2,* 149–186.

Hommel, B., Colzato, L., Fischer, R., & Christoffels, I. (2011). Bilingualism and creativity: Benefits in convergent thinking come with losses in divergent thinking. *Frontiers in Psychology, 2.* DOI: 10.3389/fpsyg.2011.00273

Hull, R., Chen, H.C., Vaid, J., & Martínez, F. (2005). Great expectations: Humor comprehension across hemispheres. *Brain and Cognition, 57,* 281–282.

Ianco-Worrall, A.D. (1972). Bilingualism and cognitive development. *Child Development, 43,* 1390–1400.

Johnson, J. (1996). Metaphor interpretations by second language learners: Children and adults. *The Canadian Modern Language Review/La Revue canadienne des langues vivantes, 53,* 219–241.

Katz, A.N., Cacciari, C., Gibbs, R.W., & Turner, M. (Eds.). (1998). *Figurative language and thought.* New York: Oxford University Press.

Kazmerski, V., Blasko, D., & Dessalegn, B. (2003). ERP and behavioral evidence of individual differences in metaphor comprehension. *Memory & Cognition, 31,* 673–689.

Kharkhurin, A. (2012). *Multilingualism and creativity*. Bristol, UK: Multilingual Matters.

Kovecses, Z. (2002). *Metaphor: A practical introduction*. New York: Oxford University Press.

Lakoff, G., & Johnson, M. (1980). *Metaphors we live by*. Chicago: University of Chicago Press.

Lakoff, G., & Turner, M. (1989). *More than cool reason: A field guide to poetic metaphor*. Chicago: University of Chicago Press.

Lambert, W.E. (1977). The effects of bilingualism on the individual: Cognitive and sociocultural consequences. In P.A. Hornby (Ed.), *Bilingualism: Psychological, social, and educational implications* (pp. 15–27). New York: Academic Press.

Littlemore, J. (2010). Metaphoric competence in the first and second language: Similarities and differences. In M. Pütz & L. Sicola (Eds.), *Cognitive processing in second language acquisition: Inside the learner's mind*. (pp. 293–315). Amsterdam: John Benjamins.

López, B., Vaid, J., & Chen, H.C. (2012, May). *Correlates of language brokering experience among Spanish-English speakers in Texas*. Poster presented at the annual meeting of the Association of Psychological Science, Chicago.

López, B., & Vaid, J. (2012, October). *Literal and figurative language processing: Differences among bilinguals varying in language brokering experience*. Poster presented at the annual meeting of the Texas Regional Cognition Conference (ARMADILLO), Texas A&M International Unversity, Laredo.

Martínez, F. (2003). *Exploring figurative language processing in bilinguals: The metaphor interference effect* (Unpublished master's thesis). Texas A&M University, Texas.

Martínez, F., Chen, H.C., Vaid, J., Wilkinson, L., & Price, E. (2004, Oct.). *Joke comprehension and detection: Is there a bilingual advantage?* Poster presented at the annual meeting of the Texas Regional Cognition Conference (ARMADILLO), University of Texas at Arlington.

Martínez, C.R., McClure, H.H., & Eddy, J.M. (2009). Language brokering contexts and behavioral and emotional adolescents. *The Journal of Early Adolescence, 29*, 71–98.

Martínez, F., Vaid, J., & Heredia, R.R. (2003, November). *Metaphoric meaning activation: Is there an effect of language status?* Poster presented at the annual meeting of the Psychonomics Society, Vancouver.

Matlock, T., & Heredia, R.R. (2002). Lexical access of phrasal verbs and verb-prepositions by monolinguals and bilinguals. In R.R. Heredia & J. Altarriba (Eds.), *Bilingual sentence processing* (pp. 251–274). Amsterdam: Elsevier.

Mednick, S.A., & Mednick, M.P. (1967). *Examiner's manual: Remote associates test*. Boston: Houghton Mifflin.

Mercado, V. (2003). *Effects of language brokering among children of Latino immigrants* (Unpublished dissertation). Pace University, New York.

Morales, A., & Hanson, W.E. (2005). Language brokering: An integrative review of the literature. *Hispanic Journal of Behavioral Sciences, 27*, 471–503.

Nelson, E.M.M. (1992). Memory for metaphor by nonfluent bilinguals. *Journal of Psycholinguistic Research, 21*, 111–125.

Pavlenko, A. (2000). New approaches to concepts in bilingual memory. *Bilingualism: Language and Cognition, 3,* 1–4.

Peal, E., & Lambert, W.E. (1962). The relation of bilingualism to intelligence. *Psychological Monographs: General and Applied, 76,* 1–23.

Pierce, R., Maclaren, R., & Chiappe, D. (2010). The role of working memory in the metaphor interference effect. *Psychonomic Bulletin & Review, 17,* 400–404.

Ricciardelli, L.A. (1992). Creativity and bilingualism. *Journal of Creative Behavior, 26,* 242–254.

Schmitz, J.R. (2002). Humor as a pedagogical tool in foreign language and translation courses. *Humor: International Journal of Humor Research. 15,* 89–113.

Titzmann, P.F. (2012). Growing up too soon? Parentification among immigrant and native adolescents in Germany. *Journal of Youth and Adolescence, 41,* 880–893.

Umaña-Taylor, A. (2003). Language brokering as a stressor for immigrant children and their families. In M. Coleman & L. Ganong (Eds.), *Points and counterpoints: Controversial relationship and family issues in the 21st century* (pp.157–159). Los Angeles, CA: Roxbury.

Vaid, J. (1984). Visual, phonetic and semantic processing in early and late bilinguals. In M. Paradis & Y. Lebrun (Eds.), *Early bilingualism and child development* (pp. 175–191). Lisse, Netherlands: Swets and Zeitlinger.

(2000). New approaches to conceptual representations in bilingual memory: The case for studying humor interpretation. *Bilingualism: Language and Cognition, 3,* 28–30.

(2006). Joking across languages: Perspectives on humor, emotion, and bilingualism. In A. Pavlenko (Ed.), *Bilingual minds: Emotional experience, expression, and representation* (pp.152–182). Clevedon, UK: Multilingual Matters.

Vaid, J., Hull, R., Heredia, R.R., Gerkens, D., & Martínez, F. (2003). Getting a joke: The time course of meaning activation in verbal humor. *Journal of Pragmatics, 35,* 1431–1449.

Vaid, J., Chen, H.C., Rao, C., & Manzano, I. (2006, May). *Joke detection: Is there a bilingual and/or brokering advantage?* Poster presented at the Conference on Language Acquisition and Bilingualism, Toronto.

Vaid, J., & Martínez, F. (2001, April). *Figurative language and thought across languages: What transfers?* Poster presented at the Third International Symposium on Bilingualism, University of the West of England, Bristol.

(2008). *Language Brokering Questionnaire.* Unpublished manuscript, Texas A&M University.

Vaid, J., Milliken, K., López, B., & Rao, C. (2011, July). *Language brokering experience affects phrase interpretation and sound segmentation: Evidence from Spanish-English bilinguals.* Poster presented at the annual meeting of the Cognitive Science Society, Boston.

Valdes, G. (2003). *Expanding definitions of giftedness: The case of young interpreters from immigrant communities.* Mahwah, NJ: Lawrence Erlbaum Associates.

Vygotsky, L.S. (1962). *Thought and language.* Cambridge, MA: M.I.T. Press.

Weisskirch, R.S. (2005). The relationship of language brokering to ethnic identity for Latino early adolescents. *The Journal of Early Adolescence, 27,* 545–561.

Wolff, P., & Gentner, D. (2000). Evidence for role-neutral initial processing of metaphors. *Journal of Experimental Psychology: Learning, Memory, and Cognition, 26,* 529–541.

(2011). Structure-mapping in metaphor comprehension. *Cognitive Science, 35,* 1456–1488.

Wray, A. (2003). *Formulaic language and the lexicon.* Cambridge, UK: Cambridge University Press.

Section II

Methodological Approaches

4 Metaphoric Reference: A Real-Time Analysis

Roberto R. Heredia and Mónica E. Muñoz
Texas A&M International University

ABSTRACT

In two experiments, we examine the processing of metaphoric reference, where a metaphoric description (e.g., *creampuff*) makes reference to an antecedent describing a *cowardly boxer* during the online comprehension of spoken sentences. We measured activation levels of figurative (e.g., *boxer*) and literal (e.g., *pastry*) interpretations of the metaphoric referential description. Experiment 1 measured meaning activation at 0 ms and 1000 ms after the metaphoric referential description. At the metaphoric reference offset, only activation for the nonliteral interpretation was observed. At 1000 ms only activation for the literal interpretation was evidenced. Experiment 2 involved Spanish-English bilinguals immersed in a bilingual community where usage of both languages is a common occurrence. Meaning activation was measured at 0 ms and 300 ms after metaphoric reference offset. Results revealed that bilinguals were much faster to name targets consistent with a figurative interpretation at 300 ms than at 0 ms after prime offset. The same pattern was observed for the literal target interpretation. Implications for theories of bilingual metaphoric language processing are discussed.

Keywords: anaphoric metaphor, cross-modal lexical priming, bilingual metaphor, referential metaphor, metaphoric reference

As a way to introduce the topic of this chapter, consider sentences (1a-c), below. The metaphoric expression, *lawyers are sharks*, in sentence (1a) is an example of the more conventionalized nominal metaphor of the form *A is B*. Nominal metaphors consist of the *tenor* or the *subject* (A) of the metaphor (e.g., *lawyers*), the *vehicle* (B; e.g., *sharks*) that serves as a comparison to the subject of the metaphor, and the *ground*, on the basis of which it is possible to infer a relationship between the tenor and the vehicle.

(1a) *The appointed defense <u>lawyer is a shark</u>, known for his questionable moneymaking schemes.*

(1b) *The appointment of the defense attorney, known for his questionable moneymaking schemes, is encouraging voters to push for a citywide referendum to stop the <u>shark from taking</u> office.*

(1c) *The appointment of the city official, known for his questionable moneymaking schemes, is encouraging voters to push for a citywide referendum to stop the <u>shark</u> from taking office.*

Sentence (1b) provides an example of a *metaphoric referential* description or an *anaphoric metaphor* (Almor, Arunachalam, & Strickland, 2007; Budiu & Anderson, 2002; Gibbs, 1990, Onishi & Muphy, 1993; Stewart & Heredia, 2002). Sentence (1c) is similar to (1b), but there is no clear subject or tenor. In Spanish, this type of metaphor is referred to as *pure metaphor*, and it is most likely plausible for highly frequent, apt, and conventionalized metaphors. Whereas the tenor and vehicle typically occur in close proximity and are readily available for nominal metaphors (sentence 1a), in metaphoric reference (sentence 1b), the tenor and vehicle occur apart from one another. In this case, the vehicle is used as a reference to a previously mentioned subject. For example, in sentence (1b), the referent of the vehicle (*shark*) is the preceding tenor or subject (*attorney*) of the metaphor located earlier in the sentence. Thus, comprehension of the referential description requires that the listener or reader establish a connection between the anaphoric metaphor (*shark*) and its antecedent (*attorney*). That is, the anaphor (vehicle) must reactivate its antecedent (tenor). Once this reactivation has occurred, the listener/reader must make an additional inference, which takes additional processing (Almor et al., 2007; Onishi & Murphy, 1993) in order to understand the meaning being intended by the metaphoric description. How are metaphoric references understood? There are two possible ways in which the metaphoric (sentence 1a) and metaphoric referential (sentence 1b) descriptions could be interpreted. These descriptions can be understood in terms of their *direct* or *literal meaning* associated with *marine carnivorous fish that swim in the ocean, are sometimes large, and are voracious*; alternatively, they could be interpreted in terms of an *indirect or nonliteral* (i.e., figurative) *meaning* describing an individual of the legal profession who is *vicious, cunning, greedy* and *knows* (or *smells*) *where the money is*. Note that the related metaphor/stereotype view of lawyers is that they are *ambulance chasers* because *they smell blood and blood is money* (Heredia & Blumentritt, 2002). How do bilingual speakers comprehend metaphorical expressions in their second language (L2)? How do bilinguals process metaphoric referential descriptions? During the course of L2 metaphor processing, is literal meaning activation obligatory for bilinguals? This chapter examines the time course of meaning activation (literal vs. nonliteral) as bilinguals comprehend metaphoric reference in L2. At issue is whether literal meaning processing is obligatory and computed before the intended meaning of the metaphor is triggered. We begin with a general overview of theories of metaphor processing, followed by a discussion of the findings in metaphoric reference.

Models of Metaphoric Processing

Two general theoretical models have been proposed in the monolingual literature to explain metaphor processing. The *Direct Access Model* assumes that in the course of language processing, the nonliteral interpretation of a metaphoric expression may be accessed directly "without first requiring [that] an initial literal interpretation [be] computed and rejected" (Blasko & Connine, 1993, p. 295; Glucksberg, 2001; see also Vaid et al., this volume). Although it is possible that a literal interpretation may be temporarily accessed to construct the nonliteral meaning of the metaphor, it is not obligatory that the literal interpretation is computed and rejected before the metaphoric comprehension process begins (Blasko & Connine, 1993, p. 295). The *Indirect Processing Model* or the *Three-Stage Model* (Searle, 1979; Swinney & Osterhout, 1990), on the other hand, assumes obligatory access to the metaphor's literal meaning, and only if the literal interpretation is defective (i.e., anomalous, illogical, does not fit context), a search for a nonliteral interpretation is initiated. Although the evidence tends to lean toward the Direct Access Model, experiments that have utilized more online methods that measure language processing in real time (e.g., Janus & Beaver, 1985; Swinney & Osterhout, 1990) have unequivocally supported the Indirect Processing Model. In one study reported by Swinney and Osterhout (1990), monolingual participants were presented with nominal metaphors embedded in sentences as in (2), below.

(2) *Mary's hair was honey* [*1] *and her* [*2] *smile gleamed.*

The participants' task was to listen to uninterrupted sentences and at designated sentence positions ([*1–*2] represented as subscripts) and make a lexical decision (i.e., decide if a presented string of letters is a legal word or nonword) to word targets that were related to the literal (*bee*) or nonliteral (*blond*) sense of the metaphor and their respective control words. Position 1 is strategically located at the end of the last word of the metaphor (*metaphor offset*), and position 2 is located 500 ms after metaphor offset. The results showed that at position 1, only the literal target (*bee*) was activated, and at position 2, only the target associated with the nonliteral meaning (*blond*) was active. This pattern of results led Swinney and Osterhout (1990) to conclude that metaphor processing is not automatic and that additional processing time is required, as suggested by the Indirect Access Model, to fully comprehend the intended meaning of a metaphorical expression. That is, the nonliteral meaning requires additional processing effort that requires additional time (i.e., 500 ms).

However, other studies in nominal metaphor (e.g., Blasko & Connine, 1993) utilizing similar methodology have found results that are difficult to account for by both theoretical frameworks. Specifically, Blasko and Connine (1993) had monolingual participants listen to sentences of the type described in (3).

(3) *The belief that hard work is a ladder* [*1] *is common* [*2] *to this generation.*

At issue was whether the Direct Access (i.e., only activation of the nonliteral meaning at position 1) or the Indirect Access Model (i.e., only activation of the literal meaning in position 1, and activation only for the nonliteral meaning at position 2) provided a better theoretical account of metaphor processing. Overall, the results showed activation for both literal and nonliteral meanings at positions 1–2. However, at position 2, there was evidence of the literal meaning fading. These findings were true for highly familiar metaphors. For low familiar metaphors, there was significant activation for the literal interpretation at positions 1–2. Although there was significant inhibition where both literal and nonliteral meanings appeared *to compete* for activation at metaphor offset (i.e., position 1), at position 2 only the literal meaning remained active. Moreover, low familiar metaphors showed activation for both literal and nonliteral meaning interpretation at position 1, but only if they were high apt metaphors (i.e., the degree to which the metaphor's vehicle [*ladder*] captures important features of the tenor [*hard work*]; Thibodeau & Durgin, 2011). Moderately apt metaphors revealed activation only for the literal interpretation at position 1.

Blasko and Connine's (1993) results are difficult to account for by indirect models of metaphor processing because the literal meaning remains active even 300 ms after metaphor offset. Direct access models, on the other hand, would have difficulty explaining differences between low/high familiar and moderate/high apt metaphors and the finding that the literal interpretation remains active regardless of familiarity and aptness. A third model, which seems to account for Blasko and Connine's results, is Giora's *Graded Salience Hypothesis* (1997, 2002,

2003). Briefly, this model posits that coded *salient meanings* in the mental lexicon are processed initially, regardless of either their literality or contextual fit (Giora, 2002, p, 490). *Salience* could be portrayed as a matter of degree or a continuum influenced by such factors as word frequency, familiarity, conventionality, and prototypicality. *Nonsalient meanings* are those that are less frequently used or are less familiar, and will take longer to be triggered, requiring extra-inferential processes (p. 491). Thus, during the course of metaphoric processing, even under nonliteral highly biasing contextual conditions, if a literal meaning is salient, it will be somewhat activated. Indeed, the Graded Salience Hypothesis captures Blasko and Connine's (1993) consistent literal meaning saliency across metaphor familiarity (low vs. high) and aptness (moderate vs. high) at metaphor offset. The nonliteral, as predicted by the hypothesis, was more active (i.e., salient) in the high familiarity, and high aptness conditions.

In general, to date, most of what is known about the comprehension of metaphor comes from research on nominal metaphor (e.g., Blasko, 1999; Cacciari & Glucksberg, 1994; Giora, 2003) and to a larger extent from psycholinguistic techniques using self-paced reading tasks that might not be sensitive enough to capture the intricacies of online language processing as it occurs moment-by-moment in real time (see García et al., this volume). The overall consensus suggests that during metaphor processing the literal and nonliteral meanings are understood equally well in conditions in which metaphors are highly frequent, highly conventional, and highly familiar (Blasko & Connine, 1993; Glucksberg, 2001). When metaphors are novel and low in familiarity, the literal interpretation may be more salient and take precedence in processing (Blasko & Connine, 1993; Glucksberg, 2001; Giora, 2002, 2003).

Metaphoric Reference

In the typical Gibbsonian paradigm (Gibbs, 1990), participants are presented with short stories, as in (4a-h), that may or may not be strongly biased toward the literal or nonliteral meaning of the metaphorical description (see for example, Almor et al., 2007; Janus & Bever, 1985; Ortony, Schallert, Reynolds, & Anton, 1978). The participant's task in these types of experiments is to read each story line by line, and depending on the experimental condition, participants are presented with a literal or a metaphoric reinstatement of the preceding context.

(4a) *Stu went to see the Saturday night fights.*
(b)   *There was one boxer that Stu hated.*

(c) *This guy always lost.*
(d) *Just as the match was about to start, Stu went to get some snacks.*
(e) *He stood in line for ten minutes.*
(f) *When he returned, the bout had been cancelled.*
(g) *"What happened?" Stu asked a friend.*
(h) *The friend replied,*

> **Literal Reinstatement:** *"The fighter didn't even show up."*
> **Metaphoric Reinstatement:** *"The creampuff didn't even show up."*
> **Baseline Control:** *"The referee didn't even show up."*

Typically, the literal reinstatement (*fighter*) is a synonym of the original antecedent *the hated and loser boxer that always lost*. The metaphoric reinstatement (*creampuff*) is the vehicle of the metaphor (*boxers are creampuffs* or *creampuff boxers*) referring to the antecedent tenor or subject of the metaphor (*boxer*). Thus the connection (i.e., the ground) between the two anaphors is provided by the preceding contextual information about the described boxer. In the original study, Gibbs (1990) noted that, unlike previous findings in metaphor processing, reading times for the metaphoric description took longer (2177 ms) than for literal reinstatements (1735 ms), compared to a baseline control sentence that took significantly less time (1867 ms) than the metaphoric but longer than the literal reinstatement. It should be noted, however, that it is not clear as to the purpose of the baseline sentence (*the referee didn't show up*) given its high associative value to the preceding context, and its relative high word frequency count compared to the low word frequencies of the metaphoric and literal reinstatements. In short, at least in metaphoric reference processing, literal meaning (re)activation takes precedence over metaphoric activation. This general finding seems to hold under highly constraining contextual conditions (e.g., Almor et al., 2007; but see Ortony et al., 1978) and noncontextual conditions (e.g., Noveck, Bianco, & Castry, 2001; Onishi & Murphy, 1993). One exception to these findings is Ortony et al.'s (1978, Experiment 1; cf. Budiu & Anderson, 2002) results showing reading advantages for literal reinstatements but only under noncontextual conditions; under contextually biasing conditions, both literal and metaphoric reinstatements were read equally fast.

One important study, and the one that we would like to underscore, is Stewart and Heredia (2002). Stewart and Heredia sought to investigate the course of metaphoric reference processing using the *Cross-Modal Naming* task (CMN; Love & Swinney, 1996; Swinney, 1979; Tabossi, 1996; see also Blasko & Connine, 1993; Cieślicka, 2006; García et al., this volume; Heredia & Blumentritt, 2002; Heredia & Stewart, 2002) to assess meaning (literal vs. metaphoric) activation moment-by-moment as the speech signal unfolds in real time. The CMN task takes advantage of the priming effect whereby response to a target (*bread*) is faster when preceded by a related (*butter*) than an unrelated word (e.g., *mirror*). Further, the priming effect is taken as a measurement of lexical activation, or the extent to which a particular meaning is activated relative to is unrelated control. Participants in Stewart and Heredia's study listened to story passages such as (4a-h), above. However, for the target or reinstatement sentence (5a), below, participants named target words that were literally (*pastry*) or nonliterally (*boxer*) related to the metaphoric referential description. Position 1 was strategically located 1000 ms before the onset of the metaphoric reference to assure that the preceding context was not driving the effect (i.e., pretest). Positions 2–3 were positioned immediately after (0 ms), and 1000 ms after the metaphoric reference (*creampuff*) to assess literal and nonliteral meaning activation down the speech signal.

(5a) *His friend* [*1] *replied, "The creampuff* [*2] *didn't even show* [*3] *up, I can't believe it!"*

Stewart and Heredia (2002) wanted to specifically localize and pinpoint the psycholinguistic processes taking place, in real time, as participants understood the metaphoric reference. At issue was whether the vehicle of the metaphor (*creampuff*) would (re)activate its antecedent (*boxer*: the nonliteral meaning) and its literal interpretation (*pastry*). One concern with previous findings in metaphoric referential descriptions is that the tasks used may not have been sensitive enough to detect meaning differences (if any), because response times reflect entire sentences, and their reading times range from as high as 2851 ms to as low as 2000 ms. The possibility that these long reading times do not reflect extra-inferential processes (e.g., meaning integration) or the possibility that the metaphoric reference (*creampuff*) is being understood in terms of its literal interpretation (i.e., *pastry*) cannot be rejected.

Overall, Stewart and Heredia (2002) revealed no meaning activation at position 1 (see sentence 5a) for both literal and nonliteral interpretation, as expected, if the preceding context is not driving the effect. At position 2 (metaphoric reference offset), only the nonliteral meaning of the metaphor was active. By 1000 ms after the end of the last word of the metaphor (position 3), the activation of both the literal and nonliteral meanings had faded away. These results provide unequivocal evidence that the metaphoric description is being understood in terms of its nonliteral meaning in which the *creampuff* is referring to a boxer, and not to some sort of *edible bread* or *pastry*. These findings contrast with other results in metaphoric reference (e.g., Gibbs, 1990; Onishi & Murphy, 1993) in that metaphoric reference processing does not necessarily involve the activation of the metaphor's literal interpretation. Thus, according to Stewart and Heredia (2002), access to the nonliteral interpretation of a metaphoric reference is possible provided that appropriate and sensitive methods that measure early stages of language processing are used.

Bilingual Figurative Language Processing

How do bilinguals comprehend metaphorical language in their L2? As an example, consider the metaphor *sermons are pills* and how a bilingual speaker might understand it. Are bilinguals likely to directly understand this metaphor in terms of its direct or intended meaning that *sermons are long, boring and put people to sleep like sleeping pills*, as opposed to one literal interpretation (somewhat unusual!) that *sermons like pills heal and cure one's problems*? Research in bilingual metaphoric processing is quite limited; however, some findings suggest that bilinguals might be able to directly access the metaphor's intended or nonliteral interpretation.

Nelson (1992) investigated memory for metaphor by nonfluent bilinguals. Spanish-English and French-English bilinguals translated Spanish (e.g., *Un árbol es un paraguas*: *A tree is an umbrella*), or French (e.g., *Un arbre est un parapluie*) metaphors and literal expressions (e.g., *Un árbol es fuerte, Un arbre est fort*) into English (*A tree is strong*). In one condition, participants were explicitly instructed to translate the figurative or literal meaning of the metaphoric expression from their first language (L1) into L2. In a second experimental condition, bilinguals were instructed to simply translate a metaphoric expression into L2. In a third condition bilinguals translated literal expressions into L2. A cued-recall task (e.g., *A tree is___*) in Spanish or French was used to measure retention. Overall, translating the figurative meaning of a metaphor into English significantly improved memory retrieval relative to translating the literal meaning of a metaphor or translating a literal expression. More significant, however, was the finding that translating the figurative meaning of the metaphor did not produce better recall than the condition in which participants were simply asked to translate a metaphoric expression to their L2. These results were interpreted as suggesting that processing the figurative meaning of a metaphor is *automatic* and that the processing of the literal interpretation of a metaphor is not obligatory, thus supporting a *Direct Access Model of Bilingual Processing* (see Glucksberg & Keysar, 1990; see also Vaid et al., this volume).

In fact, asking participants to interpret the literal meaning of a metaphor actually *interfered* with normal processing, thus resulting in poor recall performance (Nelson, 1992).

Other studies investigating differences between metaphors and similes (Harris, Tebbe, Leka, Garcia, & Erramouspe, 1999; e.g., *A tree is an umbrella vs. A tree is like an umbrella*) suggest that the likelihood of remembering metaphors and similes as their own types increased when the language of presentation and language at retrieval was English. Both figures of speech exhibited comparable performance in recall. However, there was a tendency for studied Spanish metaphors to be recalled as similes in the Spanish retrieval condition. Thus, Spanish-English bilinguals studying and remembering metaphors and similes in Spanish exhibited similar patterns to Spanish monolinguals, namely, a tendency to recall metaphors as similes. In contrast, these same bilinguals did not show the reported propensity of English monolinguals to remember similes as metaphors.

Moreover, correlational studies suggest interesting relationships between fluency in the L2 and the comprehension of figurative language. For example, Johnson and Rosano (1993) gave L2 learners metaphors such as *my shirt is a butterfly* and asked them to understand what the metaphor meant and to provide as many interpretations of the metaphorical expression as possible. Possible interpretations for this metaphor could range from *the shirt can fly* to *the shirt could be very colorful*. Results showed that metaphor fluency (the number of interpretations provided) was positively correlated with measures of L2 communicative proficiency and general language proficiency. More specifically, processing capacity and relevant knowledge were the major factors determining complexity level in the bilinguals' interpretations. Other studies, which examined experienced versus non-experienced L2 learners (bilinguals learning an L2) and metaphor interpretation, show experienced L2 learners performing at monolingual levels (e.g., Johnson, 1989; see also Bountrogianni, 1988).

To summarize, the existing evidence in bilingual metaphor processing suggests that bilinguals, like monolinguals, might have access to the direct nonliteral interpretation of metaphoric language. Moreover, it appears that language knowledge or proficiency is related to the comprehension of nonliteral language. The more experience in the L2, the easier it becomes to use and comprehend nonliteral language. How bilinguals process metaphoric language in real time and what the relationship is between literal and nonliteral meaning activation in bilinguals remain open questions and are addressed by the two experiments described next.

The Present Study

How do bilinguals comprehend figurative language and, more specifically, metaphoric referential descriptions? The primary goal of Experiment 1 was to examine processing differences between figurative and
literal language in the comprehension of metaphoric reference by
bilinguals. Participants in this experiment listened to passages as in
(4) and (5) above and named visually presented targets that were
related (figuratively vs. literally) or unrelated to the metaphoric referential description (*creampuff*). To explore the temporal course of metaphoric language processing, we tested for lexical activation at 0 ms and
1000 ms after metaphoric reference offset. Like Stewart and Heredia
(2002), we chose these time intervals because we wanted to specifically
examine the course of literal versus nonliteral activation as bilinguals
comprehend metaphorical referential descriptions. Based on the
evidence from the bilingual figurative language literature, showing
that advanced bilinguals might behave similar to monolinguals (e.g.,
Matlock & Heredia, 2002), we expected to replicate Stewart and
Heredia's (2002) findings with monolinguals showing (re)activation to
the nonliteral meaning at 0 ms condition, because this is the location
where it is more likely to establish the relationship between the topic
and the vehicle of the metaphor. Alternatively, bilinguals might show
a pattern similar to the Indirect Processing Model and the Graded
Salience Hypothesis where literal meaning might take precedence over
the metaphorical interpretation. Therefore, activation only for the
literal interpretation of the metaphoric statement is expected at metaphoric reference offset. However, at 1000 ms after offset, bilinguals
should have established the relationship between the topic and the
vehicle. In this case, only priming for the nonliteral interpretation is
expected (cf. Searle, 1979).

Experiment 1

Method

Participants
Seventy-nine University of California, San Diego, students participated in
the experiment. Bilinguals represented a wide range of L2 backgrounds.
The languages contributing with more subjects were Chinese ($N = 21$),
Spanish ($N = 19$), Japanese ($N = 11$), and Vietnamese ($N = 10$).
Languages contributing with two or more participants were English
($N = 6$), Farsi ($N = 4$), and Russian ($N = 2$). Other contributing

languages were Arabic, Armenian, Hebrew, Portuguese, Tagalog, and Thai. The majority of participants reported English as the L2. However, one bilingual reported Portuguese as the L2 and English as the third language. An additional participant reported English and Spanish as second languages. Six other participants reported English as the L1. Four of these participants reported Chinese as the L2; one reported Tagalog as the L2, and another participant reported Spanish as the L2. These six participants' language self-ratings on language usage on a 1–7 scale (1 = not fluent, 7 = very fluent) did not differ from the rest of the participants in speaking, reading, and understanding English abilities (all $ps > .05$). However, bilinguals reporting English as the L1 rated themselves higher in their writing abilities than the rest of the bilinguals (see results section for further discussion). Additional t-tests were conducted on the other bilinguals' self-rating responses. Mean self-ratings showed that participants used English ($M = 6.0$, $SD = 1.2$) more frequently than the L1 ($M = 3.8$, $SD = 1.7$), $t(69) = -8.2$, $p < .01$. Their speaking ability in English ($M = 6.3$, $SD = .97$) was rated higher than the L1 ($M = 5.8$, $SD = 1.5$), $t(70) = 2.1$, $p < .05$. Likewise, their reading ability in English ($M = 6.2$, $SD = .96$) was rated higher than their L1 ($M = 4.7$, $SD = 2.2$), $t(69) = 4.6$, $p < .01$. Their writing ability was also rated higher for English ($M = 6.0$, $SD = 1.1$) than for the L1 ($M = 4.5$, $SD = 2.1$), $t(70) = 4.4$, $p < .01$. However, their understanding of English ($M = 6.3$, $SD = .88$) and L1 ($M = 6.0$, $SD = 1.3$) was comparable, $t(75) = 1.9$, $p = .06$. As can be seen from the analyses, the bilingual participants represent a highly English proficient bilingual sample.

Materials and Design

Materials were taken from Stewart and Heredia (2002). Stimuli consisted of 40 short passages such as the one described in sentences (4–5) above, each a brief exchange between two persons discussing a mutually known person or thing. All stimulus materials were in English. The average length of each passage was 4.5 spoken sentences. Forty additional passages were constructed to serve as fillers. These passages were matched to the experimental stimuli on format and number of sentences and contained no metaphorical reference or any hint of figurative language. For all passages, the critical metaphoric referential description always appeared in either the penultimate or final sentence. Two related associates were chosen to serve as visual targets for each spoken metaphoric referential description (*creampuff*). The related literal target reflected the actual meaning of the metaphoric reference, regardless of story context (*pastry*). The related nonliteral form reflected the intended meaning of the metaphor reference implied by the context (*boxer*). Literal targets were obtained from the Nelson, McEvoy, and Schreiber's (1998) online association database. Nonliteral probes were either those used as referring nouns or generated on the basis of the referent indicated by a particular story context. Literal and nonliteral related targets were matched in lexical frequency (Francis & Kŭcera, 1982), length, onset phone, and form class. Filler passages were paired with unrelated targets chosen at random from Francis and Kŭcera's frequency counts.

A male native speaker of English recorded the stimuli. All stimuli were recorded in a soundproof chamber using an Audio-Technica ATR25 stereo microphone and a Sony TCD-D8 digital audio tape recorder. The recordings were then entered into a Macintosh computer using Macromedia SoundEdit Version 2. A sampling rate of 44.1 KHz with a 16-bit (22 KHz) format was used for digitizing. For every sound wave, the offset of the critical prime was located by using waveforms and auditory feedback. Cue markers were placed in two locations (i.e., probe position) for each item, with the first cue point (i.e., target position) located immediately 0 ms ([*1]) and 1000 ms after metaphoric referential description offset ([*2]), as shown in sentence (5b) below. Cue markers triggered the visually presented targets, appropriately counterbalanced.

(5b) *"Aw, the creampuff [*1] didn't even show [*2] up, I can't believe it."*

The design conformed to a 2 (figurativeness: literal vs. nonliteral target) x 2 (relatedness: related vs. unrelated target) x 2 (probe position: 0 ms vs. 1000 ms after metaphoric reference offset) mixed factorial design with figurativeness and relatedness as within subjects factors and probe position as a between-subjects variable. Four lists were required for each probe position to counterbalance each passage. Each target word was assigned to one of four lists, for each probe position, using a Latin square design. This procedure assured that the experimental targets (related and unrelated controls) were counterbalanced across the four lists such that a given target appeared in only one condition on each list. The 80 sentences were combined in a pseudo-random order, which imposed the constraint that no more than three experimental conditions occurred consecutively. Ten additional passages served as practice trials. These passages followed the same format as both the experimental and filler items. Overall, the proportion of related versus unrelated probes was .25. To ensure that participants were listening and understanding the passages, comprehension questions were recorded and placed pseudo-randomly into each list. These questions only followed filler stimuli and were always followed by a filler item.

Procedure

Participants were tested individually. Upon arrival, informed consent was obtained. Subsequently, participants read instructions on a computer screen. Participants were instructed to listen to sentences presented over headphones, understand them, and to name the string of letters appearing in the middle of the computer screen as quickly and as accurately as possible. Participants were then given 10 practice trials to become familiar with the task. Every participant's response was recorded to allow for monitoring of response errors.

Stimuli were delivered uninterrupted at a normal speaking rate. At the specified probe position (0 ms or 1000 ms after metaphoric reference offset), a visual target word appeared on the screen for 300 ms in lower case letters. Response time was measured from the onset of the visually presented target until the participants responded, or after a 2300 ms time response window. Following a 1500-ms inter-trial interval, the next passage began. Spoken stimuli were presented over headphones (Optimus Pro-50MX). The experiment was controlled by PsyScope (Cohen, MacWhinney, Flatt, & Provost, 1993). Participants' responses to the visually presented targets were recorded by a headset microphone connected to a voice operated relay input of a serial Carnegie Mellon University Button Box. The stimuli were played at a medium volume setting through a set of Apple speakers.

Results and Discussion

Responses 3.5 standard deviations above or below the mean were excluded from subsequent analyses. This criterion represented 2.8 percent of the overall data. Five participants were excluded from the analyses because their error rates were above 30 percent. Data from two other participants were excluded because of computer errors in recording the participants' latencies.

Accuracy Response Rates

Accuracy response rates were entered into a 2 (figurativeness) x 2 (relatedness) x 2 (probe position) analysis of variance (ANOVA). The only reliable effect in the analyses by subjects, $F_1(1, 70) = 10.3$, $p < .01$, and by items $F_2(1, 39) = 8.51$, $p < .01$ was the interaction of figurativeness by relatedness. The Least Significant Difference (LSD) multiple comparison was used to interpret the two-way interaction. Participants were more accurate in naming unrelated literal ($M = 96\%$) than related literal probes ($M = 92\%$). However, accuracy in naming related ($M = 95\%$) and unrelated ($M = 93\%$) nonliteral probes did not differ significantly.

Response Latencies

Response times were entered into a 2 x 2 x 2 mixed ANOVA. The only statistically reliable main effect was relatedness by subjects, $F_1(1, 70) = 5.50$, $p < .05$, but not by items, $F_2(1, 39) = 2.37$, $p = .132$. This significant main effect by subjects shows that participants were 14 ms faster to respond to related ($M = 714$ ms, $SD = 127$), than unrelated targets ($M = 728$ ms, $SD = 135$). More important, however, was the three-way interaction by subjects, $F_1(1, 70) = 9.0$, $p < .01$, but not by items $F_2(1, 39) = 1.8$, $p = .19$. (An additional analysis excluding the six participants reporting English as the L1 revealed a significant three-way interaction by subjects, $F_1(1, 64) = 7.2$, $p < .01$) only, and followup simple effects showed identical results as the ones reported in Table 1).

Table 1 below lists the mean response times and the priming effects for the three-way interaction. Multiple comparisons for probe position at 0 ms show a 34 ms significant priming effect suggesting that bilinguals were able to (re)activate the antecedent (*boxer*) of the metaphoric referential description. In contrast, the 6 ms priming effect for the literal related condition did not reach significance, suggesting that at this point in figurative language processing, the literal meaning of the metaphoric reference was not considered. More important, however, was the significant priming effect of 34 ms for the literal meaning at 1000 ms after listening to the metaphoric referential description. Thus, it appears that the literal meaning of the metaphoric referential description remained active even after accurately computing the intended (nonliteral) meaning of the metaphoric expression. In addition, this finding suggests that

Table 1. *Mean (M) Response Times (in ms) and Standard Deviations (SD) to Related and Unrelated Targets by Probe Position for Experiment 1*

Probe Position	M	SD	DIFF
0 ms (Metaphor Offset)			
Nonliteral Related	721	138	+38
Nonliteral Unrelated	755	140	
Literal Related	725	149	+6
Literal Unrelated	719	140	
1000 ms (After Metaphor Offset)			
Nonliteral Related	711	109	+8
Nonliteral Unrelated	719	130	
Literal Related	699	115	+23
Literal Unrelated	722	135	

Note. DIFF = Difference between related and unrelated target types or priming.

our bilingual sample was more likely to be affected by word-level information, as opposed to sentence-level (sentential priming) information. In short, results of Experiment 1, like Stewart and Heredia's (2002) results with monolinguals (see also Matlock & Heredia, 2002), reveal that highly proficient bilinguals in their L2 may have direct access to the nonliteral interpretation of metaphoric referential descriptions. The results also show that, unlike for monolinguals, the literal interpretation remains a possibility for bilinguals, even 1000 ms after they have accurately resolved the linguistic ambiguity (cf. Blasko & Connine, 1993).

Results of Experiment 1 provide evidence that bilinguals, like monolinguals, might have direct access to the nonliteral interpretation of a metaphoric referential description early on during figurative language processing. However, bilinguals in Experiment 1 were highly fluent in English and their L2 was their primary everyday language. Moreover, given their heterogeneous linguistic backgrounds, they most likely had little or no exposure to their L1. Experiment 2 involved Spanish-English and English-Spanish bilinguals recruited from a U.S.-Mexican border community where usage of both Spanish and English languages is a common occurrence. The purpose of Experiment 2 was to focus on a more homogenous and representative sample of active bilinguals in a "quasi-pure" bilingual community where Spanish and English are typically mixed during the communicative process (see, for example, Heredia & Altarriba, 2001). In addition to measuring nonliteral and literal meaning activation at metaphoric reference offset (0 ms), Experiment 2 measured activation of both interpretations at 300 ms after metaphoric reference offset (cf. Blasko & Connine, 1993; Heredia & Blumentritt, 2002). This target position was chosen because it provided a way to precisely identify where in the unfolding stream activation was taking place and the extent to which the literal interpretation of the referential metaphor was already being considered. It was hypothesized that, as early as 300 ms post-offset, the literal interpretation of the metaphoric reference might be considered as a viable candidate. In other words, there is a possibility that lexical-level influences may be present as early as 300 ms post-offset.

Experiment 2

Method

Participants
Seventy-nine Texas A&M International University (TAMIU) undergraduates participated in the experiment for extra credit or to fulfill a class requirement. Forty-one Spanish-English bilinguals reported

Table 2. *Self-Ratings (1 = Not Fluent, 7 = Very Fluent) to Language History Questionnaire for Bilingual Participants in Experiment 2*

	English-Spanish	Spanish-English
Age	22.7 (6.0)	22.6 (6.0)
Mean Age L2 Learned	4.38 (2.3)	6.46 (3.0)
Mean Years in United States	22.4 (6.1)	18.0 (8.8)
Mean Years in U.S. Schools	16.7 (3.1)	15.5 (7.7)
Mean Self-Ratings		
English Usage on a Typical Day	6.37 (1.3)	5.75 (1.3)*
Speaking English	6.84 (.44)	6.05 (1.1)**
Reading English	6.95 (.23)	6.18 (.93)**
Understanding English	6.95 (.23)	6.25 (.93)**
Writing English	6.84 (.44)	6.18 (.96)**

Note. Values in parentheses represent standard deviations; *$p < .05$. **$p < .01$.

Spanish as L1, and English as L2; 38 English-Spanish bilinguals reported English as the L1, and Spanish as the L2. Independent *t*-tests were performed between Spanish-English, and English-Spanish bilinguals to compare usage of English (speaking, reading, understanding, and writing English). Table 2 describes the participants' linguistic profile.

Although usage of English in the various linguistic activities described in Table 2 significantly differs for both groups, their relative high self-ratings suggest that these bilinguals are highly fluent in English. However, to assess possible figurative language processing differences between these two potentially distinct samples, the bilinguals' L1 (English vs. Spanish) is treated as an additional factor in the results section.

Materials and Procedure
Materials and procedure were the same as in Experiment 1. The only exception was that for every wave sound, the second cue marker (i.e., target point) was placed 300 ms after metaphoric reference offset.

Results and Discussion
Responses 3.5 standard deviations above or below the mean were excluded from the response analyses. This criterion reflected 2.2 percent of the overall data. Five participants were excluded from the analyses because their error rates were above 30 percent. Data from three other participants were excluded because of computer errors in recording participants' response latencies.

Accuracy Response Rates

Accuracy response rates were entered into a 2 (figurativeness) x 2 (relatedness) x 2 (probe position) mixed ANOVA. The only reliable effect in the analyses by subjects, $F_1(1, 69) = 4.3$, $p < .05$, was the main effect of figurativeness where literal targets were named more accurately ($M = 96\%$) than nonliteral targets ($M = 94\%$). The interaction between figurativeness and probe position approached significance by subjects, $F_1(1, 69) = 3.0$, $p = .08$, but not by items, $F_2(1, 39) = 2.3$, $p = .13$. No other effects by subjects or items reached statistical significance (all $ps > .05$).

Response Latencies

Because of the possibility that the English-Spanish and Spanish-English bilinguals represented two different populations (see Table 2), the bilinguals' reported L1 was used as a blocking variable to assess response differences, if any, between the two bilingual groups. Response times were entered into a 2 (bilingual's L1: Spanish vs. English) x 2 (figurativeness: literal vs. nonliteral), x 2 (relatedness: related vs. unrelated) x 2 (probe position: 0 ms vs. 300 ms after metaphoric reference offset) four-way mixed ANOVA. Overall, the analysis by subjects and items did not reach significance (all $Fs < 1$). All other interactions and main effects involving the bilinguals' L1 were not reliable, either (all $Fs < 1$). Given these null results, the data from both bilingual groups were collapsed across the two groups.

Collapsed response times for the bilingual groups were entered into a 2 (figurativeness) x 2 (relatedness) x 2 (probe position) three-way mixed ANOVA. The only reliable effect was an interaction between figurativeness and probe position by subjects, $F_1(1, 69) = 3.9$, $p = .05$, and marginally significant by items, $F_2(1, 39) = 3.6$, $p = .07$. Table 3 lists subjects' mean response times and standard deviations for figurativeness as a function of probe position.

Table 3. *Mean (M) Reponse Times (in ms) and Standard Deviations (SD) to Related and Unrelated Targets by Probe Position for Experiment 2*

Probe Position	M	SD
0 ms (Metaphor Offset)		
Nonliteral	725	115
Literal	717	149
300 ms (After Metaphor Offset)		
Nonliteral	693	96
Literal	703	96

The statistical interaction was followed up by LSD multiple comparisons. The 8 ms difference between the literal and nonliteral targets was not reliable at the 0 ms probe position, suggesting that both literal and nonliteral meanings of the metaphoric referential descriptions were equally active. Likewise, the 10 ms difference between the literal and nonliteral targets at the 300 ms probe position did not reach significance either. However, the 32 ms difference between nonliteral targets across probe positions shows that bilinguals were faster to respond to nonliteral targets at the 300 ms than at the 0 ms probe (sentence) position. The same pattern is observed for the literal targets, where bilinguals were 14 ms faster in responding to literal targets at the 300 ms than at the 0 ms probe position.

Overall, the results of Experiment 2 indicate that, regardless of probe position, both the literal and nonliteral meanings of the metaphoric referential description are equally accessible and involve similar processes (see, for example, Glucksberg, 2001; Onishi & Murphy, 1993). Moreover, these findings further suggest that, at least for the type of bilinguals in this experiment, the literal and nonliteral meanings are more readily accessible (i.e., retrieved faster), only after the metaphoric referential description has been analyzed and integrated at the word (i.e., literal) and sentential (i.e., contextually related nonliteral meaning) levels. Although the literal interpretation may remain substantially activated throughout the comprehension of the metaphoric referential description, at both probe positions, due to its word-level lexical saliency (see, for example, Cieślicka's, 2006, this volume, *Literal Salience Model*; Giora, 2002, 2003), (re)activation of the nonliteral meaning requires additional time for the inferential (i.e., lexical integration, top-down processes) mechanisms to take place (Swinney & Osterhout, 1990, 1990). That is, it is possible that bilinguals in this experiment required additional time (300 ms), after initial exposure, to fully consider both meanings of the metaphoric referential description.

Following Gibbs (1990) and Onishi and Murphy (1993), a *post hoc* rating task was performed to assess the extent to which bilinguals had access to the nonliteral interpretation of the metaphoric referential description. After the experimental session, 45 bilinguals were asked to read the experimental passages used in the experiment to determine if the last word of the passage (i.e., the metaphoric referential description) was related or not related to a subsequent literal (e.g., *pastry*) or nonliteral target (e.g., *boxer*). Ratings were on a 1–7 scale (where 1 = not related and 7 = very related). Ratings for the nonliteral targets were significantly higher ($M = 4.7$, SD = .76) than ratings for the literal targets ($M = 3.5$, SD = .57), both by the analysis of subjects, $t_1(44) = 2.5$, $p < .05$, and by items, $t_2(39) = 8.3$, $p < .01$. Thus, the evidence from the rating task suggests that bilinguals in this experiment were able to relate the metaphoric referential description to the nonliteral antecedent.

Summary and Discussion

How do bilinguals process metaphoric expressions? In two online experiments, we examined the comprehension of metaphoric referential descriptions by bilingual speakers. In Experiment 1, highly fluent bilinguals from heterogeneous linguistic backgrounds listened to short passages and named visually presented targets that were figuratively (e.g., *boxer*) or literally (e.g., *pastry*) related to a critical metaphoric reference mentioned previously (e.g., *creampuff* describing a *weak and soft fighter that always lost and everyone hated*). Unlike the conventionalized nominal metaphor whose tenor (subject) and vehicle are found in close proximity (e.g., *boxers are creampuffs* or *creampuff boxers*), in metaphoric reference, only the vehicle is provided and the tenor or subject has to be inferred from the preceding contextual information. Experiment 1 tested activation for figurative and literal interpretations immediately (0 ms) and 1000 ms after (post-offset) listening to the metaphoric referential description. At 0 ms post-offset, bilinguals showed evidence for the availability of the nonliteral interpretation of the metaphoric reference and no evidence for the activation of the vehicle's word-level literal related meaning. However, by 1000 ms post-offset, the results showed evidence for the availability of the literal interpretation, and no activation for the nonliteral interpretation. Experiment 2 utilized a homogenous sample of bilinguals living in a bilingual community where both Spanish and English are spoken frequently and individuals code-switch during the communicative process (Heredia & Altarriba, 2001). The evidence for these bilinguals showed no response time differences between the literal and nonliteral interpretations of the metaphoric referential description at both post-offset positions (i.e., 0 vs. 300 ms), suggesting that both interpretations were equally available. However, at 300 ms post-offset, both literal and nonliteral interpretations were responded to faster than at 0 ms after the metaphoric reference offset, suggesting that metaphoric referential descriptions are effortful and require additional processing resources (e.g., Almor et al., 2007). That is, during the course of metaphor understanding, interpretation or inferencing processes require extra time to occur (Swinney & Osterhout, 1990).

Results from the two experiments reported here are consistent with the findings from metaphoric reference research (Stewart & Heredia, 2002) suggesting that bilinguals, like monolinguals, have direct access to the nonliteral representation of metaphoric referential descriptions, especially those bilinguals who are highly fluent and possibly dominant in L2 (Heredia & Altarriba, 2001). Moreover, it appears that during figurative language processing, regardless of language proficiency and language dominance, both the literal and nonliteral interpretations remain as viable candidates well beyond the comprehension of the metaphoric referential description. In relation to the findings reported by Almor et al. (2007), Budiu and Anderson (2002), Gibbs (1990), and Onishi and Murphy (1993), showing that literal anaphoric reinstatements of the antecedent referent (*boxer*) were read faster than the metaphoric anaphoric reference (*creampuff*), the present results and those reported by Stewart and Heredia (2002) go a step further and localize the locus of activation. That is, (re)activation of the referring antecedent occurs immediately at the metaphoric reference offset for both monolinguals and bilinguals. As argued before, one major concern with global reading measures of language processing (i.e., reading times) is that such measures provide little or no information about the cognitive processes taking place as participants comprehend the anaphoric metaphor. Moreover, at least for bilinguals, it appears that lexical or word-level activation for metaphoric referential descriptions is obligatory. The finding that lexical or word-level information is made available during the online comprehension of metaphors is further supported by Blasko and Connine's (1993) results showing a tendency of multiple activation for both literal and nonliteral meanings for high-familiar metaphoric expression at both 0 and 300 ms post-offset and lexical activation of only literal interpretation for low-familiar metaphors at both probe positions. Moderate- and high-apt metaphors revealed similar activation patterns at metaphor offset.

What can existing models say about bilingual metaphoric processing? The *Direct Access Model of Bilingual Processing* (Nelson, 1992) proposes that bilinguals, like monolinguals, have direct access to the nonliteral interpretation of a metaphor and rejects the possibility that literal activation is obligatory (see also Vaid et al., this volume). A second alternative that we adapt from the monolingual literature is the *Indirect Processing Model of Bilingual Processing*. This model's basic assumptions are that literal meaning activation is obligatory and that additional processing time is required for the computation of the nonliteral only if the literal interpretation of the metaphor is rejected as a plausible candidate. Thus, during the time course of metaphoric processing, this model predicts activation of the literal only at metaphor offset (see Swinney & Osterhout, 1990) and activation only for the nonliteral interpretation 300 or 1000 ms after the metaphor offset. That is, because the literal interpretation is most likely rejected at early stages of metaphoric processing as a nonviable candidate, by 300 or 1000 ms this meaning should fade away. However, the evidence from the experiments reported here suggests that, even after the metaphoric ambiguity has been resolved for bilinguals in Experiment 1 at the metaphoric reference offset (0 ms), by 1000 ms post-offset the literal meaning remains highly active. Experiment 2 provides more impressive evidence showing comparable activation for both meanings of the metaphoric referential description immediately and 300 ms after metaphoric reference offset. This pattern of results is difficult to account for by the Direct and Indirect Processing Models of Bilingual Processing.

An alternative model, and the one that we would like to propose, is the Graded Salience Hypothesis (Giora, 2003, p. 10; see also Cieślicka's 2006, this volume). One important aspect of this model is the distinction between *salient meanings* that are readily accessible and excitable with lower activation thresholds, and *nonsalient meanings* that are less accessible and less excitable. A second and critical aspect of the model is that saliency is not a dichotomy but a continuum that can be influenced by such factors as word frequency, familiarity, conventionality, and prototypicality/stereotypicality. So, in relation to bilingualism and L2, word saliency would be also influenced by such factors as language dominance (Heredia & Cieślicka, 2014, Heredia, 1997), language proficiency, and linguistic environment (i.e., bilingual vs. monolingual community). It follows then that bilinguals who are highly proficient and whose L2 has become the dominant language would be more likely to have more access to figurative meanings that might evoke high saliency. However, even for highly fluent bilinguals, it is possible that, based on their L2 learning patterns (see for example, Heredia & Cieślicka, 2014; Kroll & Stewart, 1994), word- or lexical-level information (literal or denotative) might be highly automatized. This suggests that word meanings that are more dominant or frequent in the L2 would be more salient and more readily accessible for bilinguals and L2 learners. For example, consider the concept of *bulldozer*. As a noun, a *bulldozer* is a heavy machine used to move/push dirt or rocks, but it could be someone that operates the machine. As a verb, *to bulldoze* is to use the bulldozer to move something. However, a secondary or less dominant meaning describes the action of aggressively or ruthlessly pushing something. Now consider the nominal metaphor, *a car salesman is a bulldozer,* and how a bilingual might comprehend it. Because of its dominant or more salient meaning, the bilingual is more likely to trigger the literal related meaning (*tractor*), especially when this metaphor from bilingual norms has a familiarity rating of 3.04. That is, it appears that, at least for bilingual metaphoric referential descriptions, the literal interpretation is obligatory and highly salient (see Cieślicka, this volume for similar arguments in idiom processing).

In short, the Graded Salience Hypothesis seems to provide a better explanation for the evidence provided by the two experiments reported here. Bilinguals in Experiment 1 were highly proficient and highly dominant in their L2, and their linguistic environment was English, their L2. The pattern of results was more consistent with the patterns exhibited by monolingual English speakers reported by Stewart and Heredia (2002). Bilinguals in Experiment 2, selected from a "quasi-pure" bilingual community in which both Spanish and English are used interchangeably, exhibited different metaphoric processing profiles. Although bilinguals in Experiment 2 reported high language proficiencies in both languages, it is possible that these bilinguals were less familiar with or had less experience with nonliteral language in their L2. To address this possibility, we conducted a *post hoc* familiarity rating task in which 73 bilinguals rated on a 1–7 scale the 40 nominal metaphors (e.g., a *car salesman is a bulldozer*) used to construct the experimental stimuli (where 1 = not familiar and 7 = very familiar). The familiarity ratings for the 40 metaphors ranged from 2.0 to 6.4. Fifty-two percent of these items had a familiarity rating of less than 3.99, and 47 percent had a familiarity rating greater than 4.00. Clearly, more than half of our original experimental stimuli were of low familiarity to our participants. This is not surprising, given that our sample was drawn from a Texas-Mexico border town where 95 percent of the population is Mexican American, and it is possible that our participants lacked sufficient experience with and exposure to figurative language in English. Moreover, it is worth noting that all of the items were adapted from Stewart and Heredia (2002), a study with only monolinguals. Thus, it is possible that Experiment 2 participants in the present study had a more difficult time comprehending these items because they were normed using a markedly different population of listeners – namely, monolingual English speakers. Lack of familiarity, combined with the somewhat unique nature of figurative forms of reference, may very well have proven too difficult for Experiment 2 participants, especially considering the more limited exposure these bilinguals had to their L2 figurative processing compared to bilingual participants in Experiment 1.

How do bilinguals process metaphoric reference? The present results suggest two possible bilingual processing configurations. Bilinguals who are highly proficient and highly experienced in the L2 (Experiment 1) are able to access the figurative interpretation of the metaphoric reference directly. However, bilinguals who are highly proficient in the L2 but less experienced with figurative language in the L2 (Experiment 2) require more effort and are more likely to exhibit parallel activation, in which both the literal and nonliteral meanings are readily available. In any case, the results reported here suggest that, at least in bilingual anaphoric metaphor processing, literal meaning activation is not only necessary but also obligatory due to its high saliency.

Acknowledgments

The authors are grateful to Mark Stewart, the late Elizabeth Bates, and David Swinney for helpful input during the gestation of Experiment 1 and to the Center for Research in Language (CRL) for invaluable assistance with data collection in Experiment 1. Special thanks to our students Kristina M. Alcalá, Laura Palacios, Lorena Martínez, Liliana García, and Melanie Moreno for their assistance in data collection and analysis of Experiment 2. Part of the first author's work was supported by National Science Foundation, Grant SBR-9520489.

List of Keywords

Anaphoric metaphor, Cross-modal lexical priming, Cross-modal naming, Cued-recall, Direct Access Model, Direct Access Model of Bilingual Processing, Direct meaning, Figurative meaning, Graded Salience Hypothesis, Ground of the metaphor, Indirect meaning, Literal meaning, Literal Salience Model, Metaphoric reference, Nominal metaphor, Nonsalient meaning, Referential metaphor, Salience, Self-paced reading tasks, Simile, Tenor, Three-Stage Model, Top-down processes, Topic of the metaphor, Vehicle of the metaphor

Thought Questions

1. Harris et al. (1999) suggest that in languages such as Spanish, similes (e.g., *lawyers are like sharks*) are more frequent than the conventionalized nominal English metaphors of the type *lawyers are sharks*. What is your intuition about the relationship between metaphors and similes in your L1 and L2?
2. Which of the theories discussed in this chapter, in your view, best describe how bilinguals might comprehend metaphor?
3. If you are a *Mac person*, you should know that the *trash icon* is often referred to as a *real-world metaphor*, and the *desktop* is also a metaphor of your actual working desk. The *working bench* is also used as a metaphor

to understand the functions of short-term/working memory. Can you think of any other metaphors we use, in general, that help us understand/explain conceptually difficult ideas or theories?

4. Have you ever wondered if there is something universal about metaphors? For instance, metaphors such as, *You are a flower between two thorns, love is a rose, love is a thorn* (or the simile *love is like a thorn*), and *love is a crystal* have direct Spanish equivalents but transformed into similes, *Eres como una flor entre dos espinas, el amor es como una flor, el amor es como una espina, el amor es como un cristal.* Can you think of any other domains (e.g., emotions, expletives, bodily functions, nature) in which metaphoric representations might be shared across languages (see also Zoltán et al., this volume)?

Suggested Student Research Projects

1. *Textbook assignment.* Choose an introductory psychology or a cognitive psychology textbook. Select two or three chapters at random from one of these books and locate as many metaphors as you possibly can. How many metaphors and what types of metaphors were you able to find? To assist you in your metaphor classification, please use the links provided below. Consider some of the metaphors you identified and think about how these metaphors helped you understand the material presented in the chapter. If you came across the *mind as a computer* metaphor, think about how this metaphor helped you visualize or understand the intricacies of the human mind. Share your findings with your class.

2. *Memory and metaphor processing.* In this project, you will replicate Nelson's (1992) bilingual metaphor experiment. Nelson's findings are discussed in the chapter (see also the reference section). Follow the procedures outlined in the methods section as closely as possible. However, you can improve on this experiment by using OpenSesame (http://osdoc.cogsci.nl) or PsyScope (http://psy.ck.sissa.it), two free software/open source experiment builders. These applications, unlike the original study, will allow you to measure reading times at the millisecond level. Simplify the experiment by utilizing only one language. English metaphors can be obtained from Katz et al., (1988; see suggested further readings). For other languages, please consult the existing databases such as PsycInfo, and the Internet. If you have to come up with your own materials, see (3) below and follow the same procedures to properly norm your metaphoric stimuli. Analyze and graph your results. Were you able to replicate Nelson's (1992) results? Did you find evidence for the Direct Access Model of Bilingual Processing?

3. *Imagery and metaphor processing.* A major concern in bilingual research is the lack of stimuli norms for bilinguals. In this project you will

create your own norms for *metaphor imagery*, and most important of all, you will correlate your results with the existing monolingual norms to determine how "good" your norms are, where "good" would be determined by a high positive correlation coefficient (+.5 or higher). Download *GNU PSPP* (www.gnu.org/software/pspp/pspp. html), or *R* (http://www.r-project.org), two free/open source statistical programs. Because your study will be a rating task, to facilitate the data gathering process, consider using OpenSesame. Choose 30–40 nominal metaphors that are moderately to highly familiar (familiarity ratings from 4.5 to 7). For example, the nominal metaphor (A is B) *Clouds are puffballs* has a familiarity rating of 6.10 and a metaphor imagery rating of 6.37. This metaphor is very familiar and highly imageable. Select 10–15 bilinguals, at random, from your class and have them rate the selected metaphors in terms of metaphor imagery. You might want to also consider the possibility of having your bilingual participants rate metaphors for familiarity. Use the monolingual ratings provided by Katz et al. (1988) to perform your correlation analysis between your bilingual ratings and Katz et al.'s monolingual ratings. Using PSPP, graph your results using a scatter plot diagram. What did you find? What is the correlation between your ratings and the ones reported by Katz et al.? Are the measurements positively correlated? Discuss your findings with your class.

Related Internet Sites

Anaphora and Reference: http://www.phon.ucl.ac.uk/home/dick/tta/anaphora/anaphora.htm

ATT-Meta Project Databank: http://www.cs.bham.ac.uk/~jab/ATT-Meta/Databank

Metaphors: http://reglaespanol.about.com/od/figurasretoricas/a/ejemplos-de-metafora.htm

Metaphors by Reference: https://en.wikipedia.org/wiki/Category:Metaphors_by_reference

Rhetorical Figures: http://www.retoricas.com/2009/06/principales-figuras-retoricas.html

The Association for Researching and Applying Metaphor: http://www.raam.org.uk

The Mind Is a Metaphor: http://metaphors.lib.virginia.edu

Thirteen Types of Metaphors: http://grammar.about.com/od/rhetoricstyle/a/13metaphors.htm

Types of Metaphors: http://reglaespanol.about.com/lr/tipos_de_metafora/1917828/4

Suggested Further Readings

Diaz, M.T., & Hogstrom, L.J. (2011). The influence of context on hemispheric recruitment during metaphor processing. *Journal of Cognitive Neuroscience,* 23, 3586–3597.

Gong, S-P., & Ahrens, K. (2007). Processing conceptual metaphors in on-going discourse. *Metaphor & Symbol,* 22, 313–330.

Katz, A.N., Paivio, A., Marschark, M., & Clark, J.M. (1988). Norms for 204 literary and 260 nonliterary metaphors on 10 psychological dimensions. *Metaphor and Symbolic Activity,* 3, 191–214. *Behavior Research Methods, Instruments, & Computers,* 36, 371–383.

Kövecses, Z. (2000). *Metaphor and emotion: Language, culture, and body in human feeling.* Cambridge, UK: Cambridge University Press.

Lakoff, G. (1987). *Women, fire, and dangerous things: What categories reveal about the mind.* Chicago, IL: The University of Chicago Press.

Lakeoff, G., & Johnson, M. (1980). *Metaphors we live by.* Chicago, IL: The University of Chicago Press.

Ortony, A. (1993). *Metaphor and thought* (2nd ed.). New York: Cambridge University Press.

REFERENCES

Almor, A., Arunachalam, S., & Strickland, B. (2007). When *the creampuff* beat the boxer: Working memory, cost, and function in reading metaphoric reference. *Metaphor and Symbol,* 22, 169–193.

Blasko, D.G. (1999). Only the tip of the iceberg: Who understands what about metaphor? *Journal of Pragmatics,* 31, 1675–1683.

Blasko, D.G., & Connine, C.M. (1993). Effects of familiarity and aptness on metaphor processing. *Journal of Experimental Psychology: Learning, Memory, and Cognition,* 19, 295–308.

Bountrogianni, M. (1988). Bilingualism and metaphor comprehension. *European Journal of Education,* 11, 53–64.

Budiu, R., & Anderson, J.R. (2002). Comprehending anaphoric metaphors. *Memory & Cognition,* 30, 158–165.

Cacciari, C., & Glucksberg, S. (1994). Understanding figurative language. In M. Gernsbacher (Ed.), *Handbook of psycholinguistics* (pp. 447–477). San Diego, CA: Academic Press.

Cieślicka, A.B. (2006). Literal salience in on-line processing of idiomatic expressions by L2 speakers. *Second Language Research,* 22, 115–144.

Cohen, J.D., MacWhinney, B., Flatt, M., & Provost, J. (1993). PsyScope: A new graphic interactive environment for designing psychology experiments. *Behavioral Research Methods, Instruments, and Computers,* 25, 257–271.

Francis, W.N., & Kučera, H. (1982). *Frequency analysis of English usage: Lexicon and grammar.* Boston: Houghton Mifflin.

Gibbs, R.W. (1990). Comprehending figurative referential descriptions. *Journal of Experimental Psychology: Learning, Memory, and Cognition,* 16, 56–66.

Giora, R. (1997). Understanding figurative and literal language: The graded salience hypothesis. *Cognitive Linguistics*, *7*, 183–206.

(2002). Literal vs. figurative language: Different or equal? *Journal of Pragmatics*, *34*, 487–506.

(2003). *On our mind: Salience, context, and figurative language*. New York: Oxford University Press.

Glucksberg, S. (2001). *Understanding figurative language*. New York: Oxford University Press.

Glucksberg, S., & Keysar, B. (1990). Understanding metaphorical comparisons: Beyond Similarity. *Psychological Review*, *97*, 3–18.

Harris, R.J., Tebbe, M.R., Leka G.E., García, R.C., & Erramouspe, R. (1999). Monolingual and bilingual memory for English and Spanish metaphors and similes. *Metaphor and Symbol*, *14*, 1–16.

Heredia, R.R. (1997). Bilingual memory and hierarchical models: A case for language dominance. *Current Directions in Psychological Science*, *6*, 34–39.

Heredia, R.R., & Altarriba, J. (2001). Bilingual language mixing: Why do bilinguals code-switch? *Current Directions in Psychological Science*, *10*, 164–168.

Heredia, R.R., & Blumentritt, T.L. (2002). On-line processing of social stereotypes during spoken language comprehension. *Experimental Psychology*, *49*, 208–221.

Heredia, R.R., & Cieślicka, A.B. (2014). Bilingual memory storage: Compound-coordinate and derivatives. In R.R. Heredia & J. Altarriba (Eds.), *Foundations of bilingual memory* (pp. 11–39). New York: Springer.

Heredia, R.R., & Stewart, M.T. (2002). On-line methods in bilingual spoken language research. In R.R. Heredia & J. Altarriba (Eds.), *Bilingual sentence processing* (pp. 7–28). North Holland: Elsevier.

Janus, R.A., & Bever, T.G. (1985). Processing of metaphoric language: An investigation of the three-stage model of metaphor comprehension. *Journal of Psycholinguistic Research*, *14*, 473–487.

Johnson, J. (1989). Factors related to cross-language transfer and metaphor interpretation in bilingual children. *Applied Psycholinguistics*, *10*, 157–177.

Johnson, J., & Rosano, T. (1993). Relation of cognitive style to metaphor interpretation and second language proficiency. *Applied Psycholinguistics*, *14*, 159–175.

Kroll, J.F., & Stewart, E. (1994). Category interference in translation and picture naming: Evidence for asymmetric connections between bilingual memory representations. *Journal of Memory and Language*, *33*, 149–174.

Love, T., & Swinney, D. (1996). Coreference processing and levels of analysis in object-relative constructions: Demonstration of antecedent reactivation with the cross-modal priming paradigm. *Journal of Psycholinguistic Research*, *25*, 5–24.

Matlock, T., & Heredia, R.R., (2002). Understanding phrasal verbs in monolinguals and bilinguals. In R.R. Heredia & J. Altarriba (Eds.), *Bilingual sentence processing* (pp. 251–274). North Holland: Elsevier.

Nelson, E.M. (1992). Memory for metaphor by nonfluent bilinguals. *Journal of Psycholinguistic Research*, *21*, 111–125.

Nelson, D.L., McEvoy, C.L., & Schreiber, T.A. (1998). *The University of South Florida wordassociation, rhyme, and word fragment norms.* http://www.usf.edu/FreeAssociation

Noveck, I.A., Bianco, M., & Castry, A. (2001). The costs and benefits of metaphor. *Metaphor and Symbol, 16,* 109–121.

Onishi, K.A., & Murphy, G.O. (1993). Metaphoric reference: When metaphors are not understood as easily as literal expressions. *Memory & Cognition, 21,* 763–772.

Ortony, A., Schallert, D.L., Reynolds, R.E., & Antos, S.J. (1978). Interpreting metaphors and idioms: Some effects of context comprehension. *Journal of Verbal Learning and Verbal Behavior, 17,* 465–477.

Searle, J. (1979). Metaphor. In A. Ortony (Ed.), *Metaphor and thought* (pp. 92–123). New York: Cambridge University Press.

Swinney, D.A. (1979). Lexical access during sentence comprehension: (Re) consideration of context effects. *Journal of Verbal Learning and Verbal Behavior, 18,* 645–659.

Swinney, D.A., & Osterhout, L. (1990). Inference generation during auditory language comprehension. *The Psychology of Learning and Motivation, 25,* 17–33.

Stewart, M.T., & Heredia, R.R. (2002). Comprehending spoken metaphoric reference: A real-time analysis. *Experimental Psychology, 49,* 34–44.

Tabossi, P. (1996). Cross-modal semantic priming. *Language and Cognitive Processes, 11,* 569–576.

5   Nonliteral Language Processing and Methodological Considerations

Omar García, Anna B. Cieślicka, and Roberto R. Heredia
Texas A&M International University

ABSTRACT

This chapter explores the various methodological tasks employed in the study of bilingual figurative language processing. In the first part of the chapter, we discuss classic behavioral reading paradigms such as *rapid serial visual presentation, visual* and *auditory moving windows,* and the newly developed reading integration *maze* task, as well as eye tracking. The second section focuses on the *cross-modal lexical priming* task (Swinney, 1979). Finally, we provide an overview on what *event-related potentials* (ERPs) can tell us about how bilinguals process figurative language. Advantages and disadvantages of these experimental techniques, as well as the implications of task demands for bilingual figurative language processing, are also discussed.

Keywords: bilingual figurative language, cross-modal lexical priming, event related potentials, online tasks, reading tasks

A fundamental characteristic of language is that, over time, it evolves and adapts to readily fit different linguistic needs. Figurative language is linguistic evolution at its best because it describes concrete and abstract ideas by moving beyond literal constructs and using nonliteral meanings to reach an effect. Expressions such as *kick the bucket* or *stop bulldozing me* reflect this capacity. We laugh (as in puns and jokes), learn and share life experiences or wisdom (as in idioms and proverbs), emphasize certain messages (e.g., irony and hyperbole), and compare our worlds (e.g., similes and metaphors), as figures of speech enhance our communicative effort. How do bilingual or multilingual speakers comprehend figurative expressions? To illustrate, consider the interaction between a Spanish-English bilingual comedian asking another Spanish-English bilingual colleague to *go to the grain*. The comedian being addressed appears mystified at first but could not help but laugh as he realizes that the not-so-novel linguistic expression is a direct translation of the Spanish idiom, *ir al grano* or *get to the point*. Likewise, bilingual speakers not familiar with the English referential metaphoric expression *ambulance chasers* might require additional time and context to figure out that this metaphor refers to lawyers manipulating certain events to obtain clients, as in *if you or your loved ones believe you have been exposed to triclosan, found in hand sanitizers, please call our Law Offices because you may be entitled to monetary compensation!* A literal reading of this expression might suggest a member of the legal profession actually chasing ambulances looking for ways to have access to clients. How do bilinguals understand metaphoric expressions? Are they more likely to access the literal sense of a metaphor followed by the figurative interpretation?

While theories of figurative language developed for monolingual language users differ in whether they view figurative expressions as stored holistically or in a distributed fashion (see Cieślicka, this volume), the existence of a second language (L2) in the mental lexicon adds another conundrum to the issue of storage and language processing. This chapter is about the research techniques used to study bilingual figurative language processing. Some of the issues addressed in this chapter include (1) What is the best way, *if any*, to study bilingual language processing? (2) What is the difference between the so called *offline tasks*, in which participants typically make subjective judgments about some aspect of a figurative expression (e.g., familiarity, imagery), and *online tasks* measuring the time (in milliseconds) taken to determine if an idiomatic expression is grammatical (e.g., *kick the bucket*) or ungrammatical (e.g., *bucket the kick*; e.g., Swinney & Cutler, 1979)? (3) What are some differences between the methodologies used to study bilingual figurative language processing?

Offline versus Online Methods

Several experimental *paradigms* or techniques have been developed to explore figurative language processing. The goal of these experimental techniques is to measure tacit (i.e., unconscious) mental processes that are, in essence, beyond our awareness (Gibbs, 1994; Schacter, 1987), such as *online tasks*, described below. What are the optimal experimental techniques to study bilingual figurative language processing? Ultimately, which technique is more appropriate would depend on the research questions and hypotheses being addressed. Offline tasks explore how individuals interpret language, but their main limitation is that they cannot explain language processing (e.g., Sanford, Sturt, Moxey, Morrow, & Emmott, 2004). In a typical offline study, an individual is given a task, such as reading a sentence, and then asked to paraphrase or interpret its meaning. Online tasks, in contrast, measure moment-to-moment processing variations in sentence reading comprehension (e.g., Mitchell, 2004; Swinney, 1979). Although the offline versus online distinction is often characterized as a dichotomy, more accurately, this distinction should be viewed as a continuum (Veldhuis & Kurvers, 2012). As shown in Figure 1, while some tasks can be classified as offline (e.g., sentence *ratings* or sentence *paraphrasing*; see Table 1) or online (see Table 2), other tasks could be very well situated in the middle of the continuum. One such example is the *discourse completion task*, used by Irujo (1986) to examine comprehension and production of English idioms by Spanish learners of English. Idioms in this study were classified as either identical or similar in form and meaning to their Spanish equivalents, or different from the corresponding Spanish expressions. Participants were instructed to read sentences and supply the missing word (e.g., *Tim's parents were tired of hearing loud music all the time. "Turn that music down," his mother yelled, "I'm____ (fed) up with your music!"*).

Overall, identical idioms were produced more correctly in significantly more cases than similar or different idioms. Notice, however, that the discourse completion task, as used in this study, could become *more* offline if participants were provided with choices as in a multiple-choice test. Indeed, a common misconception in the language research literature is the widespread assumption that tasks involving some type of reaction time (RT) measurements can be considered online tasks. As an example, consider a study reported by Cook (1997), in which bilinguals and monolinguals read sentences of the type described in 1a-b, below.

(1a) *The skier said the doctor helps himself.*
(1b) *The boxer said the skier helps him.*

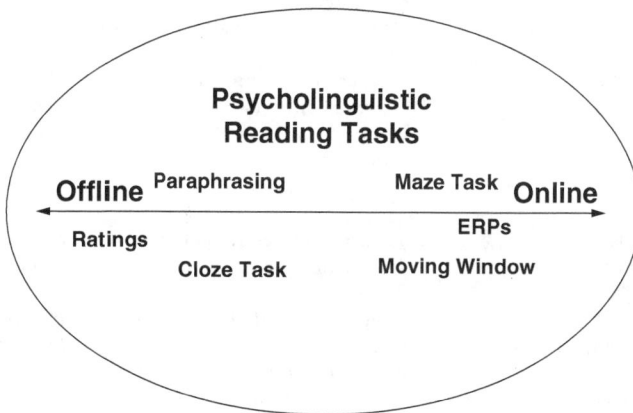

Figure 1. The offline-online task continuum. Adapted from "Offline Segmentation and Online Language Processing Units: The Influence of Literacy," by D. Veldhuis and J. Kurvers, 2012, *Written Language and Literacy, 15*, p. 172. Copyright 2012 by John Benjamins.

Table 1. *Examples of Offline Figurative Language Studies*

Bilingual Study	Task	Stimulus Types
Abel (2003)	Familiarity rating/Decomposability decision task	Idioms
Blais & Gonnerman (2013, Experiment 1 & 3)	Similarity rating	Verb particles
Bortfeld (2002, Experiment 1)	Sentence generation/Mental image interview	Idioms
Bortfeld (2002, Experiment 3)	Mental image questionnaire	Idioms
Blair & Harris (1981)	Recall test	Idioms
Bromberek-Dyzman & Ewert (2010)	Implicature test	Idioms
Cieślicka (2002)	Definition matching/Mental imagery	Proverbs
Cieślicka (2003)	Comprehensibility rating/ Paraphrasing/Generation	Metaphors
Cieślicka (2006)	Word-fragment completion test	Idioms
Curco (2005, Experiment 2)	Interpretation questionnaire	Proverbs
Dagut & Laufer (1985)	Cloze task	Phrasal verbs
Harris et al. (1999)	Stem completion task/Cloze task	Proverbs/Idioms
Hulstijn & Marchena (1989)	Multiple choice/Translation/ Memorization	Phrasal verbs
Irujo (1986)	Completion Task/Translation/ Define-the-idiom/Multiple choice	Idioms
Irujo (1993)	Translation	Idioms
Johnson (1989)	Interpretation task	Metaphors
Johnson & Rosano (1993)	Interpretation task	Metaphors
Laufer (2000)	Fill-in translation test/Passive knowledge test	Idioms
Liao & Fukuya (2004)	Multiple choice/Translation/Recall test	Phrasal verbs
Liontas (2002)	Paraphrasing/Interpretation	Idioms
Littlemore (2010)	Meaningfulness rating/ Interpretation/Sentence completion	Metaphors
Matlock & Heredia (2002, Experiment 1)	Sentence completion	Phrasal verbs
Nelson (1992)	Translation/Cued recall test	Metaphors
Saygin (2001)	Translation	Metaphors
Skoufaki (2008)	Rating	Idioms
Sjöholm (1995)	Multiple-choice/Fill-in-the-blank	Phrasal verbs
Vaid & Martínez (2001)	Paraphrasing or Translation/ Recognition test	Proverbs
Van Lancker-Sidits (2003)	Translation/Paraphrasing/ Recognition test	Proverbs

Table 2. *Examples of Online Bilingual Studies*

Bilingual Study	Task	Stimulus Type
Blair & Harris (1981)	Phoneme-monitoring	Idioms
Blais & Gonnerman (2013, Experiment 4)	Masked lexical decision	Verb particles
Cieślicka (2006)	Cross-modal lexical priming	Idioms
Cieślicka (2007)	Self-paced reading/Naming	Idioms
Cieślicka (2013)	Cross-modal lexical priming	Idioms
Cieślicka & Heredia (2011)	Modified RSVP	Idioms
Cieślicka & Heredia (2013)	Eye tracking	Idioms
Conklin & Schmitt (2008)	Self-paced reading	Idioms
Gerard (2007)	Eye tracking	Formulaic language
Heredia et al. (2007, Experiment 1)	Self-paced reading	Idioms
Heredia et al. (2007, Experiment 2)	Lexical decision	Idioms
Ibáñez et al. (2010)	ERP	Metaphor
Matlock & Heredia (2002, Experiment 2)	Self-paced reading	Phrasal verbs
Moreno et al. (2002)	ERP	Idioms
Siyanova-Chanturia et al. (2011)	Eye tracking	Idioms
Underwood et al. (2004)	Eye tracking	Idioms/Proverbs

Note. RSVP = Rapid serial visual presentation; ERP = Event-related potentials.

The participants' task in this study was to determine to whom the reflexive pronoun *himself* (sentence 1a) and the pronoun *him* (sentence 1b) referred. Bilinguals took approximately 7100 ms and 7600 ms, respectively, to establish the link between *himself* and its antecedent *doctor*, and *him* and *boxer*. These unusually long responses, well above any automatic processing, suggest that these measurements reflect other cognitive processes, such as strategic or metacognitive processing. According to Figure 1, this task described by Cook (1997) could be positioned close to the middle of the continuum. Indeed, the offline-online continuum contrasts with the *explicit-implicit* memory task continuum (e.g., Schacter, 1987), in which *explicit memory tasks* (e.g., free recall) measure explicit, or conscious recollection of an event (e.g., *what did you have for breakfast this morning?*), and *implicit* memory tasks (e.g., lexical decision) measure nonconscious (i.e., automatic) aspects of memory, or knowledge that we are not aware we possess (e.g., native speakers of English "knowing" that verbs such as *give* require a direct object).

In a typical *offline task*, participants are required to use their language knowledge (i.e., explicit knowledge) to assess their metalinguistic perception (Sanford et al., 2004; Sekerina, Fernandez, & Clahsen, 2008; Veldhuis & Kurvers, 2012). Moreover, participants are able to examine different language aspects and provide thoughtful and effortful responses to a given linguistic characteristic. It has been argued that these tasks provide researchers with important data on bilinguals' skills and competence (Bromberek-Dyzman & Ewert, 2010; Veldhuis & Kurvers, 2012; see Table 1 for a summary and examples of offline tasks used in bilingual figurative language). In short, although offline studies provide an important insight into how bilinguals comprehend figurative language, they fail to provide a clear picture of *how* processing is carried out, because they rely exclusively on *ex post facto* strategies (Bolger & Zapata, 2011; Carreiras & Clifton, 2004).

One advantage of online research techniques is that they offer insights into how language is processed as it unfolds in real time (Carreiras & Clifton, 2004; Mitchell, 2004; Sanford et al., 2004; Swinney, 1979; Tanenhaus, 2004). Most, if not all, online methods require extremely controlled settings and time-limit constraints as an accurate data collection prerequisite. These elements, in fact, are almost absent in offline techniques. Due to their real-time processing nature, most online procedures tend to involve some measure of speed and accuracy, unlike offline tasks, which value *how much* the participant knows instead (Bolger & Zapata, 2011). Sekerina et al. (2008) note a late movement toward online methods in L2 acquisition research and bilingualism (see, for example, Heredia & Stewart, 2002; Cieślicka & Heredia, 2011). The next section elaborates on some of the most typical online tasks used in the figurative language processing literature, particularly in bilingualism. We underscore these tasks' strengths and weaknesses and provide a brief account of their use.

Online Behavioral Paradigms

Online methodologies aimed at measuring language processing range from the more traditional (e.g., self-paced reading paradigms), to the more advanced behavioral tasks (e.g., eye tracking), to the technologically advanced ERPs. A majority of these techniques have been used to investigate figurative language processing in monolinguals, and only a few of these tasks have been employed in bilingual studies (see Table 2).

According to Bolger and Zapata (2011), there are three important dimensions regarding most online behavioral tasks: (a) response modes, (b) stimulus presentation manipulations, and (c) conditions proper to task executions. The first dimension, response mode, deals with how participants respond to a presented stimulus. During an experimental session, a participant may be engaged in production (e.g., naming a target word), confirmation (e.g., pressing a button to move to the next stimulus as in the visual moving window), or judgment/classification (e.g., a lexical decision task in which participants determine if a string of letters is a word [*house*] or nonword [*fouse*]). In the second dimension, stimulus presentation manipulation relies on how participants perceive the material being presented. There are five critical stimulus manipulations commonly utilized in psycholinguistic research. The first one is auditory or visual language modes. This characteristic involves the way a given stimulus is presented to participants (e.g., a spoken word or a sentence on a computer screen). The second characteristic is priming. Priming refers to the facilitation effect in which a target word (e.g., *butter*) is responded to faster if preceded by a related (*bread*) than an unrelated word (*carpet*). The third characteristic refers to degrading a stimulus presentation through changed fonts or background, such as in forward versus backward masking. For example, in backward masking a visual stimulus (or mask) is briefly presented immediately after a target, thus disrupting perception of the latter. The fourth characteristic is the timing manipulations between presentations, such as varying stimulus onset asynchrony (SOA) and/or interstimulus interval (ISI). SOA refers to the time interval between the presentation of one stimulus and the beginning of a subsequent stimulus (i.e., between stimuli onsets). ISI, on the other hand, refers to the time delay between the offset of one stimulus and the onset of the subsequent one. The final characteristic includes the addition of distractions, such as performing two or more tasks at the same time; for example, the *Stroop task*, which measures reading interference. Finally, Bolger and Zapata (2011) argue that there are specialized manipulations and/or task executions, which are designed to address specific research hypotheses. One example is the Go/No-Go task, which measures inhibition of responses after certain conditions are met (e.g., press a designated button if the flashing string of letter is a word and withhold response if it is not).

Reading Paradigms

Self-Paced Reading Task

One of the most basic online behavioral techniques utilized in figurative language research is the *self-paced reading* task, in which participants are simply asked to read sentences or phrases, and their reading times (in ms) are recorded. That is, this task is often classified as a global reading processing task, because an entire sentence or phrase is measured. Using the self-paced reading task, Conklin and Schmitt (2008) measured the amount of time taken to read idiomatic (e.g., *Hit the nail on the head*), literal (*Hit the nail on the side*), or control literal expressions (*Hit his head on the nail*). Control literal expressions were a rearrangement of the words of the original idiom with some of the function words (e.g., *the*) replaced by other words (e.g., *his*), equally high or higher in word frequency. Idiomatic and literal expressions were always preceded by a context biasing toward the literal or figurative interpretation. Of critical importance was to determine processing differences between native and non-native speakers of English. The overall results showed that, for both groups, idiomatic expressions exhibited significantly shorter reading times than control phrases. However, literal and idiomatic phrases were equally fast for both groups. In general, native speakers of English exhibited shorter comprehension times than non-natives; however, both groups revealed similar patterns when processing literal and nonliteral language. These results showed that idiomatic expressions were no different than literal expressions and that they most likely involve the same cognitive processing mechanisms. Still, we must add that, based on the somewhat high reading times reported, ranging from 1112 to 1376 ms for native, and 2035 to 2292 ms for the non-native speakers, it is likely that these results represent other nonautomatic processes due to the nature of the task used. As Conklin and Schmitt pointed out, these results await replication using other more sensitive tasks such as eye movements.

Other studies using the self-paced reading task have specifically looked at idiom similarity across languages by bilingual speakers. Heredia, García, and Penecale (2007, Experiment 1) had Spanish-English bilinguals read highly familiar English idiomatic expressions that were (a) direct translations of Spanish (e.g., *point of view* vs. *punto de vista*); (b) similar idioms (e.g., *to kill two birds with one stone*) with a close Spanish translation in which at least one key word was not a direct translation (e.g., *matar dos pájaros de un tiro* vs. *to kill two birds with one shot*); and (c) different idioms that had different translations, and no key words in common (e.g., *to pull his/her leg* vs. *tomar el pelo*: "take someone's hair").

The purpose of this experiment was to explore reading/comprehension facilitation effects among identical and similar expressions, relative to different idiomatic expressions across Spanish and English. Based on *Transfer Theory* (Irujo, 1986), reading times for identical/similar idioms were predicted to be faster than different idioms. This ease of comprehension for identical and similar idioms is presumably due to cross-language transfer. Accordingly, during the comprehension of idiomatic expressions that are identical and similar across languages, bilinguals use the information from their L1 to help them arrive at an interpretation of

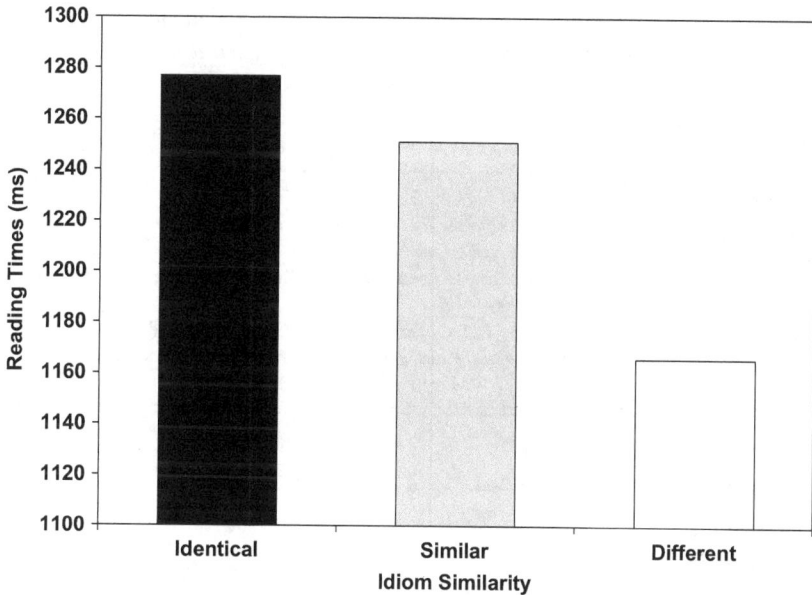

Figure 2. Reading Times as a Function of Idiom Similarity

the idiomatic expression in their L2 (Irujo, 1986). As a consequence, the intended meanings of the identical and similar idioms are retrieved more readily. When reading different idioms, on the other hand, bilinguals are unable to take advantage of this one-to-one mapping between the two languages, and any attempts to use the L1 to make sense of the idiomatic expression cause interference errors and slow down the comprehension process. The results are summarized in Figure 2.

Unlike Irujo's (1986) offline results, Spanish-English bilinguals were actually faster in reading idiomatic expressions that were different across Spanish and English. Reading times between identical and similar idioms did not differ. One reason that different idioms were faster than identical and similar might be due to the possibility that idioms that are different across languages (e.g., *kick the bucket*) are learned and memorized as a word, and thus retrieved as a *single lexical item* as posed by the *Lexical Representation Hypothesis* (Swinney & Cutler, 1979). In contrast, identical and similar idioms took longer due to the possibility that, given their similarity across the two languages, both lexicons were readily active, thus slowing down the retrieval process due to inter-language competition.

In another standard self-paced reading study (Heredia, Athanatou, & Tuttle, 2004), Spanish-English bilinguals read idiomatic expressions

Table 3. *Sample Stimuli of Idiomatic Expressions as a Function of Idiom Type (Different, Identical, and Similar) between Spanish and English and Preceding Context (Literal, Figurative, and Unbiased)*

Type	Idiom
Different	*Kick the bucket*: "Estirar la pata"
Identical	*Adds fuel to the fire*: "Echar leña al fuego"
Similar	*Hit the nail on the head*: "Dar en el clavo"
	Preceding Biased Context Biased Context
	Kick the bucket
	Literal: The soccer player spilled the water and ...
	Figurative: Mary went to the funeral because her uncle had ...
	Unbiased: Mary's very nice uncle ...

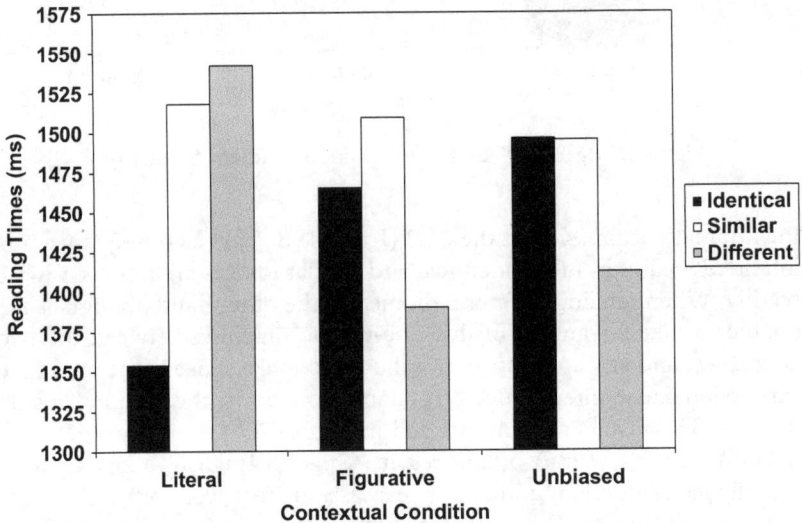

Figure 3. Reading Times as a Function of Contextual Conditions and Idiom Type in a Self-Paced Reading Task

followed by preceding contextual information that was either biased toward the literal or figurative meaning or unbiased (see Table 3). Results exhibited patterns similar to those in Heredia et al. (2007).

The participants' task was to read the first part of a sentence followed by the idiomatic expression. Only reading times for the idiomatic expressions were measured. As can be seen from Figure 3, different idioms were faster under figurative and unbiased contextual conditions.

However, for the literal contextual condition, they took longer to read. Although the standard self-paced reading task might be sensitive enough for measuring participants' reading ability, language proficiency, and dominance, it appears to be a very general task in which it is difficult to determine what is being measured. It could be argued that this task is fairly low on the online continuum described in Figure 1, because participants read entire sentences as opposed to individual words (see Conkling & Schmitt, 2008; Heredia et al., 2007). Although idiom-type differences across Spanish and English appear to be robust, other results from our laboratory experiments, employing more sensitive online tasks (e.g., eye movements and the *cross-modal lexical priming task*, discussed below; see also Cieślicka, 2006), provide more insight into these effects. We next discuss two main variants of the self-paced reading task: the visual moving window and the stationary moving window.

Visual Moving Window

The *visual moving window* and the *stationary moving window* are two self-paced reading techniques used in figurative language research (Katz & Ferretti, 2001; Mitchell, 2004). In the visual moving window technique, participants read sentences word by word, or phrase by phrase on a computer screen, from left to right. Latency or RT is the critical measurement, with an increase in reading times taken to reflect difficulty in comprehension (Katz & Ferreti, 2001). The participant's task is to press a button (typically the space bar) as fast as possible in order to move from one word/phrase to the next, from left to right (see Figure 4). In some versions of the visual moving window, nonspace characters (i.e., individual letters that compose a word) are replaced by a dash (e.g., – – for *cold feet*) and every button press reveals the first word of the sentence while replacing the previous word with dashes (see, for example, Katz & Ferreti, 2001). In other cases (e.g., cumulative presentation), words appear on the computer screen without disappearing, unlike the non-cumulative presentation, in which nonspace characters may be replaced with dashes. In the stationary or center non-cumulative presentation, stimuli appear in the middle of the screen in the same location for each

XXX > Victor > was > feeling > uncomfortable > and > he > had > cold > feet. > [Blank Screen]

Figure 4. Example of a Self-Paced Reading Moving Window Presentation of a Sentence
Note. Greater than (>) symbols denote a self-activated transition to the next stimulus presentation.

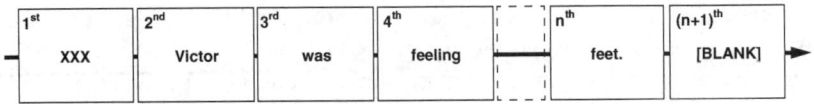

Figure 5. Example of Self-Paced Reading Stationary Moving Window Presentation of a Sentence

Note. Screens (1st – n^{th}) illustrate successive stimuli appearing in the same location in the middle of the screen represented by the broken rectangle.

word (see Figure 5; Just, Carpenter, & Woolley, 1982; Mitchell, 2004). The stationary visual moving window is to a certain extent similar to the rapid serial visual presentation technique, reviewed below, the only difference being that in the latter, item presentation is typically fixed at a predetermined rate of time. For example, for the idiom described in Figures 4 and 5, the investigator might be interested in measuring reading times for the first and second words of the idiomatic expression (e.g., *to have*), followed by the noun phrase (*cold feet*), and other indexes combining entire idioms, and comparing them to a nonidiomatic expression containing the noun phrase (e.g., *cold hands*).

To assess comprehension and attention error rates (e.g., percentage of missed questions due to poor attention), from time to time participants are presented with comprehension questions based on information presented visually. This is obviously not particular to the moving window technique, because it is a general practice in reading research. As pointed out by Bolger and Zapata (2011) and Mitchell (2004), the visual moving window is a fairly low-cost task to implement, it has ecological validity, and its results are comparable to eye movement findings (cf. Witzel, Witzel, & Forster, 2012). One important advantage of this task is that it is a fair approximation of normal reading, and it can significantly reduce participants' reading strategies (Witzel et al., 2012).

A few experiments in bilingual figurative language processing have implemented some variation of the visual moving window (e.g., Cieślicka, 2007; see also Libben & Titone, 2008). For example, Cieślicka (2007) investigated Polish-English bilinguals using this technique combined with a naming task. Participants were presented with Polish and English idioms varying along the dimension of literality (i.e., the extent to which an idiomatic expression possesses a literal interpretation) and transparency (i.e., the extent to which the original figurative meaning of an idiomatic phrase can be deduced from its literal analysis). For example, idiomatic expressions such as *add fuel to the fire* could be understood both literally and figuratively; this phrase is also transparent because its figurative interpretation can be abstracted from its individual components. In contrast, the idiom *he battled the storm* is literally implausible but transparent, and the idiom *kick the bucket* is literally plausible but opaque, because its meaning cannot be deduced from analyzing the meaning of its constituent words. Idioms were embedded in sentences biasing their figurative meaning (e.g., *Rather than providing a solution, their statements merely added fuel to the fire*) and followed by three types of target stimuli: idiomatic (related to the figurative meaning of the whole phrase, e.g., *worse*), literal (related to the literal meaning of the last word of the idiom, e.g., *heat*), and unrelated, which served as a baseline condition for the idiomatic and literal targets (e.g., *hole*). Targets were displayed either immediately after the end of the sentence (0 ms) or after an 850 ms ISI. Each trial consisted of a visual presentation of a sentence that remained on the screen until the participant pressed a designated key. The task required participants to name a target word appearing in the center of a computer screen. At the 0 ms ISI, significant priming (i.e., activation) was found, but only for the literal interpretation of both Polish and English idioms. At the 850 ms ISI, not only literal but also idiomatic targets were primed in both the Polish and English conditions, and the priming effects obtained for literal targets were significantly larger for English than for Polish idioms. These results were interpreted as suggesting that both literal and figurative meanings of idioms are still active after the idiom has been accessed and that literal activation is more prominent in the non-native than native language idiom processing.

Another variant of the visual moving window technique, the *auditory moving window* (Ferreira, Anes, & Horine, 1996; Ferreira, Henderson, Anes, Weeks, & McFarlane, 1996) provides yet another alternative to studying bilingual figurative language processing. In this task, participants listen to sentences one or two words at a time and are required to press a button to receive successive segments, as in sentences 2a-b (spoken word segments are depicted with carets "ˆ"; Heredia & Stewart, 2002; Heredia, Stewart, & Cregut, 1997). Times between button presses or inter-response times (IRTs) are recorded. Analysis can be performed on the IRTs or difference times (DTs). DTs are computed by subtracting the IRTs from the duration of the segment during the digitizing of the word. For example, if the IRT for the phrasal verb *ran over* in sentence 2a is 950 ms, and the time taken to record the target (duration time) is 500 ms, then the DT would be 450 ms.

(2a) *Mr. ˆSmithˆ [the Olympicˆ athleteˆ] <u>ran overˆ</u> the oldˆ bridgeˆ earlyˆ this morning.*

(2b) *Mr. ˆSmith [the serialˆ killerˆ] <u>ran overˆ</u> the oldˆ farmerˆ earlyˆ this morning.*

Although this task has been mostly utilized in the monolingual literature (e.g., Little, Prentice, Darrow, & Wingfield, 2005; Titone, Prentice, & Wingfield, 2000; Titone, Wingfield, Caplan, Waters, & Prentice, 2001), work by Heredia et al. (1997) in bilingual sentence processing suggests that this task might be well suited to study figurative language processing among bilinguals exhibiting different proficiency levels or language dominance (i.e., which language is more readily activated due to language use) in speaking and reading English. Future studies might consider looking at the comprehension of ambiguous phrasal verbs (e.g., *run over*: "walking over something," in sentence 2a, vs. "killing someone by driving" in sentence 2b; see also, Matlock & Heredia, 2002; Paulmann et al., this volume) under contextually biased and unbiased conditions among bilinguals varying in the degrees of language dominance and language proficiency. However, a possible disadvantage with these reading techniques is that the researcher must trust that the participant has read or listened to the presented stimuli (Bolger & Zapata, 2011). Researchers employing these paradigms will not know if participants are paying attention to the presented stimuli unless they employ "comprehension checks," such as random comprehension questions embedded in the trials, as discussed in earlier sections.

To summarize, even though the visual moving window task and its variants offer a fair approximation to normal reading (or listening), one disadvantage is their clear deviation from natural reading because stimuli are presented one word or phrase at a time (Witzel et al., 2012). Like most online tasks, the moving window technique employs RT as the dependent measure; however, it might not be exempt from *repetition blindness*, or the inability to detect certain stimuli due to recurrent presentation (Altarriba & Soltano, 1986; Kanwisher, 1987), and other confounding variables such as misinterpretation of sentence meaning (Marinis, 2003). Indeed, future research would benefit from a task analysis in which the moving window is compared to other tasks (e.g., the rapid serial visual presentation task) under similar experimental conditions. Moreover, Mitchell (2004) argues that the unnatural segmentation of the reading material might actually slow down the reading process and RT, as well as leading to possible *spill-over effects*, where the processing of previous words influences decisions on subsequent words (Witzel et al., 2012). Another considerable issue with this task involves the button-pressing needed to move between stimulus presentations. Witzel et al. (2012) point out that participants can adopt different button-pushing strategies (e.g., fast vs. delayed), which could result in incongruent reading times, thus affecting their interpretation. For instance, participants adopting a faster (as quick as possible) button-pushing strategy will exhibit shorter reaction times compared to participants who delay their responses. Participants could also develop a consistent rhythm as they push the button to move to the next word (Witzel et al., 2012). More recent tasks, discussed below, have been developed to help decrease participants' response strategies.

Rapid Serial Visual Presentation

The *rapid serial visual presentation* (RSVP) technique measures visual information processing via the viewers' word recognition, recollection, and levels of awareness (Wyble, Potter, & Mattar, 2012). In RSVP, stimulus information is presented in text or images in a series of computer screens. For instance, phrases or sentences (e.g., Cieślicka & Heredia, 2011; see also Altarriba & Soltano, 1996) are presented one word at a time, at a fixed point and at a constant pace, in a series of screens (see Figure 6).

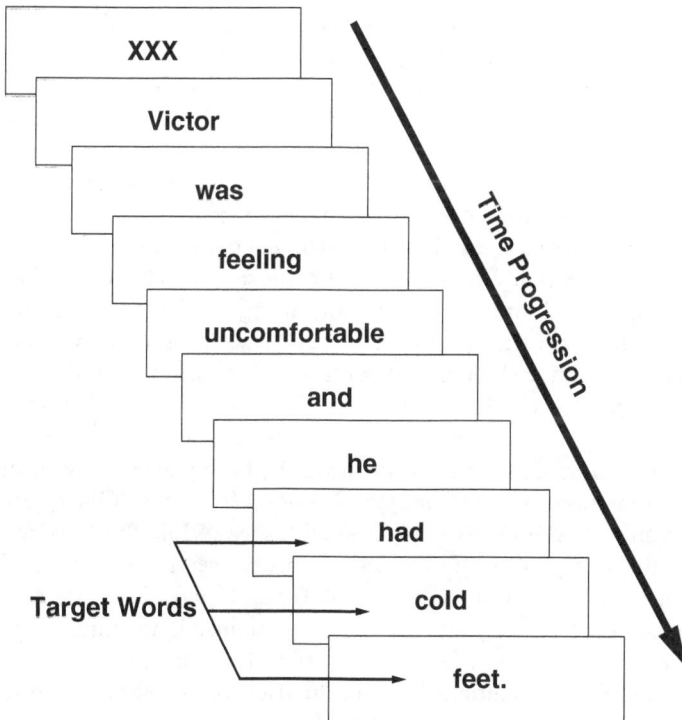

Figure 6. Example of an RSVP Presentation of a Sentence

In some instances (see Schwartz & Kroll, 2006), the target word is set to stand out from the rest of the stimuli by displaying distinct characteristics (e.g., font color). Nonetheless, efforts to make a target distinct might introduce undesirable third variables, such as expectations or *demand characteristics*, making this task *less* online, in relation to the offline-online continuum (see Figure 1). For instance, a researcher might be interested in measuring the time taken to understand the noun phrase *cold feet* (see Figure 6) in the idiom *to have cold feet* and comparing it to a control noun phrase (e.g., *cold hands*) that turns the original idiomatic phrase into a literal statement (e.g., *to have cold hands*). One prediction would be that if idiomatic expressions are indeed lexicalized and retrieved as chunks from the mental lexicon, they should show a processing advantage over newly created literal phrases, whose meaning must be computed through a compositional analysis of their constituent words. Indeed, this is essentially what the evidence seems to support (Swinney & Cutler, 1979; see also Cieślicka, this volume).

In some experimental conditions, a stimulus presentation might follow duration times that are calculated depending on the stimulus' character count plus a constant, as suggested by Faust and Gernsbacher (1996). These presentation times commonly last a few hundred milliseconds. For example, in Cieślicka and Heredia's (2011) study, presentation duration was set to 300 ms for Polish words stimuli and 400 ms for English words. Other studies (e.g., Altarriba & Soltano, 1996) have utilized presentations rates of 117 ms per word.

A few studies have employed the RSVP technique in bilingual figurative language research. For example, Cieślicka and Heredia (2011) tested Polish-English bilingual participants using a divided visual field paradigm, where presentation of a sentence was followed by a Go/No-Go lexical decision task (i.e., Go for a word decision requiring pressing a button and No-Go for a non-word decision not requiring any action). The goal of the study was to investigate the role of salience and context in the processing of idiomatic expressions by bilingual language users and to test predictions of the *Graded Salience Hypothesis* (Giora, 1997) and Beeman's (1998) *Fine-Coarse Coding Theory*. While the Graded Salience Hypothesis capitalizes on the distinction between *salient* (more frequent, familiar, prototypical, conventional) and *nonsalient* (less frequent, familiar, prototypical, and less conventionalized) meanings, postulating differential sensitivity of the left and right hemisphere to these meanings, the Fine-Coarse Coding Theory focuses on cerebral asymmetries in response to context and qualitative differences in the type of semantic processing the two hemispheres employ.

Table 4. *Sample Stimuli from Cieślicka and Heredia (2011)*

Condition	Stimulus Sentence	Target
Ambiguous context-idiomatic target	As soon as possible, she let the cat out of the bag	REVEAL
Ambiguous context- literal target	As soon as possible, she let the cat out of the bag	SHOP
Unambiguous context-idiomatic target	Unable to keep secrets, she let the cat out of the bag	REVEAL
Unambiguous context-literal target	Unable to keep secrets, she let the cat out of the bag	SHOP
Control context-idiomatic target	Last week we went to the theater, but the play was awful	REVEAL
Control context-literal target	My sister has just got a new job and she is happy	SHOP

In Cieślicka and Heredia's (2011) study, idioms were inserted in an ambiguous (i.e., where the idiom could be read both figuratively and literally) and unambiguous (i.e., biased toward the idiomatic interpretation) sentence context (see Table 4). Idiomatic (e.g., *reveal*) and literal (e.g., *shop*) target words were paired with each idiom. Participants were assigned to three different conditions in which target words were displayed at 0, 300, and 800 ms ISIs. Overall, both context and salience were found to significantly contribute to idiom processing, and their effects were modulated by the language (L1 vs. L2) of the stimulus materials. Whereas literal meanings of ambiguous idioms were found to be particularly active for L2 idioms, suggesting that idiom literal meanings are more salient than figurative in the course of their processing by L2 users, no differences were found between the right and left hemisphere in terms of their sensitivity to contextual constraints.

One advantage of RSVP is that, at least in the bilingual language processing domain, this task produces results comparable to eye tracking techniques (e.g., Altarriba, Kroll, Sholl, & Rayner, 1996). RSVP avoids typical eye movements that happen during reading that limit reading speed rates (Potter, 1984). Another advantage of RSVP is that experimenters can manipulate reading times word by word, even to reflect natural moderate reading speed rates (i.e., around 6 words per second).

However, Mitchell (1984) argues that RSVP's main limitation in measuring reading is that this task may not be sensitive enough to capture immediate processes, because it tends to rely on the *accuracy of recall* response (i.e., how well different sentence stimulus fragments are stored, retrieved, or reconstructed in memory). As a result, RSVP data may be open to contamination because stimulus recall, the task's main performance measure, might not reflect immediate reading processing *per se* (Mitchell, 1984). Not only does the RSVP task lack enough sensitivity in certain cases (i.e., potential participants not responding to presented stimuli as fast as they could), but it also suffers from possible repetition blindness and *attentional blink*, or failure to perceive subsequent target stimuli presented after the first case (see Raymond, Shapiro, & Arnell, 1992; Wyble et al., 2012), which are both confounding variables. Moreover, as a reading task, RSVP is low on ecological validity, because it does not represent the manner in which reading takes place in the natural setting. Responses to RSVP stimulus presentations also run the risk of becoming habitual as participants learn to respond in a certain way. In addition, distinctive target stimulus features such as special font sizes or colors may introduce participants' effects. To overcome some of these shortcomings, researchers have turned to more sensitive reading methodologies in which the participant can exert direct control over presentation speed rates.

Maze Task

The *reading maze* task in monolingual (Bolger & Zapata, 2011; Forster, 2010; Forster, Guerrera, & Elliot, 2009; Qiao, Shen, & Forster, 2012; Witzel et al., 2012) and bilingual homograph studies (Heredia, Altamira, Cieślicka, & García, 2012) provides another alternative to RSVP and reading moving window variants, and it circumvents some of their weaknesses (Forster et al., 2009), such as being unable to determine if participants are indeed paying attention as they move from one trial (word) to the next. Additionally, the reading maze also controls for eye tracking limitations, such as repeated eye jumping between words and article (*a, the*) omissions (see Forster, 2010 for a detailed discussion). This control is achieved because the task requires, and thus fosters, incremental processing in order to move forward (Bolger & Zapata, 2011; Forster et al., 2009). There are two variants of the reading *maze task*: the *grammaticality maze* (G-maze) task and the *lexicality maze* (L-maze) task.

Figures 7 and 8 illustrate the presentation of a sentence in the *grammaticality maze* (G-maze) task. After seeing the beginning of the sentence (e.g., *The XXX*), the participant is presented with a series of screen frames displaying two possible choices at the same time (e.g., *are* vs. *student*) on the left and right of the computer screen. The participant's task is to select the word that continues the preceding fragment in a

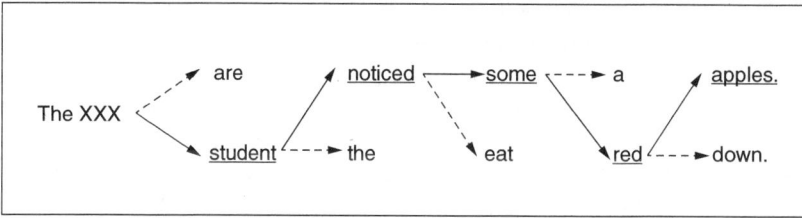

Figure 7. Representation of the G-Maze
Note. Solid lines represent a coherent and grammatical sentence.

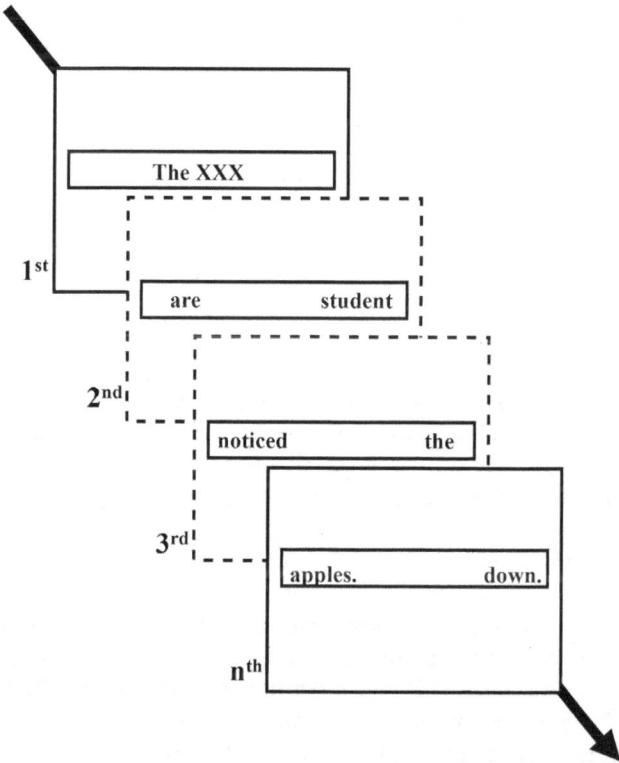

Figure 8. Representation of Common Screen Schematics Displayed
in Reading Maze Experiments. Adapted from "The Maze Task:
Measuring Forced Incremental Sentence Processing Time,"
by K.I. Forster, C. Guerrera, & L. Elliot, 2009, *Behavior Research
Methods, 41*, p. 164. Copyright 2009 by Springer.

grammatically correct way by pressing a keyboard key or button. One of the choices is ungrammatical (see Figures 7 and 8). Each new trial decision is meant to build upon the previous selected stimulus, which in the end will result in forming a complete, grammatically correct sentence. In the maze task, stimulus presentation resembles that of a moving window, because sentences are fragmented and presented on the computer screen in a series of word pairs. RTs are collected to grammatical judgments or decisions constructing meaningful and correct sentences resulting from selecting between two possible choices (Witzel et al., 2012).

Dotted lines in Figure 7 represent paths that would either cancel the experiment and restart the trial or move to the subsequent fragment of the sentence. Because this paradigm fosters incremental word-to-sentence analysis, it has the capacity of minimizing participant response strategies (Witzel et al., 2012) and spillover effects, unlike other reading tasks (Forster et al., 2009). No comprehension questions (avoiding their implications, see Forster et al., 2009 for a brief review) are needed by the maze because a comprehension measure is built in (i.e., if a participant makes a mistake, the trial stops and it is recorded as an error). When compared to the eye tracking and moving window techniques, the maze has the most reading restrictions due to the word-pair presentation it employs and the inability to go back to previous stimuli, which considerably decreases participant reading strategies (Witzel et al., 2012). Participants have no access either to the preceding or following stimuli; therefore, they need to focus only on the words currently displayed and integrate them with the prior information, so as to avoid mistakes and trial cancelation. This behavioral method is based on basic operant conditioning principles, because it provides positive reinforcement (e.g., sentence continuation) and negative punishment (e.g., trial cancelation).

The second variant of the maze task, the *lexicality maze* (L-maze) task is for all purposes similar to the G-maze, the only difference being that, instead of a grammatical judgment, participants continuously make lexical decisions between words (e.g., *noticed*) and nonwords (*jempud*).

However, like the RSVP and moving window variants, the maze task deviates even more from natural reading (Witzel et al., 2012) and might require a large number of experimental stimuli to construct unrelated word pairs. Moreover, RTs tend to increase as participants appear to take more time processing the fragmented stimuli. Because participants cannot predict the length of a given sentence, they might be tempted to shorten some of its compoments (Witzel et al., 2012). For example, for the noun phrase *post office*, participants experience difficulties responding to *office* after *post* is presented because *the post* could serve as a closed constituent. RTs are longer as participants must read both presented choices and then reach a decision. This might mute other important reading effects (Forster, 2010). Another issue with this paradigm and running software is its higher complexity to program when compared to self-paced reading tasks (Bolger & Zapata, 2011; but see Heredia et al., 2012). Moreover, this task has very little ecological validity because the reading technique it utilizes is highly unnatural. There are no studies exploring bilingual figurative language processing with the maze task. The following section deals with a more advanced methodology that measures eye movements recorded in real time as the participant reads a given sentence.

Eye Tracking

Eye tracking is a more sensitive gaze-contingency technique that lies at the higher end of the online continuum (see Figure 1) and has been recently used in cross-linguistic figurative language research (see Cieślicka & Heredia, 2013; Gerard, 2007; Siyanova-Chanturia, Conklin, & Schmitt, 2011; Underwood, Galpin, & Schmitt, 2004). Through a recording computer, fixation (the amount of time a person spent looking at a region of interest), fixation count (the number of all fixations made within a region of interest), first pass reading time (or gaze duration, defined as the sum of all fixations made prior to exiting the region), total reading time (the sum of all fixation durations made within a region of interest), among others, are recorded as participants are exposed to words, phrases, or entire passages (Frenck-Mestre, 2005; Marian, 2008; Underwood et al., 2004; see Figure 9).

The eye tracking paradigm measures more natural-occurring reading and comprehension based eye movement behaviors (Gordon, Camblin, & Swaab, 2004). One of the advantages of eye tracking is that it does not restrict reading strategies because participants are allowed to go back to the presented stimuli, unlike the other reading tasks discussed earlier. In addition, eye tracking avoids potential problems associated with sentence segmentation, because it measures continuous reading, as opposed to the previously mentioned moving window paradigm (Sanford et al., 2004).

Although eye tracking has been successfully employed in monolingual figurative language processing research (e.g., Cieślicka, O'Rourke, & Singleton, 2008; Titone & Connine, 1999), little work has been done on bilingual/L2 figurative processing (see, for example, Cieślicka, Heredia, & Olivares, 2014; Conklin & Schmitt, 2008; Siyanova-Chanturia et al., 2011; Underwood et al., 2004). The few L2 eye tracking

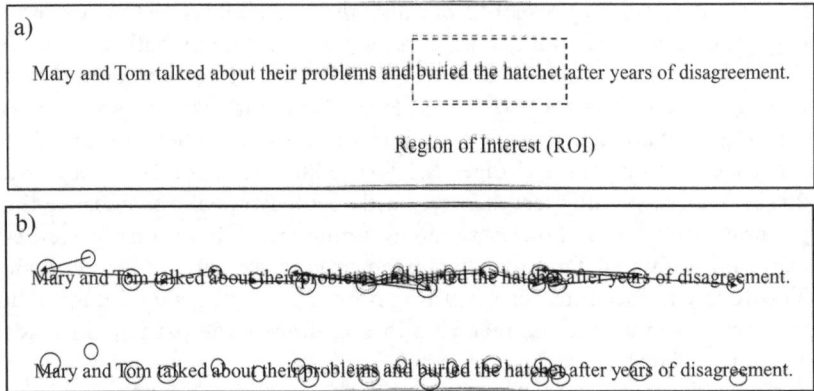

Figure 9. Representation of (a) Region of Interest (ROI) in Online Eye Tracking Reading Experiments and (b) Fixations and Regressions

figurative processing studies reported so far have mostly focused on the role of context, salience, and language status (native vs. non-native or dominant in L1 or L2), as well as on the question of whether idioms are lexicalized (i.e., stored as chunks in the mental lexicon) and retrieved holistically, as opposed to novel, nonfigurative phrases that undergo a compositional analysis.

In one of these studies, Underwood et al. (2004) recorded fixation count and fixation duration as native and non-native speakers of English read idiomatic expressions and novel non-formulaic sequences. The critical region of interest (ROI) was the last word of the idiomatic phrase (e.g., *policy*) when this word occurred in an idiom (e.g., *honesty is the best policy*) or when it was embedded in a control sentence used literally (*it seems that his policy of...*). If idioms are stored as chunks and retrieved holistically from the mental lexicon, then they should enjoy a processing advantage over novel, non-formulaic sequences that must be assembled through a compositional analysis. Thus, fewer and shorter fixations should be expected on the last idiom word when the word is part of the idiom than when it occurs in the novel phrase. Overall, the results for native speakers showed a clear processing advantage for formulaic over non-formulaic phrases. However, the non-native speaker data were mixed – no differences were found in the duration of fixations on the target words, regardless of whether the words were part of the idiom or control literal phrase.

In a recent eye tracking study, Cieślicka et al. (2014) looked at how the activation of idiom's literal and figurative meanings varies as a function of context and language dominance. Spanish-English bilinguals, dominant either in Spanish or in English, were presented with ambiguous idioms (i.e., idioms with a plausible literal interpretation, such as *a piece of cake*). The idioms were used in sentences in which context biasing the literal or figurative interpretation of the idiom either preceded the idiom or followed it. For example, the literally biasing context preceding the idiom *piece of cake* was: *On Sunday, I went to my uncle's birthday party, but I only ate one piece of cake because it was vanilla with chocolate icing and it filled me up*, whereas the figuratively biasing context preceding the idiom read: *With foolproof instructions from "Homemaker" magazine, home decorating is a piece of cake, so that even beginners can produce amazing results*. When the biasing context followed the idiom, the beginning of the sentence was ambiguous with regard to how the idiom should be interpreted, and it was only the part of the sentence following the idiom that disambiguated its reading toward either a figurative (e.g., *It's not a piece of cake for smaller newspapers to maintain a comprehensive website featuring fresh news and features*) or a literal reading (e.g., *It's not a piece of cake, it's an apple tart, and I'd also appreciate it if you'd bring me the cappuccino I ordered ten minutes ago*). The eye measures recorded were total reading time, fixation count, and regressions (fixations going back to the idiom region) for both the idiom region and the post-idiom region, which was the disambiguating part of the sentence when the idiom was preceded by the neutral context.

Overall, the results showed a significant effect of context in all the reading measures, which strongly affected idiom processing, regardless of language dominance. This effect held true for idioms used both figuratively and literally, suggesting that a rich context can successfully facilitate the comprehension of idiomatic phrases, no matter whether they are used in their conventionalized, figurative meanings, or literally. In addition, the study showed differences in the pattern of activation of idiom's literal and figurative meanings, with Spanish-dominant bilinguals processing literally used idioms faster than figuratively used ones, and English-dominant bilinguals showing shorter reading times for figuratively than literally used idioms. While those differences did not manifest consistently across all the three reading measures, they do point to the importance of language dominance in modulating figurative processing and suggest that language status is an important factor determining how idioms are represented in the mental lexicon and retrieved in online processing. Despite its numerous advantages, the eye tracking paradigm is not free from limitations. One possible drawback includes spillover effects in which earlier-occurring stimulus words influence the perception of later words, thus affecting subsequent reading time measurements (Forster et al., 2009). Another limitation is that participants can adopt multiple strategies, such as skimming, which could impact reading measures and thus overall data analysis (Witzel et al., 2012). While analyses of eye data might help answering the "when" processing question more precisely, this technique fails at explaining "how" language is being processed (Pickering, Frisson, McElree, & Traxler, 2004). The next section discusses the lexical decision task typically used on its own or in conjunction with other tasks (e.g., the *cross-modal lexical priming* task).

Lexical Decision Task

In the traditional *lexical decision task* (LDT; Meyer & Schvaneveldt, 1971), participants are presented with a visual or auditory *prime* (e.g., the word *bread*), followed by a related (e.g., *butter*) or unrelated (e.g., *carpet*) *target* word. Depending on the experimental condition, prime presentation may vary. The participant's task is simply to determine if the presented target is a word (*butter*) or a nonword (*botter*). The assumption underlying this task is that a target word that is related to the preceding prime is responded to faster than a target word that is unrelated. This robust effect is known as the *priming effect*. The priming effect has been used in the figurative language processing literature as an index of *lexical activation*, or whether a particular meaning of a word is active or not active. Priming is the difference between the unrelated and the related target (i.e., unrelated − related target). A difference of zero signifies that a given meaning was not facilitated, relative to a control word, and a difference greater than zero signifies lexical facilitation or activation.

French-English bilinguals in the Blais and Gonnerman's (2013) experiment participated in a masked priming lexical decision task investigating L2 sensitivity to different verb particles ranging from more transparent (e.g., *finish up*) to less transparent or opaque (e.g., to *chew out*). Participants were first presented with an asterisk "*" as a fixation point for 1000 ms, followed by a visual mask (a pattern symbol characters) lasting for 500 ms (see Figure 10). The prime (e.g., *cover up*) remained on the screen for 35 ms and the target (e.g., *cover*) was subsequently presented for 200 ms. Briefly, in masked priming, a prime is exposed for a few ms between a pattern symbol mask (e.g., ####) and a target, rendering this form of priming nearly invisible (Forster et al., 2003). The results suggested that, as L2 proficiency increases, bilinguals tend to exhibit RTs similar to those of monolingual speakers, regardless of the absence of such word constructions in their L1.

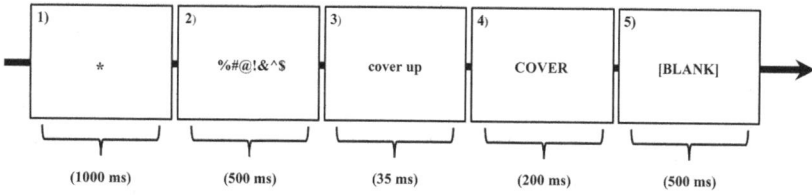

Figure 10. Example of a Trial in a Priming Lexical Decision Task (Duration Times For Stimuli Presentation Are Noted below the Respective Screen)
Note. Screens Illustrate (1) fixation point, (2) visual mask, (3) prime, (4) target; and (5) ISI or delay before next trial.

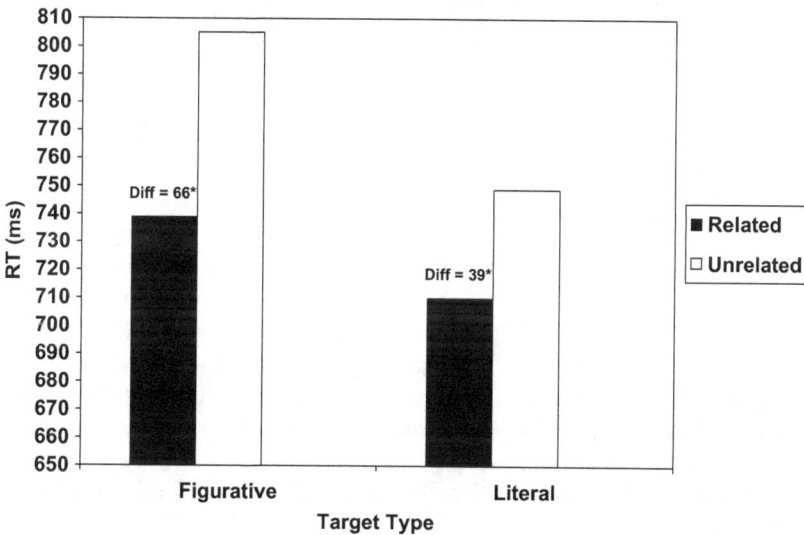

Figure 11. RT as a Function of Target Type and Relatedness (Diff = Unrelated – Related)

In another bilingual study, Heredia et al. (2007, Experiment 2) utilized the lexical decision task to investigate priming effects for *identical*, *similar*, and *different* idioms across Spanish and English (see the section *self-paced reading task* for further details). Participants in this task were presented with idiomatic expressions as primes (e.g., *kick the bucket*) that remained on the computer screen for 4500 ms, followed by a 300-ms presentation of a figurative-related (*die*) or literal-related (*water*) target and their respective controls. Figure 11 summarizes the results of the priming study. Facilitatory priming was revealed, showing that both the

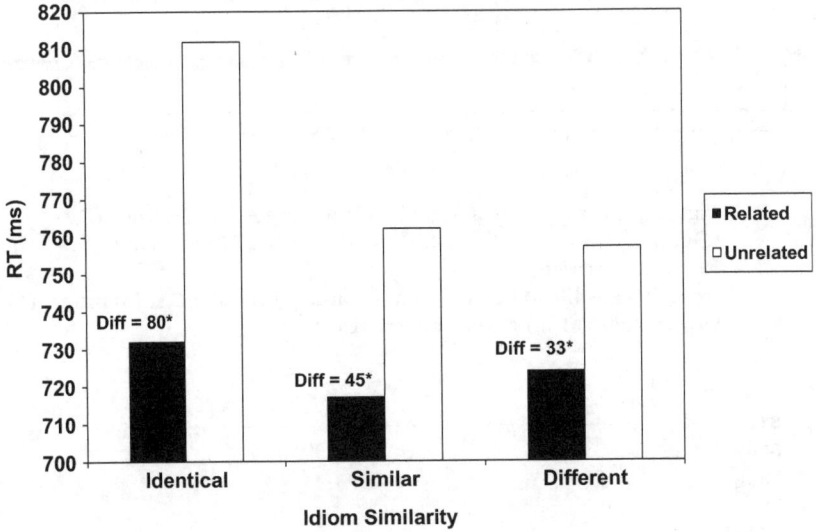

Figure 12. RT as a Function of Idiom Similarity Target Type and Relatedness (Diff = Unrelated − Related)

figurative and literal meanings of the idiomatic expression were active immediately after the offset of the idiomatic expression. More impressive, however, was the two-way interaction between idiom similarity and relatedness (see Figure 12) showing facilitatory priming among the three types of idioms, with identical idioms exhibiting substantially more priming. These results also show that identical and similar idioms enjoy more priming than different ones across languages. This idiom type facilation may be congruent with the Tranfer Hypothesis described earlier.

Another related task that has been used in the monolingual figurative language processing literature and is currently beeing used in our laboratory with bilinguals is Swinney and Cutler's (1979) *phrase classification task*. Briefly, in this task, participants are presented with an idiomatic expression (e.g., *kick the bucket*) or a controlled literal phrase (e.g., *lift the bucket*) in which the first or last word of the idiom is replaced by another word comparable in length and frequency. The participant's task is to decide, as quickly as possible, whether a string of letters forms a "natural" (e.g., *kick the bucket*) or a nonnatural (e.g., *bucket the kick*) phrase in English.

Overall, the lexical decision task has been used in the bilingual and monolingual figurative language literature to assess meaning activation.

Table 5. *Examples of Methodological Issues Associated with Semantic-Priming Techniques*

Variable	Methodological Issue
Language Skills	Poor collection of participant's language profile (e.g., how and where the L2 was acquired, proficiency, and language dominance in reading and writing) might add unaccounted variation.
Word Type	Deliberate or accidental inclusion of cross-linguistic words (unrelated to a study's goal) that are identical (e.g., cognates) or that look identical (e.g., false cognates) among the experimental stimuli might also add unaccounted variation.
Masking Effects	Awareness of the experimental prime words might lead to participant use of response strategies.
Word Frequency and Length	Dissimilarity between word primes, targets, and other stimuli might lead to different word recognition and processing speeds.
SOA	Longer SOAs (Greater than 200 ms) could develop expectancy strategies among participants or other strategies such as stimulus translation.
Relatedness Proportion	Higher inclusion of prime-target trials might show increased priming facilitation responses due to expectancy among participants, while lower proportion could have the opposite effect.
Nonword Ratio	Inclusion of nonword items below or above the suggested ratio level (.5) might result in higher participant error rates.

There are some issues associated with the LDT and priming-related tasks, however, that bilingual researchers must consider (see, for example, Altarriba & Basnight-Brown, 2007; see Table 5 for examples of participant and other methodological/procedural factors that might influence the priming effect in bilingual research). Failure to control for these potential confounds would results in inconsistent and questionable priming effects.

Cross-Modal Lexical Priming

The final behavioral task that we discuss is the *cross-modal lexical priming task* (CMLP: Swinney, 1979; Swinney, Onifer, Prather, & Hirshkowitz, 1979). This task has proven to be reliable and accurate in the monolingual (e.g., Blasko & Connine, 1993; Cacciari & Tabossi, 1988; Stewart & Heredia, 2002; Tabossi, 1996; Tabossi, Fanari, & Wolf, 2005; Titone & Connine, 1994) and bilingual figurative language processing literature (Cieślicka, 2006; Heredia & Blumentritt, 2002; Heredia & Stewart, 2002; see also Li & Yip, 1998). In the typical CMLP experiment, participants listen uninterruptedly to a sentence presented aurally and, at designated point throughout the sentence, a target word is presented briefly (typically for 300 ms to discourage participants from developing strategies or expectations) in the middle of a computer screen. Participants make a timed response or a lexical decision to the target word. RTs to the target words and their matched controls are then compared to determine meaning activation.

Indeed, it could be argued that the CMLP is a purely online task capable of taking "snapshots" of the psycholinguistic/cognitive processes taking place, as the spoken sentence temporarily unfolds, moment-to-moment in real time. For example, one theoretical issue in the metaphor literature concerns the manner in which metaphoric expressions (e.g., *her hair is honey*) are understood. The metaphor, *her hair is honey*, in sentence (3), below, could be understood in terms of its literal meaning, in which the described hair could be "sweet" (as in "bees") or "blond" like the color of honey (i.e., the nonliteral meaning). Using the CMLP, Swinney and Osterhout (1990) measured meaning facilitation (i.e., priming) of both the literal and nonliteral meanings at sentence positions 1–3 (designated by subscripts [*1 – *3]). Swinney and Osterhout (1990) found that at position 2, immediately after metaphor offset, the literal meaning of the metaphor associated with "bee" was the only one active, and by position 3, which represented a delay of 500 ms after the last word of the metaphor, the nonliteral or intended meaning (*blond*) had become active. This pattern of results led Swinney and Osterhout to suggest that metaphor processing is not automatic and that additional time (i.e., position 3) is required to fully comprehend the intended meaning of the metaphorical expression (cf. Blasko & Connine, 1993; see also Heredia & Muñoz; Vaid et al., this volume). Thus, using the CMLP, it would be possible to probe for meaning activation pre (position 1), and post (position 3) metaphor, idiom, or proverbial expressions.

(3) *Jeff told his friend that Mary's hair was* [*1] *honey* [*2] *and her* [*3] *smile gleamed.*

In one of the first bilingual figurative language studies to utilize the CMLP, Cieślicka (2006) measured activation of literal and nonliteral meanings in sentences of the type described in (4) below.

(4) *Peter was planning to tie the* [*1] *knot* [*2] *later that month.*

As bilinguals listened to spoken sentence presented aurally, they made lexical decisions to visually presented words related to the literal (e.g., *rope*), the nonliteral interpretation (e.g., *marry*) and their respective unrelated control words. Visual targets were presented immediately after the penultimate word of the idiom (position [*1]) and at the end of the idiom (subscript [*2]). Idiomatic expressions varied in regards to literality (i.e., the extent to which the phrase can be interpreted literally). Overall, the results replicated McPartland-Fairman's (1989) findings showing activation of both the literal and nonliteral meanings at idiom offset (position [*2]). Moreover, although no activation for the literal and nonliteral meanings of the idiom was found at position 1, inspection of the response times showed longer processing times for both literal and idiomatic interpretations at this position than at idiom offset. This increase in processing time may be indicative that, at this position, the two meanings of the idiom were being considered. However, the most important finding was that, regardless of idiom type (i.e., literal vs. nonliteral), the literal interpretation appeared to be more active, or more salient, than the nonliteral interpretation of the idiom. Indeed, these findings were interpreted as supporting the Graded Salience Hypothesis suggesting that for bilinguals, activation or the computation of the literal interpretation of the idiom is obligatory and automatic.

Preliminary work in our laboratory employing the CMLP to further explore idiom similarity across Spanish and English shows that idioms that are different (5c), as opposed to identical (5a) or similar idioms (5b) across Spanish and English, are responded to faster. Specifically, in this study, Spanish-English bilinguals listened to sentences of the type described in sentences (5a-c).

(5a) *The teacher requested the students' point of view [*1] and no one cared to respond back.*

(5b) *Joe was glad that he killed two birds with one stone [*1] and his mom was impressed.*

(5c) *Lisa learned that Dr. White had kicked the bucket [*1] and the next day she took an early flight to attend the funeral.*

For the different idiom language condition, immediately after the offset of the idiomatic phrase (position 1, depicted by subscript "[*1]") participants made lexical decisions to targets that were related to the figurative (*died*), or the literal (*water*) meanings of the idiom, and their respective controls (*made* and *country*). Figure 13 summarizes the two-way interaction. Bilinguals made lexical decisions faster to literal related words for sentences that contained different than identical/similar idiomatic expressions. The opposite was true for figurative expressions. That is, participants were slower in responding to figurative related targets for different idiomatic expressions, thus suggesting a possible transfer or facilitation effect in the comprehension of idiomatic expressions that are identical/similar across languages (cf. Irujo, 1986). Clearly, this is a

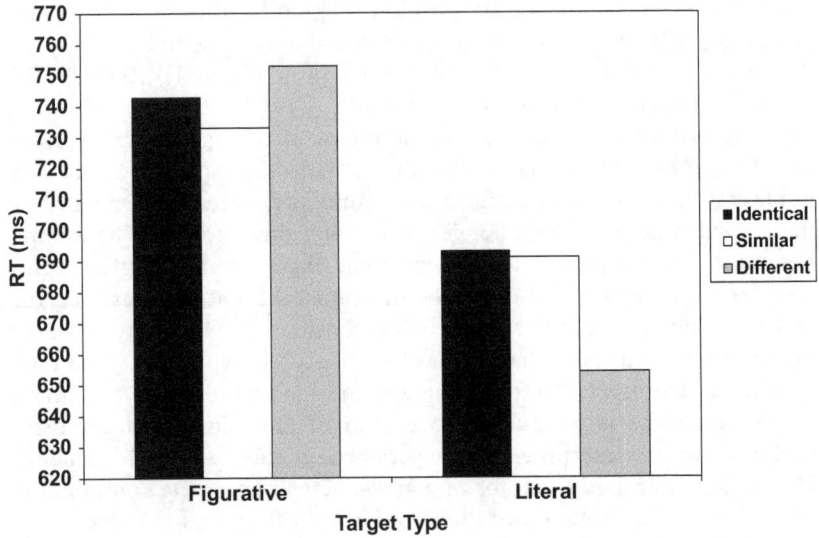

Figure 13. RTs a Function of Target Type and Idiom Type in the CMLP Task

somewhat mixed set of results regarding language processing differences between idiom type that may very well be explained based on task effects, in which the reading tasks reported by Heredia et al. (2007) are at the low end of the offline-online continuum in Figure 1.

Overall, the CMLP (and its various forms; see, for example, Tabossi, 1996) has proven to be reliable and its empirical and theoretical bases have been successfully validated in the monolingual ambiguity resolution and figurative language processing literature (Stewart & Heredia, 2002; Tabossi, 1996; but see Glucksberg, Kreuz, & Rho, 1986; Peterson & Simpson, 1989), as well as in the bilingual sentence processing (see Heredia, 1998, 2000; Heredia & Stewart, 1998, 2002; Li & Yip, 1998;), and figurative language literature (e.g., Cieślicka, 2006; Heredia & Blumentritt, 2002). One important aspect of this task is that its measurements reflect local (i.e., "snapshots") language processing effects rather than global or generalized sentence processing effects (cf. self-paced reading task). A critical aspect of the CMLP is that it relies on semantic priming effects and is capable of measuring semantic or meaning activation during the unfolding of the speech signal. Moreover, it is high on ecological validity because it mirrors the manner in which participants listen and understand language as it unfolds in real time. The CMLP also overcomes language proficiency and reading difficulties often experienced by bilingual speakers whose L1 becomes less dominant and whose L1 reading ability is far less developed than their dominant L2 (Heredia, 1997; Heredia & Altarriba, 2001).

Neurophysiological Paradigms

Event-Related Potentials

Using *event-related potentials* (ERPs) is a noninvasive neurophysiological technique measuring brain function through electroencephalography (EEG) by recording electrical activity occurring within pyramidal neurons (a type of neuron found in the cerebral cortex) of the brain. ERP studies have been used extensively to resolve theoretical debates concerning the mental architecture of language processing. These studies have examined stimulus-locked averages, or event-related potentials (ERPs), which are scalp-recorded changes in electrical activity occurring in response to a particular cognitive, motor, or sensory event (Osterhout, McLaughlin, Kim, Greenwald, & Inoue, 2004). ERPs provide a continuous millisecond-by-millisecond record of electrical changes in the brain related to the perceptual and cognitive processes underlying real-time language comprehension and word recognition. Different neurocognitive processes are manifested in electrophysiological studies as different ERP components, and differences in the degree of effort or difficulty associated with processing a given stimulus are reflected as amplitude variations in a specific component (Arzouan, Goldstein, & Faust, 2007a, 2007b). Given their perfect temporal resolution and sensitivity, ERPs are superior to other behavioral and neuropsychological methodologies in exploring neurobiological underpinnings of language and addressing complex processing issues that are not available through other existing methods (see Kutas & Delong, 2008; Mueller, 2005; Osterhout et al., 2004).

A number of ERP components have been identified in the literature. Traditionally, ERP components are named after their polarity (i.e., positive- or negative-going) and ordinal position (first, second, etc.). Alternatively, they are named after their polarity and peak latency with respect to the stimulus onset (e.g., 100 ms after stimulus presentation). For example, the N100 is a negative-going potential peaking around 100 ms after the stimulus presentation and viewed as an index of attentional processes (Harter & Aine, 1984). P200 is a positive-going component peaking around 150–275 ms and related to the mechanisms of feature detection and selective attention accompanying early encoding processes (see Oren & Breznitz, 2005). Another early, negative-going component identified in the ERP literature is the N200, which has been related to response inhibition, the processing of orthographic information, and phonological mismatch (see Elston-Güttler, Paulmann, & Kotz, 2005 for review). After 200 ms, especially at the N400 component, meaning-related attributes of words are extracted. The N400 is a negative deflection in the event-related potential that is known to be an index of semantic processes and linguistic expectations. It peaks around 400 ms after the presentation of a content word, and its size depends on a number of factors, such as word frequency, repetition, word concreteness, number of a word's orthographic neighbors, semantic relatedness, sentence position, and contextual expectancy (Kutas & Delong, 2008; Kutas & Federmeier, 2000, 2011; Kutas & Hillyard, 1980b). Thus, incongruent or unexpected sentence endings and unrelated word pairs elicit larger N400 responses than congruent or expected sentence endings and related word pairs (e.g., Gunter, Friederici, & Schriefers, 2000; Kutas & Hillyard, 1980b, 1984; Rommers, 2010). For example, Federmeier and Kutas (1999) found that unexpected endings (e.g., *tulips*) of highly constraining sentences (e.g., *They wanted to make the hotel look more like a tropical resort. So along the driveway they planted rows of...*) elicited larger N400 effects compared to expected endings (e.g., *palms*). The amplitude of the N400 differed depending on whether the unexpected ending was semantically related to the expected word and contextually appropriate (e.g., *pines*) or semantically unrelated and contextually inappropriate (e.g., *tables*). The N400 to unexpected words belonging to the same semantic category as the expected word was significantly smaller than the N400 elicited to unexpected words that belonged to a different semantic category than the expected word.

In contrast, unexpected changes of a nonsemantic nature (i.e., changes in the physical attributes of words, such as size or color, or grammatical violations) have been linked to positive-going potentials occurring either around 300 ms (P300) or 600 ms (P600) after stimulus presentation (Kutas & Hillyard, 1980a; Osterhout & Holcomb, 1992). The P300 component is a marker of updating the internal representation of the environmental context (Donchin, 1981) and reflects the processes occurring between the classification and preparation of responses (Verleger, Jaśkowski, & Wascher, 2005). Like the N400, it is also sensitive to word frequency effects (Hauk & Pulvermüller, 2004; King & Kutas, 1998; Polich & Donchin, 1988; Rugg, 1990). The P600, on the other hand, is a large positive-going wave peaking between 500 and 1000 ms after the presentation of a syntactic anomaly, as in *the cat will eating the food* (Friederici, 1995; Osterhout & Mobley, 1995). The P600 has been shown to reflect syntactic violations (Hahne & Friederici, 1999;

Neville, Nicol, Baarss, Forster, & Garret, 1991), memory retrieval (Paller & Kutas, 1992; Rugg, Cox, Doyle, & Wells, 1995), the processing of well-formed but syntactically complex sentences (Kaan, Harris, Gibson, & Holcomb, 2000), and processes of reanalysis and syntactic repair (Friederici, 1995, 2002; Osterhout, Holcomb, & Swinney, 1994).

Despite the abundance of ERP studies in bilingual language processing (e.g., Hahne & Friederici, 2001; Leikin, 2008; Federmeier & Kutas 2002; Kotz, 2001; Kotz & Elston- Güttler, 2004; Moreno, Federmeier, & Kutas 2002; Frenck-Mestre, German, & Foucart, 2014; Palmer, van Hooff, & Havelka, 2010; Paulmann, Elston-Güttler, Gunter, & Kotz, 2006; Schoonbaert, Holcomb, Grainger, & Hartsuiker, 2011), the domain of bilingual figurative language processing remains relatively unexplored (see Paulmann et al., this volume). In one of the few published studies in bilingual figurative language processing, Moreno et al. (2002) looked at ERPs to context-ually expected and unexpected words in literal and idiomatic expressions. The critical regions involved the expected (highly predictable) words, literal synonyms of the expected words (i.e., *lexical switches*), or L2 (Spanish) translations (i.e., code switches). Results showed larger N400 amplitudes to lexical switches than to the expected words in both literal and idiomatic sentences. Code switches, however, did not elicit semantic N400 effects, but instead a Late Positive Component (LPC) 450–850 ms post stimulus onset, which was taken to support the idea that language switches do not pose challenges at the lexical-semantic level but rather are treated as unexpected events and therefore are associated with decision-related processes. Generally, the LPC refers to a group of positive-going components peaking after the N400 and lasting until around 900 ms after stimulus onset. The LPC is viewed as a marker of continued analysis or reanalysis of the input (De Grauwe, Swain, Holcomb, Ditman, & Kuperberg, 2010). It has been observed in response to words violating syntactic constraints of the preceding context, where it has been labeled P600 (Osterhout & Holcomb, 1992), as well as elicited by severe semantic violations and implausibil-ities (Hoeks, Stowe, & Doedens, 2004; Kim & Osterhout, 2005; Kolk, Chwilla, Van Herten, & Oor, 2003; Kuperberg, 2007).

In the domain of bilingual language switching, a large N400 has been observed when bilinguals perform a task in one specific language and are asked to suppress the non-target language (see Moreno, Rodriguez-Fornells, & Laine, 2008 for a review). In short, these studies have shown that the N400 is related to the enhanced cognitive control, which is required when bilinguals have to either deal with mixed-language stimuli, thus having to switch between one language and another (e.g., Proverbio, Leoni, & Zani, 2004; Rodriguez-Fornells, Rotte, Heinze, Nosselt, & Münte, 2002; Rodriguez-Fornells et al., 2005; Rodriguez-Fornells, De Diego Balaguer, & Münte, 2006), or when they perform a task in their less fluent language, and thus inhibit the more dominant language (e.g., De Diego Balaguer, Toro, Rodriguez-Fornells, & Bachoud-Levy, 2007). In a study measuring ERP responses to within- and cross-language repetitions (i.e., either the same word presented twice in English, the L1, or Spanish, the L2, or a word in English/Spanish followed by its translation equivalent), Alvarez, Holcomb, and Grainger (2003) found an increased N400 amplitude for L1 to L2 switches. Generally, the ERP literature on language switching is not unanimous. While some studies report both N400 and LPC effects in response to code-switching (e.g., Van Der Meij, Cuetos, Carreiras, & Barber, 2011), others show only LPC effects (e.g., Moreno et al., 2002). In addition, factors like the degree of proficiency in the L2 (e.g., Van Der Meij et al., 2011) or direction of switching, from L1 to L2 or from L2 to L1 (e.g., Alvarez et al., 2003; Proverbio et al., 2004), have been shown to crucially affect brain's responses to code switches. Green (2011) has argued that cortical structures involved in language control will be dependent on whether bilingual speakers originate from code-switching or non-code-switching communities.

In sum, ERPs have been widely used to study language processing of spoken or visually presented words, as well as other cognitive phenomena (van Berkum, 2004). Aside from its noninvasiveness, this paradigm is highly successful, because it provides accurate time-processing responses, or fine temporal resolution (Fabiani, Gratton, & Coles, 2000; Gordon et al., 2004), thus being able to catch elements that behavioral (RTs or DTs) or eye tracking paradigms might miss (Bolger & Zapata, 2011). Similar to previous tasks and techniques, the ERP paradigm has some methodological issues. One drawback is the considerable amount of time it requires when collecting data, primarily because of the need for individual application of multiple electrodes throughout the scalp and the time needed to run a given experiment. Increased costs and setup also are considered ERPs' drawbacks (Mitchell, 2004).

Summary and Conclusions

This chapter provides an overview of some of the psycholinguistic tasks used in the bilingual and monolingual literature that we believe can be successfully employed in exploring bilingual processing. In our discussion, we started off by describing the self-paced reading task and some of its variants, such as the visual moving window and the stationary moving window. Whereas the self-paced reading task provides a global (or general) measure of language processing, the moving window and its variants yield a much more refined measurement of language comprehension by analyzing each phrase or sentence word by word for any possible language processing effects. The auditory moving window, an auditory variant of the visual moving window, in our view, shows an added advantage for bilinguals exhibiting different reading and speaking proficiency levels. However, taken together, the self-paced techniques provide a rather limited insight into real-time visual (or auditory) processing because participants are in complete control of the stimulus presentation rate (i.e., leaving these tasks open to the development of participants' response strategies). Although described as a significant alternative to the self-paced reading tasks, the RSVP task might not reflect the natural reading process. How is this task different than the moving window techniques? Clearly, future research would benefit from carrying out task analyses comparing the RSVP against the moving reading window techniques.

Next, we moved on to the two variants of the reading maze task and reviewed how this task not only minimizes participant response strategies seen in previous techniques, but also how its design measures reading integration more accurately, hence tapping into real-time processing. However, this technique is yet to be employed in the bilingual figurative language processing domain. We also explored the role of meaning activation as measured by the lexical decision and the CMLP tasks. While the lexical decision task has been traditionally utilized at the word level and, to a certain extent, at the phrasal level (e.g., the phrase classification task), the CMLP task and its variants (e.g., cross-modal naming) utilize the spoken sentence as the experimental unit and the lexical decision task to measure meaning activation moment by moment and word by word, as participants process language in real time. Finally, we provided a general overview of the findings in bilingual figurative language processing from eye tracking and ERP studies. In the eye tracking reading domain, there has been a recent significant increase in studies exploring bilingual figurative language processing. However, at the neuropsychological level, bilingual figurative language processing research is significantly behind.

As is clear from the overview of the existing research in bilingual figurative language processing provided in this chapter, the overwhelming majority of the bilingual figurative processing studies have utilized offline tasks. Moreover, it appears that most of what we know about how bilingual speakers process figurative language derives from experiments utilizing idiomatic expressions as experimental stimuli. This may be problematic due to the possibility that bilingual metaphor comprehension might be fundamentally different from idiom comprehension (see for example, Heredia & Muñoz, this volume). It is possible that metaphors may be more language dependent or language specific. As some evidence shows (e.g., Harris et al., 1999), it appears that in some languages (e.g., Spanish) similes are more frequent than metaphor, and nominal metaphors (e.g., *clouds are puffballs*) are less frequent than what is referred to as "pure metaphor," where the topic of the metaphor (*clouds*) is omitted as in *those puffballs are really showing good signs of rain*. In this case, the topic of the metaphor must be derived from the given contextual information. In contrast, idiomatic expressions, especially those which are highly conventionalized and familiar, may be more lexicalized in storage and retrieved and processed more automatically than the less frequently used metaphors. In addition, as preliminary research in cross-linguistic interactions in the course of idiom processing seems to suggest, comprehension and production of L2 idioms is strongly affected by the degree of their similarity to L1 translation equivalents.

One purpose of this chapter, as alluded to in the introduction, was *to go to the grain* and present a general overview of the existing findings, theoretical perspectives, and psycholinguistic techniques used in the bilingual figurative domain. The information provided in this chapter, we hope, will provide bilingual researchers with the tools to undertake and expand our limited knowledge of bilingual figurative language processing. Clearly, empirical work would benefit from task analysis (i.e., comparisons between experimental tasks; Witzel et al., 2011) and distinguishing between those tasks that measure explicit versus implicit knowledge. As has been made clear in our overview of the experimental techniques, not all response-time-dependent tasks measure automatic language processing because other confounds (e.g., demand characteristics) are likely to significantly affect the experimental results, unless properly controlled.

In the introduction to this chapter, we asked whether there is a *best way* to study bilingual figurative language processing. Although it is very clear that some tasks are more suitable than others and more sensitive to assess online aspects of bilingual figurative language processing, the choice of the task will ultimately depend on the research question being investigated. Clearly, work in bilingual online figurative language comprehension is limited, and more research is needed to increase our understanding of the bilingual brain by utilizing more technologically advanced brain-mapping technologies such as positron emission tomography (PET) and functional magnetic resonance imaging (fMRI).

List of Key Words and Concepts

Auditory moving window (AMW), Compositional analysis, Cross-modal lexical priming task (CMLP), Difference time (DT), Eye tracking, Event related potentials (ERPs), Electroencephalography (EEG), Figurative language processing, Fine-Coarse Coding Theory, First pass reading time, Fixation count, Fixation duration, Fixation point, Gaze-contingency paradigm, Gaze duration, Go/No-Go protocol, Graded Salience Hypothesis, Late positive component (LPC), Lexical decision task (LDT), Masking effects, Maze task, N200, N400, Naming task, Offline/Online tasks, P300, P600, Priming effect, Rapid serial visual presentation (RSVP), Region of interest (ROI), Self-paced reading, Stationary moving window, Stimulus onset asynchrony (SOA), Total reading time, Transfer Theory, Visual moving window (VMW), Word frequency

Thought Questions

1. What are the main differences between online and offline paradigms?
2. What is the difference between stationary and moving window self-paced reading tasks?
3. What are some advantages of the cross-modal lexical priming task (CMLP) over other online experimental techniques?
4. What are some advantages and disadvantages of eyen tracking over RSVP and other self-paced reading tasks?
5. What are some possible reasons that bilingual research in figurative language is so limited in comparison to mainstream monolingual research?
6. Evaluate the following statements: *Bilingual and monolingual figurative language processing are fundamentally the same. There is no need to examine bilingualism. We already know the answer.*

Suggested Research Projects

1. In this project, you will learn how to make/modify experiment scripts using PsyScope (http://psy.ck.sissa.it), a free/open source experiment builder. If you do not have an Apple computer, please visit www. tamiu.edu/~rheredia/software.html for OS X emulation software for the Windows environment. Your task is to modify the visual moving window script (http://psy.ck.sissa.it/psy_cmu_edu/scripts/ Moving.sit) and make it run on your computer. Next, download the

auditory moving window or any other script of your choosing from the PsyScope sample scripts link below and make them operational. Were you able to run your scripts? If you need assistance, the PsyScope webpage provides excellent tips on how to create experiment scripts. You can also join the PsyScope newsgroup.

2. *Task analysis*: In this project, you will compare a version of the self-paced reading task, and Swinney and Cutler's (1979) phrasal classification task (see references). For this task, you need to locate Katz et al. (1988; see suggested readings) article to select metaphors of the type A is B (*lawyers are sharks*) that are moderate to highly familiar. Select 25–30 metaphors with familiarity ratings ranging from 5 to 7. Because you are going to run the experiment using an experiment builder, visit PsyScope's webpage for additional scripts. Alternatively you can use the multi-platform OpenSesame software application (see related sites below), which is also free and open source with excellent documentation. E-prime (http://www.pstnet. com/demos/eprime/RequestDemo.aspx) is another experiment builder application and you can download a free demo evaluation version. Visit http://step.psy.cmu.edu for additional ready-to-use experiment scripts that you can modify. For this project, you will be using Meyer & Schvaneveldt's (1971) original lexical decision task (http://step.psy.cmu.edu/scripts/Linguistics/Meyer1971.html). For the self-paced reading task, modify the script so that participants simply press the space bar when they finish reading the metaphoric expression displayed on the computer screen. Once they press the space bar, the computer will measure the time taken to read the metaphoric expression. So, for this task, assure that your instructions are very clear before you start your experiment. For both experiments, assure that you measure the response or reading time from the metaphor's time onset (i.e., the exact moment in which the metaphor appears on the computer screen) until the participant presses the designated key signaling that he/she has completed a trial. Swinney and Cutler provide very clear procedural instructions, so please follow them carefully. The phrase classification task is very similar to the lexical decision task. You will be presenting participants with a metaphoric phrase and participants will be asked to decide if the presented phrase is a grammatical (e.g., *lawyers are sharks*) or ungrammatical phrasal expression (e.g., *lawyers sharks is*). To randomly scramble your phrases to make them ungrammatical, perform a Google search for a word or phrase scrambler. For the phrase classification task, you will need to select 30–40 additional metaphoric expressions of the same familiarity as the critical stimuli to scramble. Keep your

professor informed about your experiment and contact your university's Institutional Review Board (IRB) to obtain permission to run your experiment. From your class select 30 participants. Randomly assign half of the participants to the self-paced reading and the other half to the phrase classification task. After completing your experiment, analyze your data utilizing the free/open source statistical package PSPP (www.gnu.org/software/pspp/pspp.html) or R (www.r-project.org). For the purpose of this experiment, perform a bivariate correlation analysis. Before running the analysis, make sure that you check your data for outliers and assure that you have met the appropriate statistical assumptions required to compute *Pearson's correlation coefficient*. Are the two measurements correlated? If both tasks are measuring the same psycholinguistic processes, the correlation between the two tasks should be significantly large, well above a correlation of $+.5$. What correlation did you obtain? Discuss the results of the experiment with your classmates.

3. *Bilingual vs. Monolingual*: Using the two tasks discussed in the second project (or if you want to simplify the study, use only one task), select two groups of bilinguals, one for each task, and two groups of monolinguals, one for each task. Assure that participants are assigned into the groups at random. Run the experiment and analyze your results using R or an alternative statistical program. Your professor should be able to assist you with the analysis. The purpose of your analysis is to compare the tasks between the monolingual groups and between the bilingual groups, as well as across the two groups and two tasks. Assure that your bilingual groups are homogenous in such a way that the two bilingual groups learned the L2 about the same time. Analyze your results and report them to your class. What did you find? Did you find differences between the monolingual group and between the bilingual groups? Did you find any other interesting differences across the tasks and across the two different groups? Did your variables interact? That is, were you able to find an interaction between tasks (self-paced reading vs. phrase classification) and bilinguals versus monolinguals? Write your results in APA style sixth edition and report them to your class.

Related Internet Sites

Experimental Materials: www.tamiu.edu/~rheredia/materials.html

Masked Priming: www.u.arizona.edu/~kforster/priming/index.htm

Maze Task: www.u.arizona.edu/~kforster/MAZE/index.htm

OpenSesame Scripts: http://osdoc.cogsci.nl/examples

PsyScope Sample Scripts: http://psy.ck.sissa.it/psy_cmu_edu/scripts/index.html

Runtime for Android: http://osdoc.cogsci.nl/getting-opensesame/android

STEP E-Prime Scripts: http://step.psy.cmu.edu/scripts/index.html

Suggested Further Readings

Bolger, P.A., & Zapata, G.C. (2011). Psycholinguistic approaches to language processing in heritage speakers. *Heritage Language Journal, 8*,1–29.

Grosjean, F., & Frauenfelder, U.H. (Eds). (1996). A guide to spoken word recognition paradigms. [Special issue]. *Language and Cognitive Processes, 11,* 553–558.

Forster, K.I. (2010). Using a maze task to track lexical and sentence processing. *The Mental Lexicon, 5,* 347–357.

Katz, A.N., Paivio, A., Marschark, M., & Clark, J.M. (1988). Norms for 204 literary and 260 nonliterary metaphors on 10 psychological dimensions. *Metaphor and Symbolic Activity, 3,* 191–214. *Behavior Research Methods, Instruments, & Computers, 36,* 371–383.

Marinis, T. (2003). Psycholinguistic techniques in second language acquisition research. *Second Language Research, 19,* 144–161.

Veldhuis, D., & Kurvers, J. (2012). Offline segmentation and online language processing units: The influence of literacy. *Written Language and Literacy, 15,* 165–184.

REFERENCES

Abel, B. (2003). English idioms in the first language and second language lexicon: A dual representation approach. *Second Language Research, 19,* 329–358.

Altarriba, J., & Basnight-Brown, D.M. (2007). Methodological considerations in performing semantic- and translation-priming experiments across languages. *Behavior Research Methods, 39,* 1–18.

Altarriba, J., & Soltano, E.G. (1996). Repetition blindness and bilingual memory: Token individuation for translation equivalents. *Memory & Cognition, 24,* 700–711.

Altarriba, J., Kroll, J.F., Sholl, A., & Rayner, K. (1996). The influence of lexical and conceptual constraints on reading mixed-language sentences: Evidence from eye fixations and naming times. *Memory & Cognition, 24,* 477–492.

Alvarez, R.P., Holcomb, P.J., & Grainger, J. (2003). Accessing word meaning in two languages: An event-related brain potential study of beginning bilinguals. *Brain and Language, 87,* 290–304.

Ardal, S., Donald, M.W., Meuter, R., Muldrew, S., & Luce, M. (1990). Brain responses to semantic incongruity in bilinguals. *Brain and Language, 39,* 187–205.

Arzouan, Y., Goldstein, A., & Faust, M. (2007a). Dynamics of hemispheric activity during metaphor comprehension: Electrophysiological measures. *NeuroImage, 36,* 222–231.

(2007b). Brainwaves are stethoscopes: ERP correlates of novel metaphor comprehension. *Brain Research, 1160,* 69–81.

Beeman, M. (1998). Coarse semantic coding and discourse comprehension. In M. Beeman & C. Chiarello (Eds.), *Right hemisphere language comprehension: Perspectives from cognitive neuroscience* (pp. 255–284). Mahwah, NJ: Lawrence Erlbaum Associates.

Binder, K.S. &. Morris, R.K. (1995). Eye movements and lexical ambiguity resolution: Effects of prior encounter and discourse topic. *Journal of Experimental Psychology: Learning, Memory, and Cognition, 21,* 1186–1196.

Blair, D., & Harris, R.J. (1981). A test of interlingual interaction in comprehension by bilinguals. *Journal of Psycholinguistic Research, 10,* 457–467.

Blais, M.J., & Gonnerman, L.M. (2013). Explicit and implicit semantic processing of verb-particle constructions by French-English bilinguals. *Bilingualism: Language and Cognition, 16,* 829–846.

Blasko, D.G., & Connine, C.M. (1993). Effects of familiarity and aptness on metaphor processing. *Journal of Experimental Psychology: Learning, Memory, and Cognition, 19,* 295–308.

Boland, J.E. (2004). Linking eye movements to sentence comprehension in reading and listening. In M. Carreiras, & C. Clifton (Eds.), *The on-line study of sentence comprehension: Eye-tracking, ERP and beyond* (pp. 51–76). New York: Psychology Press.

Bolger, P.A., & Zapata, G.C. (2011). Psycholinguistic approaches to language processing in heritage speakers. *Heritage Language Journal, 8,* 1–29.

Bortfeld, H. (2002). What native and non-native speakers' images for idioms tell us about figurative language. In R.R. Heredia, & J. Altarriba (Eds.), *Advances in psychology: Bilingual sentence processing* (pp. 275–295). Amsterdam: Elsevier Science.

Breznitz, Z., Oren, R., & Shaul, S. (2004). Brain activity of regular and dyslexic readers while reading Hebrew as compared to English sentences. *Reading and Writing, 17,* 707–737.

Bromberek-Dyzman, K., & Ewert, A. (2010). Figurative competence is better developed in l1 than in L2, or is it? Understanding conversational implicatures in L1 and L2. In M. Pütz, & L. Sicola (Eds.), *Cognitive processing in second language acquisition: Inside the learner's mind* (pp. 317–334). Amsterdam: John Benjamins.

Cacciari, C., & Tabossi, P. (1988). The comprehension of idioms. *Journal of Memory and Language, 27,* 668–683.

Carreiras, M., & Clifton, C. (2004). On the on-line study of language comprehension. In M. Carreiras, & C. Clifton (Eds.), *The on-line study of sentence comprehension: Eyetracking, ERPs, and beyond* (pp. 1–14). New York: Psychology Press.

Cieślicka, A.B. (2002). Comprehension and interpretation of proverbs in L2. *Studia Anglica Posnaniensia: An International Review of English Studies*, *37*, 173–200.

(2003). On understanding metaphorical expressions in the bilingual mode. *Linguistica Silesiana*, *24*, 143–68.

(2006). Literal salience in on-line processing of idiomatic expressions by second language learners. *Second Language Research*, *22*,115–144.

(2007). Language experience and fixed expressions: Differences in the salience status of literal and figurative meanings of L1 and L2 idioms. In M. Nenonen, & S. Niemi (Eds.), *Collocations and idioms 1: Papers from the First Nordic Conference on Syntactic Freezes* (pp. 55–70). Joensuu, Finland: Joensuu University Press.

(2013). Do nonnative language speakers chew the fat and spill the beans with different brain hemispheres? Investigating idiom decomposability with the divided visual field paradigm. *Journal of Psycholinguistic Research*, *42*, 475–503.

Cieślicka, A.B., & Heredia, R.R. (2011). Hemispheric asymmetries in processing L1 and L2 idioms: Effects of salience and context. *Brain & Language*, *116*, 136–150.

(2013, May). *The multiple determinants of eye movement patterns in bilingual figurative processing*. Paper presented at the 25th APS Annual Convention, Washington, DC.

Cieślicka, A.B., Heredia, R.R., & Olivares, M. (2014). The eyes have it: How language dominance, salience, and context affect eye movements during idiomatic language processing. In L. Aronin, & M. Pawlak (Eds.), *Essential topics in applied linguistics and multilingualism. Studies in honor of David Singleton* (pp. 21–42). Switzerland, Springer.

Conklin, K. & Schmitt, N. (2008). Formulaic sequences: Are they processed more quickly than nonformulaic language by native and non-native speakers? *Applied Linguistics*, *29*, 72–89.

Cook, V.J. (1997). The consequences of bilingualism for cognitive processing. In A. de Groot, & J.F. Kroll (Eds.), *Tutorials in bilingualism: Psycholinguistic perspectives* (pp. 270–300). Mahwah, NJ: Lawrence Erlbaum Associates.

Curco, C. (2005). On mosquitoes and camels: Some notes on the interpretation of metaphorically transparent popular sayings. In H. Colston, & A. Katz (Eds.), *Figurative language comprehension: Social and cultural language* (pp.283–308). Mahwah, NJ: Lawrence Erlbaum Associates.

Cutler, A. (1983). Lexical complexity and sentence processing. In G. B. F. d'Arcais, & R.J. Jarvella (Eds.), *The process of language understanding* (pp. 43–79). New York: John Wiley & Sons.

Dagut, M., & Laufer, B. (1985). Avoidance of phrasal verbs: A case for contrastive analysis. *Studies in Second Language Acquisition*, *7*, 73–79.

De Diego Balaguer, R., Toro, J.M., Rodriguez-Fornells, A., & Bachoud-Lévy, A.C. (2007). Different neurophysiological mechanisms underlying word and rule extraction from speech. *PLOS One*, *2*, e1175.

De Grauwe, S., Swain, A., Holcomb, P.J., Ditman, T., & Kuperberg, G.R. (2010). Electrophysiological insights into the processing of nominal metaphors. *Neuropsychologia*, *48*, 1965–1984.

Donchin, E. (1981). Surprise! Surprise? *Psychophysiology*, *18*, 493–513.

Dopkins, S., Morris, R.K., & Rayner, K. (1992). Lexical ambiguity and eye fixations in reading: A test of competing models of lexical ambiguity resolution. *Journal of Memory and Language*, *31*, 461–476.

Elston-Güttler, K.E., Paulmann, S., & Kotz, S.A. (2005). Who's in control? Processing and L1 influence on L2 processing. *Journal of Cognitive Neuroscience*, *17*, 1593–1610.

Fabiani, M., Gratton, G., & Coles, M.G.H. (2000). Event related brain potentials: Methods, theory, and application. In J.T. Cacioppo, L.G. Tassinary, & G.G. Berntson (Eds.), *Handbook of psychophysiology* (pp. 53–84). Cambridge, UK: Cambridge University Press.

Faust, M.E., & Gernsbacher, A.M. (1996). Cerebral mechanisms for suppression of inappropriate information during sentence comprehension. *Brain and Language*, *53*, 234–259.

Federmeier, K.D., & Kutas, M. (1999). Right words and left words: Electrophysiological evidence for hemispheric differences in meaning processing. *Cognitive Brain Research*, *8*, 373–392.

Ferreira, F., Anes, M.D., & Horine, M.D. (1996). Exploring the use of prosody during language comprehension using the auditory moving window technique. *Journal of Psycholinguistic Research*, *25*, 273–290.

Ferreira, F., Henderson, J.M., Anes, M.D., Weeks, J.P.A., & McFarlane, D.K. (1996). Effects of lexical frequency and syntactic complexity in spoken-language comprehension: Evidence from the auditory moving-window technique. *Journal of Experimental Psychology. Learning, Memory, and Cognition*, *22*, 324–335.

Forster, K.I. (2010). Using a maze task to track lexical and sentence processing. *The Mental Lexicon*, *5*, 347–357.

Forster, K.I., & Davis, C. (1984). Repetition priming and frequency attenuation in lexical access. *Journal of Experimental Psychology: Learning, Memory, and Cognition*, *10*, 680–698.

Forster, K.I., Guerrera, C., & Elliot, L. (2009). The maze task: Measuring forced incremental sentence processing time. *Behavior Research Methods*, *41*, 163–171.

Forster, K.I., Mohan, K., & Hector, J. (2003). The mechanics of masked priming. In S. Kinoshita, & S.J. Lupker (Eds.), *Masked priming: The state of the art* (pp. 2–20). New York: Psychology Press.

Frenck-Mestre, C., German, E.S., & Foucart, A. (2014). Qualitative differences in native and nonnative semantic processing as revealed by ERPS. In R.R. Heredia & J. Altarriba (Eds.), *Foundations of bilingual memory* (pp. 237–255). New York: Springer.

Frenck-Mestre, C. (2005). Eye-movement recording as a tool for studying syntactic processing in a second language: A review of methodologies and experimental findings. *Second Language Research*, *21*, 175–198.

Friederici, A.D. (1995). The time course of syntactic activation during language processing: A model based on neuropsychological and neurophysiological data. *Brain and Language*, *50*, 259–284.

(2002). Towards a neural basis of auditory sentence processing. *Trends in Cognitive Sciences*, *6*, 78–84.

Gerard, J.E. (2007). *The reading of formulaic sequences in a native and non-native language: An eye movement analysis.* (Doctoral dissertation). Retrieved from http://arizona.openrepository.com/arizona/bitstream/10150/195865/1/azu_etd_2387_sip1_m.pdf

Gibbs, R.W. (1994). *The poetics of mind: Figurative thought, language, and understanding.* Cambridge, UK: Cambridge University Press.

Giora, R. (1997). Understanding figurative and literal language: The graded salience hypothesis. *Cognitive Linguistics, 8,* 183–206.

Gordon, P.C., Camblin, C.C., & Swaab, T.Y. (2004). On-line measures of conferential processing. In M. Carreiras, & C. Clifton (Eds.), *The on-line study of sentence comprehension: Eye-tracking, ERP and beyond* (pp. 139–150). New York: Psychology Press.

Glucksberg, S., Kreuz, R.J., & Rho, S.H. (1986). Context can constrain lexical access: Implications for models of language comprehension. *Journal of Experimental Psychology: Learning, Memory, and Cognition, 12,* 323–335.

Green, D.W. (2011). Language control in different contexts: The behavioral ecology of bilingual speakers. *Frontiers in Psychology, 2.*

Gunter, T.C., Friederici, A.D., & Schriefers, H. (2000). Syntactic gender and semantic expectancy: ERPs reveal early autonomy and late interaction. *Journal of Cognitive Neuroscience, 12,* 556–568.

Hahne, A., & Friederici, A.D. (1999). Electrophysiological evidence for two steps in syntactic analysis: Early automatic and late controlled processes. *Journal of Cognitive Neuroscience, 11,* 193–204.

(2001). Processing a second language: Late learners' comprehension mechanisms as revealed by event-related brain potentials. *Bilingualism: Language and Cognition, 4,* 123–141.

Harris, R.J., Tebbe, M.R., Leka, G.E., Garcia, R.C., & Erramouspe, R. (1999). Monolingual and bilingual memory for English and Spanish metaphors and similes. *Metaphor and Symbol, 14,* 1–16.

Harter, M.R., & Aine, C.J. (1984). Brain mechanisms of visual selective attention. In R. Parasuraman, & D.R. Davies (Eds.), *Varieties of attention.* (pp. 293–321). New York: Academic Press.

Hauk, O., & Pulvermüller, F. (2004). Effects of word length and frequency on the human event-related potential. *Clinical Neurophysiology, 115,* 1090–1103.

Heredia, R.R. (1997). Bilingual memory and hierarchical models: A case for language dominance. *Current Directions in Psychological Science, 6,* 34–39.

(1998, August). *Cross-modal approaches to the investigation of bilingual spoken language comprehension.* Paper presented at the meeting of the International Association for Cross-Cultural Psychology, Western Washington University, Bellingham, WA.

(2000, May). *Bilingual lexical access and code-switching.* Paper presented at the Fifth Conference on Applied Linguistics, Universidad de Las Américas-Puebla, Mexico.

Heredia, R.R., Altamira, W.A., Cieślicka, A.B., & García, O. (2012, November). *Bilingual lexical access: Interlingual homographs and the grammaticality maze task.* Poster presented at the 53rd Annual Meeting of the Psychonomic Society, Minneapolis, MN.

Heredia, R.R., & Altarriba, J. (2001). Bilingual language mixing: Why do bilinguals code-switch? *Current Directions in Psychological Science, 10*, 164–168.

Heredia, R.R., & Blumentritt, L.T. (2002). On-line processing of social stereotypes during spoken language comprehension. *Experimental Psychology, 49*, 208–221.

Heredia, R.R., Athanatou, E., & Tuttle, S. (2004, November). *Bilingual figurative processing: Comprehension of idiomatic expressions*. Poster presented at the 45th annual meeting of the Psychonomic Society, Minneapolis, MN.

Heredia, R.R., García, O., & Penecale, M.R. (2007, November). *The comprehension of idiomatic expressions by Spanish-English bilinguals*. Paper Presented at the 48th Annual Meeting of the Psychonomic Society, Long Beach, CA.

Heredia, R.R., & Stewart, M.T. (1998, November). *Bilingual on-line sentence processing: A moment-to-moment processing approach*. Poster presented at the 39th annual meeting of the Psychonomic Society, Dallas, TX.

Heredia, R.R., & Stewart, M.T. (2002). On-line methods in spoken language research. In R.R. Heredia & J. Altarriba (Eds.), *Bilingual sentence processing* (pp. 7–28). Amsterdam: Elsevier Science Publishers B.V.

Heredia, R.R., Stewart, M.T., & Cregut, I. (1997, November). *Bilingual online sentence processing: Frequency and context effect in code switching*. Poster presented at the 38th annual meeting of the Psychonomic Society, Philadelphia, PA.

Hoeks, J. C. J., Stowe, L.A., & Doedens, G. (2004). Seeing words in context: The interaction of lexical and sentence level information during reading. *Cognitive Brain Research, 19*, 59–73.

Hulstijn, J.H., & Marchena, E. (1989). Avoidance: Grammatical or semantic causes? *Studies in Second Language Acquisition, 11*, 241–255.

Ibáñez, A., Manes, F., Escobar, J., Trujillo, N., Andreucci, P., & Hurtado, E. (2010). Gesture influences the processing of figurative language in non-native speakers: ERP evidence. *Neuroscience Letters, 471*, 48–52.

Irujo, S. (1986). Don't put your leg in your mouth: Transfer in the acquisition of idioms in a second language. *TESOL Quarterly, 20*, 281–304.

(1993). Steering clear: Avoidance in the production of idioms. *International Review of Applied Linguistics in Language Teaching, 31*, 205–219.

Johnson J. (1989). Factors related to cross-language transfer and metaphor interpretation in bilingual children. *Applied Psycholinguistics, 10*, 157–177.

Johnson, J., & Rosano, T. (1993). Relation of cognitive style to metaphor interpretation and second language proficiency. *Applied Psycholinguistics, 14*, 159–175.

Just, M., Carpenter, P., & Woolley, J. (1982). Paradigms and processes in reading comprehension. *Journal of Experimental Psychology: General, 111*, 228–238.

Kaan, E., Harris, A., Gibson, E., & Holcomb, P.J. (2000). The P600 as an index of syntactic integration difficulty. *Language and Cognitive Processes, 15*, 159–201.

Kanwisher, N.G. (1987). Repetition blindness: Type recognition without token individuation. *Cognition, 27*, 117–143.

Katz, A.N., & Ferretti, T.R. (2001). Moment-by-moment reading of proverbs in literal and nonliteral contexts. *Metaphor and Symbol, 16*, 193–221.

Kim, A., & Osterhout, L. (2005). The independence of combinatory semantic processing: Evidence from event-related potentials. *Journal of Memory and Language, 52*, 205–225.

King, J.W., & Kutas, M. (1998). Neural plasticity in the dynamics of human visual word recognition. *Neuroscience Letters, 244*, 61–64.

Kolk, H.H., Chwilla, D.J., Van Herten, M., & Oor, P.J. (2003). Structure and limited capacity in verbal working memory: A study with event-related potentials. *Brain and Language, 85*, 1–36.

Kotz, S.A. (2001). Neurolinguistic evidence for bilingual language representation: A comparison of reaction times and event-related brain potentials. *Bilingualism: Language and Cognition, 4*, 143–154.

(2009). A critical review of ERP and fMRI evidence on L2 syntactic processing. *Brain and Language, 109*, 68–74.

Kotz, S.A., & Elston-Güttler, K.E. (2004). The role of proficiency on processing categorical and associative information in the L2 as revealed by reaction times and event-related brain potentials. *Journal of Neurolinguistics, 17*, 215–235.

Kroll, J.F., Bobb, S.C., Misra, M., & Guo, T. (2008). Language selection in bilingual speech: Evidence for inhibitory processes. *Acta Psychologica, 128*, 416–430.

Kuperberg, G.R. (2007). Neural mechanisms of language comprehension: Challenges to syntax. *Brain Research, 1146*, 23–49.

Kutas, M., & Delong, K.A. (2008). A sampler of event-related brain potential (ERP) analyses of language processing. *Brain Research in Language*, 153–186.

Kutas, M., & Federmeier, K.D. (2000). Electrophysiology reveals semantic memory use in language comprehension. *Trends in Cognitive Sciences, 4*, 463–470.

(2011). Thirty years and counting: Finding meaning in the N400 component of the event-related brain potential (ERP). *Annual Review of Psychology, 62*, 621–647.

Kutas, M., & Hillyard, S.A. (1980a). Event-related potentials to semantically inappropriate and surprisingly large words. *Biological Psychology, 11*, 99–116.

(1980b). Reading senseless sentences: Brain potentials reflect semantic incongruity. *Science, 207*, 203–205.

(1984). Brain potentials during reading reflect word expectancy and semantic association. *Nature, 307*, 161–163.

Kutas, M., & Kluender, R. (1991). What is who violating? A reconsideration of linguistic violations in the light of event-related potentials. In H.J. Heinze, T.F. Münte, & G.R. Mangun (Eds.), *Cognitive electrophysiology: Basic and clinical applications* (pp. 183–210). Boston: Birkhauser.

Laufer, B. (2000). Avoidance of idioms in a second language: The effect of L1-L2 degree of similarity. *Studia Linguistica, 54*, 186–196.

Leikin, M. (2008). Syntactic processing in two languages by native and bilingual adult readers: An ERP study. *Journal of Neurolinguistics, 21*, 349–373.

Li, P., & Yip, M.C. (1998). Context effects and the processing of spoken homophones. *Reading and Writing: An Interdisciplinary Journal, 10*, 223–243.

Liao, Y., & Fukuya, Y.J. (2004). Avoidance of phrasal verbs: The case of Chinese learners of English. *Language Learning, 54*, 193–226.

Libben, M., & Titone, D. (2008). The multidetermined nature of idiomatic expressions. *Memory & Cognition, 36*, 1103–1131.

Liontas, J. (2002). Context and idiom understanding in second languages. In S.H. Foster-Cohen, T. Ruthenberg, & M.L. Poschen (Eds.), *EUROSLA Yearbook* (Vol. 2, pp. 155–185). Amsterdam: John Benjamins.

Little, D.M., Prentice, K.J., Darrow, A.W., & Wingfield, A. (2005). Listening to spoken text: Adult age differences as revealed by self-paced listening. *Experimental Aging Research, 31*, 313–330.

Littlemore, J. (2010). Metaphoric competence in the first and second language: Similarities and differences. In M. Pütz, & L. Sicola (Eds.), *Cognitive processing in second language acquisition: Inside the learner's mind* (pp. 293–315). Amsterdam: John Benjamins.

Marian, V. (2008). Bilingual research methods. In J. Altarriba, & R.R. Heredia (Eds.), *An introduction to bilingualism: Principles and processes* (pp. 13–37). New York: Lawrence Erlbaum Associates.

Marinis, T. (2003). Psycholinguistic techniques in second language acquisition research. *Second Language Research, 19*, 144–161.

Matlock, T., & Heredia, R.R. (2002). Lexical access of phrasal verbs and verb-prepositions by monolinguals and bilinguals. In R.R. Heredia, & J. Altarriba (Eds.), *Bilingual sentence processing* (pp. 251–303). Amsterdam: Elsevier Science Publishers B.V.

McPartland-Fairman, P. (1989). *The processing of phrasal verbs by native and nonnative speakers of English.* (Unpublished doctoral dissertation). The City University of New York, NewYork.

Meuter, R. (2009). Neurolinguistic contributions to understanding the bilingual mental lexicon. In A. Pavlenko (Ed.), *The bilingual mental lexicon: Interdisciplinary approaches* (pp. 1–25). Bristol: Multilingual Matters.

Meyer, D.E., & Schvaneveldt, R.W. (1971). Facilitation in recognizing pairs of words: Evidence of a dependence between retrieval operations. *Journal of Experimental Psychology, 90*, 227–234.

Midgley, K.J., Holcomb, P.J., Van Heuven, W.J.B., & Grainger, J. (2008). An electrophysiological investigation of cross-language effects of orthographic neighborhood. *Brain Research, 1246*, 123–135.

Mitchell, D.C. (1984). An evaluation of subject-paced reading tasks and other methods for investigating immediate processes in reading. In D.E. Kieras, & M.A. Just (Eds.), *New methods in reading comprehension research* (pp. 69–89). Hillsdale, NJ: Lawrence Erlbaum Associates.

(2004). On-line methods in language processing: Introduction and historical review. In M. Carreiras, & C. Clifton (Eds.), *The on-line study of sentence comprehension: Eye-tracking, ERP and beyond* (pp. 15–32). New York: Psychology Press.

Moreno, E.M., Federmeier, K.D., & Kutas, M. (2002). Switching languages, switching palabras (words): An electrophysiological study of code switching. *Brain and Language, 80*, 188–207.

Moreno, E.M., Rodriguez-Fornells, A., & Laine, M. (2008). Event-related potentials (ERPs) in the study of bilingual language processing. *Journal of Neurolinguistics*, *21*, 477–508.

Mueller, J.L. (2005). Electrophysiological correlates of second language processing. *Second Language Research*, *21*, 152–174.

Nelson, E.M.M. (1992). Memory for metaphor by nonfluent bilinguals. *Journal of Psycholinguistic Research*, *21*, 111–125.

Neville, H.J., Nicol, J.L., Barss, A., Forster, K.I., & Garret, M. (1991). Syntactically based sentence processing classes: Evidence from event-related brain potentials. *Journal of Cognitive Neuroscience*, *3*, 151–165.

Neville, H.J., Mills, D.L., & Lawson, D.S. (1992). Fractionating language: Different neural subsystems with different sensitive periods. *Cerebral Cortex*, *2*, 244–258.

Oren, R., & Breznitz, Z. (2005). Reading processes in L1 and L2 among dyslexic as compared to regular bilingual readers: Behavioral and electrophysiological evidence. *Journal of Neurolinguistics*, *18*, 127–151.

Osterhout, L., & Holcomb, P.J. (1992). Event-related brain potentials elicited by syntactic anomaly. *Journal of Memory and Language*, *31*, 785–806.

Osterhout, L., Holcomb, P.J., & Swinney, D.A. (1994). Brain potentials elicited by garden-path sentences: Evidence of the application of verb information during parsing. *Journal of Experimental Psychology: Learning, Memory, and Cognition*, *20*, 786–803.

Osterhout, L., McLaughlin, J., Kim, A., Greenwald, R., & Inoue, K. (2004). Sentences in the brain: Event-related potentials as real-time reflections of sentence comprehension and language learning. In M. Carreiras & C. Clifton (Eds.), *The on-line study of sentence comprehension: Eyetracking, ERPs, and beyond* (pp. 271–308). New York: Psychology Press.

Osterhout, L., & Mobley, L.A. (1995). Event-related brain potentials elicited by failure to agree. *Journal of Memory and Language*, *34*, 739–773.

Paller, K.A., & Kutas, M. (1992). Brain potentials during memory retrieval provide neurophysiological support for the distinction between conscious recollection and priming. *Journal of Cognitive Neuroscience*, *4*, 375–391.

Palmer, S.D., van Hooff, J.C., & Havelka, J. (2010). Language representation and processing in fluent bilinguals: Electrophysiological evidence for asymmetric mapping in bilingual memory. *Neuropsychologia*, *48*, 1426–1437.

Paulmann, S., Elston-Güttler, K.E., Gunter, T.C., & Kotz, S.A. (2006). Is bilingual lexical access influenced by language context? *NeuroReport*, *17*, 727–731.

Peterson, R.R., & Simpson, G.B. (1989). Effect of backward priming on word recognition in single-word and sentence contexts. *Journal of Experimental Psychology: Learning, Memory, and Cognition*, *15*, 1020–1032.

Pickering, M.J., Frisson, S., McElree, B., & Traxler, M.J. (2004). Eye movements and semantic composition. In M. Carreiras, & C. Clifton (Eds.), *The on-line study of sentence comprehension: Eye-tracking, ERP and beyond* (pp. 33–50). New York: Psychology Press.

Potter, M.C. (1984). Rapid serial visual presentation (RSVP): A method for studying language processing. In D.E. Kieras, & M.A. Just (Eds.), *New methods in reading comprehension research* (pp. 91–118). Hillsdale, NJ: Lawrence Erlbaum Associates.

Polich, J., & Donchin, E. (1988). P300 and the word frequency effect. *Electroenceph. Clinical Neurophysiology, 70,* 33–45.

Proverbio, A.M., Čok, B., & Zani, A. (2002). Electrophysiological measures of language processing in bilinguals. *Journal of Cognitive Neuroscience, 14,* 994–1017.

Proverbio, A.M., Leoni, G., & Zani, A. (2004). Language switching mechanisms in simultaneous interpreters: An ERP study. *Neuropsychologia, 42,* 1636–1656.

Qiao, X., Shen, L., & Forster, K.I. (2012). Relative clause processing in Mandarin: Evidence from the maze task. *Language and Cognitive Processes, 27,* 611–630.

Raymond, J.E., Shapiro, K.L., & Arnell, K.M. (1992). Temporary suppression of visual processing in an RSVP task: An attentional blink? *Journal of Experimental Psychology: Human Perception and Performance, 18,* 849–860.

Rayner, K., & Duffy, S.A. (1986). Lexical complexity and fixation times in reading: Effects of word frequency, verb complexity, and lexical ambiguity. *Memory & Cognition, 14,* 191–201.

Rayner, K., & Frazier, L. (1989). Selection mechanisms in reading lexically ambiguous words. *Journal of Experimental Psychology: Learning, Memory, and Cognition, 15,* 779–790.

Rodriguez-Fornells, A., Rotte, M., Heinze, H.J., Nosselt, T., & Münte, T.F. (2002). Brain potential and functional MRI evidence for how to handle two languages with one brain. *Nature, 415,* 1026–1029.

Rodriguez-Fornells, A., van Der Lugt, A., Rotte, M., Britti, B., Heinze, H.J., & Münte, T.F. (2005). Second language interferes with word production in fluent bilinguals: Brain potential and functional imaging evidence. *Journal of Cognitive Neuroscience, 17,* 422–433.

Rodriguez-Fornells, A., De Diego Balaguer, R., & Münte, T.F. (2006). Executive control in bilingual language processing. *Language Learning, 359,* 133–190.

Rommers, J. (2010). Semantic expectancy in the comprehension of idiomatic expressions: An ERP study. *Nijmegen CNS, 5,* 51–75.

Rugg, M. (1990). Event-related brain potentials dissociate repetition effects of high- and low-frequency words. *Memory & Cognition, 18,* 367–379.

Rugg, M.D., Cox, C.J.C., Doyle, M.C., & Wells, T. (1995). Event-related potentials and the recollection of low and high frequency words. *Neuropsychologia, 33,* 471–484.

Sanders, L.D., & Neville, H.J. (2003). An ERP study of continuous speech processing. Segmentation, semantics, and syntax in non-native speakers. *Cognitive Brain Research, 15,* 214–227.

Sanford, A.J., Sturt, P., Moxey, L., Morrow, L., & Emmott, C. (2004). Production and comprehension measures in assessing plural object formation. In M. Carreiras & C. Clifton (Eds.), *The on-line study of sentence comprehension: Eye-tracking, ERP and beyond* (pp.151–166). New York: Psychology Press.

Saygin, A.P. (2001, March). *Processing figurative language in multi-lingual task: Translation, transfer and metaphor.* Paper presented in Proceedings of Corpus-Based and Processing Approaches to Figurative Language Workshop, Corpus Linguistics. Lancaster, UK: Lancaster University.

Sereno, S.C. (1995). Resolution of lexical ambiguity: Evidence from an eye movement priming paradigm. *Journal of Experimental Psychology: Learning, Memory, and Cognition, 21,* 582–595.

Sereno, S.C., Pacht, J.M., & Rayner, K. (1992). The effect of meaning frequency on processing lexically ambiguous words: Evidence from eye fixations. *Psychological Science, 3,* 296–300.

Schacter, D.L. (1987). Implicit memory: History and current status. *Journal of Experimental Psychology: Learning, Memory, and Cognition, 13,* 501–518.

Schoonbaert, S., Holcomb, P.J., Grainger, J., & Hartsuiker, R.J. (2011). Testing asymmetries in noncognate translation priming: Evidence from RTs and ERPs. *Psychophysiology, 48,* 74–81.

Schwartz, A.I., & Kroll, J.F. (2006). Bilingual lexical activation in sentence context. *Journal of Memory and Language, 55,* 197–212.

Sekerina, I.A., Fernández, E.M., & Clahsen, H. (2008). *Developmental psycholinguistics: On-line methods in children's language processing.* Amsterdam: John Benjamins.

Siyanova-Chanturia, A., Conklin, K., & Schmitt, N. (2011). Adding more fuel to the fire: An eye-tracking study of idiom processing by native and non-native speakers. *Second Language Research, 27,* 251–272.

Sjöholm, K. (1995). *The influence of crosslinguistic, semantic, and input factors on the acquisition of English phrasal verbs: A comparison between Finnish and Swedish learners at an intermediate and advanced level.* Åbo: Åbo Akademi University Press.

Skoufaki, S. (2008). Investigating the source of idiom transparency intuitions. *Metaphor and Symbol, 24,* 20–41.

Stewart, M.T., & Heredia, R.R. (2002). Comprehending spoken metaphoric reference: A real-time analysis. *Experimental Psychology, 49,* 34–44.

Swinney, D.A. (1979). Lexical access during sentence comprehension. *Journal of Verbal Learning and Verbal Behaviour, 18,* 645–659.

Swinney, D.A., & Osterhout, L. (1990). Inference generation during auditory language comprehension. *The Psychology of Learning and Motivation, 25,* 17–33.

Swinney, D.A., & Cutler, A. (1979). The access and processing of idiomatic expressions. *Journal of Verbal Learning and Verbal Behavior, 18,* 523–534.

Swinney, D.A., Onifer, W., Prather, P., & Hirshkowitz, M. (1979). Semantic facilitation across sensory modalities in the processing of individual words and sentences. *Memory & Cognition, 7,* 159–165.

Tabossi, P. (1996). Cross-modal semantic priming. *Language and Cognitive Processes, 11,* 569–576.

Tabossi, P., Fanari, R., & Wolf, K. (2005). Spoken idiom recognition: Meaning retrieval and word expectancy. *Journal of Psycholinguistic Research, 34,* 465–495.

Tanenhaus, M.K. (2004). On-line sentence processing: Past, present, and future. In M. Carreiras, & C. Clifton (Eds.), *The on-line study of sentence comprehension: Eye-tracking, ERP and beyond* (pp. 371–393). New York: Psychology Press.

Titone, D.A., & Connine, C.M. (1994). The comprehension of of idiomatic expressions: Effects of predictability and literality. *Journal of Experimental Psychology: Learning, Memory, and Cognition, 20,* 1126–1138.

(1999). On the compositional and nonconpositional nature of idiomatic expressions. *Journal of Pragmatics, 31,* 1655–1674.

Titone, D., Prentice, K., & Wingfield, A. (2000). Resource allocation strategy and recall performance during self-paced listening of discourse. *Memory & Cognition, 28,* 1029–1040.

Titone, D., Wingfield, A., Caplan, D., Waters, G., & Prentice, K. (2001). Memory and encoding of spoken discourse following right hemisphere damage: Evidence from the auditory moving window (AMW) technique. *Brain and Language, 77,* 10–24.

Underwood, G., Galpin, A., & Schmitt, N. (2004). The eyes have it: An eye-movement study into the processing of formulaic sequences. In N. Schmitt (Ed), *Formulaic sequences: Acquisition, processing, and use* (pp. 23–45). Amsterdam: John Benjamins.

Vaid, J. (2008). The bilingual brain: What is right and what is left. In J. Altarriba, & R.R. Heredia (Eds.), *An introduction to bilingualism: Principles and processes* (pp. 129–144). New York: Lawrence Erlbaum Associates.

Vaid, J., & Martínez, F. (2001, April). *Figurative language and thought across languages: What transfers?* Poster presented at the Third International Symposium on Bilingualism, University of the West of England, Bristol, UK.

van Berkum, J.J.A. (2004). Sentence comprehension in a wider discourse: Can we use ERPs to keep track of things? In M. Carreiras & C. Clifton (Eds.), *The on-line study of sentence comprehension: Eye-tracking, ERP and beyond* (pp. 229–270). New York: Psychology Press.

Van Der Meij, M., Cuetos, F., Carreiras, M., & Barber, H.A. (2011). Electrophysiological correlates of language switching in second language learners. *Psychophysiology, 48,* 44–54.

Van Lancker-Sidits, D. (2003). Auditory recognition of idioms by native and nonnative speakers of English: It takes one to know one. *Applied Psycholinguistics, 24,* 45–57.

Veldhuis, D., & Kurvers, J. (2012). Offline segmentation and online language processing units: The influence of literacy. *Written Language and Literacy, 15,* 165–184.

Verleger, R., Jaśkowski, P., & Wascher, E. (2005). Evidence for an integrative role of P3b in linking reaction to perception. *Journal of Psychophysiology, 19,* 165–181.

Weber-Fox, C.M., & Neville, H.J. (1996). Maturational constraints on functional specializations for language processing: ERP and behavioral evidence in bilingual speakers. *Journal of Cognitive Neuroscience, 8,* 231–256.

(2001). Sensitive periods differentiate processing of open- and closed-class words: An ERP study of bilinguals. *Journal of Speech, Language and Hearing Research, 44,* 1338–1353.

Witzel, N., Witzel, J., & Forster, K.I. (2012). Comparisons of online reading paradigms: Eye tracking, moving-window, and maze. *Journal of Psycholinguistic Research, 41,* 105–128.

Wyble, B., Potter, M.C., & Mattar, M. (2012). RSVP in orbit: Identification of single and dual targets in motion. *Attention, Perception & Psychophysics, 74,* 553–562.

Section III

Figurative Language Processing

6 Contrasting Bilingual and Monolingual Idiom Processing

Debra Titone, Georgie Columbus, Veronica Whitford,
Julie Mercier, and Maya Libben
McGill University, Canada

ABSTRACT

In this chapter, we survey what is currently known about bilingual idiom processing and present data from a study that investigates three questions about the comprehension of idioms in English-French bilinguals. First, do the linguistic factors that control monolingual idiom comprehension (e.g., familiarity, literal plausibility, semantic decomposability; Libben & Titone, 2008) similarly control bilingual comprehension? Second, does an idiom's cross-language similarity affect comprehension? Third, does native language status interact with idiom processing in these respects? To address these questions, we conducted a comprehension study where English-French bilinguals read English sentences that included idioms from a prior normative first-language study that were further coded for their similarity to idioms in French. We also manipulated whether the idiom-final word was presented in English (intact condition) or French (code-switched condition). The results suggest that bilinguals are sensitive to the same linguistic factors that control idiom processing for monolinguals (i.e., familiarity) and that previous work suggesting an increased role for semantic decomposability (Abel, 2003) may actually be due to cross-language overlap. The implications for bilingual lexical representation and processing are discussed.

Keywords: bilingualism, idiom processing, code-switching, figurative language processing, idiomatic expressions

When Joan Foster visited her Polish lover, Paul, she stumbled upon several English novels penned by an improbably named Mavis Quilp. As Joan thumbed through the novels, she noted the signs of a second-language writer, who turned out to be Paul: *"For instance, someone said 'They're selling like pancakes' instead of hotcakes. Someone else said, 'Keep a stiff upper jaw'"* (Atwood, 1976, p. 152). As Joan's creator, Margaret Atwood, aptly illustrates, knowledge and appropriate use of idioms and other formulaic language contribute greatly to perceptions of native-like fluency (Boers, Eyckman, Kappel, Stengers, & Demecheleer, 2006; Gatbonton & Segalowitz, 1988; Segalowitz, 2010; Wood, 2006). Indeed, idiomatic competence is essential to first-language (L1) and second-language (L2) acquisition, as idioms comprise a substantial portion of natural language (Jackendoff, 1995, 1997, 2003; Nattinger & DeCarrico, 1989, 1992; Pawley & Syder, 1983; Sinclair, 1991).

In this chapter, we review several factors that are relevant to our understanding of bilingual idiom processing. These include the many ways that idioms differ, how idioms have been framed theoretically over the years, and what we currently know about L1 and L2 idiom processing. We also offer a preliminary empirical study of bilingual idiom processing that focuses on a dimension of potential importance, cross-language overlap, along with other dimensions that are historically relevant to the monolingual idiom processing literature, including familiarity and decomposability. Our overall conclusions are that an understanding of bilingual idiom processing has much to gain from an appreciation of the processes involved in monolingual idiom processing and has much to offer with respect to understanding formulaic and non-formulaic language processing more generally.

Defining Idioms and How They Vary

Idioms are usually defined as multiword units whose figurative meanings are distinct from their component words, for example, *kick the bucket, spill the beans, be on cloud nine,* and others (Abel, 2003; Cacciari & Glucksberg, 1991; Gibbs, Nayak, & Cutting, 1989; Libben & Titone, 2008; Nunberg, 1978; Titone & Connine, 1999). Idioms have been important to linguistic theory precisely because of their dual nature as conventionalized sequences, subject to rapid direct retrieval from the mental lexicon, and as decomposable sequences, subject to normal syntactic and semantic analysis. Of note, idioms are also important members of a larger class of formulaic language or *multiword expressions* (MWEs), which have received a considerable amount of recent attention (e.g., Arnon & Snider, 2010; Bannard & Matthews, 2008; Columbus, 2010, 2012, 2013; Siyanova-Chanturia, Conklin, & Schmitt, 2011; Siyanova & Schmitt, 2007; Tremblay & Tucker, 2011; Tremblay, Derwing, Libben & Westbury, 2011; Tremblay & Baayen, 2010; Wulff, 2008). Indeed, there are striking parallels with respect to the theoretical controversies found in both literatures.

Similar to theoretical alternatives now entertained for MWEs, early approaches in linguistics adhered to a strongly noncompositional view of idioms (Chomsky, 1981, 1965; Fraser, 1970), largely based on a working definition of idioms as nondecomposable (e.g., *kick the bucket*, where the figurative meaning *to die* cannot be directly inferred from the literal interpretation). However, not all idioms conform to this definition (e.g., *save your skin, throw up your hands*, where the literal interpretation is related to the figurative meaning; Nunberg, 1978; Nunberg, Sag, & Wasow, 1994). While subsequent approaches within linguistics better accommodated differences among idioms, many adhered to a strongly compositional position (Marantz, 2005; McGinnis, 2002), which under-emphasizes the conventionalized fixed nature of idioms (Jackendoff, 1995, 1997, 2003). Psycholinguistic investigations can clarify these issues by determining whether factors related to direct retrieval or com-positional analysis are relevant to comprehension; however, the extant literature is riddled with conflicting findings and methods. Thus, despite a long-standing interest in idioms, and MWEs more generally, across many disciplines (theoretical and applied linguistics, L1 and L2 language learning, psycholinguistics, corpus linguistics), fundamental questions remain about L1, L2, and bilingual idiom processing.

Idioms optimally represent the larger class of MWEs because they vary along all linguistic dimensions relevant to MWEs generally, including familiarity, literal plausibility, semantic decomposability, and other lin-guistic attributes (Abel, 2003; Caillies, 2009; Libben & Titone, 2008; Schweigert & Cronk, 1993; Titone & Connine, 1994a; Wulff, 2008). *Familiarity* refers to the comprehender's subjective impression of how often an idiom is encountered in its written or spoken form, regardless of whether the figurative meaning of the phrase is known. Highly familiar idioms (e.g., *kick the bucket*) are easier to understand than unfamiliar or less familiar idioms (e.g., *a pig in a poke*), presumably because compre-henders can retrieve the meaning directly and rapidly from memory. *Literal plausibility* refers to an idiom's potential to have a literal interpret-ation. For example, some idioms have a readily available, well-formed literal meaning (e.g., *bite the bullet*), whereas others do not (e.g., *shoot the breeze*). Literal plausibility generally interferes with idiom processing; however, facilitation arises with increased literal plausibility, where idiomatic interpretations are not required (e.g., Libben & Titone, 2008). *Semantic decomposability* refers to how the individual meanings of the idiom's component words relate to the figurative meaning of the phrase. In *pop the question*, for example, the literal meaning of *question* contributes to the figurative meaning (*a marriage proposal*). In contrast, neither *kick* nor *bucket* contributes to the meaning of the idiom *to kick the bucket*. As we will see, the role of semantic decomposability in idiom processing is more contentious than familiarity or literal plausibility, in that some studies find facilitation from semantic decomposability in the early stages of idiom processing, (e.g., Gibbs, 1992; Gibbs & Nayak, 1989; Gibbs, Nayak, Bolton & Keppel, 1989; Gibbs, Nayak & Cutting, 1989), while others do not (Abel, 2003; Cieślicka, 2012; Tabossi, Fanari & Wolf, 2008; Titone & Connine, 1994a).

A Constraint-Based Model of Idiom Processing

Building upon early linguistic theories (Chomsky, 1981, 1965; Fraser, 1970), several psycholinguistic models emphasize the fixed noncompositional nature of idioms (Bobrow & Bell, 1973; Cacciari & Tabossi, 1988; Cutting & Bock, 1997; Sprenger, Levelt & Kempen, 2006; Swinney & Cutler, 1979). While these models differ in detail, they generally agree that idioms are stored holistically in the lexicon and directly retrieved during language processing. For example, previous studies have shown that highly familiar or predictable idioms, which are most likely to have directly retrievable word-like representations, are processed more rapidly than literal phrases or unfamiliar idioms (Cacciari, Padovani, & Corradini, 2007; Cacciari & Tabossi, 1988; Conklin & Schmitt, 2008; Cronk, Lima, & Schweigert, 1993; Cronk & Schweigert, 1992; Libben & Titone, 2008; Schmitt, 2004; Schweigert, 1991; Schweigert & Cronk, 1993; Schweigert & Moates, 1988; Tabossi, Fanari, & Wolf, 2005; Tabossi & Zardon, 1993; Titone & Connine, 1994a, 1994b). Thus, compelling evidence supports the fixed nature of idioms and the notion that figurative meanings are directly retrieved from the lexicon at the earliest stages of comprehension. However, the role of compositional processes is more contentious.

Building upon later linguistic theories (Nunberg, 1978; Nunberg, Sag, & Wasow, 1994), other psycholinguistic accounts emphasize the flexible or compositional nature of idioms (Burt, 1992; Caillies & Butcher, 2007; Gibbs et al., 1989; Gibbs & Nayak, 1989; Gibbs, Nayak, & Cutting, 1989; Hamblin & Gibbs, 1999). The *Direct Access Model*, for example, posits that idioms whose component words relate to their figurative meaning (decomposable idioms such as *save your skin*) are directly and more rapidly understood through a normal compositional analysis compared to idioms whose figurative and literal meanings are distinct (nondecomposable idioms such as *kick the bucket*; Gibbs, Nayak, & Cutting, 1989).

Several pieces of evidence cohere with a strong compositional view. First, idioms differ in semantic decomposability and syntactic flexibility, and people can identify these differences reliably (Libben & Titone, 2008; Titone & Connine, 1994a). Second, people successfully interpret idioms presented in noncanonical, non-adjacent, or novel forms, suggesting that direct retrieval of fixed lexicalized word sequences is not the only route to comprehension (Everaert, van der Linden, Schenk, & Schreuder,1995; Gonnerman & Hayes, 2005; Knobloch, 2009; McGlone, Glucksberg, & Cacciari, 1994; Vespignani, Canal, Molinaro, Fonda, & Cacciari, 2010). Third, literal processing does not simply stop when we encounter idioms; rather, we semantically process their constituent words (Cacciari & Tabossi, 1988; Titone & Connine, 1994b), anticipate their words' syntactic class (Peterson, Burgess, Dell, & Eberhard, 2001), and generate literal phrasal interpretations (Libben & Titone, 2008; Popiel & McRae, 1988; Titone & Connine, 1994b).

It is unclear, however, whether the products of this normal compositional analysis are necessary for understanding an idiom's figurative interpretation, the main prediction of compositional models, or whether direct retrieval of the idiom as a whole is sufficient. While there is some evidence for this prediction, it typically comes from experimental tasks that involve meta-linguistic or overt semantic judgments about idioms as a whole (Gibbs et al., 1989; Gibbs, Nayak, & Cutting, 1989; Hamblin & Gibbs, 1999), which may lack ecological validity or have small numbers of idioms that vary in many ways. Other studies using similar methods fail to find decomposability advantages (Fanari, Cacciari, & Tabossi, 2010; Tabossi, Fanari, & Wolf, 2005, 2008; Tabossi, Wolf, & Koterle, 2008), while yet other studies suggest more nuanced effects of decomposability. For example, Titone and Connine (1999) and Libben and Titone (2008) have shown that decomposability does not facilitate the initial comprehension of idioms but does facilitate later stages involving the integration of particular meanings into a relevant context. Thus, decomposability aids in resolving competition between figurative and literal phrasal meanings but does not initiate the activation of figurative meanings.

To illustrate this point in more detail, Libben and Titone (2008) examined the simultaneous influence of decomposability and familiarity for over 200 VERB-X-NOUN English idioms across several comprehension tasks in native English participants. These included offline meaningfulness judgments, online whole sentence meaningfulness judgments, word-by-word fixed-rate meaningfulness judgments, and word-by-word self-paced reading. Libben and Titone found that increased familiarity facilitated comprehension for native English users across all dependent measures, consistent with previous work (Cronk & Schweigert, 1992; Gibbs, 1980; Nippold & Taylor, 2002; Titone & Connine 1994a; Schweigert, 1986). Increased literal plausibility also facilitated comprehension, but likely because participants were able to make meaningfulness judgments without interpreting the phrase idiomatically in this particular task.

In contrast with familiarity and literal plausibility, the effects of semantic decomposability on comprehension were less consistent. Increased decomposability facilitated comprehension in tasks requiring overt semantic judgments about idiom meaningfulness (e.g., *pop the question* would be easier to understand than *kick the bucket*); however, it did not facilitate reading in tasks less likely to direct attention to idiomatic meanings as a whole (i.e., predictability ratings and moving window reading). Thus, when native English speakers encounter the verb of VERB-X-NOUN idioms, they generate simultaneous activation for the semantic representation of its literal interpretation and also directly retrieve its fixed phrasal meaning. These results are consistent with prior work on idiom compositionality showing facilitative compositionality effects on comprehension only for relatively offline or metalinguistic tasks (Gibbs et al., 1989; Gibbs & Nayak, 1989; Gibbs, Nayak, & Cutting, 1989) and at later integrative stages of processing (Titone & Connine, 1999).

Such findings led to the proposal of a *Hybrid* (Titone & Connine, 1999) or *Constraint-Based* (Libben & Titone, 2008) *Model of Idiom Processing*, which could readily encompass MWEs generally or other elements of figurative language (e.g., metaphor). Within this view, people simultaneously use all available information during comprehension, resulting from direct retrieval and compositional analysis. Different kinds of information may be available at different time-courses, and different classes of information may interact over time. Thus, assuming that direct retrieval is a fast process that may occur prior to the idiom's offset (Cacciari & Tabossi, 1988; Titone & Connine, 1994b), variables that modulate the ease of direct retrieval (familiarity or predictability) will affect very early comprehension stages such as initial figurative activation. Similarly, assuming that on-demand compositional analyses are slower and more effortful than direct retrieval, in that they necessitate that all component words of an idiom are encountered, variables that modulate the ease of compositional processing (decomposability, syntactic flexibility) will affect comprehension stages subsequent to initial meaning activation. Because all sources of information interact, if the products of direct retrieval are particularly strong or salient, they may attenuate the products of compositional processes. In contrast, if the products of direct retrieval are weak, as they might be for low or moderately familiar idioms, the products of an ongoing compositional analysis might be heightened.

Consistent with this view, Titone and Connine (1994b) showed that non-idiomatic literal word meaning activation is reduced for highly predictable and literally implausible idioms and that figurative meanings of highly predictable idioms are retrieved prior to encountering their phrase-final words. Conversely, as just described, Libben and Titone (2008) also found that increased decomposability facilitated meaningfulness judgments for unfamiliar idioms, but not highly familiar idioms. An important corollary of this constraint-based approach is that any factor that independently modulates direct retrieval or compositional processes should also modulate figurative meaning generation and integration during comprehension; these include individual differences among idioms or people. Thus, many untested questions remain, particularly with respect to L2 or bilingual idiom processing, to which we now turn.

Constraint-Based Idiom Processing in the L2

Despite the pervasiveness of idioms in everyday language (Cowie, 1992), they often go unnoticed by L1 speakers. Accordingly, idiom processing is relatively easy for L1 speakers; however, this subjective ease of processing is not the case for L2 speakers. As illustrated by Margaret Atwood's *selling like pancakes* example above, L2 speakers, especially those who acquired their L2 later in life (i.e., late bilinguals), have great difficulty with conventional idioms in terms of learning, production, and comprehension (Abel, 2003; Bortfeld, 1998; Charteris-Black, 2002; Cieślicka, 2006; Conklin & Schmitt, 2008; Durrant & Schmitt, 2010; Ellis, Simpson-Vlach, & Maynard, 2008; Eskildsen, 2009; Irujo, 1993; Jiang & Nekrasova, 2007; Kecskes, 2000; Laufer, 2000; Li & Schmitt, 2009; Matlock & Heredia, 2002; Nekrasova, 2009; Rossiter, Derwing, Manimtim, & Thomson, 2010; Steinel, Hulstijn, & Steinel, 2007; Tabossi, Wolf, & Koterle, 2008; Vanlancker-Sidtis, 2003; Weinert, 1995; Wood, 2006; Wray, 2000). Indeed, most studies of bilingual idiom processing have emphasized the disadvantage associated with idiom comprehension during L2 processing.

For example, in a cross-modal priming study where asymmetric Polish-English bilinguals heard sentences containing English idioms and saw visual targets requiring a lexical decision response, Cieślicka (2006) found more priming for literal targets than for idiomatic targets across different probe positions. Thus, the participants had difficulty retrieving idiomatic meanings for idioms in their L2. Similarly, Vanlancker-Sidtis (2003) found that both fluent and less fluent English L2 bilinguals had more difficulty than English native speakers in deciding whether literally plausible idioms were intended figuratively as a function of prosodic bias. Finally, two recent studies underscore the advantages for literal over figurative interpretations in L2 speakers. Siyanova-Chanturia, Conklin, and Schmitt (2011) conducted an eye tracking study where L2 speakers read paragraphs containing a variety of idioms or literal control sentences preceded by a disambiguating context. The authors found no differences in first-pass reading times for idiom versus control phrase regions, suggesting no differences during early-stage processing. However, differences in total reading times (reflecting late-stage processing and/or semantic integration) were found for idiom versus control phrase regions, suggesting that figurative uses of idioms were read more slowly than literal uses. L2 speakers also reread the idiom regions more than the literal control regions (see also, Cieślicka & Heredia, 2011, for similar results using a divided visual field priming study).

While the studies reviewed above are consistent with the idea that L2 versus L1 idiom processing is more difficult, particularly when idioms are used in a figurative context, it is unclear whether this conclusion is warranted for all types of idioms. Indeed, L2 idiom processing also appears to be affected by factors such as decomposability and cross-language overlap, and differences among idioms in these dimensions may increase or decrease the burden of L2 idiom processing (Abel, 2003; Charteris-Black, 2002; Irujo, 1993; Laufer, 2000; Nippold & Duthie, 2003; Nippold & Taylor, 2002; Nippold, Taylor, & Baker, 1996; Steinel, Hulstijn, & Steinel, 2007). For example, Abel (2003) showed that L2 English learners were more likely to rate English idioms as semantically decomposable compared to the L1 English speakers in Titone and Connine's study (1994a). Similarly, Steinel, Hulstijn, and Steinel (2007) showed that L2 speakers value idiom imagery more heavily (which is related to decomposability) during L2 processing. Moreover, and of relevance here, several findings indicate that L2 idiom processing is easier if an idiom is dually represented across all known languages. For example, Irujo's (1993) study of idiom translation during language production showed that L2 Spanish learners were more likely to translate Spanish (L2) idioms into English (L1) idioms when the idioms had similar forms in English (see also García et al., this voume). Further, cross-language similarity was a better predictor of whether Spanish idioms would be translated into English idioms than phrasal frequency or semantic decomposability (see also Laufer, 2000). Comprehension studies (e.g., Charteris-Black, 2002) similarly indicate that cross-language similarity of form and concept is important for idiom processing, although more studies are needed that investigate the earliest stages of comprehension rather than later comprehension stages or the outcome of comprehension.

Facilitative effects of cross-language overlap for idioms are consistent with the bilingual word processing literature, where single word processing is subject to similar cross-language effects in the form of *cognate facilitation* (e.g., Dijkstra, Grainger, & Van Heuven, 1999; Lemhöfer & Dijkstra, 2004; Libben & Titone, 2009; Schwartz, Kroll, & Diaz, 2007; Titone, Libben, Mercier, Whitford, & Pivneva, 2011). Cognates are words that overlap across languages in terms of both orthography and semantics (although their phonology often differs, sometimes significantly). Cognates (e.g., French-English) are typically easier to process than noncognate words (e.g., *cabin* and *cabine*, compared to *building* and *bâtiment*). For example, in a study that measured eye movements while participants read L2 sentences containing cognates, Libben and Titone (2009) found significant cognate facilitation for neutral sentence contexts during the earliest stages of comprehension (i.e., first fixation duration) that persisted through the later stages of comprehension (i.e., total reading time; see also Titone et al., 2011). Thus, it is an open question whether immediate cognate facilitation at a multiword level would also occur for idiomatic expressions. Given that idioms are dually represented across languages and are analogous to lexical cognates, one would expect to observe similar facilitation effects for idioms. However, idioms are intriguingly different from lexical cognates given that cross-language overlap is more abstract or structural (i.e., depending on the relation of words within a phrase) rather than based on form (i.e., depending on low-level orthographic or phonological overlap). In either case, any facilitative effect of cross-language overlap on bilingual idiom processing would presumably reflect a kind of direct retrieval process, only unlike L1 direct retrieval of idioms, the information being retrieved would derive from non-target language knowledge rather than target-language knowledge.

Also relevant to an understanding of bilingual idiom processing is the presumed learning processes involved in mastering L2 idioms. Wray's (2000, 2002) theoretical framework posits that L2 learners may process idioms differently based on when and how L2 was acquired, their communicative goals, and cognitive and language learning style. Indeed, Wray's theoretical treatment of L1 and L2 language acquisition dovetails well with the *Constraint-Based* or *Hybrid* view previously described (Libben & Titone, 2008; Titone & Connine, 1999). Following others (Nattinger & DeCarrico, 1989, 1992; Pawley & Syder, 1983; Sinclair, 1991), Wray characterizes language acquisition and processing as a dynamic, needs-driven balance between holistic (memory-based) and analytic (composition-based) processes. Prior to children's word explosion around age 2, Wray argues that close to 100 percent of linguistic processing is holistic. Thus, children at this age tacitly learn and imitate holistic utterances, and they induce the lexical and syntactic properties of language through this knowledge (Tomasello, 2003). However, once a child begins to learn grammatical rules, the balance swings in the analytical direction. Thus, children between 2 and 8 years old have difficulty with nonliteral forms, are overly literal or concrete, and make language errors consistent with the rigid overapplication of grammatical rules. Once grammatical rules are mastered, however, there is a gradual return to holistic processes, which also helps to minimize effort while planning more adult-like complex utterances.

According to Wray (2000, 2002), L2 acquisition is superimposed on this basic L1 learning framework. If an L2 is acquired early, the holistic-analytical balance and idiomatic competence ultimately attained may be indistinguishable from that of an L1 user. However, if the L2 is acquired late in life (i.e., late bilinguals), the ultimate balance attained will be shifted away from the holistic end of the spectrum, partly because adults learn L2 more analytically than young children. Moreover, the cognitive infrastructure supporting late L2 acquisition is biased away from unconscious tacit (procedural) learning and more toward conscious and effortful memory-based (declarative) learning (J. Paradis, 2010; J. Paradis, Nicoladis, & Crago, 2007; M. Paradis, 2008a, 2008b; Prado & Ullman, 2009; Ullman, 2001, 2006).

The net effect is that adult L2 users will comprehend and produce idioms differently from L1 users. In production, they may substitute words in idioms that are related and more frequent in their L1 (*They sold like pancakes*), or produce an incomprehensible form (*Keep a stiff upper jaw*). Because people vary significantly in language aptitude, and may be more or less holistic or analytical (Andreou, Vlachos, & Andreou, 2005; Hummel, 2009; Robinson, 2005; Rysiewicz, 2008a, 2008b; Skehan, 1991, 2009; Sparks, Patton, Ganschow, & Humbach, 2009a, 2009b;), L2 success may also depend on both when a person acquires an L2 and what linguistic or cognitive capacities are brought to the learning context (for similar issues in the context of monolingual research, see, Carpenter, Miyake, & Just, 1995; Duchek et al., 1992; Faust & Gernsbacher, 1996; Gernsbacher & Faust, 1991; Gernsbacher, Varner, & Faust, 1990; Gunter, Wagner, & Friederici, 2003; Miyake, Just, & Carpenter, 1994; Wagner & Gunter, 2004; Wagner, Gunter, & Friederici, 2000).

Thus, couching these ideas about learning within the language of a Constraint-Based Idiom Processing Model (Libben & Titone, 2008; Titone & Connine, 1999), L2 users may more heavily weigh information generated by compositional processes over direct retrieval of precompiled idioms, either because direct retrieval provides less information for L2 users or because L2 users are inherently more analytical or compositional. As well, other factors that are important for the bilingual situation (i.e., the activation of a nontarget language) may alter the relative balance of compositional versus direct retrieval processes during idiom L2 reading. These could include whether an idiom overlaps across the L1 and L2 or whether the language processing context is comprised of one language exclusively or contains code-switches that may increase saliency of the nontarget language (Altarriba, Kroll, Sholl, & Rayner, 1996; Heredia & Altarriba, 2001). Under such circumstances, bilinguals may rely more heavily on direct retrieval processes (i.e., accessing idiomatic knowledge from the current target language or another known language, most likely the L1) over compositional processes (i.e., building the figurative interpretation of an idiom within a target language in real time).

A Preliminary Study of Bilingual Idiom Processing

To begin to address some of these issues, we now turn to a preliminary study of bilingual idiom processing that poses two questions about the comprehension of idioms in English-French bilinguals based on the Constraint-Based Model (Libben & Titone, 2008). First, do the cognitive-linguistic processes that govern monolingual idiom comprehension (e.g., direct retrieval vs. compositional analysis; Libben & Titone, 2008), similarly govern bilingual idiom comprehension? Second, is comprehension affected by an idiom's cross-language similarity, which is another potential source of knowledge that may be directly retrieved? To address these questions, we conducted a preliminary study where English-French bilinguals read English sentences containing 120 idioms taken from Libben and Titone's (2008) normative study that were further coded for their similarity to idioms in French. We also manipulated whether the idiom-final word was presented in English (intact condition) or French (code-switched condition). We then embedded these sentences in a speeded task that required bilinguals to decide whether sentences containing idioms were meaningful. We presented a large set of structurally homogeneous English idioms that varied systematically in several dimensions known to affect comprehension, such as cross-language overlap, compositionality, and English familiarity.

Our hypotheses are as follows. To the extent that idioms are understood through direct retrieval from target language knowledge rather than a compositional analysis, consistent with the Constraint-Based Model (Libben & Titone, 2008), a code-switch on the phrase-final word should have a significantly more disruptive effect for idioms than for literal sentences. This would occur because the introduction of a code-switch would disrupt recognition of a holistic idiomatic form and encourage a more compositional strategy by making individual words within an idiom more salient. However, cross-language overlap of idioms should facilitate idiom processing generally, and particularly when a code-switch explicitly cues the nontarget language. Indeed, it is possible that a code-switch cost that is particular to idioms may be reduced in cases where idioms have high cross-language overlap because the holistic idiomatic form exists in both languages. These predictions are somewhat different from those of Abel (2003), according to which bilinguals should rely more heavily on compositional processes for understanding idioms, particularly when they are encountering idioms in their L2. While we agree that compositional processes may be more necessary for bilingual idiom processing under circumstances where idioms are relatively unknown in either their L1 or L2, our view here emphasizes that direct retrieval can also occur from the L1 to L2 direction and vice versa (cf. Cieślicka; García et al., this volume).

Methods

A total of 26 English-French bilingual McGill University students participated for course credit as part of the Psychology Participant Pool or for monetary compensation at a rate of $10 per hour. Seventeen had English as their L1, and 6 had French as their L1. Background data for the remaining 3 participants was missing. All participants had normal or corrected vision.

We selected 120 English idioms having a PRONOUN-VERB-X-NOUN structure where x could be an article, preposition, or determiner (e.g., *she kicked the bucket, he took a beating, he used his head*). We also created 120 literal sentences that were individually matched to the idiomatic sentences in terms of length in words, syntactic structure, word length, the Kučera-Francis (1967) word frequency, and the cloze probability of the sentence-final word. For example, the literal sentence *She told a lie* was based on the idiomatic sentence *She lived a lie*. Sentence-final words for idiomatic and literal sentences were translated into French to create code-switched versions for each sentence, for example, *He played with feu (fire)*. French-final words across the idiom and literal conditions were matched on length and word frequency using the Lexique database (New, Pallier, Brysbaert, & Ferrand, 2004). Finally, 120 semantically anomalous filler sentences were also included to provide clear *no* responses in the meaningfulness judgment task. These sentences were similar in form and lexical characteristics as the idiom and literal sentences and were not anomalous until the final word of the sentence (e.g., *He published the doughnut*).

Libben and Titone's (2008) idioms were rated on a variety of linguistic dimensions, which included familiarity, literal plausibility, and global decomposability, as defined earlier. For the purposes of this experiment, all English idioms were also systematically coded with respect to their overlap with French. Idioms were coded for cross-linguistic overlap by two native speakers of Canadian French, in consultation with online and published French-English idiom dictionaries. As seen in Table 1 below, the code used a scale that ranged from 1 to 5, where a value of 1 designated idioms that did not have a French equivalent idiomatic meaning; a value of 2 designated idioms that had the same idiomatic meaning but did not share component words; a value of 3 designated idioms that shared the same idiomatic meaning with one shared component word; a value of 4 designated idioms that shared the same idiomatic meaning with two component words overlapping; and a value of 5 designated idioms that had an identical meaning and complete word-to-word overlap (for content words only). See Table 2 for sample idioms with their English-French overlap ratings, along with their literal plausibility, familiarity, and decomposability ratings taken from Libben and Titone (2008). Table 3 lists the correlations between the different ratings for this particular set of idioms.

Table 1. *Categories of L1 and L2 Idiom Overlap*

Category	Definition	English example	French representation
1	Idiom does not exist in French	*He coined the phrase*	N/A
2	French idiom with same meaning but different words	*She pocketed her pride*	*Elle a fait taire son amour-propre*
3	French idiom with same meaning and one word in common	*He broke his back*	*Il s'est cassé les reins*
4	French idiom with same meaning and two words in common	*They weathered the storm*	*Ils ont surmonté la tempête*
5	Idiom exists in French as a direct word-to-word translation	*He bit the dust*	*Il a mordu la poussière*

Table 2. *Examples of Idioms Categorized by Their Cross-language Overlap, Familiarity, Literal Plausibility, and Semantic Decomposability Ratings*

Idiom Type	Sample Sentences	N	Familiarity	Literal Plausibility	ProportionSemantic Decomposability
No Overlap	*He coined the phrase (No French equivalent)*	13	2.72	3.03	0.34
Same Meaning	*She pocketed her pride (Elle a fait taire son amour-propre)*	34	3.41	2.82	0.44

Note. Familiarity (1 = Low, 5 = High); Literal plausibility (1 = Low, 5 = High); Semantic decomposability (1.0 = Decomposable).

Table 3. *Pearson Correlation Values for the Independent Variables Used in the Linear Mixed Models*

Pearson Correlation	Cross-Language Overlap	Familiarity	Literal Plausibility	Semantic Decomposability
Cross-language overlap	1.0	–	–	–
Familiarity	0.24**	1.0	–	–
Literal Plausibility	0.11	–0.15	1.0	–
Semantic Decomposability	0.31**	0.42**	–0.18*	1.0

Note. $* p < .05$; $** p < .01$.

Sentences were presented visually in a word-by-word fashion using E-Prime software (Schneider, Eschman, & Zuccolotto, 2002). Each word appeared in the center of the computer screen for 300 ms, with a 200 ms interval between each word. Participants were instructed to judge (Yes/No) whether each sentence was meaningful by pressing the appropriate key on a button box as quickly as possible. The final word remained on the screen (with 3 red question marks appearing below it) until the participant provided a Yes/No response. To prevent anticipation effects, the intertrial intervals varied randomly between 1000 ms and 1250 ms, during which time participants saw a white fixation cross.

The experiment was approximately 30 minutes in duration. Participants were informed that they would see English sentences word by word, and that some sentences would contain French words. They were instructed to respond to each sentence as quickly and as accurately as possible. Participants completed a practice block consisting of 10 trials prior to beginning the test session.

Results and Discussion

We examined accuracy and the reaction times for the correct meaningfulness judgement responses. We excluded all trials with latencies longer than five seconds. The data were analyzed *using linear mixed effects* models within the lme4 package (version 0.999999-2; Bates, Maechler, & Bolker, 2013) of R (version 3.0.0; R Development Core Team, 2013). Across all models, participants and items (words) were random effects, and random slope adjustments were included for sentence type and code-switch condition (Barr, Levy, Scheepers, & Tily, 2013). $Pr|z|$-values are reported for the accuracy data; approximate p-values are reported for the response time data based on degrees of freedom (26 participants), because there is no function in R yet to produce p-values from models involving complex random effects structures.

Effects of code-switches on idiomatic sentences and literal sentences

To investigate whether idiom processing was differentially affected by the presence of a code-switch for English L1 and French L1 speakers, we computed linear mixed effects models that included the following fixed effects: Sentence type (idiom vs. literal), Language of sentence-final noun (English vs. French), Group (English L1, French L1) and their interactions, for both accuracy and correct meaningfulness judgment reaction times. Details of the statistical results are presented in Table 4.

As can be seen in Table 4 and Figure 1, whether the sentence was idiomatic or literal made a difference to readers in both accuracy and correct response reaction times, as did whether the final noun was presented in French or in English. As expected, code-switches on idiom-final words caused significantly greater disruptions for sentences containing idioms than for literal control sentences in terms of correct meaningfulness judgment reaction times (interaction between sentence type and language of sentence-final noun, $t = 3.63$, $p = 0.05$). The upper panel of Figure 1 illustrates this effect: Idioms took longer to read than literal sentences, and also took longer when the final noun was presented in French. In the accuracy data, this interaction was not significant, but there were

Table 4. *Effect Sizes (b), Standard Errors (SE), and P-Values for Code-Switch Effect Linear Mixed Effects Model (Correct Response Time), and Pr(> |z|) Values for Code-Switch Effect Logistic Linear Mixed Effects Model (Accuracy)*

	Correct Response Times			Accuracy		
Fixed Effects	*b*	*SE*	*p*	*b*	*SE*	*Pr(|z|)*
Sentence Type (Idiom vs. Literal)	0.05	0.01	$\leqslant 0.01$	0.04	0.09	< 0.01
Language (Final Word English vs. French)	−0.22	0.02	$\leqslant 0.01$	1.06	0.26	< 0.01
Group (French L1 vs. English L1)	−0.01	0.06	0.92	0.69	0.44	0.12
Sentence Type*Language	0.03	0.01	$\leqslant 0.01$	−0.14	0.12	0.25
Sentence Type*Group	0.03	0.02	0.13	−0.36	0.20	0.07
Language*Group	−0.03	0.05	0.48	0.88	0.53	0.10
Sentence Type*Language*Group	−0.01	0.02	0.47	−0.28	0.24	0.24
Control Predictors	*b*	*SE*	*p*	*b*	*SE*	*Pr(|z|)*
(Intercept)	6.74	0.03	< 0.01	1.07	0.23	< 0.01
Random Effects	**Variance**			**Variance**		
Subject	0.002			1.05		
Item	0.004			0.40		
Subject | Sentence Type	0.002			0.21		
Subject | Language	0.003			1.17		
Subject | Sentence Type | Language	0.000			0.25		
Residual	0.108			*n/a*		

significant main effects indicating that judgment accuracy was reduced for idioms versus literal sentences ($t = 4.17$, $p < .01$) and for French versus English sentence final words ($t = 4.01$, $p < .01$). The lower panel of Figure 1 illustrates this effect. Unexpectedly, there were no differences between English L1 and French L1 bilinguals. However, there may not have been enough participants to sufficiently test for a group effect.

Interactions with familiarity, semantic decomposability, or cross-language overlap

To investigate whether differences among idioms significantly interacted with the above basic effects, we computed models for English sentence-final words and French sentence-final words alone that tested for the interaction of each idiom attribute (i.e., familiarity, decomposability, and

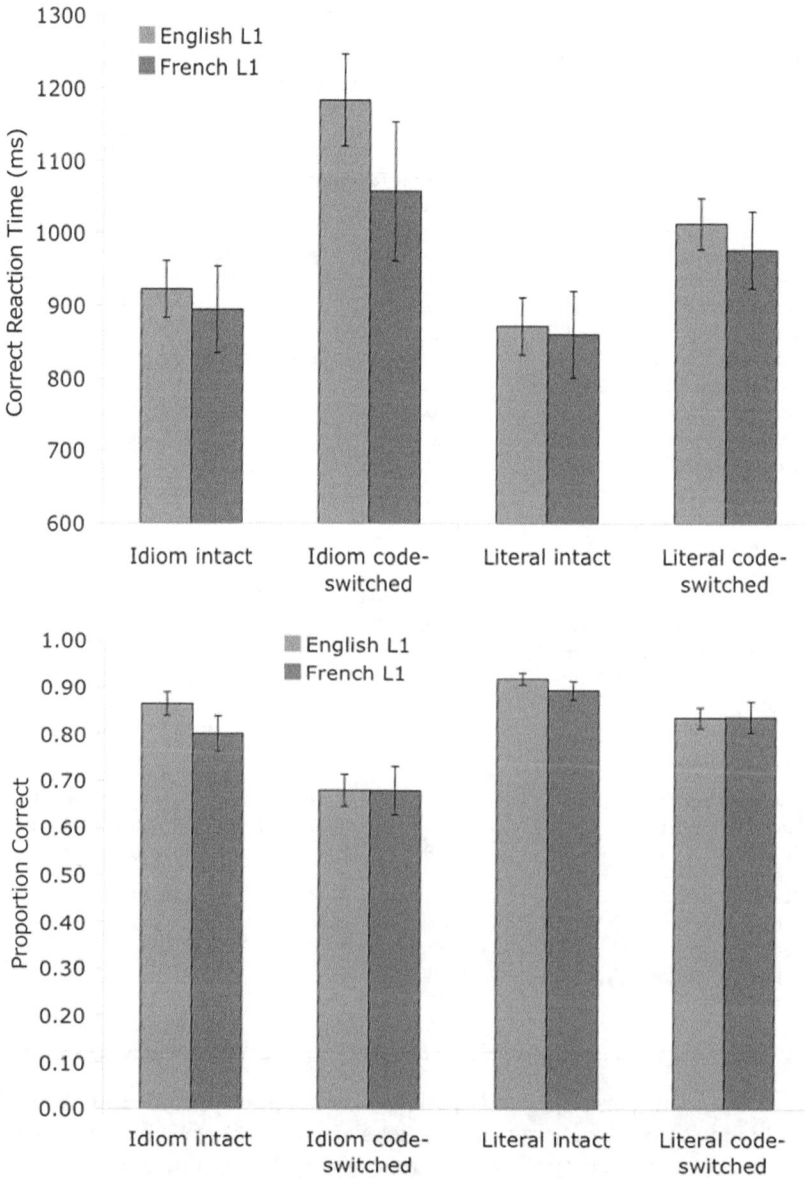

Figure 1. Correct Reaction Time (Upper Panel) and Accuracy (Lower Panel) as a Function of Sentence Type by Final Noun Language

Table 5. *Effect Sizes (b), Standard Errors (SE), and P-Values for Idiom Effects Linear Mixed Effects Models (Correct Response Time), and $Pr(>|z|)$ Values for Idiom Effects Logistic Linear Mixed Effects Models (Accuracy) When Final Word Is in English*

Fixed effects	Correct Response Times			Accuracy		
	b	*SE*	*p*	*b*	*SE*	*Pr(|z|)*
Group (French L1 vs. English L1)	0.01	0.07	0.86	1.53	0.67	0.02
Sentence Type (Idiom vs. Literal)	−0.05	0.02	0.01	0.09	0.18	< 0.01
Familiarity (Scaled)	−0.14	0.03	< 0.01	2.14	0.23	< 0.01
Cross-Language Overlap (Scaled)	−0.02	0.03	0.50	0.21	0.22	0.34
Decomposability (Scaled)	0.03	0.03	0.27	−0.28	0.23	0.22
Group*Sentence Type	−0.01	0.03	0.95	−0.62	0.33	0.06
Group*Familiarity	−0.00	0.05	0.23	0.20	0.45	0.66
Sentence Type*Familiarity	−0.06	0.02	< 0.01	−1.13	0.18	< 0.01
Group*Cross-Language Overlap	0.06	0.04	0.36	−0.05	0.42	0.91
Sentence Type*Cross-Language Overlap	0.04	0.02	0.63	−0.04	0.17	0.81
Group*Decomposability	0.01	0.04	0.72	0.29	0.44	0.51
Sentence Type*Decomposability	−0.02	0.02	0.23	0.17	0.17	0.32
Group*Sentence Type*Familiarity	0.04	0.03	0.20	0.07	0.31	0.82
Group*Sentence Type*Cross-Language Overlap	−0.03	0.03	0.27	0.18	0.29	0.54
Group*Sentence Type*Decomposability	0.01	0.03	0.65	−0.38	0.30	0.20
Control Predictors	*b*	*SE*	*p*	*b*	*SE*	*Pr(|z|)*
Literality (Scaled)	−0.01	0.01	0.21	0.06	0.11	< 0.01
(Intercept)	6.8	0.04	< 0.01	1.30	0.34	< 0.01
Random Effects	Variance			Variance		
Subject	0.02			1.65		
Item	0.02			0.00		
Subject | Sentence Type	0.00			0.19		
Item | Sentence Type	0.01			0.42		
Residual	0.10			*n/a*		

cross-language overlap) and sentence type. Specifically, each model included three three-way interactions (sentence type by familiarity by group, sentence type by decomposability by group, sentence type by cross-language overlap by group), as well as the lower-order two-way interactions and main effects. In what follows, we only focus on interactions involving each idiom attribute of interest and whether it interacted with sentence type. None of the three-way interactions involving group were significant. Details of the statistical results are presented in Table 5.

With respect to correct judgment response time for sentences containing English sentence-final words, only idiom familiarity interacted with sentence type ($t = 3.56$, $p < .05$; see middle column of Table 5). As seen in the left panel of Figure 2, this interaction suggests that as familiarity increased, idioms were responded to more quickly, thus reducing the difference between idiom and literal sentences. As can be seen in the center panel of Figure 2, this effect did not occur for decomposability. While the right panel of Figure 2 suggests that cross-language overlap may have functioned similarly to familiarity, this interaction was not significant ($t < 1$). A similar pattern of data also occurred for response accuracy. Again, only the interaction between sentence type and familiarity was significant ($t = -6.41$, $p < .05$; see left panel of Figure 3, and third column of Table 5).

In contrast to what was found for sentences containing English final words, which uniformly showed significant interactions with familiarity and none for decomposability or cross-language overlap, sentences containing French final words showed a greater effect of cross-language overlap (see Table 6). In the response time data, sentence type significantly interacted with cross-language overlap ($t = 2.68$, $p < .05$).

As can be seen in the right panel of Figure 4, responses to idioms became progressively faster as cross-language overlap increased, thus reducing the difference between idioms and literal sentences. Neither familiarity nor decomposability interacted with sentence type for

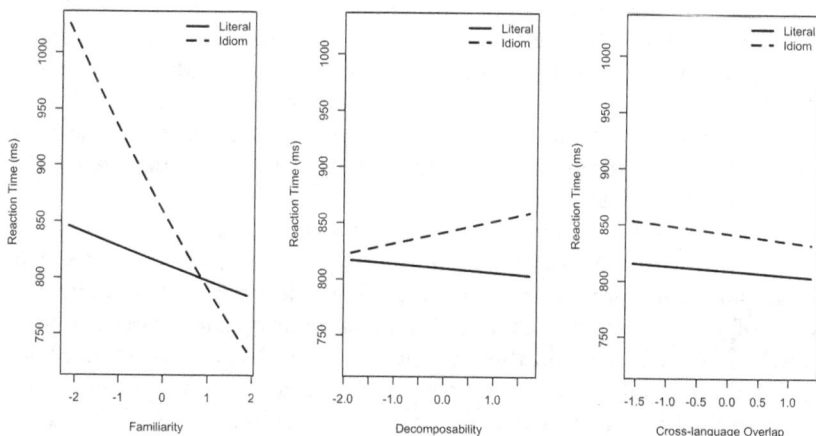

Figure 2. Partial Correct Response Time Effects in Sentences with English Final Nouns for Idiom versus Literal Sentences as a Function of Familiarity (Left), Decomposability (Center), and Cross-Language Overlap (Right)

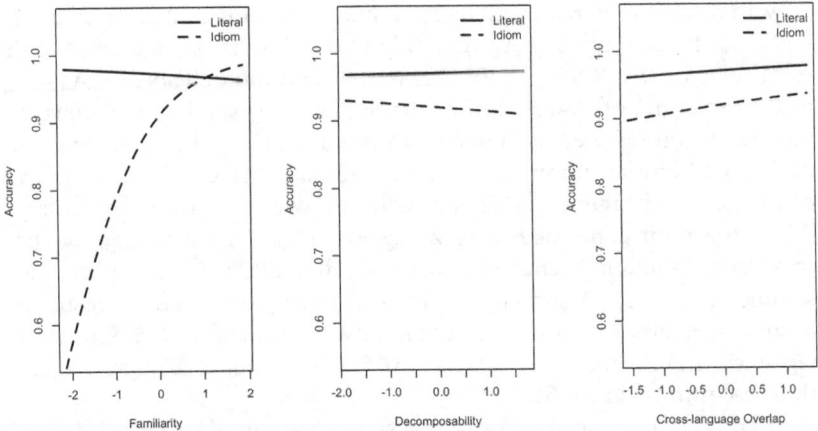

Figure 3. Partial Accuracy Effects in Sentences with English Final Nouns for Idiom versus Literal Sentences, as a Function of Familiarity (Left), Decomposability (Center), and Cross-Language Overlap (Right)

sentences containing French final words (left and center panels of Figure 4). Similarly, the accuracy data showed a significant interaction between sentence type and cross-language overlap ($t = 2.64$, $p < .01$), whereby increased overlap was associated with increased idiom accuracy, thus again reducing the difference between idiom and literal sentences (see third column of Table 6). Unlike the response time data, however, sentence type also interacted with familiarity for sentences containing French final words ($t = -2.60$, $p < .01$). As can been seen in the left panel of Figure 5, increased familiarity led to increased idiom accuracy. Finally, decomposability did not interact with sentence type. The significant interaction with idiom familiarity suggests that there is a substantial direct retrieval component during the comprehension of language-intact idioms in bilinguals.

Taken together, these results are consistent with an extension of the Constraint-Based Model (Libben & Titone, 2008), which posits that bilingual idiom processing is facilitated by factors that modulate the ease of direct retrieval, that is, idiom familiarity and cross-language overlap (cf. García et al., this volume). Specifically, increased familiarity facilitated bilingual idiom processing regardless of whether sentences contained code-switched final words (as seen in the left panels of Figures 2–5). Moreover, increased cross-language overlap facilitated bilingual idiom processing when idioms were presented in sentences that had code-switched final words (as seen in the right panels of Figures 4 and 5), although inspection of the data suggests that this

Table 6. *Effect Sizes (b), Standard Errors (SE), and P-Values for Idiom Effects Linear Mixed Effects Models (Correct Response Time), and Pr(> |z|) Values for Idiom Effects Logistic Linear Mixed Effects Models (Accuracy) When Final Word Is in French*

	Correct Response Times			Accuracy		
Fixed effects	*b*	*SE*	*p*	*b*	*SE*	*Pr(|z|)*
Group (French L1 v. English L1)	0.11	0.01	0.33	−0.10	0.59	0.87
Sentence Type (Idiom v. Literal)	=0.13	0.03	< 0.01	1.18	0.23	< 0.01
Familiarity (scaled)	=0.08	0.04	0.06	1.17	0.36	< 0.01
Cross-Language Overlap (Scaled)	=0.12	0.04	< 0.01	1.03	0.35	< 0.01
Decomposability (Scaled)	=0.01	0.04	0.90	−0.24	0.37	0.52
Group*Sentence Type	−0.01	0.04	0.48	0.02	0.27	0.94
Group*Familiarity	0.08	0.05	0.15	−0.41	0.36	0.25
Sentence Type*Familiarity	0.04	0.02	0.16	−0.63	0.24	0.01
Group*Cross-Language Overlap	=0.01	0.05	0.80	0.31	0.35	0.38
Sentence Type*Cross-Language Overlap	0.06	0.02	0.01	−0.62	0.24	< 0.01
Group*Decomposability	=0.00	0.05	0.99	0.41	0.38	0.28
Sentence Type*Decomposability	0.01	0.02	0.77	0.17	0.25	0.50
Group*Sentence Type*Familiarity	−0.04	0.03	0.19	0.30	0.25	0.23
Group*Sentence Type*Cross-Language Overlap	0.02	0.03	0.47	−0.16	0.24	0.51
Group*Sentence Type*Decomposability	0.00	0.03	0.98	−0.27	0.25	0.28
Control Predictors	*b*	*SE*	*p*	*b*	*SE*	*Pr(|z|)*
Literality (scaled)	−0.03	0.01	0.02	0.49	0.11	< 0.01
(Intercept)	7.11	0.06	< 0.01	0.01	0.41	0.99
Random Effects	**Variance**			**Variance**		
Subject	0.05			1.47		
Item	0.09			9.25		
Subject | Sentence Type	0.01			0.13		
Item | Sentence Type	0.03			4.08		
Residual	0.10			*n/a*		

effect may also be true for non-code-switched sentences. The effects of cross-language overlap and familiarity suggest that there is a substantial direct retrieval component during the comprehension of code-switched idioms in bilinguals.

It is possible that the task used in this preliminary experiment was not sensitive enough to detect an effect of cross-language overlap on non-code-switched sentences for several reasons. First, the majority of bilinguals tested were English L1, thus, they may have had a very high

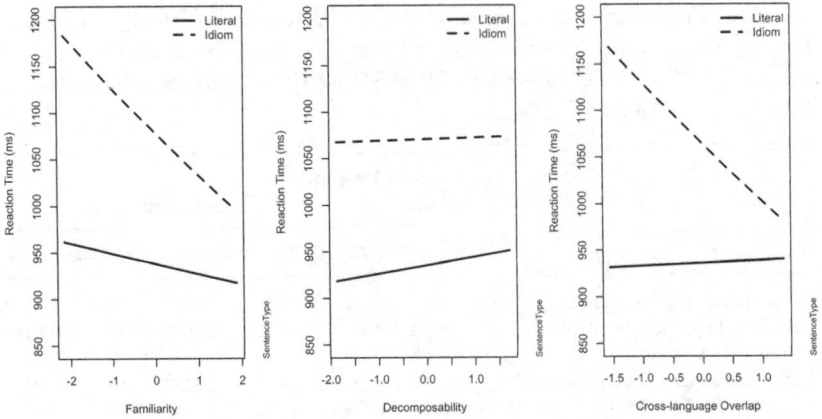

Figure 4. Partial Correct Response Time Effects in Sentences with French Final Nouns for Idiom versus Literal Sentences, as a Function of Familiarity (Left), Decomposability (Center), and Cross-Language Overlap (Right)

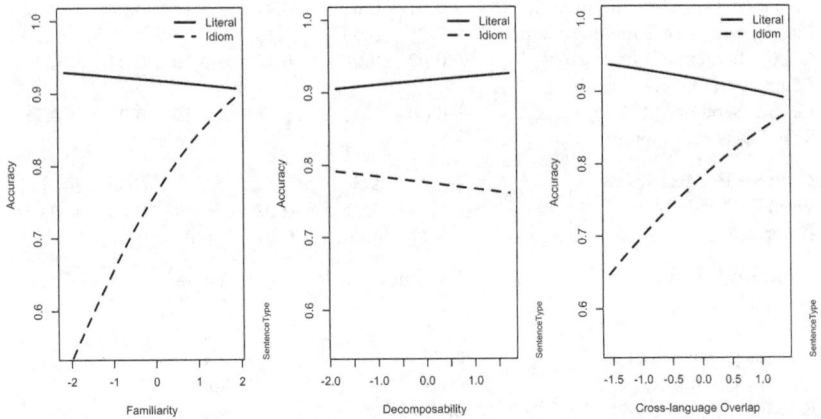

Figure 5. Partial Accuracy Effects in Sentences with French Final Nouns for Idiom versus Literal Sentences, as a Function of Familiarity (Left), Decomposability (Center), and Cross-Language Overlap (Right)

level of familiarity with these English idioms that diluted the effect of cross-language overlap. Second, the task may have lacked sensitivity to detect such effects either because the nature of the judgment decision was too coarse or because the sentences did not require people to interpret the idioms in a specific way (i.e., idiomatically or literally).

Thus, future work that improves upon these limitations might show stronger effects of cross-language overlap. Indeed, such aspects of the task may also relate to why decomposability failed to play a role in any condition and also why there were no significant effects arising from group status (i.e., English vs. French L1).

Summary and Conclusion

In this chapter, we reviewed several factors that are relevant to our understanding of bilingual idiom processing. This included the many ways idioms differ, how idioms have been framed theoretically over the years, and what we currently know about L1 and L2 idiom processing. We also presented data from a preliminary empirical study of bilingual idiom processing that investigates what factors modulate bilingual idiom processing. Taken together, these efforts lead us to the working hypothesis that bilingual idiom processing bears many similarities to monolingual idiom processing and indeed may be explained by the same theoretical approaches. Thus, we believe that bilingual idiom processing has much to gain from an appreciation of the processes involved in monolingual idiom processing and also has much to offer with respect to understanding formulaic and non-formulaic language processing more generally.

We believe that empirical findings to date on both L1 and L2 idiom processing are most consistent with a Constraint-Based Model of Idiom Processing (Libben & Titone, 2008; Titone & Connine, 1999; see also, Sprenger et al., 2006). As previously described, this view asserts that people simultaneously use all available information during comprehension (resulting from direct retrieval and compositional analysis); different kinds of information may be available at different time-courses; and different classes of information interact over time. Thus, assuming that direct retrieval is a fast process that may occur prior to the idiom's offset (Cacciari & Tabossi, 1988; Titone & Connine, 1994b), variables that modulate the ease of direct retrieval will affect the earliest comprehension stages of idiom processing. Thus, the degree to which idioms are familiar to comprehenders, which is presumably a function of how often they are encountered in either the L1 or L2, will have a direct bearing on whether and how information about idioms can be directly retrieved from memory. This information may have different levels of representation. For example, people may have knowledge of the formal co-occurrence properties of idioms, without necessarily knowing their meaning (e.g., they know that *kick the bucket* is a phrase, but may not know that it means *to die* in English). However, what is known about idioms likely also includes information about what the phrase normally refers to, or at the very least, the appropriate places in conversation or discourse when use of the sequence is appropriate.

Distinguishing between these different levels of representation, the formal, the semantic or conceptual, and the pragmatic, are extremely important because idioms, or MWEs generally, can vary dramatically and independently at all of these levels, for both L1 and L2 language users. With respect to the formal properties of idioms, some are rigidly fixed and never appear in varied forms (e.g., *by and large*, *She twiddled her thumbs*, *It rained cats and dogs*), whereas others are highly flexible structurally and indeed function in a slot-filler kind of way (e.g., *She took X to the cleaners*). With respect to the semantic or conceptual properties of idioms, some have multiple phrasal interpretations (e.g., you can literally and figuratively *kick the bucket*), others only have a plausible figurative interpretation (e.g., you can only figuratively *pay through the nose*), and others still have virtually no semantic content independent of pragmatic principles guiding their use (e.g., *by and large*). Finally, as amply demonstrated by the more recent work on MWEs (e.g., Arnon & Cohen-Priva, 2013; Arnon & Snider, 2010; Columbus, 2010, 2012, 2013; Shaoul, 2012; Shaoul & Westbury, 2011; Snider & Arnon, 2012; Tremblay, 2009; Tremblay & Baayen, 2010), multiword sequences that can also be thought of as idiomatic have only a single normal literal interpretation that is very frequently encountered (e.g., conversational statements, such as, *How do you do?* or n-gram sequences such as *at the end*). Indeed, it is quite difficult to draw definitive lines in the sand regarding typologies of MWEs, and of note, many recent papers on MWEs generally include a vast array of types such as idioms of the type used here, conversational statements, or n-grams that reduce to frequently occurring sentence fragments (Arnon & Snider, 2010; Columbus, 2010, 2012, 2013; Shaoul, 2012; Shaoul & Westbury, 2011; Tremblay, 2009; Tremblay & Baayen, 2010).

Idioms have the potential to track the ways in which all aspects of language vary normally over these different levels of linguistic representation, a point that is foundational in recent usage-based approaches that are now becoming increasingly mainstream across psychology and different branches of linguistics (e.g., Bybee, 2006; Goldberg, 1995, 2006; Pierrehumbert, 2001, Tomasello, 2003; Wulff, 2008). For example, Goldberg has nicely illustrated how idiomaticity and the tension between part-whole processing exist at the sub-word and word levels in terms of how morphological units combine (e.g., are words like *unbearable* or *cowboy* morphologically decomposed or retrieved holistically?), idioms with and without slots to be filled (e.g., *get his/her/their goat* vs. *bat out of hell*), to more structurally abstract forms at the syntax/ idiom interface (e.g., *the X-er they have* [some attribute], *the Y-er they* [engage in some action]), to abstract structural forms that many of us would normally think of as non-idiomatic, but nevertheless, may have some level of constructional meaning (e.g., ditransitive forms, such as *She gave him a kiss*). Indeed, when one adopts a usage-based perspective, one proceeds down a road where all forms of language differ at multiple independent levels in terms of how parts accumulate to make wholes and how parts and wholes may be discovered through language use, stored in memory, and retrieved somewhat independently during comprehension and production.

This approach to idioms is well stated in a recent corpus linguistic treatment of idioms by Wulff (2008). According to Wulff, we selectively attend to statistical or distributional information in the linguistic environment that makes form-meaning relationships between linguistic units at any level salient and code this information into long-term memory. Of note, there are many more statistical or distributional links between form and meaning in the linguistic environment than what people may selectively attend to at any given point in time. To provide an example from the traditional idiom-processing literature, we know that native language users readily characterize differences among idioms in decomposability. However, this does not mean that they use this sensitivity to decomposability in the moment while they are processing idiomatic language (e.g., Libben & Titone, 2008; the results of the present study). Moreover, as detailed by many developmental researchers (e.g., Tomasello, 2003; Wray 2002), children may be more likely to attend to certain dimensions of language over others. Specifically, children (and L2 learners) may be more likely than L1 adults to initially selectively attend to the multiword or holistic level rather than the analytic or compositional level. Then, once enough linguistic knowledge is built up in memory, it becomes possible for language learners to induce how lesser-known linguistic parts relate to better known linguistic wholes.

These ideas cohere with a final important point raised by Wulff (2008), which is that idiomaticity is fundamentally a psychological construct that emerges from how people encode or weight different form- or meaning-based linguistic cues in the environment during initial language learning and ongoing life. Thus, an important direction for future work on both L1 and L2 idiom processing, and L1 and L2 language learning generally, is to determine a core set of cues people selectively attend to in linguistic environments that inform their subsequent comprehension and production of language. Some possibilities would likely include both absolute frequency of occurrence in the linguistic environment, as well as more nuanced kinds of conditional frequency that depend on the frequency of particular words in the context of particular constructions versus language generally. For example, the word *twiddled* is highly infrequent in English generally, yet it is highly frequent in the context of co-occurring with the noun phrase, *her thumbs*.

To conclude, while much is known about idiom processing, there are many important new frontiers that are waiting to be explored, for which the study of bilinguals will be crucially important. What we believe is essential, however, is a much wider view of what idioms are and the interdependent dimensions along which they vary for L1 and L2 learners and monolingual and bilingual adults. Indeed, as the field starts thinking about idiomaticity as foundational to language proper, our models of L1 and L2 idiom processing will inevitably grow more unified with general models of language. As well, we will likely make greater advances in applications of these models to promoting L1 and L2 learning, understanding how L1 and L2 interact in the bilingual brain, and discovering new insights about how language processing can break down in pathological populations.

List of Keywords

Bilingual idiom comprehension, Cloze probability, Code-switched condition, Cognate facilitation, Compositional models, Constraint-Based Model of Idiom Processing, Conventional idioms, Cross-language similarity, Declarative learning, Decomposability, Direct Access Model, Early-stage processing, Ecological validity, Facilitative effects, Familiarity, Formulaic language, Global decomposability, Hybrid Model of Idiom Processing, Late bilinguals, Lexical decision task, Literal meaning, Literal plausibility, Meaningfulness judgment task, Multiword Expressions (MWEs), Nondecomposable idioms, Offline meaningfulness judgments, Predictable idioms, Procedural learning, Semantic analysis, Semantic decomposability, Semantically decomposable, Syntactic flexibility

Thought Questions

1. Are idioms and other multiword expressions merely special cases of language or do they represent the ground upon which all of human linguistic knowledge is based?

2. What are the many different ways that idioms and multiword expressions generally can vary, and which dimensions may be related to each other or independent?
3. How easy is it to identify idioms and multiword expressions generally in our environment? Would this be more or less difficult to do in an L1 or L2 and why?
4. In your L1 or L2, do you ever hear an idiom or other multiword sequence that you recognize as a unit but do not understand? What strategies do you use to try to interpret its meaning?
5. When using your L2, how often do you explicitly use knowledge from your L1 to interpret idioms or multiword sequences that you read or hear? Are there other cues that you use to help make sense of novel idioms or multiword sequences?

Suggested Student Research Projects

1. *Class idiom database.* In groups, find examples of idioms or other multiword expressions from as many different languages as you can. If there aren't many other languages in your class, make a list of languages and assign one language to each person. That person should then research idioms or common sayings in that language using the Internet or family and friends in the community. Bring together all the idioms you have found and see if they have a meaning equivalent in your L1, using the ratings of Table 1 on page 183. For example, if they do not have a meaning equivalent, rate them as "1"; if they have a meaning equivalent, rate how closely the words relate from the L1 to the L2. Compile the rated results into one worksheet. Then compile the results from across the class into one large worksheet. How many languages are represented? How many idioms occur in more than two languages? How closely are the idioms related from the L1 to the L2?
2. *Spot the idiom.* Find bilinguals who speak at least two particular languages (e.g., English and French) and collect at least 3–5 page-length articles from different sources for each language (e.g., newspapers, magazines). Then, ask the bilinguals to read each paragraph and circle as many idioms or multiword expressions as they can in each language sample. How successful are these bilinguals at doing this task in their L1 or L2? Do differences among your bilingual group in how proficient they are in each language, or other potentially relevant measures, alter the results?

Related Internet Sites

Fun list of Spanish and English idioms: www.tomisimo.org/
idioms

Idiom and Bilingual Research Conducted in Our Laboratory:
www.debratitone.org

Interesting Idiom Translation Tool: http://expressions.ccdmd.
qc.ca/index.html

Suggested Further Readings

Allen, D., & Conklin, K. (2013). Cross-linguistic similarity and task
demands in Japanese-English bilingual processing. *PLOS one.* Retrieved
from: www.plosone.org/article/info%3Adoi%2F10.1371%2Fjournal.
pone.0072631

Charteris-Black, J. (2002). Second language figurative proficiency:
A comparative study of Malay and English. *Applied Linguistics, 23,* 104–133.

Cieślicka, A.B., & Heredia, R.R. (2011). Hemispheric asymmetries in processing
L1 and L2 idioms: Effects of salience and context. *Brain and Language, 116,*
136–150.

Irujo, S. (1993). Steering clear: Avoidance in the production of idioms.
International Review of Applied Linguistics in Language Teaching, 31, 205–219.

Laufer, B. (2000). Avoidance of idioms in a second language: The effect of
L1-L2 degree of similarity. *Studia Linguistica, 54,* 186–196.

Libben, M., & Titone, D. (2008). The multidetermined nature of idiom
processing. *Memory & Cognition, 36,* 1103–1121.

Martin-Jones, M., Blackledge, A., & Creese, A. (Eds.). (2012). *The Routledge
handbook of multilingualism.* Oxford/New York: Routledge.

REFERENCES

Abel, B. (2003). English idioms in the first language and second language
lexicon: A dual representation approach. *Second Language Research, 19,*
329–358.

Altarriba, J., Kroll, J., Sholl, A., & Rayner, K. (1996). The influence of lexical
and conceptual constraints on reading mixed-language sentences: Evidence
from eye fixations and naming times. *Perception and Psychophysics, 63,*
875–890.

Andreou, G., Vlachos, F., & Andreou, E. (2005). Affecting factors in second
language learning. *Journal of Psycholinguistic Research, 34,* 429–438.

Arnon, I., & Cohen-Priva, U. (2013). More than words: The effect of multi-word
frequency and constituency on phonetic duration [Special Issue]. *Parsimony
and redundancy in usage-based models of linguistic knowledge, Language and
Speech, 56,* 349–371.

Arnon, I., & Snider, N. (2010). More than words: Frequency effects for
multi-word phrases. *Journal of Memory and Language, 62,* 67–82.

Atwood, M. (1976). *Lady Oracle*. Toronto: McClelland & Stewart.

Bannard, C., & Matthews, D. (2008). Stored word sequences in language learning: The effect of familiarity on children's repetition of four-word combinations. *Psychological Science, 19*, 241–248.

Barr D., Levy, R., Scheepers, C., & Tily, H. (2013). Random effects structure for confirmatory hypothesis testing: Keep it maximal. *Journal of Memory and Language, 68*, 255–278.

Bates, D.M., & Bolker, B. (2013). lme4: Linear mixed-effects modeling using S4 classes R package [Computer Software]. Vienna, Austria: R Foundation for Statistical Computing. Available online at: http://CRAN.R-project.org/package=lme4 (R package version 0.999999-2).

Bobrow, S., & Bell, S. (1973). On catching on to idiomatic expressions. *Memory & Cognition, 1*, 343–346.

Boers, F., Eyckmans, J., Kappel, J., Stengers, H., & Demecheleer, M. (2006). Formulaic sequences and perceived oral proficiency: Putting a lexical approach to the test. *Language Teaching Research, 10*, 245–261.

Bortfeld, H. (1998). *A cross-linguistic analysis of idiom comprehension by native and non-native speakers* (Unpublished doctoral dissertation). State University of New York, Stony Brook, NY.

Burt, J. (1992). Against the lexical representation of idioms. *Canadian Journal of Psychology/Revue Canadienne De Psychologie, 46*, 582–605.

Bybee, J. (2006). From usage to grammar: The mind's response to repetition. *Language, 82*, 711–733.

Cacciari, C., & Glucksberg, S. (1991). Understanding idiomatic expressions: The contribution of word meanings. In G.B. Simpson (Ed.), *Understanding word and sentence* (pp. 217–240). Amsterdam: Elsevier.

Cacciari, C., Padovani, R., & Corradini, P. (2007). Exploring the relationship between individuals' speed of processing and their comprehension of spoken idioms. *European Journal of Cognitive Psychology, 19*, 417–445.

Cacciari, C., & Tabossi, P. (1988). The comprehension of idioms. *Journal of Memory and Language, 27*, 668–683.

Caillies, S. (2009). Descriptions of French idiomatic expressions: Familiarity, literality, compositionality predictability, and knowledge of meaning. *Année Psychologique, 109*, 463–508.

Caillies, S., & Butcher, K. (2007). Processing of idiomatic expressions: Evidence for a new hybrid view. *Metaphor and Symbol, 22*, 79–108.

Carpenter, P., Miyake, A., & Just, M. (1995). Language comprehension: Sentence and discourse Processing. *Annual Review of Psychology, 46*, 91–120.

Charteris-Black, J. (2002). Second language figurative proficiency: A comparative study of Malay and English. *Applied Linguistics, 23*, 104–133.

Chomsky, N. (1965). *Aspects of the theory of syntax*. Cambridge, MA: The MIT Press.

(1981). Principles and parameters in syntactic theory. In N. Hornstein & D. Lightfoot (Eds.), *Explanation in linguistics: The logical problem of language acquisition* (pp. 32–75). London: Longman.

Cieślicka, A. (2006). Literal salience in on-line processing of idiomatic expressions by second language learners. *Second Language Research, 22,* 115–144.

   (2012). Do nonnative language speakers chew the fat and spill the beans with different brain hemispheres? Investigating idiom decomposability with the divided visual field paradigm. *Journal of Psycholinguistic Research.* doi: 10.1007/s10936-012-9232-4.

Cieślicka, A.B., & Heredia, R.R. (2011). Hemispheric asymmetries in processing L1 and L2 idioms: Effects of salience and context. *Brain & Language, 116,* 136–150.

Columbus, G. (2010). Processing MWUs: Are different types of MWUs psycholinguistically valid? An eye-tracking study. In D. Wood (Ed.), *Perspectives on formulaic language in communication and acquisition* (pp. 194–210). New York: Continuum.

   (2012). An analysis of the processing of multiword units in sentence reading and unit presentation using eye movement data: Implications for theories of MWUs (Unpliblished doctoral dissertation). University of Alberta, Canada.

   (2013). In support of multiword unit classifications: Corpus and human rating data validate phraseological classifications of three different multiword unit types. *Yearbook of Phraseology, 4,* 23–44.

Conklin, K., & Schmitt, N. (2008). Formulaic sequences: Are they processed more quickly than nonformulaic language by native and nonnative speakers. *Applied Linguistics, 29,* 72–89.

Cowie, A. (1992). Multiword lexical units and communicative language teaching. In P. Arnaud & H. Béjoint (Eds.), *Vocabulary and applied linguistics* (pp.1–12). London: Macmillan.

Croft, W. (2001). *Radical construction grammar: Syntactic theory in typological perspective.* Oxford,UK: Oxford University Press.

Cronk, B., Lima, S., & Schweigert, W. (1993). Idioms in sentences: Effects of frequency, literalness, and familiarity. *Journal of Psycholinguistic Research, 22,* 59–82.

Cronk, B., & Schweigert, W. (1992). The Comprehension of Idioms: The effects of familiarity, literalness, and usage. *Applied Psycholinguistics, 3,* 131–146.

Cutting, J., & Bock, K. (1997). That's the way the cookie bounces: Syntactic and semantic components of experimentally elicited idiom blends. *Memory & Cognition, 25,* 57–71.

Dijkstra, T., Grainger, J., & Van Heuven, W. (1999). Recognition of cognates and interlingual homographs: The neglected role of phonology. *Journal of Memory and Language, 41,* 496–518.

Duchek, J., Balota, D., Ferraro, F., Gernsbacher, M., Faust, M., & Connor, L. (1992). The inhibition of irrelevant information in young and older adults. *International Journal of Psychology, 27,* 35–35.

Durrant, P., & Schmitt, N. (2010). Adult learners' retention of collocations from exposure. *Second Language Research, 26,* 163–188.

Ellis, N.C., Simpson-Vlach, R., & Maynard, C. (2008). Formulaic language in native and second language speakers: Psycholinguistics, corpus linguistics, and TESOL. *TESOL Quarterly, 42,* 375–396.

Eskildsen, S. (2009). Constructing another language: Usage-based linguistics in second language acquisition. *Applied Linguistics, 30,* 335–357.

Everaert, M., van der Linden, E-J., Schenk, A., & Schreuder, R. (Eds.). (1995). *Idioms: Structural and psychological perspectives.* Hillsdale, NJ, England: Lawrence Erlbaum Associates.

Fanari, R., Cacciari, C., & Tabossi, P. (2010). The role of idiom length and context in spoken idiom comprehension. *European Journal of Cognitive Psychology, 22,* 321–334.

Faust, M., & Gernsbacher, M. (1996). Cerebral mechanisms for suppression of inappropriate information during sentence comprehension. *Brain & Language, 53,* 234–259.

Fraser, B. (1970). Idioms within a transformational grammar. *Foundations of Language, 6,* 22–42.

Gatbonton, E., & Segalowitz, N. (1988). Creative automatization: Principles for promoting fluency within a communicative framework. *TESOL Quarterly, 22,* 473–492.

Gernsbacher, M., & Faust, M. (1991). The mechanism of suppression: A component of general comprehension skill. *Journal of Experimental Psychology: Learning, Memory, and Cognition, 17,* 245–262.

Gernsbacher, M., Varner, K., & Faust, M. (1990). Investigating differences in general comprehension skill. *Journal of Experimental Psychology: Learning, Memory, and Cognition, 16,* 430–445.

Gibbs, R. (1980). Spilling the beans on understanding and memory for idioms in conversation. *Memory & Cognition, 8,* 149–156.

(1992). What do idioms really mean? *Journal of Memory and Language, 31,* 485–506.

Gibbs, R., & Nayak, N. (1989). Psycholinguistic studies on the syntactic behavior of idioms. *Cognitive Psychology, 21,* 100–138.

Gibbs, R., Nayak, N., Bolton, J., & Keppel, M. (1989). Speakers' assumptions about the lexical flexibility of idioms. *Memory & Cognition, 17,* 58–68.

Gibbs, R., Nayak, N., & Cutting, C. (1989). How to kick the bucket and not decompose: Analyzability and idiom processing. *Journal of Memory and Language, 28,* 576–593.

Goldberg, A. (1995). *Constructions.* Chicago: University of Chicago Press.

(2006). *Constructions at work: The nature of generalization in language.* Oxford, UK: Oxford University Press.

Gonnerman, L., & Hayes, C. (2005). The professor chewed the students out: Effects of dependency, length, and adjacency on word order preferences in sentences with verb particle constructions. In *Proceedings of the Twenty-Seventh Annual Conference of the Cognitive Science Society* (pp. 785–790). Mahwah, NJ: Lawrence Erlbaum Associates.

Gunter, T., Wagner, S., & Friederici A. (2003). Working memory and lexical ambiguity resolution as revealed by ERPs: A difficult case for activation theories. *Journal of Cognitive Neuroscience, 15,* 643–657.

Hamblin, J., & Gibbs, R. (1999). Why you can't kick the bucket as you slowly die: Verbs in idiom comprehension. *Journal of Psycholinguistic Research, 28*, 25–39.

Heredia, R.R., & Altarriba, J. (2001). Bilingual language mixing: Why do bilinguals code-switch? *Current Directions in Psychological Science, 10*, 164–168.

Hummel, K. (2009). Aptitude, phonological memory, and second language proficiency in nonnovice adult learners. *Applied Psycholinguistics, 30*, 225–249.

Irujo, S. (1993). Steering clear: Avoidance in the production of idioms. *International Review of Applied Linguistics in Language Teaching, 31*, 205–219.

Jackendoff, R. (1995). The boundaries of the lexicon. In M. Everaert, E-J. van der Linden, A. Schenk, & R. Schreuder (Eds.), *Idioms: Structural and psychological perspectives* (pp. 133–165). Hillsdale, NJ: Lawrence Erlbaum Associates.

(1997). *The architecture of the language faculty.* Cambridge, MA: The MIT Press.

(2003). *Foundations of language: Brain, meaning, grammar, evolution.* New York: Oxford University Press.

Jiang, N., & Nekrasova, T. (2007). The processing of formulaic sequences by second language speakers. *Modern Language Journal, 91*, 433–445.

Kecskes, I. (2000). A cognitive-pragmatic approach to situation-bound utterances. *Journal of Pragmatics, 32*, 605–625.

Knobloch, C. (2009). Once more: Particle verb constructions. *Zeitschrift Fur Germanistische Linguistik, 37*, 544–564.

Kučera, H., & Francis, W. (1967). *Computational analysis of present day American English.* Providence, RI: Brown University Press.

Laufer, B. (2000). Avoidance of idioms in a second language: The effect of L1-L2 degree of similarity. *Studia Linguistica, 54*, 186–196.

Lemhöfer, K., & Dijkstra, T. (2004). Recognizing cognates and interlingual homographs: Effects of code similarity in language-specific and generalized lexical decision. *Memory & Cognition, 32*, 533–550.

Li, J., & Schmitt, N. (2009). The acquisition of lexical phrases in academic writing: A longitudinal case study. *Journal of Second Language Writing, 18*, 85–102.

Libben, M., & Titone, D. (2008). The multidetermined nature of idiom processing. *Memory & Cognition, 36*, 1103–1121.

(2009). Bilingual lexical access in context: Evidence from eye movements during reading. *Journal of Experimental Psychology: Learning, Memory, and Cognition, 35*, 381–390.

Marantz, A. (2005). Generative linguistics within the cognitive neuroscience of language. *The Linguistic Review, 22*, 429–445.

Matlock, T., & Heredia, R.R. (2002). Understanding phrasal verbs in monolinguals and bilinguals. In R.R. Heredia & J. Altarriba (Eds.), *Bilingual sentence processing* (pp. 251–274). Amsterdam, Netherlands: Elsevier.

McGinnis, M. (2002). On the systematic aspect of idioms. *Linguistic Inquiry, 33*, 665–672.

McGlone, M., Glucksberg, S., & Cacciari, C. (1994). Semantic productivity and idiom comprehension. *Discourse Processes*, *17*, 167–190.

Miyake, A., Just, M., & Carpenter, P. (1994). Working-memory constraints on the resolution of lexical ambiguity: Maintaining multiple interpretations in neutral contexts. *Journal of Memory and Language*, *33*, 175–202.

Nattinger, J., & De Carrico, J. (1989). Lexical phrases, speech acts and teaching conversation: Vocabulary acquisition. *AILA*, *6*, 118–139.

Nattinger, J., & DeCarrico, J. (1992). *Lexical phrases and language teaching*. New York: Oxford University Press.

Nekrasova, T. (2009). English L1 and L2 speakers' knowledge of lexical bundles. *Language Learning*, *59*, 647–686.

New, B., Pallier, C., Brysbaert, M., & Ferrand, L. (2004). Lexique 2: A new French lexical database. *Behavior Research Methods, Instruments, & Computers*, *36*, 516–524. http://www.lexique.org

Nippold, M., & Duthie, J. (2003). Mental imagery and idiom comprehension: A comparison of school-age children and adults. *Journal of Speech Language & Hearing Research*, *46*, 788–799.

Nippold, M., & Taylor, C. (2002). Judgments of idiom familiarity and transparency: A comparison of children and adolescents. *Journal of Speech Language & Hearing Research*, *45*, 384–391.

Nippold, M., Taylor, C., & Baker, J. (1996). Idiom understanding in Australian youth: A cross-cultural comparison. *Journal of Speech Language & Hearing Research*, *39*, 442–447.

Nunberg, G. (1978). *The pragmatics of reference*. Bloomington: Indiana University Linguistics.

Nunberg, G., Sag, I., & Wasow, T. (1994). Idioms. *Language*, *70*, 491–538.

Paradis, J. (2010). Bilingual children's acquisition of English verb morphology: Effects of language exposure, structure complexity, and task type. *Language Learning*, *60*, 651–680.

Paradis, J., Nicoladis, E., & Crago, M. (2007). French-English bilingual children's acquisition of the past tense. *Proceedings of the 31st Annual Boston University Conference on language development* Vols 1 and 2 (pp. 497–507). Somerville, MA: Cascadilla Press.

Paradis, M. (2008a). Bilingual effects are not unique, only more salient. *Bilingualism: Language & Cognition*, *11*,181–183.

(2008b). Bilingualism and neuropsychiatric disorders. *Journal of Neurolinguistics*, *21*, 199–230.

Pawley, A., & Syder, F. (1983). Two puzzles for linguistic theory: Nativelike selection and nativelike fluency. In J. Richards & R. Schmidt (Eds.), *Language & Communication* (pp. 191–226). New York: Longman.

Peterson, R., Burgess, C., Dell, G., & Eberhard, K. (2001). Dissociation between syntactic and semantic processing during idiom comprehension. *Journal of Experimental Psychology: Learning, Memory, and Cognition*, *27*, 1223–1237.

Popiel, S., & McRae, K. (1988). The figurative and literal senses of idioms, or all idioms are not used equally. *Journal of Psycholinguistic Research, 17,* 475–487.

Prado, E., & Ullman, M. (2009). Can imageability help us draw the line between storage and composition? *Journal of Experimental Psychology: Learning, Memory, and Cognition, 35,* 849–866.

R Development Core Team. (2013). *R: A language and environment for statistical computing.* (Version 3.0.0) [Computer Software]. Vienna, Austria: R Foundation for Statistical Computing.

Robinson, P. (2005). Cognitive abilities, chunk-strength, and frequency effects in implicit artificial grammar and incidental L2 learning: Replications of Reber, Walkenfeld, and Hernstadt (1991) and Knowlton and Squire (1996) and their relevance for SLA. *Studies in Second Language Acquisition, 27,* 235–268.

Rossiter, M., Derwing, T., Manimtim, L., & Thomson, R. (2010). Oral fluency: The neglected component in the communicative language classroom. *Canadian Modern Language Review/La Revue Canadienne Des Langues Vivantes, 66,* 583–606.

Rysiewicz, J. (2008a). Cognitive profiles of (un)successful FL learners: A cluster analytical study. *Modern Language Journal, 92,* 87–99.

    (2008b). Measuring foreign language learning aptitude. Polish adaptation of the modern language aptitude test by Carroll and Sapon. *Poznań Studies in Contemporary Linguistics, 44,* 569–595.

Schmitt, N. (2004). *Formulaic sequences: Acquisition, processing, and use.* Philadelphia, PA: John Benjamins.

Schneider, W., Eschman, A., & Zuccolotto, A. (2002). *E-Prime: A user's guide.* Pittsburgh: Psychology Software Tools.

Schwartz, A., Kroll, J., & Diaz, M. (2007). Reading words in Spanish and English: Mapping orthography to phonology in two languages. *Language & Cognitive Processes, 22,* 106–129.

Schweigert, W. (1986). The comprehension of familiar and less familiar idioms. *Journal of Psycholinguistic Research, 15,* 33–45.

    (1991). The muddy waters of idiom comprehension. *Journal of Psycholinguistic Research, 20,* 305–314.

Schweigert, W., & Cronk, B. (1993). Ratings of the familiarity of idioms figurative meanings and the likelihood of literal meanings among United States college-students. *Current Psychology-Research & Reviews, 11,* 325–345.

Schweigert, W., & Moates, D. (1988). Familiar idiom comprehension. *Journal of Psycholinguistic Research, 17,* 281–296.

Segalowitz, N. (2010). *Cognitive bases of second language fluency.* New York: Routledge.

Shaoul, C., & Westbury, C. (Eds.). (2011). Formulaic sequences: Do they exist and do they matter? Methodological and analytic frontiers in lexical research (Part II) [Special issue]. *The Mental Lexicon, 6,* 1.

Shaoul, C. (2012). *The processing of lexical sequences* (Unpublished doctoral dissertation). University of Alberta, Canada.

Sinclair, J. (1991). *Corpus, concordance, collocation*. Oxford, UK: Oxford University Press.

Siyanova-Chanturia, A., Conklin, K., & Schmitt, N. (2011). Adding more fuel to the fire: An eye-tracking study of idiom processing by native and non-native speakers. *Second Language Research, 27,* 251–272.

Siyanova, A., & Schmitt, N. (2007). Native and nonnative use of multi-word vs. one-word verbs. *International Review of Applied Linguistics in Language Teaching, 45,* 119–139.

Skehan, P. (1991). Individual differences in second language learning. *Studies in Second Language Acquisition, 13,* 275–298.

(2009). Modelling second language performance: Integrating complexity, accuracy, fluency, and lexis. *Applied Linguistics, 30,* 510–532.

Snider, N., & Arnon, I. (2012). A unified lexicon and grammar? Compositional and non-compositional phrases in the lexicon. In D. Divjak & S. Gries (Eds.), *Frequency effects in language* (pp. 127–264). Berlin: Mouton de Gruyter.

Sparks, R., Patton, J., Ganschow, L., & Humbach, N. (2009a). Long-term crosslinguistic transfer of skills from L1 to L2. *Language Learning, 59,* 203–243.

(2009b). Long-term relationships among early first language skills, second language aptitude, second language affect, and later second language proficiency. *Applied Psycholinguistics, 30,* 725–755.

Sprenger, S., Levelt, W., & Kempen, G. (2006). Lexical access during the production of idiomatic phrases. *Journal of Memory and Language, 54,* 161–184.

Steinel, M., Hulstijn, J., & Steinel, W. (2007). Second language idiom learning in a paired-associate paradigm: Effects of direction of learning, direction of testing, idiom imageability, and idiom transparency. *Studies in Second Language Acquisition, 29,* 449–484.

Swinney, D., & Cutler, A. (1979). The access and processing of idiomatic expressions. *Journal of Verbal Learning and Verbal Behavior, 18,* 522–534.

Tabossi, P., Fanari, R., & Wolf, K. (2005). Spoken idiom recognition: Meaning retrieval and word expectancy. *Journal of Psycholinguistic Research, 34,* 465–495.

(2008). Processing idiomatic expressions: Effects of semantic compositionality. *Journal of Experimental Psychology: Learning, Memory, and Cognition, 34,* 313–327.

Tabossi, P., Wolf, K., & Koterle, S. (2008). Idiom syntax: Idiosyncratic or principled? *International Journal of Psychology, 43,* 415–415.

Tabossi, P., & Zardon, F. (1993). The activation of idiomatic meaning in spoken language comprehension. In C. Cacciari & P. Tabossi, (Eds.), *Idioms: Processing, structure, and interpretation* (pp. 145–162). Hillsdale, NJ: Lawrence Erlbaum Associates.

Titone, D., & Connine, C. (1994a). Comprehension of idiomatic expressions: Effects of predictability and literality. *Journal of Experimental Psychology: Learning, Memory, and Cognition, 20,* 1126–1138.

(1994b). Descriptive norms for 171 idiomatic expressions: Familiarity, compositionality, predictability, and literality. *Metaphor and Symbolic Activity*, *9*, 247–270.

(1999). On the compositional and noncompositional nature of idiomatic expressions. *Journal of Pragmatics*, *31*, 1655–1674.

Titone, D., Libben, M., Mercier, J., Whitford, V., & Pivneva, I. (2011). Bilingual lexical access during L1 sentence reading: The effects of L2 knowledge, semantic constraint and L1-L2 intermixing. *Journal of Experimental Psychology: Learning, Memory, and Cognition 37*, 1412–1431.

Tomasello, M. (2003). *Constructing a language: A usage-based theory of language acquisition*. Cambridge, MA/London: Harvard University Press.

Tremblay, A. (2009). *Processing advantages of lexical bundles: Evidence from self-paced reading, word and sentence recall, and free recall with event-related brain potential recordings* (Unpublished doctoral dissertation). University of Alberta, Canada.

Tremblay, A., & Baayen, R.H. (2010). Holistic processing of regular four-word sequences: A behavioral and ERP study of the effects of structure, frequency, and probability on immediate free recall. In D. Wood (Ed.), *Perspectives on formulaic language: Acquisition and communication* (pp. 151–173). London and New York: Continuum.

Tremblay, A., Derwing, B.L., Libben, G., & Westbury, C. (2011). Processing advantages of lexical bundles: Evidence from self-paced reading experiments, word and sentence recall tasks, and off-line semantic ratings. *Language Learning*, *61*, 569–613.

Tremblay, A., & Tucker, B.V. (2011). The effects of n-gram probabilistic measures on the recognition and production of four-word sequences. *The Mental Lexicon*, *6*, 302–324.

Ullman, M. (2001). The declarative/procedural model of lexicon and grammar. *Journal of Psycholinguistic Research*, *30*, 37–69.

(2006) The declarative/procedural model and the shallow structure hypothesis. *Applied Psycholinguistics*, *27*, 97–105.

Vanlancker-Sidtis, D. (2003). Auditory recognition of idioms by native and nonnative speakers of English: It takes one to know one. *Applied Psycholinguistics*, *24*, 45–57.

Vespignani, F., Canal, P., Molinaro, N., Fonda, S., & Cacciari, C. (2010). Predictive mechanisms in idiom comprehension. *Journal of Cognitive Neuroscience*, *22*, 1682–1700.

Wagner, S., Gunter, T., & Friederici, A. (2000). Working memory and the processing of ambiguous words in compounds. *Journal of Cognitive Neuroscience*, *35*, 125–125.

Wagner, S., & Gunter, T. (2004). Determining inhibition: Individual differences in the 'lexicon context' trade-off during lexical ambiguity resolution in working memory. *Experimental Psychology*, *51*, 290–299.

Weinert, R. (1995). The role of formulaic language in second language acquisition: A review. *Applied Linguistics*, *16*, 180–205.

Wood, D. (2006). Uses and functions of formulaic sequences in second language speech: An exploration of the foundations of fluency. *Canadian Modern Language Review/La Revue Canadienne Des Langues Vivantes, 63*, 13–33.

Wray, A. (2000). Formulaic sequences in second language teaching: Principle and practice. *Applied Linguistics, 21*, 463–489.

(2002). *Formulaic language and the lexicon.* Cambridge, UK: Cambridge University Press.

Wulff, S. (2008). *Rethinking idiomaticity: A usage-based approach.* London/New York: Continuum.

7   Idiom Acquisition and Processing by Second/ Foreign Language Learners

Anna B. Cieślicka
Texas A&M International University

ABSTRACT

Acquiring competence in figurative language is a challenging aspect of the second/foreign (L2) language learning process. A crucial component of figurative competence is the knowledge of idiomatic expressions. The present chapter focuses on the acquisition and processing of idioms by L2 learners. It first discusses the different dimensions along which idiomatic expressions vary and reviews theoretical accounts of the representation and processing of idioms by native language (L1) and L2 speakers. A parasitic mechanism of L2 idiom acquisition is suggested as the most plausible cognitive strategy in building the L2 figurative competence. Factors affecting L1 idiom processing such as idiom literal plausibility, semantic decomposability, salience, and context are analyzed, and their potential role in L2 idiomatic processing is discussed. In addition, factors uniquely relevant for L2 idiom acquisition and processing, such as cross-language similarity, are identified.

Keywords: foreign language idioms, lexical acquisition, parasitism, second language figurative competence, second language idiom processing

We have the ability to speak in riddles ... We call these special riddles idioms ... [W]e use them so readily that we are usually unaware of their special character-unless we have the misfortune not to be a native speaker (Johnson-Laird, 1993, p. x)

The quote above captures the prevalence of figurative language in everyday communication. It also points to an important contrast between native and non-native speakers: While the former use figurative language effortlessly and mostly unconsciously, for non-native speakers, idioms often constitute a major stumbling block on their way toward achieving a full mastery in the foreign language or second language (L2). Note that the terms "second language" and "foreign language" are used interchangeably throughout this chapter; however, the two denote different linguistic environments. Whereas second language refers to the situation when the learner's target language is used extensively in the community in which he or she lives (e.g., learning English in England), in the foreign language environment, the target language is not spoken in the learner's community (e.g., learning English in Poland). In addition, second language learners who learn an L2 have different native language (L1) backgrounds, whereas foreign language learners all share the same L1 and they learn the L2 in a formal (classroom-based) setting (Kecskes & Papp, 2000). Pervasiveness of figurative language is best reflected in the estimates concerning the number of figurative expressions that an average native speaker produces on a daily basis. Accordingly, a person utters approximately 4.7 million novel and 21.4 million frozen (i.e., conventional) metaphors over a sixty-year lifespan (e.g., Pollio, Barlow, Fine, & Pollio, 1977). Jackendoff (1997) noted that the number of fixed expressions in a native speaker's mental lexicon is roughly similar to that of single words. Given those figures, Searle's (1975) informal rule of conversation, *Speak idiomatically unless there is some reason not to do so*, should come as no surprise.

Thus, it follows that figurative competence is an important component of L2 fluency and that, in order to be proficient in a foreign/second language, an L2 learner needs to build a large repertoire of conventionalized expressions such as idioms, collocations, compounds, phrasal verbs, and other so-called multiword lexical items. Acquiring figurative competence in L2 is a very difficult and slow process (e.g., Alexander, 1987; Boers, 2000; Charteris-Black, 2002; Fernando, 1996; Gairns & Redman, 1986; Kövecses & Szabo, 1996; Lattey, 1986; Lazar, 1996; Littlemore, 2001; Low, 1988; McCarthy, 1990; Moon, 1997; Yorio, 1989; Zughoul, 1991). L2 learners' knowledge of idiomatic expressions lags significantly behind their general L2 vocabulary proficiency (Steinel, Hustijn, & Steinel, 2007), and their performance in formal written language displays a very low level of collocational knowledge (i.e., knowledge of the sequences of words that frequently occur together) when compared to native speaker writing (Howarth, 1998). Danesi (1992) claims that lack of metaphorical competence is a major reason why foreign language learners fail to attain native-like fluency and that competence in using figurative language is inadequate in typical classroom language learners even after three or four years of foreign language learning (see also Kecskes & Papp, 2000).

Idioms are one of the most frequent figurative language tropes; hence, their mastery constitutes an essential component of L2 learners' figurative competence. Idioms have been traditionally defined as multiword items whose figurative interpretation cannot be derived from the compositional analysis of the individual words (e.g., Chafe, 1970; Fraser, 1970; Katz, 1973; Makkai, 1972). On this account, idioms were therefore considered to be *dead metaphors* that might have been innovative when they were first coined, but with time lost their novelty and became *frozen*, in the sense that it is impossible to determine their original metaphorical motivation. For example, unless a person possesses specific knowledge about the origin of the idiom *to bark up the wrong tree* (referring to the practice of raccoon hunting with the aid of dogs where occasionally dogs would bark at the bottom of the tree thinking mistakenly that the raccoon is hiding there), there is no way the intended meaning of the idiom (i.e., waste one's efforts by pursuing the wrong thing or path) could be inferred from the compositional analysis of its constituent words.

Idiom Compositionality in L1 Processing Theories

The traditional definition of idioms is reflected in early psycholinguistic theories proposing how native speakers store idioms in their mental dictionary and process them in the course of language comprehension. Those *noncompositional* theories of idiom processing, also referred to as *direct look-up* models (Glucksberg, 1993), assume that idiom meanings are arbitrary and understood by retrieving the meaning of an idiomatic phrase as a whole, rather than by processing their component parts. The major noncompositional models include the *Idiom List Hypothesis* (Bobrow & Bell, 1973), the *Lexical Representation Hypothesis* (Swinney & Cutler, 1979), and the *Direct Access Model* (Gibbs, 1980, 1985, 1993, 2002). Briefly, under those accounts, idioms are retrieved holistically from a special idiom lexicon (the Idiom List Hypothesis), or from a general word lexicon, where they are stored as long words (the Lexical Representation Hypothesis). Literal analysis of idiom constituents is unnecessary and not undertaken, because figurative meanings can be accessed directly (the Direct Access Model). Alternatively, literal analysis is viewed as obligatory, in that literal meaning of an idiom needs to be rejected as inappropriate before retrieving its figurative meaning (the Idiom List Hypothesis), or the two meanings (literal and figurative) are processed simultaneously (the Lexical Representation Hypothesis).

A number of problems have emerged with the noncompositional view of idiom processing, a major one being its inability to account for the fact that idiom constituents can be modified and undergo internal transformations without significantly altering the gist of idiom's intended meaning. Such transformations apply to idioms as they do to literal language and suggest that idioms have some kind of internal structure. For example, idiom parts can be quantified (e.g., *He didn't spill a single bean*), modified by insertion of adjectives (e.g., *You should kick that filthy habit once and for all*), or emphasized through topicalization (e.g., *Those strings he wouldn't pull for you*). Because each of these operations only changes part of the idiom's meaning and not the whole idiom (e.g., *We needed to pull a couple of strings to get her a job* does not mean *A couple of times we needed to pull strings to get her a job*), each component must make its own contribution to the idiom's figurative interpretation. In addition, parts of idioms can serve as antecedents to pronouns and ellipsis, which means that they must be individually meaningful, as in *He turned the tables on me and then I turned them on him*, or *They said the tide would turn, and eventually it did* (see Gibbs & Nayak, 1989; Glucksberg, 2001; Nunberg, Sag, & Wasow, 1994; Pulman, 1993).

A growing strand of research has demonstrated that individual meanings of idiom constituent words do indeed actively contribute to their figurative interpretation (Cacciari, 1993; Cacciari & Glucksberg, 1991; Cacciari & Tabossi, 1988, 1993; Gibbs, 1993; Gibbs & Nayak, 1989; Gibbs, Nayak, Bolton, & Keppel, 1989; Nunberg, 1979; Wasow, Sag, & Nunberg, 1983). All these research findings have contributed to the emergence of *compositional* models of idiom processing, which propose that idiomatic meaning unfolds both from the literal analysis of idiom constituents and the specific figurative interpretation of these constituent word meanings within a given context. Major compositional theories of L1 idiom processing are the *Idiom Decomposition Model* (Gibbs & Nayak, 1989; Gibbs, Nayak, & Cuting, 1989), the *Configuration Model* (Cacciari & Tabossi, 1988; Cacciari & Glucksberg, 1991; Vespignani, Canal, Molinaro, Fonda, & Cacciari, 2010), and the *Phrase-Induced Polysemy Model* (Glucksberg, 1993, 2001). The most recent approach is the *Hybrid Model* (Caillies & Butcher, 2007; Cutting & Bock, 1997; Sprenger, Levelt, & Kempen, 2006) or *Constraint-Based Model* (Libben & Titone, 2008; Titone & Connine, 1999; see also Titone et al. this volume for discussion of L1 idiom-processing models), which assumes that idioms behave both compositionally and noncompositionally. Accordingly, idioms are noncompositional because they are highly automatized multiword phrases whose meaning can be accessed directly from the mental lexicon. At the same time, some idioms can be described as compositional because literal analysis of their constituents allows inferring the original motivation of their figurative meaning. For example, it is easy to guess from the literal analysis of the idiom *play with fire* that it means to do dangerous things, as playing with fire is literally a dangerous thing to do. People use different types of information simultaneously during idiomatic processing, making use of many factors that affect both direct retrieval and compositional analysis of idioms.

Heterogeneity of Idioms

Overall, unlike the traditional view of idioms as *dead metaphors* and frozen linguistic expressions, compositional and hybrid models of idioms recognize that idioms are highly heterogeneous and vary along a number of dimensions. Some idioms have a plausible literal meaning (e.g., you can literally *skate on thin ice* or *wear the pants*), whereas others do not (e.g., you cannot literally *go bananas* or *come a cropper*). Some idioms are highly predictable or quickly recognized as having a figurative meaning. For example, upon encountering the sequence, *He turned a blind...*, the language user is likely to complete the phrase idiomatically with *eye*, even before reaching the end of the sentence. On the other hand, some idioms are low predictable and cannot be recognized as idiomatic before the whole idiom string has been processed. For instance, for the sentence fragment, *He passed the...*, the language user would not very likely predict that the missing word is *buck*, unless the sentence occurred in the idiom-biasing context. In such low-predictable idioms, the last word must be accessed in order for the idiom to be recognized as a figurative phrase. Idiom predictability constitutes the major determinant of idiom recognition in the *Configuration Model* and has been shown to affect idiom comprehension in a number of monolingual studies (Cacciari & Tabossi, 1988, Flores d'Arcais, 1993; Tabossi & Zardon, 1993, 1995; Titone & Connine, 1994a).

Furthermore, idioms may be highly familiar and frequently used in the language (e.g., *keep an eye on someone*), which makes their figurative meaning *salient* (or prominent) for a language user, or they may be less familiar (e.g., *the goose hangs high*), in which case their literal meaning might be the first to come to mind (i.e., be more salient than the less frequently encountered figurative interpretation). The *salient* meaning of a word or an expression can be viewed as the meaning primarily on our mind and easily retrievable from the mental lexicon, as suggested by the *Graded Salience Hypothesis* (GSH; Giora, 1997, 1999, 2002, 2003). In addition, other factors that make a particular meaning more salient are conventionality, frequency, and prototypicality. The GSH further assumes that salient meanings are always processed first and accessed via a direct look-up in the mental lexicon. Thus, for well-known, highly conventionalized, and frequent idiomatic expressions (e.g., *hit the road*), the figurative meaning is the first one to be retrieved and will therefore be accessed faster than the literal meaning. On the other hand, when coming across a less familiar and less frequently used idiom (e.g., *five o'clock shadow*), the language user is likely to first analyze it literally and then try to figure out what its figurative meaning might be. In this case, the literal meaning of the idiom would be more salient than its less well-known figurative meaning. Idiom familiarity and salience are hence strictly related.

One controversial dimension of idioms that has been extensively investigated in the monolingual literature is their *semantic decomposition* (Nunberg, 1979), also referred to as *semantic analyzability* (Gibbs & Nayak, 1989; Gibbs et al., 1989), or the degree to which individual meanings of an idiom contribute to its overall figurative interpretation. For example, the idiom *spill the beans* is said to be semantically decomposable because its individual word components contribute to the figurative meaning, where *spill* corresponds to *divulge something* and *beans* to *secret*. In comparison, components of the idiom *kick the bucket* do not map in the same way onto the figurative meaning of *to die*, so the idiom is viewed as nondecomposable. Decomposability is often confused with transparency, even if the two describe different aspects of idiom meaning. Specifically, transparency refers to the extent to which the original metaphorical motivation of an idiomatic phrase can be deduced from its literal analysis (Nunberg, Sag, & Wasow, 1994). For instance, it is possible to infer the meaning of *saw logs* based on the similarity of the sound produced by a snoring person to that resulting from the action of cutting wood with a saw (Cacciari & Glucksberg, 1991; Glucksberg, 1993). On the other hand, meanings of opaque idioms (e.g., *take the gilt off the gingerbread*) cannot be inferred by analyzing their literal constituents.

In general, people tend to view transparent idioms as more decomposable (see Tabossi, Fanari, & Wolf, 2008), and the two characteristics have sometimes been used interchangeably (e.g., Abel, 2003; Briner, 2010; Vega Moreno, 2005). However, it should be emphasized that the two dimensions are not interchangeable, because some idioms can be transparent and nondecomposable (*jump the gun*), whereas others can be opaque and decomposable (*pop the question*). Thus, the idiom *jump the gun* can be viewed as transparent, because its metaphorical motivation (i.e., starting to run before the gun has been fired to start the race) can be recovered from its literal analysis. At the same time, the idiom is nondecomposable, because its figurative meaning is not distributed among its constituents (e.g., *jump the gun* ≠ *do something too soon*). In turn, literal analysis of the idiom *pop the question* does not render its figurative meaning obvious, so the idiom is opaque. Despite being opaque, it is decomposable, in that correspondences can be established between literal meanings of its components and the figurative meanings they convey in an idiomatic phrase (*pop* = *utter* and *question* = *marriage proposal*).

L2 Idiom Learning

How can we account for the acquisition of idiomatic expressions by L2 learners? One way to do this is by looking at what we already know about L2 lexical development in general. After all, idiomatic expressions are part of the L2 lexical repertoire and can be viewed as a peculiar case of long words. Many L2 lexical studies emphasize the role the native language conceptual and lexical systems play in L2 lexical development (e.g., Arabski, 2001; Dagut, 1977; Ellis & Beaton, 1995; Graham & Belnap, 1986; Ijaz, 1986; Kellerman, 1983; Laufer, 1991, 1997; Meara, 1980, 1993; Meara & Ingle, 1986; Nation, 1993, 2001; Singleton, 1987, 1999; Singleton & Little, 1991; Sonaiya, 1991). When faced with the task of learning a new language, L2 learners are likely to rely heavily on their already established L1 lexical and conceptual networks. This view has been long supported in linguistic research (cf. Lado, 1957; Odlin, 1989) and is succinctly captured by MacWhinney's (1992, 1997, 2002, 2005, 2008) *Competition Model*, which views L2 lexical development as strongly parasitic on L1 (see also Hall's, 2002 *Parasitic Hypothesis* of vocabulary development).

In this parasitic view, the initial referent of a new L2 vocabulary item is a conceptual structure of the most closely corresponding L1 word. A newly acquired L2 word has no separate meaning representation but instead relies on the conceptual structure of L1. Gradually such L1-based representations are replaced, as the learner establishes L2 conceptual representations and direct connections are developed between L2 word forms and their corresponding L2 concepts. Thus, the learning process starts with a parasitic lexicon, which is subsequently restructured in the course of L2 learner's developing proficiency. Over time, the initial parasitic associations disappear as between-language links are replaced with within-language links (see also Jiang, 2000; Kecskes, 2000, 2001, 2003). The parasitic account of the developing L2 learner's mental lexicon is also reflected in hierarchical bilingual memory models (see for example, Kroll & Stewart, 1994). In these models, initial processing of L2 items relies on the mediation of corresponding L1 translation equivalents, only later to be replaced with direct conceptual connections between L2 items and concepts (cf. Heredia & Cieślicka, 2014).

Can the Parasitic Hypothesis explain L2 idiom acquisition? It seems reasonable to assume that it can; after all, when faced with a novel expression, the learner is likely to resort to whatever linguistic means are available in order to make sense of it. Translating the idiom literally and trying to find its native language equivalent appear to be obvious choices in carrying out this task. For example, a Polish learner of English coming across the unfamiliar idiomatic string *play with fire* is very likely to start by activating literal meanings of its constituents, retrieving their L1 translation equivalents (*play = bawić się, with = z, fire = ogień*) and analyzing conceptual information associated with the individual words. At the same time, the learner will search his or her mental lexicon for the closest corresponding L1 idiom. Because a similar idiom exists in Polish (*igrać z ogniem* = literal: "toy with fire"), its L1 meaning representation stored at the conceptual level is initially "borrowed" and serves as an L2 conceptual representation for the L2 idiom meaning. With the learner's repeated exposure to the L2 idiom, this L1-based conceptual representation will gradually become modified and restructured so as to be fully compatible with the intricacies of L2 idiom's meaning. When the idiom becomes well-established in the learner's mental lexicon, the L1-based conceptual information is replaced with an L2 concept. At a more advanced stage, the learner no longer needs to resort to the translation-based strategy when processing the idiom. Instead, the L2 idiom meaning can be accessed directly through active within-language connections that have been built between the idiom entry at the lexical level and its L2 conceptual representation at the conceptual level.

A study by Matlock and Heredia (2002; see also Paulmann et al., this volume) supports the Parasitic Hypothesis account of idiom acquisition in L2. The study measured how long it took monolinguals and bilinguals to comprehend sentences with phrasal verbs used idiomatically (e.g., *look up*, as in *Teri looked up the pilot's address on the computer*) and literally as verb+preposition combinations (e.g., *look up*, as in *Teri looked up her friend's chimney with a flashlight*). Based on the reading time data, Matlock and Heredia suggested that less advanced L2 learners first translated the L2 idiom into L1 and then attempted to make sense of it before they accessed its figurative meaning. At a more advanced level of L2, it was hypothesized that learners might process idiomatic expressions by directly retrieving their figurative meaning, consistent with the Direct Access Model proposed by Gibbs for monolingual language users (1980).

Moreover, the more similar an L2 idiom is to its native language counterpart, the easier it will be for the learner to understand and learn via the parasitic strategy, described above, by mapping the idiom directly onto the L1 concept corresponding to its word-for word translation. If an L2 idiom lacks lexical and conceptual counterparts in the learner's native language, the L1-based parasitic processing strategy will not be of much assistance in deriving the idiom's figurative interpretation. In this case, the learner will most likely resort to analyzing the idiom in a piecemeal fashion and will attempt to determine its figurative interpretation solely from the literally based analysis, as one Polish learner of English who concluded that the idiom *chew the fat* meant someone being on a diet (*When a person is on a diet, their body is deprived of calories and chews its own fat*). The degree of idiom translatability, or cross-language overlap, has indeed been shown to play an important role in L2 idiom processing, with similar idioms reported easier to comprehend than different ones, but more prone to negative transfer from L1 in production tasks (e.g., Charteris-Black, 2002; Cieślicka, 2006a; Deignan, Gabryś, & Solska, 1997; Irujo, 1986b; Laufer, 1989, 2000; Laufer & Eliasson, 1993; Liontas, 2002; Yorio, 1989). For example, Irujo (1986a) examined comprehension and production of English idioms by Spanish learners of English. The idioms were either identical or similar in form and meaning to their Spanish equivalents or different from the corresponding Spanish expressions. Idioms that were simple in terms of vocabulary and structure (i.e., transparent) and identical or similar across languages were comprehended much better than different ones. In the production task, identical idioms were produced more correctly in significantly more cases than similar or different idioms, whereas similar idioms showed interference from the participants' native language. In a related study by Yorio (1989), including native speakers of various language backgrounds learning English as a second language, the level of idiomaticity was shown to increase with the increase in the learner's proficiency, and the easiest idioms turned out to be those that were semantically transparent and lexically or syntactically simple. In another study involving the comprehension of English figurative expressions by advanced Polish learners of English, Deignan, Gabryś, and Solska (1997) found that the easiest idiomatic expressions were those that shared the same conceptual metaphor and equivalent form as the corresponding L1 translation. English expressions lacking semantically similar equivalents in the students' L1 were most difficult to understand. Consistent with these findings, Charteris-Black (2002) suggested that identification of conceptual and linguistic similarities and differences between L1 and L2 figurative expressions might help identify potential problems that learners may encounter in the acquisition of L2 figurative language. Results of a comprehension and production task conducted with Malay learners of English showed that figurative expressions with equivalent linguistic forms and an equivalent conceptual basis were the easiest to comprehend and produce. The most difficult expressions turned out to be those with an equivalent linguistic form and a different conceptual basis, as well as culture-specific expressions with a different linguistic form and a different conceptual basis.

In cases in which L2 idioms lack similar or identical counterparts in the learner's L1, the learner's hypotheses concerning their meaning can be derived either from the literal analysis of idiom constituents or from considering the broader (i.e., sentential, situational) context in which the idiom is embedded. With transparent idioms, a literal analysis of idiom constituents can help identify the figurative reading of the expression. As noted earlier, idiom transparency indicates the degree to which the original motivation of the figurative meaning can be inferred from the literal meaning of the idiom's constituent words or the trope that it represents, such as, for instance, metaphor or hyperbole (e.g., *to take the bull by the horns*; see Nunberg et al., 1994). The degree of idiom transparency can be influenced by a number of factors, such as the idiom's clear etymological origin (e.g., *bury the hatchet* referring to the symbolic act when making peace), a common metaphorical theme, where one conceptual domain (e.g., anger) is expressed in terms of another (e.g., heat), as in he *blew his top* or he *let off steam* (e.g., Katz & Bower this volume; Kövecses et al., this volume), or idiom imageability (i.e., how easy it is to evoke an image depicting the idiom's meaning) clearly suggesting its figurative interpretation (as in *foam at the mouth* evoking the image of a person being very angry). A number of studies in L2 idiom learning have indeed shown a facilitating influence of idiom transparency on recognition and production (e.g., Irujo, 1986 a-b; Steinel, Hulstijn, & Steinel, 2007; Yorio, 1989). In their paired-associate learning study, Steinel et al. (2007) had Dutch university students learn English idioms in L1-L2 or L2-L1 pairs. In addition to the direction of learning, idiom imageability and transparency were manipulated. It was hypothesized that transparency should be particularly facilitative for participants' performance on a recognition task, because the overlap between literal and figurative meanings would provide the learners with sufficient clues to deduce the figurative interpretation of the idiom. In addition, the literal meaning of a transparent idiom might constitute an extra memory-aid-boosting performance. In line with those predictions, transparency facilitated the comprehension of idioms, but high transparent idioms did not differ much from low transparent ones on the production task. In a study by Skoufaki (2008), transparent idioms were shown to be easier to comprehend even if they were unfamiliar to L2 learners. Skoufaki had advanced learners of English guess at the meaning of unknown English idioms varying along the dimension of transparency. High transparent idioms had significantly more correct guesses than low transparent idioms (see also Boers & Demecheleer, 2001).

What if the L2 idiom not only lacks a word-for-word equivalent in the learner's L1 but is in addition opaque? To address this issue, let's return to the idiom *chew the fat* and speculate on a possible course of events that could be involved in processing this idiom by a Polish learner of English.

Let's further assume that the learner is exposed to this idiom in the following sentence, *Every time they met, they would chew the fat for hours on end, sipping beer and smoking their cigars*. The learner might access the literal meaning of the word *fat* as a starting point of inference. Upon activating the literal meaning of *fat*, the learner would likely start considering its properties in order of their relevance for the utterance. Thus, the property of being something that can be consumed would probably be more highly activated than the property of *fat* being located in the human adipose tissue or being the major culprit of one's high cholesterol level. Semantic properties of the word *fat* hypothesized by the learner to be relevant for the idiom's meaning would next be combined with the information obtained from a literal analysis of the word *chew* (i.e., the fact that *chewing* involves movements of the mouth and often signals an idle activity, as when people chew gum). In addition, based on the available contextual information, the learner might decide that the idiom is unlikely to mean *eat*, because the two people are chewing fat while drinking and smoking and they do so for an extended period of time. Based on his or her background knowledge, the learner might conclude that if the action is performed hours on end, with two people drinking and smoking, and because it involves moving one's mouth, then it might plausibly be talking. The end product of these processes would thus be the hypothesized meaning of the L2 idiom, provided the learner indeed drew all the correct inferences. It would be unlikely for a learner to arrive at a correct meaning of this idiom if it occurred in isolation or in a linguistically limited context. Because the idiom lacks a native language translation equivalent and is opaque, accessing the literal meaning of its individual constituents would be insufficient to derive the idiom's figurative interpretation.

Overall, similar or identical idioms and idioms with a transparent meaning derivable from the literal analysis of their constituents will be easier to comprehend for L2 learners than different and opaque ones. In addition, idiom processing will be affected by the presence of a supportive context. It is very likely that, in line with Vega Moreno's (2007) *pragmatic inferential* approach to comprehending idioms, language users aim at optimal relevance and follow the path of least cognitive effort when trying to infer the figurative meaning of an idiom. They do it by searching for contextual implications, analyzing the concepts encoded by the utterance, and testing the most relevant meanings activated upon accessing the word. It is also evident from the L2 idiom learning studies that a default strategy that L2 learners resort to when processing idioms is analyzing them literally and assuming that the idiom component words in some way contribute to the idiom's overall figurative interpretation.

Those factors (i.e., cross-language similarity, context, reliance on literal processing) figure prominently in the few L2 idiom-processing models that have been proposed in the psycholinguistic literature.

L2 Idiom-Processing Theories

The interaction of cross-language idiom similarity and context in L2 idiom comprehension forms the core of Liontas' (2002, see also this volume) *Idiom Diffusion Model of Second Languages*, which proposes that L2 idiom comprehension consists of two stages. In the first, prediction stage, the L2 learner constructs a number of hypotheses about the L2 idiom's figurative interpretation. The hypotheses constructed at the prediction stage will vary depending on the degree of idiom transparency, its semantic distance from the corresponding L1 idiomatic expression, and the presence of the supporting context. In the absence of context, the learner relies solely on the literal analysis of the idiom's constituents. L2 idioms with identical L1 equivalents (referred to as *lexical-level*) are the easiest to understand, because the learner can refer to L1 lexical entries and comprehend the idiom via a one-to-one match between the L2 and the corresponding L1 expression (e.g., *take the bull by the horns = tomar al toro por los cuernos*). Context is hence unnecessary for understanding lexical-level idioms. More cognitive effort and some contextual support will be required when comprehending idioms with slightly different L1 equivalents (referred to as *semi-lexical level* idioms, for example, *pull someone's leg = tomarle el pelo a alguien*; literal: "pull someone's hair"). In such idioms, the meaning of one or more lexical items, those not present in the corresponding L1 idiom, has to be inferred, thus incurring additional processing effort. Comprehension of L2 idioms that have no direct equivalents in the learner's L1 (*post-lexical level* idioms, e.g., *to save someone's neck = sacar a alguien las castañas del fuego*; literal: "pull for someone the chestnuts out of the fire") relies quite heavily on contextual support. Whereas the learner at first attempts to interpret the idiom via a literal analysis of its constituents, successful comprehension of such idioms requires the use of the larger discourse context and top-down processing strategies. The hypotheses created in the prediction stage are verified in the second, confirmation or replacement, reconstructive stage, as the learner fully analyzes information available in the input, focusing on the most relevant contextual constraints and rejecting unlikely interpretations.

Another model of L2 idiom processing, *Model of Dual Idiom Representation* (Abel, 2003), focuses on the role of idiom decomposability and familiarity. In this model, how an idiom is represented in the lexicon is determined by its decomposability. While nondecomposable idioms have separate lexical entries (referred to as *idiom entries*), decomposable idioms do not need to develop a separate idiom entry because they can be represented via lexical entries of their individual constituents (*constituent entries*). The more frequently an L2 learner sees or hears an idiom, the more likely it is for such an idiom to develop its own idiom entry. The model thus capitalizes on the role that frequency and familiarity play in the developing L2 figurative competence. Because L2 learners encounter idioms much less frequently than native speakers, they do not develop as many idiom entries in their mental lexicon as native speakers do and have to rely on the analysis of idiom constituents in order to derive the idiom's figurative meaning.

Predictions of the model have been verified in the idiom decomposability study conducted by Abel (2003) with non-native English speakers. In this study, German learners of English were presented with English idioms and asked to make a decomposability judgment about them, that is, say to what extent individual components of the idiom contributed to the idiom's overall figurative interpretation. The obtained data were compared to the norms established for native speakers of English (Titone & Connine, 1994b). The results showed differences in decomposability judgments between both groups. Whereas native speakers of English tended to judge idioms as nondecomposable, L2 learners rated more idioms as decomposable, even if the English expressions were nondecomposable and opaque. This reflects the strategy of reliance on literal meanings of idiom constituents when decoding their meaning by non-native language users and points to the possibility that figurative meanings of idioms are less salient for non-native speakers than for native speakers. It is important to note, however, that support for this model is limited to offline ratings (see García et al., this volume).

The strategy of reliance on literal analysis in the course of L2 idiom processing constitutes the major assumption of Cieślicka's (2006a) *Literal Salience Model*. The model has been developed to account for the acquisition and processing of idiomatic expressions by foreign language learners who acquire their L2 in a formal setting and live in the country where the L2 is not spoken outside of the classroom environment. One important difference between learning a new lexical item and learning a multiword expression, such as an idiom, is that learning the latter rarely implies having to establish novel formal representations for its constituent words. The idiom constituents are usually already known by the L2 learner and their meanings well established in the learner's lexicon. To provide an example, the learner of English encountering the idiom *chew the fat* is very likely to be already familiar with its individual component words, *chew* and *fat*. This simple observation has important implications for modeling the acquisition and processing of L2 idioms.

Accordingly, the major assumption of the Literal Salience Model is that literal meanings of idiom constituents are more salient than the idiom's overall figurative meaning (see Kecskes, 2006 for a similar argument). Following Giora's (1997) Graded Salience Hypothesis, salient meanings are taken here as those meanings that are activated automatically and most strongly, regardless of contextual bias. Because foreign language learners acquiring their L2 in a formal setting are likely to know the literal meanings of words before they see those words used in a figurative phrase, those literal meanings are more strongly coded in their lexicon (and hence more salient) than the newly acquired figurative ones. As argued by Kecskes (2006), salience is a function of familiarity and experience with a given meaning. As such, it captures an essentially dynamic property of the human cognitive system. What started off as a nonsalient meaning (i.e., a newly coined metaphor, such as *She is a sugar mom*, to refer to the owner of a diabetic cat, or a newly learned unfamiliar L2 idiom), an expression can with time, repeated exposure, or change in the linguistic environment (e.g., the novel metaphor becoming highly conventionalized and frequently used in the language community) evolve to become highly salient. This view of salience is akin to a dynamic concept of the learner's lexicon, which can be seen as an evolving network that is constantly changing with the increase in the learner's proficiency (see the *Dynamic Model of Multilingualism*; Herdina & Jessner, 2002; see also Meara, 1978, 1980; Meara & Ingle, 1986; Nation, 1993, 2001; Singleton & Little, 1991; Söderman, 1993).

A gradual shift in salience status is likely to occur as a function of idiom familiarity, such that the initially more salient literal meaning of a newly acquired idiomatic phrase becomes less *privileged* as the language user encounters the phrase repeatedly in its figurative sense and uses the idiom figuratively in many different contexts. As a result, the figurative meaning becomes more salient and likely to be activated faster and more strongly than the literal meaning, which becomes less salient. Such a complete shift in salience status, however, is unlikely to occur for foreign language learners whose only exposure to the L2 happens in the classroom setting. Support for the idea that literal meanings enjoy a higher salience status in the course of L2 idiom processing has been demonstrated in a number of behavioral studies (see, for example, Cieślicka, 2006a, 2010; Cieślicka, Heredia, & Olivares, 2014; Siyanova-Chanturia, Conklin, & Schmitt, 2011). For example, Siyanova-Chanturia et al. (2011) recorded eye-movement data as native and non-native speakers of English read ambiguous idioms used in a figurative-biasing story context (e.g., *at the end of the day* meaning "eventually"), in a literal-biasing context (*at the end of the day* meaning "in the evening"), or novel control phrases (e.g., *at the end of the war*). Results revealed that native speakers processed idioms faster than they did novel phrases, suggesting that idioms were lexicalized and quickly retrieved from the mental lexicon as whole chunks. In contrast, non-native speakers did not show a comparable processing advantage of idioms over novel phrases, suggesting that L2 idioms were not very well established in their lexicon. Whereas there was no distinction in terms of eye movement patterns between the processing of idioms used figuratively and literally by native speakers, non-native language users tended to process idioms used literally faster than when idioms were intended figuratively, which points to the possibility that literal meanings were more salient in online L2 idiom processing than figurative ones.

As an extension of the Graded Salience Hypothesis, Giora, Zaidel, Soroker, Batori, and Kasher (2000) have suggested that the left and right hemispheres process salient and nonsalient meanings differently. Given that the figurative meaning of highly conventionalized expressions such as idioms or familiar metaphors is salient and coded in the mental lexicon, its processing should primarily engage the left hemisphere, which stores linguistic knowledge. On the other hand, processing nonsalient figurative expressions, such as newly coined metaphors or less well-known idioms, should involve initial activation of their more salient (i.e., literal) meanings, followed by a reinterpretation process, which is the domain of the right hemisphere. In keeping with those predictions, Giora et al. (2000) found differential effects of right and left brain lesions on understanding salient conventional metaphors and nonsalient sarcasm in patients with right hemisphere damage and left hemisphere damage. The view that the left hemisphere is more likely to engage in processing salient meanings whereas the right hemisphere is more active when interpreting novel, less salient meanings has been supported in a number of neuropsychological L1 figurative processing studies (Eviatar & Just, 2006; Giora et al., 2000; Laurent, Denhieres, Passerieux, Iakimova, & Hardy-Bayle, 2006; Lee & Dapretto, 2006; Mashal, Faust, & Hendler, 2005; Mashal, Faust, Hendler, & Jung-Beeman, 2008a, 2008b; Rapp, Leube, Erb, Grodd, & Kircher, 2004; Stringaris, Medford, Giora, Giampietro, Brammer, & David, 2006; Stringaris, Medford, Giampietro, Brammer, & David, 2007).

Given Giora et al.'s (2000) findings that the left and right hemispheres process salient and nonsalient meanings differently, Cieślicka and Heredia (2011) investigated whether cerebral asymmetries for salient versus nonsalient meanings would differ as a function of language (native vs. nonnative). A series of experiments with fluent Polish speakers of English were conducted using the divided visual field technique. Briefly, the divided visual field technique involves presentation of stimuli to the right visual field/left hemisphere and left visual field/right hemisphere. Typically, some stimuli are presented centrally (for example, a sentence that sets up a context) and other stimuli, such as the targets that are the focus of the study, are displayed laterally. Lateral presentation ensures initial selective stimulation of the visual cortex in only one hemisphere. Participants may be asked to make a word/nonword decision about the target (i.e., decide if the target is a legitimate word) or a meaningfulness judgment decision (i.e., decide if the target is meaningfully related with the preceding sentence that has been displayed centrally). While the information presented laterally is in healthy individuals quickly transmitted to the contralateral hemisphere, the divided visual field technique can successfully capture hemisphere-specific computations in the initial stages of language processing by shifting the balance of processing to the hemisphere contralateral to the presentation side (Coulson & Van Petten, 2007). In Cieślicka and Heredia's (2011) study, literally plausible Polish and English idioms were embedded in unconstraining ambiguous (e.g., *I knew he kept an ace up his sleeve*) or constraining unambiguous context (e.g., *The debating president kept an ace up his sleeve*) and presented centrally, followed by laterally presented targets related to the idioms figuratively (e.g., *gain*) or literally (e.g., *shirt*). Targets were displayed at interstimulus intervals (ISI) of 0, 300, and 800 ms. Salience effects turned out to be significantly modulated by the language (native vs. non-native) of the stimulus materials, as well as by context. Results showed the literal meanings of L2 idioms were more salient than figurative meanings, in line with predictions of the Literal Salience Model. Literal L2 targets were significantly facilitated in both hemispheres and throughout all ISIs, with the exception of the 300 ms where they were only primed (i.e., recognized faster) when presented in the right visual field corresponding to the left hemisphere. Overall, more facilitation was found for L2 literal meanings in the left hemisphere than in the right hemisphere, and more facilitation was found for L2 figurative meanings in the right than in the left hemisphere. These findings are consistent with the Literal Salience Model, under which literal meanings are more salient than figurative ones in L2 idiom processing, and also with the GSH, since more salient meanings received more facilitation in the left hemisphere and the less salient ones were more highly activated in the right hemisphere.

Factors Affecting L2 Idiom Processing

While there has been an abundance of pedagogically oriented research in idioms and other multiword expressions (e.g., Boers, Demecheleer, &

Eyckmans, 2004; Boers, Kappel, Stengers, & Demecheleer, 2006; Bortfeld, 2003; Cooper, 1999; Grant & Bauer, 2004; Liontas, 2003; Laufer, 1989; Schmitt, 2004; Spötl & McCarthy, 2003; Wray, 2000), very few studies have explored the factors influencing the online (i.e., real-time) dynamics of L2 idiom processing. Most, if not all, of what we know about psycholinguistic factors influencing idiom processing comes from the monolingual domain. This section reviews psycholinguistic and neuropsychological findings and the factors identified as crucial in online idiom processing. Some of those factors (e.g., literal plausibility and decomposability) have been shown to be particularly relevant in L1 idiom processing, and they are only now becoming the focus of the still limited L2 idiom research. Others, such as cross-language similarity, are unique for L2 idiom processing and offer an exciting area for future research.

Idiom Literal Plausibility

The dimension of idiom literal plausibility (i.e., the extent to which the idiom can be interpreted in a literal fashion), also called *literality*, or *literalness* (Cronk & Schweigert, 1992), has been investigated in a number of L1 idiom-processing studies (e.g., Cronk, Lima, & Schweigert, 1993; Forrester, 1995; Mueller & Gibbs, 1987; Titone & Connine, 1994a). Recent neuropsychological research suggests that literally plausible and implausible idioms may actually be processed in different brain regions because of a differential sensitivity of both hemispheres to semantically ambiguous information. Differences in patterns of semantic processing between the left and right hemispheres are captured by the *Fine-Coarse Coding Theory* (e.g., Beeman 1998, Jung-Beeman 2005). According to this view, the left hemisphere activates only a small set of semantic fields closely related to the dominant meaning of a stimulus word, whereas the right hemisphere engages in coarse coding, that is, activation of large and diffuse semantic fields related only peripherally to the word being processed. For example, when presented with the word *foot*, the left hemisphere is likely to activate only the words that are strongly related and belong to the same semantic field (e.g., *toe*). The right hemisphere, on the other hand, will activate more distantly related words, such as *glass* or *cry* (as in stepping with one's foot on glass can make one cry). The theory further suggests that in the course of processing ambiguous language stimuli possessing several meanings, the left hemisphere activates only a few salient (dominant) meanings, while the right hemisphere activates a wide range of weakly related nonsalient meanings and maintains their activation for a longer time. These asymmetries in processing semantic information would make the right hemisphere superior at processing ambiguous (literally plausible) idioms, where multiple meanings have to be activated and considered for interpretation. In contrast, the left hemisphere, which engages in fine coding and focuses on close semantic relations, would be more efficient at processing unambiguous (literally implausible) idioms.

Support for the suggestion that ambiguous and unambiguous idioms might be processed differently by the left and right hemispheres comes from a case study of an Italian patient with selective atrophy of left hemisphere regions (Papagno & Cacciari, 2010). In this study, the patient showed impairment in the comprehension of unambiguous, but not ambiguous idioms. The crucial role of the left hemisphere in processing unambiguous idioms has been also demonstrated in a repetitive Transcranial Magnetic Stimulation (rTMS) study by Oliveri, Romero, and Papagno (2004). In this study, participants saw idiomatic or literal sentences followed by a pair of pictures, one of which corresponded to the correct and the other to incorrect meanings of the stimulus expressions, and were asked to choose the picture depicting the meaning of the sentence. Reaction times were unaffected by right hemisphere rTMS and significantly slowed by left hemisphere rTMS, comparably for both literal and idiomatic sentences, which indicated that a similar neural substrate, the left temporal cortex subserved the processing of unambiguous idioms and literal sentences. Similarly, Fogliata, Rizzo, Reati, Miniussi, Oliveri, and Papagno (2007) showed reduced comprehension accuracy in processing unambiguous idioms following rTMS applied to the left but not right prefrontal and temporal cortex, which suggests that unambiguous idioms are processed in the left hemisphere. In addition, Zempleni, Haverkort, Renken, and Stowe (2007) found in their functional Magnetic Resonance Imaging (fMRI) study that, while the comprehension of both ambiguous and unambiguous idioms is supported by both hemispheres, there is additional activation in the right hemisphere solely when processing ambiguous idioms. However, other studies (e.g., Hillert & Buraças, 2009; Romero Lauro, Tettamanti, Cappa, & Papagno, 2008) did not support the claim that ambiguous and unambiguous idioms are processed in different brain hemispheres. For example, Hillert and Buraças (2009) examined comprehension of spoken ambiguous and unambiguous idioms in an event-related fMRI experiment. Both idiom types were found to mainly activate the left hemisphere. Romero Lauro et al. (2008) found bilateral prefrontal activation for both ambiguous and unambiguous idioms, suggesting a common network of neural activity for both idiom types. Similarly, Rizzo, Sandrini, and Papagno (2007) found that both left and right hemispheres (dorsolateral prefrontal cortext) were involved in processing unambiguous idioms. All in all, the question of whether ambiguous and unambiguous idioms are processed differently in the two cerebral hemispheres remains unanswered in the L1 idiom-processing literature. The question has not been addressed as of yet in the L2 idiom-processing studies.

Behavioral studies into the role of idiom literal plausibility seem to imply that it affects the speed of idiom processing (Mueller & Gibbs, 1987) and the degree to which literal meanings of idiom constituents get activated (Titone & Connine, 1994a). In the L2 idiom-processing domain, the few studies conducted so far have been inconclusive. For example, Cieślicka (2006a) had fluent Polish speakers of English listen to English idioms embedded in neutral sentences that did not provide any clear bias toward the figurative interpretation (e.g., *Peter was going to tie the knot later that month*). While listening to the sentences, the L2 participants made a lexical decision on a visually presented target word related either to the figurative meaning of the idiom (e.g., *marry*) or the literal meaning of the last word in the idiom (e.g., *rope*). Visual targets were presented at one of two positions: (1) immediately at the offset of the penultimate word of the idiom (i.e., after *the* in *tie the[*] knot*), and (2) at the idiom offset (i.e., after *knot* in *tie the knot[*]*). Results showed an overall priming advantage for literal targets consistent with the assumption that literal meanings of idioms are highly salient in the course of L2 idiom processing. More surprisingly, idiom literal plausibility did not significantly affect the degree of activation of idiom literal meanings. While activation of literal targets was nonsignificant at the penultimate position of both literally plausible and implausible idioms, there was robust and highly comparable activation for literal targets at the offset of both idiom types. In addition, the priming effects (i.e., difference between the activation obtained for a target related word and its unrelated control) for literal targets were significantly higher than for idiomatic targets for both literally plausible and implausible idioms, which provided support for the Literal Salience Model discussed earlier.

Idiom Semantic Decomposability

As discussed earlier, the degree to which idiom meaning is decomposable may be particularly relevant for non-native language users, given their tendency to analyze fixed phrases into constituent parts (e.g., Abel, 2003). It appears that the monolingual evidence available so far is inconclusive with regard to processing differences between decomposable and nondecomposable idioms. The Idiom Decomposition Model (Gibbs &

Nayak, 1989; Gibbs et al., 1989) originally predicted that nondecomposable idioms (e.g., *kick the bucket*) are highly lexicalized (i.e., stored as a long word) and should therefore be easy to retrieve and processed faster than decomposable ones (e.g., *spill the beans*), which call for additional processing effort during the computation of meanings of their individual components. Using a phrase classification task, Gibbs et al. (1989) found that nondecomposable idioms took significantly more time to process than decomposable ones. To account for these unexpected findings, Gibbs et al. suggested that such idioms might take longer to comprehend because assigning independent meanings to the idiom's components, which is obligatory during language processing, does not yield the figurative interpretation of the idiom. In contrast, compositional analysis of decomposable idioms overlaps with their idiomatic interpretation, because in those idioms literal meanings of individual words directly map onto their figurative senses in the idiomatic phrase. This latest formulation of the Idiom Decomposition Hypothesis, which is supported by some empirical findings (Caillies & Butcher, 2007; Titone & Connine, 1994a, 1999), thus suggests that decomposable idioms are faster and easier to comprehend than nondecomposable ones. However, other findings (Cutting & Bock, 1997; Libben & Titone, 2008; Sprenger et al., 2006; Tabossi, Fanari, & Wolf, 2008; Tabossi, Wolf, & Koterle, 2009) have challenged this claim and showed no processing differences between both idiom types.

In addition, it has been suggested in the monolingual idiom-processing literature (Titone, 1998) that decomposable and nondecomposable idioms might be processed differently by the two cerebral hemispheres. Based on the Fine-Coarse Coding Theory (Beeman, 1998), Titone (1998) has suggested that hemispheric differences in sensitivity to central and peripheral semantic relationships might cause asymmetries in the processing of decomposable and nondecomposable idioms by both hemispheres. Because the left hemisphere engages in fine coding and activates only a small set of closely related meanings, it might be more efficient at processing decomposable idioms in which there are close semantic relations between literal meanings of idiom components and their corresponding figurative senses. On the other hand, because the right hemisphere engages in coarse coding and is sensitive to peripheral semantic relationships, it might be superior for the processing of nondecomposable idioms in which semantic relations between literal meanings of idiom components and the overall figurative meaning are either extremely weak and distant, or absent altogether.

The few existing studies exploring the role of idiom decomposability in online L2 processing have failed to demonstrate any processing differences between decomposable and nondecomposable idioms. For example, Cieślicka (2010) looked at whether idiom decomposability affects the degree of activation of literal meanings of idiom constituents in language production. The study employed a variant of the completion and naming task used by Sprenger et al. (2006). This task measures the time taken by a language user to complete an idiomatic phrase (e.g., *Jack pulled my* _____) in which the last word (e.g., *leg*) of the idiom has been replaced with a semantically related (e.g., *foot*), phonologically related (e.g., *lend*), or unrelated control word (e.g., *peas*). The rationale behind this task is that if idioms are processed via a literal analysis of their constituents, then semantically and phonologically related words substituted for last idiom's words would be named faster than unrelated controls. This would be the case because the language comprehension system would be *prepared* to activate the idiom *pull the leg*, and, even if its last word is missing, idiom components would have already co-activated those lexical items with which they were semantically or phonologically related. In Cieślicka's (2010) study, naming latencies for semantically and phonologically related targets were significantly shorter than the latencies obtained for unrelated controls. This effect was true irrespective of idiom compositionality, suggesting that both decomposable and non-decomposable idioms are stored and processed in a similar manner.

In another study employing the divided visual field methodology, Cieślicka (2013) explored possible cerebral asymmetries in the storage and processing format of decomposable and nondecomposable idioms. L1 (Polish) and L2 (English) idioms varying in decomposability were embedded in neutral (e.g., *I do not particularly like the idea of skating on thin ice*) and figurative-biasing context (e.g., *Signing a contract with him is really skating on thin ice*) and presented centrally, followed by laterally presented target words related to the figurative (e.g., *risk*) or literal (e.g., *snow*) meaning of an idiom. Targets appeared either immediately at sentence offset (0 ms) or 300 ms after the end of the sentence. Contrary to the previous monolingual findings (Caillies & Butcher, 2007; Gibbs et al., 1989; Titone & Connine, 1999), L1 decomposable idioms were not faster to recognize than nondecomposable ones. Cerebral asymmetries were found for both idiom types, but they were significantly modulated by context. For example, the right hemisphere was found to process L1 and L2 nondecomposable idioms faster than decomposable ones, in line with Titone's (1998) suggestion, but this right hemisphere advantage held true only in the unambiguous context condition. On the other hand, advantage for the left hemisphere in processing decomposable idioms was only found in the L1 and the ambiguous context condition. From the limited L2 data obtained so far, it seems that decomposability by itself does not affect online idiom processing, and it might have an effect only in combination with other factors, such as context.

Cross-Language Similarity

While similar idioms have an identical meaning and close word-for-word correspondence across languages, different idioms express a similar concept but vary substantially in their lexical makeup. For example, the English idiom *look for a needle in a haystack* has an identical word-for-word translation equivalent in Polish, *szukać igły w stogu siana*, where *szukać= look for; igły= a needle; w=in; stogu siana=haystack*). In contrast, the closest equivalent of the English idiom *a piece of cake* in Polish would be *bułka z masłem* (literal: "bread roll with butter"). As mentioned earlier, L2 learners are likely to resort to their native language when interpreting and learning novel idiomatic expressions. A number of classroom-oriented studies reviewed earlier have indicated that similar idioms are easier than different ones in comprehension tasks, but might pose difficulty in production tasks, where negative transfer (i.e., interference from the learner's L1) is likely to occur (e.g., Charteris-Black, 2002; Cieślicka, 2006b; Liontas, 2002, Yorio, 1989). How will cross-language similarity affect online idiomatic processing?

To address this question, an eye-tracking experiment was conducted in which Spanish-English bilinguals were presented with English idiomatic sentences (Cieślicka & Heredia, 2013). English idioms (e.g., *point of view*) that have a direct translation and express the same meaning in Spanish (e.g., *punto de vista*) were classified as similar. Idioms classified as different were those lacking any written or spoken similarity but expressing the same concept (e.g., *hit the sack* vs. *planchar oreja*; literal: "to iron one's ear"). All idioms conformed to the syntactic structure, verb + (determiner/adj) + noun, and differed along the dimension of transparency, with half of the idioms being transparent and half opaque. Each idiom was embedded in two context types: (1) context biasing the idiom's literal meaning, *Grandpa was told by the doctor that his circulation problems are the reason why he often gets cold feet and becomes tired quickly*; (2) context biasing the idiom's figurative meaning, *Even though he is a seasoned conference speaker, every time he is about to get on stage he gets cold feet and fears a panic attack*. In addition, a novel, idiom's control phrase was included, in which the last word of the idiom was replaced with a matched control (e.g., *Grandpa was told by the doctor that his circulation problems are the reason why he often gets cold hands and becomes tired quickly*). The critical values measured were first pass reading time (gaze duration, defined as the sum of all fixations made prior to exiting the region), total reading time (the sum of all fixation durations made within a region of interest), and fixation count (the number of all fixations made within a region of interest), both for the whole idiom (*gets cold feet*) and its matched control phrase (*gets cold hands*) and for the final word of an idiomatic phrase (*feet*) and the final word (*hands*) of a matched control phrase. Overall, cross-language similarity was found to significantly affect idiom processing, and this effect was present in all the reading measures, both for the whole phrase analysis and the last word analysis. For example, in the first-pass reading time data, similar idioms took significantly longer to read than different ones. Consistent with these findings, similar idioms had significantly more fixations than different idioms in the whole phrase analysis. Likewise, in the total reading time data, different, but not similar idioms demonstrated a processing advantage over matched control phrases, in that their reading time was significantly shorter. These results suggest that the presence of a word-for-word translation equivalent results in its automatic activation in the course of idiom processing. The activated lexical items from L1 subsequently need to be suppressed, which slows down the processing time for similar, as compared to different, idioms, where no competing lexical items from L1 get activated. In contrast, when no direct L1 counterpart exists, as is the case for different idioms, they are more likely to be processed faster than their matched control phrases, because the processing mechanism is not slowed down by the necessity to suppress the activated cross-language translation equivalent. This explains the demonstrated advantage for different idioms over novel matched phrases in the total reading time data (see also García et al., this volume; Titone et al., this volume).

To summarize, results obtained from Cieślicka and Heredia's (2013) eye-tracking experiment are generally supportive of the previous offline research that showed a significant role that cross-language similarity plays in L2 idiom processing (e.g., Irujo, 1985a, b). However, previous research has employed primarily offline measures and has shown mixed effects of idiom similarity, mostly depending on the task type, with facilitation for similar idioms in comprehension/recognition tasks and some amount of interference in production tasks. Unlike the offline comprehension tasks, where the presence of a cross-language translation equivalent turned out to be facilitative, the eye measures recorded in the online experiment described here showed that similar idioms take longer to process than different ones. These data indicate the presence of a cross-language interaction, where the existing native language equivalent is automatically activated and calls for the extra processing time needed for its suppression (see also Heredia, García, & Penecale, 2007 and García et al., this volume for similar results).

Summary and Conclusions

In the words of Johnson-Laird (1993, x), idioms are "mysterious...,
pervasive, poetic, and easy," and it is precisely their complex, colorful
nature that has fascinated linguists and psycholinguists for such a long
time. This chapter started with a definition of idioms and discussion of
their heterogeneous nature. Idioms are pervasive in language, yet they
have consistently proven difficult to define, as reflected in the changing
views and theories summarized in this chapter. This difficulty has been
directly related to the fact that idioms cross the literal versus figurative
continuum, and the issue of what should be labeled *literal* and *figurative*
has itself been debated by language scholars (see Ariel, 2002).

To summarize, this chapter first offered a brief overview of idiom
processing theories developed in the monolingual literature. It then
looked at how second/foreign language learners understand and learn
idioms and specifically emphasized the importance of analyzing idioms in
a piecemeal fashion and relying on the native language translation
equivalent. Parasitism has been offered as the most plausible strategy
employed by L2 learners to make sense of idioms and incorporate them
into their developing L2 mental lexicon. This has brought up the question of factors determining idiom processing that are unique for L2
learners, such as cross-language similarity. The few studies in online
aspects of L2 idiom processing carried out so far provide important steps
toward understanding the mechanisms underlying the acquisition,
mental representation, and comprehension of idioms by non-native
language users.

Overall, review of the L2 idiom processing research provided in this
chapter suggests that a number of factors dynamically interact in determining how second/foreign language learners comprehend idiomatic
expressions. Studies employing eye-tracking and hemifield paradigms
have helped shed some light into the interplay of those factors. For
example, while idiom decomposability *per se* might not affect the time
course of their recognition by L2 learners, it may influence the online
processing of idioms in conjunction with context. It is also likely that
cross-language similarity will interact with transparency in affecting the
ease or difficulty of L2 idiom acquisition, recognition, and production.
Similar transparent idioms might be more likely to evoke cross-language
interference than similar opaque ones, as our preliminary eye-tracking
data exploring the interaction of those two dimensions seem to suggest.

Given the importance of figurative competence for achieving fluency
and communicative competence in the second/foreign language, one of
the goals of this chapter has been to emphasize the need for further

psycholinguistic and neuropsychological research in L2 idiom acquisition, storage, and processing. Despite the prevalence of advanced neurocognitive techniques, such as event-related potentials (ERPs) and fMRI and rTMS in investigating figurative language in the monolingual domain, there are almost no studies to date with the use of those methodologies that explored the processing of idiomatic language by second/foreign language learners. Our future goal should be to bridge this gap through interdisciplinary effort that could lead to more successful pedagogical approaches to teaching idioms in the L2 classroom.

List of Key Words

Cerebral asymmetries, Competition Model, Compositional models, Conceptual domain, Configuration Model, Constituent entries, Constraint-Based Model, Cross-language similarity, Decomposability, Direct Access Model, Direct look-up models, Divided visual field, Dynamic Model of Multilingualism, Figurative competence, Fine-Coarse Coding Theory, First pass reading time, Fixation count, Gaze duration, Graded Salience Hypothesis, Hybrid Model, Idiom Decomposition Model, Idiom Diffusion Model of Second Languages, Idiom List Hypothesis, Idiom predictability, Imageability, Lexical Representation Hypothesis, Lexical-level, Literal plausibility, Literal Salience Model, Literality, Model of Dual Idiom Representation, Multiword lexical items, Negative transfer, Noncompositional theories, Nonsalient meaning, Parasitic Hypothesis, Phrase-Induced Polysemy Model, Post-lexical level, Repetitive Transcranial Magnetic Stimulation (rTMS), Salient meaning, Semantic analyzability, Semantic decomposition, Semi-lexical level, Total reading time, Transparency

Thought Questions

1. Because literal analysis of idiom component words seems to constitute an obligatory aspect of L2 idiom processing, do you think that providing a learner with a picture depicting a literal meaning of an idiom might help him or her remember the idiom better? Why or why not? Do you think that providing an explanation of the idiom origin could also help learners remember it better? For example, the origin of the idiom *let the cat out of the bag* relates to the practice of selling livestock at markets and the fraud of substituting a cat for a piglet. To avoid buying a cat, the bag needed to be inspected before finalizing

the transaction – thus, *letting the cat out of the bag* was disclosing the trick. Do you think learners might benefit from such explanations? Why or why not? Read the article by Boers et al. (2009) concerning the use of pictorial elucidation in L2 idiom learning/teaching. Read the article by Szczepaniak and Lew (2011) exploring the usefulness of imagery (i.e., pictorial illustrations of idioms) and etymological notes (explanations of idiom origins) in idiom dictionaries. What did you find out in the articles? Were your predictions confirmed?

2. Think of your own experience learning a foreign or a second language and how you encountered, remembered, and produced idioms in the L2. Based on your own experience, which of the theories of idiom processing described in this chapter sounds most appealing to you? Which one would do the best job describing your own path toward achieving L2 figurative competence?

3. The chapter presented a number of dimensions along which idioms can vary. It has also reviewed research showing how some types of idioms might be easier/more difficult to process than others. From your own L2 learning experience, which idiom types have posed most/least difficulty for you to remember and recall? Can you explain why, based on the previous research? Do your experiences confirm findings from the L2 idiom research reviewed in this chapter?

Suggested Student Research Projects

1. Prepare a list of idioms in English and another language you know. Categorize idioms into three groups, following Liontas (2002): *lexical-level idioms*, *semi-lexical level idioms*, and *post-lexical level idioms*. Run a comprehension and production experiment with learners of the language you chose for the experiment. For the comprehension experiment, present a list of idioms and ask your participants to explain what they think the idiom means, either by paraphrasing it or providing an L1 equivalent. For a production experiment, use a *discourse completion task* (see Irujo, 1986a, for an example of a discourse completion task with L2 idioms). What results did you obtain? Which idioms were the easiest to comprehend? Which category had the highest correct number of responses in the discourse completion task? Did you observe any instances of negative transfer from the learners' L1? What were they? What can you conclude from your study about how cross-language idiom similarity affects their comprehension and production?

2. One of the ways to explore the structure of the L2 learner's lexicon is to conduct a word association task. In this task, you provide participants with a list of expressions and ask them to generate the first

response that comes to their mind. Compile a list of English idioms (e.g., http://www.usingenglish.com/reference/idioms/cat). Make sure the list includes idioms varying along the following dimensions: *literal plausibility*, *transparency*, and *semantic analyzability*. Consult norms for English idiomatic expressions (e.g., Cronk, Lima, & Schweigert, 1993; Gibbs, Nayak, & Cutting, 1989; Titone & Connine, 1994b) to ensure you have the right categories. Get a group of native speakers of English to generate word association responses to the idioms. Find a group of learners of English and repeat the task. What association responses were most typical? Were they predominantly semantically related to the overall figurative meaning of the idiom (for example, response *luck* provided to the idiom *break a leg*), or were they literally related (e.g., the word *pain* in response to *break a leg*)? Did you observe any differences in the type of responses provided by native versus non-native speakers of English? Read Söderman (1993) to find out more about word association responses in native and non-native language speakers. What conclusions can you draw about the way idioms are stored in the mental dictionary of native versus non-native language users? If idioms are stored as single chunks (i.e., long words) in the mental lexicon of native language users, what kind of responses should be most typical in your opinion? Figuratively or literally related? Did you find any differences as a function of the idiom category? For example, did literally plausible and transparent idioms evoke more literally related responses than literally implausible and/or opaque idioms? Did idiom semantic analyzability have any effect on the responses provided?

3. For this experiment, you will need to use E-Prime or another software for measuring reaction time (RT). Please note that a demo version of E-Prime can be downloaded from http://www.pstnet.com/eprime.cfm. In this experiment you will measure RT to words literally or figuratively related to idioms. RTs to literal and figurative targets will be indicative of the degree of activation of the literal meanings of idiom component words and of the figurative meaning of the idiom. Prepare a basic lexical decision task experiment with idioms and related words as your stimuli. In the lexical decision experiment participants see words (e.g., *cat*) and nonwords (e.g. *crat*) and make a decision as to whether what they see on the computer screen is a word or a nonword. The simple stimulus set should consist of at least 15–20 idiomatic expressions. Each idiom should be paired with two target words, one of which will be related literally and another related figuratively to the idiom. For example, for the idiom *let the cat out of the bag*, your literally related target word could be *meow* and your figuratively related target could be

reveal. Next, you will need to develop sentences in which to use your idioms, as well as to prepare control sentences for your literal and figurative targets. For example, a set of stimuli for the idiom *let the cat out of the bag* might be the following:

(a) Idiomatic sentence: *I was preparing a surprise birthday party for Andrea and trying to keep it secret, but my talkative friend went ahead and let the cat out of the bag.*

(b) Literal sentence: *Bambi, my hyperactive kitty, escaped again last night, but my neighbor caught her, brought to my apartment, and let the cat out of the bag.* Suggested targets for the lexical decision task might include *meow*, and *reveal*.

(c) Control sentence: *I was making pierogi for our get-together, but I ran out of mushrooms and replaced them with grilled artichokes.*

In addition, you will need around 15–20 control sentences that will be paired with nonwords. The nonwords should be pronounceable (e.g. *plink, froat*). In your analysis, you will be comparing RTs to literal and figurative targets when those targets are paired with idiomatic sentences versus when the targets are paired with the control sentences. The differences in RTs will constitute the *priming effect*. Run the experiment with at least 15 participants who are advanced learners of English. Did you observe differences in the priming effect for literal versus figurative targets? Which targets were recognized faster? Were literal targets recognized faster for idioms used in their literal sense than in figurative sense, or were they equally primed in both contexts? What does it tell you about the salience of literal and figurative meanings of idioms for this group of participants? Do your data provide support for any of the idiom models discussed in the chapter?

Related Internet Sites

Learn English Today: http://www.learn-english-today.com/idioms/idioms_proverbs.html

Readwritethink: http://www.readwritethink.org/classroom-resources/lesson-plans/figurative-language-teaching-idioms-254.html

The Phrase Finder: http://phrases.org.uk/meanings/index.html

Suggested Further Readings

Blais, M-J., & Gonnerman, L.M. (2013). Explicit and implicit semantic processing of verb-particle constructions by French-English bilinguals. *Bilingualism: Language and Cognition, 16*, 829–846.

236 Bilingual Figurative Language Processing

Boers, F., Piquer Píriz, A.M., Stengers, H., & Eyckmans, J. (2009). Does pictorial elucidation foster recollection of idioms? *Language Teaching Research*, 13, 367–382.

Conklin, K., & Schmitt, N. (2008). Formulaic sequences: Are they processed more quickly than nonformulaic language by native and nonnative speakers? *Applied Linguistics*, 29, 72–89.

Jiang, N., & Nekrasova, T.M. (2007). The processing of formulaic sequences by second language speakers. *The Modern Language Journal*, 91, 433–445.

Langlotz, A. (2006). *Idiomatic creativity: A cognitive-linguistic model of idiom-representation and idiom-variation in English*. Philadelphia, PA: John Benjamins.

Szczepaniak, R., & Lew, R. (2011). The role of imagery in dictionaries of idioms. *Applied Linguistics*, 32, 323–347.

Underwood, G., Schmitt, N., & Galpin, A. (2004). The eyes have it: An eye-movement study into the processing of formulaic sequences. In N. Schmitt (Ed.), *Formulaic sequences: Acquisition, processing, and use* (pp. 153–172). Amsterdam/Philadelphia: John Benjamins.

REFERENCES

Abel, B. (2003). English idioms in the first language and second language lexicon: A dual representation approach. *Second Language Research*, 19, 329–358.

Alexander, R.J. (1987). Problems in understanding and teaching idiomaticity in English. *Anglistik und Englischunterricht*, 32, 105–122.

Arabski, J. (Ed.). (2001). *Time for words: Studies in foreign language vocabulary acquisition*. Katowice: Śląsk Sp. z o.o.

Ariel, M. (2002). The demise of a unique concept of literal meaning. *Journal of Pragmatics*, 34, 361–402.

Beeman, M. (1998). Coarse semantic coding and discourse comprehension. In M. Beeman & C. Chiarello (Eds.), *Right hemisphere language comprehension: Perspectives from cognitive neuroscience* (pp. 255–284). Mahwah, NJ: Lawrence Erlbaum Associates.

Bobrow, S.A., & Bell, S.M. (1973). On catching on to idiomatic expressions. *Memory & Cognition*, 1, 342–346.

Boers, F. (2000). Metaphor awareness and vocabulary retention. *Applied Linguistics*, 21, 553–571.

Boers, F., & Demecheleer, M. (2001). Measuring the impact of cross-cultural differences on learners' comprehension of imageable idioms. *ELT Journal*, 55, 255–262.

Boers, F., Demecheleer, M., & Eyckmans, J. (2004). Cross-cultural variation as a variable in comprehending and remembering figurative idioms. *European Journal of English Studies*, 8, 375–388.

Boers, F., Kappel, J., Stengers, H., & Demecheleer, M. (2006). Formulaic sequences and perceived oral proficiency: Putting a Lexical Approach to the test. *Language Teaching Research*, 10, 245–261.

Bortfeld, H. (2003). Comprehending idioms cross-linguistically. *Experimental Psychology*, 50, 217–230.

Briner, S. (2010). *Hemisphere differences in idiom comprehension: The influence of ambiguity, transparency, and familiarity* (Doctoral dissertation). Retrieved from Theses and dissertations: http://via.library.depaul.edu/etd/45

Cacciari, C. (1993). The place of idioms in literal and metaphorical world. In C. Cacciari & P. Tabossi (Eds.), *Idioms: Processing, structure, and interpretation* (pp. 27–56). Hillsdale, NJ: Lawrence Erlbaum Associates.

Cacciari, C., & Glucksberg, S. (1991). Understanding idiomatic expressions: The contribution of word meanings. In G.B. Simpson (Ed.), *Understanding word and sentence* (pp. 217–240). Amsterdam, Netherlands: Elsevier.

Cacciari, C., & Tabossi, P. (1988). The comprehension of idioms. *Journal of Memory and Language, 27*, 668–683.

(Eds.). (1993). *Idioms: Processing, structure, and interpretation*. Hillsdale, NJ: Lawrence Erlbaum Associates.

Caillies, S., & Butcher, K. (2007). Processing of idiomatic expressions: Evidence for a new hybrid view. *Metaphor and Symbol, 22*, 79–108.

Chafe, W. (1970). *Meaning and the structure of language*. Chicago: University of Chicago Press.

Charteris-Black, J. (2002). Second language figurative proficiency: A comparative study of Malay and English. *Applied Linguistics, 23*, 104–133.

Cieślicka, A.B. (2006a). Literal salience in on-line processing of idiomatic expressions by L2 speakers. *Second Language Reserach, 22*, 115–144.

(2006b). On building castles on the sand, or exploring the issue of transfer in the interpretation and production of L2 fixed expressions. In J. Arabski (Ed.), *Cross-linguistc influences in the second language lexicon* (pp. 226–245). Clevedon: Multilingual Matters.

(2010). Formulaic language in L2: Storage, retrieval and production of idioms by second language learners. In M. Pütz & L. Sicola (Eds.), *Cognitive processing in second language acquisition: Inside the learner's mind* (pp. 149–168). Amsterdam/Philadelphia: John Benjamins.

(2013). Do nonnative language speakers *chew the fat* and *spill the beans* with different brain hemispheres?: Investigating idiom decomposability with the divided visual field paradigm. *Journal of Psycholinguistic Research, 42*, 475–503.

Cieślicka, A.B., & Heredia, R.R. (2011). Hemispheric asymmetries in processing L1 and L2 idioms: Effects of salience and context. *Brain and Language, 116*, 136–150.

(2013, May). *The multiple determinants of eye movement patterns in bilingual figurative processing*. 25th APS Annual Convention, Washington, DC.

Cieślicka, A.B., Heredia, R.R., & Olivares, M. (2014). The eyes have it: How language dominance, salience, and context affect eye movements during idiomatic language processing. In L. Aronin & M. Pawlak (Eds.), *Essential topics in applied linguistics and multilingualism. Studies in honor of David Singleton* (pp. 21–42). New York: Springer.

Cooper, T.C. (1999). Processing of idioms by L2 learners of English. *TESOL Quarterly, 33*, 233–262.

Coulson, S., & Van Petten, C. (2007). A special role for the right hemisphere in metaphor comprehension? ERP evidence from hemifield presentation. *Brain Research, 1146*, 128–145.

Cronk, B.C., Lima, S.D., & Schweigert, W.A. (1993). Idioms in sentences: Effects of frequency, literalness, and familiarity. *Journal of Psycholinguistic Research, 22*, 59–81.

Cronk, B.C., & Schweigert, W.A. (1992). The comprehension of idioms: The effects of familiarity, literalness, and usage. *Applied Psycholinguistics, 13*, 131–146.

Cutting, J.C., & Bock, K. (1997). That's the way the cookie bounces: Syntactic and semantic components of experimentally elicited idiom blends. *Memory & Cognition, 25*, 57–71.

Danesi, M. (1992). Metaphorical competence in second language acquisition and second language teaching: The neglected dimension. In J.E. Alatis (Ed.), *Georgetown University Round Table on Languages and Linguistics* (pp. 489–500). Washington, DC: Georgetown University Press.

Dagut, M. (1977). Incongruencies in lexical "gridding" and application of contrastive semantic analysis to language teaching. *International Review of Applied Linguistics, 15*, 221–229.

Deignan, A., Gabryś, D., & Solska, A. (1997). Teaching English metaphors using cross-linguistic awareness-rasing activities. *ELT Journal, 51*, 352–360.

Ellis, N.C., & Beaton, A. (1995). Psycholinguistic determinants of foreign language vocabulary learning. In B. Harley (Ed.), *Lexical issues in language learning* (pp. 107–165). Ann Arbor/Amsterdam/Philadelphia: John Benjamins Publishing Company.

Eviatar, Z., & Just, M.A. (2006). Brain correlates of discourse processing: An fMRI investigation of irony and conventional metaphor comprehension. *Neuropsychologia, 44*, 2348–2359.

Fernando, C. (1996). *Idioms and idiomaticity*. Oxford, UK: Oxford University Press.

Flores d'Arcais, G.B. (1993). The comprehension and semantic interpretation of idioms. In C. Cacciari & P. Tabossi (Eds.), *Idioms: Processing, structure, and interpretation* (pp. 79–98). Hillsdale, NJ: Lawrence Erlbaum Associates.

Fogliata, A., Rizzo, S., Reati, F., Miniussi, C., Oliveri, M., & Papagno, C. (2007). The time course of idiom processing. *Neuropsychologia, 45*, 3215–3222.

Forrester, M.A. (1995). Tropic implicature and context in the comprehension of idiomatic phrases. *Journal of Psycholinguistic Research, 24*, 1–22.

Fraser, B. (1970). Idioms within a tranformational grammar. *Foundations of Language, 6*, 22–42.

Gairns, R., & Redman, S. (1986). *Working with words: A guide to teaching and learning vocabulary*. Cambridge, UK: Cambridge University Press.

Gibbs, R.W. (1980). Spilling the beans on understanding and memory for idioms in conversation. *Memory & Cognition, 8*, 149–156.

(1985). On the process of understanding idioms. *Journal of Psycholinguistic Research, 14*, 465–472.

(1993). Why idioms are not dead metaphors. In C. Cacciari & P. Tabossi (Eds.), *Idioms: Processing, structure, and interpretation* (pp. 57–77). Hillsdale, NJ: Lawrence Erlbaum Associates.

(2002). A new look at literal meaning in understanding what is said and implicated. *Journal of Pragmatics, 34*, 457–486.

Gibbs, R.W., & Nayak, N.P. (1989). Psycholinguistic studies on the syntactic behavior of idioms. *Cognitive Psychology, 21*, 100–138.

Gibbs, R.W., Nayak, N., Bolton, J., & Keppel, M. (1989). Speakers' assumptions about the lexical flexibility of idioms. *Memory & Cognition, 17*, 58–68.

Gibbs, R.W., Nayak, N.P., & Cutting, C. (1989). How to kick the bucket and not decompose: Analyzability and idiom processing. *Journal of Memory and Language, 28*, 576–593.

Giora, R. (1997). Understanding figurative and literal language: The graded salience hypothesis. *Cognitive Linguistics, 8*, 183–206.

(1999). On the priority of salient meanings: Studies of literal and figurative language. *Journal of Pragmatics, 31*, 919–929.

(2002). Literal vs. figurative language: Different or equal? *Journal of Pragmatics, 34*, 487–506.

(2003). *On our mind: Salience, context, and figurative language.* Oxford, UK: Oxford University Press.

Giora, R., Zaidel, E., Soroker, N., Batori, G., & Kasher, A. (2000). Differential effects of right- and left-hemisphere damage on understanding sarcasm and metaphor. *Metaphor and Symbol, 15*, 63–83.

Glucksberg, S. (1993). Idiom meanings and allusional content. In C. Cacciari & P. Tabossi (Eds.), *Idioms: Processing, structure, and interpretation* (pp. 3–26). Hillsdale, NJ: Lawrence Erlbaum Associates.

(2001). *Understanding figurative language: From metaphors to idioms.* New York: Oxford University Press.

Graham, C., & Belnap, R. (1986). The acquisition of lexical boundaries in English by speakers of Spanish. *International Review of Applied Linguistics, 24*, 273–281.

Grant, L., & Bauer, L. (2004). Criteria for re-defining idioms: Are we barking up the wrong tree? *Applied Linguistics, 25*, 38–61.

Hall, C. (2002). The automatic cognate form assumption: Evidence for the parasitic model of vocabulary development. *IRAL, 40*, 69–87.

Heredia, R.R., Cieślicka, A.B. (2014). Bilingual memory storage: Compound-coordinate and derivatives. In R.R. Heredia & J. Altarriba (Eds.). *Foundations of bilingual memory* (pp. 11–39). New York: Springer.

Heredia, R.R., García, O., & Penecale, M. R. (2007, November). *The comprehension of idiomatic expressions by Spanish-English bilinguals.* Paper Presented at the 48th Annual Meeting of the Psychonomic Society, Long Beach, CA.

Herdina, P., & Jessner, U. (2002). *A dynamic model of multilingualism: Perspectives of change in psycholinguistics.* Clevedon: Multilingual Matters Ltd.

Hillert, D.G., & Buraças, G.T. (2009). The neural substrates of spoken idiom comprehension. *Language and Cognitive Processes, 24*, 1370–1391.

Howarth, P. (1998). Phraseology and second language proficiency. *Applied Linguistics, 19*, 24–44.

Ijaz, H. (1986). Linguistics and cognitive determinants of lexical acquisition in a second language. *Language Learning, 36*, 401–451.

Irujo, S. (1986a). Don't put your leg in your mouth: Transfer in the acquisition of idioms in a second language. *TESOL Quarterly, 20*, 287–304.

(1986b). A piece of cake: Learning and teaching idioms. *ELT Journal, 40*, 236–242.

(1993). Steering clear: Avoidance in the production of idioms. *International Review of Applied Linguistics, 21*, 205–219.

Jackendoff, R. (1997). *The architecture of language faculty*. Cambridge, MA: MIT Press.

Jiang, N. (2000). Lexical representation and development in a second language. *Applied Linguistics, 21*, 47–77.

Johnson-Laird, P.N. (1993). Foreword. In C. Cacciari & P. Tabossi (Eds.), *Idioms: Processing, structure, and interpretation* (pp. VII–X). Hillsdale, NJ: Lawrence Erlbaum Associates.

Jung-Beeman, M. (2005). Bilateral brain processes for comprehending natural language. *Trends in Cognitive Sciences, 9*, 512–518.

Katz, J.J. (1973). Compositionality, idiomaticity and lexical substitution. In S. R. Anderson & P. Kiparsky (Eds.), *A festschrift for Morris Halle* (pp. 357–376). New York: Holt, Reinhart and Winston.

Kecskes, I. (2000). A cognitive-pragmatic approach to situation-bound uterrances. *Journal of Pragmatics, 32*, 605–625.

(2001). "The graded salience hypothesis" in second language acquisition. In S. Niemeier & M. Puetz (Eds.), *Applied cognitive linguistics* (pp. 249–271). Berlin: Mouton de Gruyter.

(2003). *Situation-bound uterances in L1 and L2*. Berlin/New York: Mouton de Gruyter.

(2006). On my mind: Thoughts about salience, context, and figurative language from a second language perspective. *Second Language Research, 22*, 219–237.

Kecskes, I., & Papp, T. (2000). Metaphorical competence in trilingual language production. In J. Cenoz & U. Jessner (Eds.), *English in Europe: The acquisition of a third language* (pp. 99–120). Clevedon: Multilingual Matters Ltd.

Kellerman, E. (1983). Now you see it, now you don't. In S. Gass & L. Selinker (Eds.), *Language transfer in language learning* (pp. 112–134). Rowley, MA: Newbury House.

Kövecses, Z., & Szabo, P. (1996). Idioms: A view from cognitive semantics. *Applied Linguistics, 17*, 326–355.

Kroll, J.F., & Stewart, E. (1994). Category interference in translation and picture naming: Evidence for asymmetric connections between bilingual memory representations. *Journal of Memory and Language, 33*, 149–174.

Lado, R. (1957). *Linguistics across cultures*. Ann Arbor: University of Michigan Press.

Lattey, E. (1986). Pragmatic classification of idioms as an aid for the language learner. *International Review of Applied Linguistics, 24*, 217–233.

Laufer, B. (1989). A factor of difficulty in vocabulary learning: Deceptive transparency. *AILA Review, 6*, 10–20.

(1991). *Similar lexical forms in interlanguage*. Tübingen: Narr.

(1997). What's in a word that makes it hard or easy: Some intralexical factors that affect the learning of words. In N. Schmitt & M. McCarthy (Eds.),

Vocabulary: Description, acquisition, and pedagogy (pp. 140–155). Cambridge, UK: Cambridge University Press.

(2000). Avoidance of idioms in a second language: The effect of L1-L2 degree of similarity. *Studia Linguistica, 54,* 186–196.

Laufer, B., & Eliasson, S. (1993). What causes avoidance in L2 learning: L1-L2 difference, L1-L2 similarity, or L2 complexity? *Studies in Second Language Acquisition, 15,* 35–48.

Laurent, J.-P., Denhieres, G., Passerieux, C., Iakimova, G., & Hardy-Bayle, M.-C. (2006). On understanding idiomatic language: The salience hypothesis assessed by ERPs. *Brain Research, 1068,* 151–160.

Lazar, G. (1996). Using figurative language to expand students' vocabulary. *ELT Journal, 50,* 43–51.

Lee, S.S., & Dapretto, M. (2006). Metaphorical vs. literal word meanings: fMRI evidence against a selective role of the right hemisphere. *NeuroImage, 29,* 536–544.

Libben, M.R., & Titone, D.A. (2008). The multidetermined nature of idiom processing. *Memory & Cognition, 36,* 1103–1121.

Liontas, J.I. (2002). Context and idiom understanding in second languages. In S. H. Foster-Cohen, T. Ruthenberg, & M.-L. Poschen (Eds.), *EUROSLA Yearbook: Annual conference of the European Second Language Association* (pp. 155–185). Amsterdam/Philadelphia: John Benjamins Publishing Company.

(2003). Killing two birds with one stone: Understanding Spanish VP idioms in and out of context. *Hispania, 86,* 289–301.

Littlemore, J. (2001). Metaphoric competence: A language learning strength of students with a holistic cognitive style? *TESOL Quarterly, 35,* 459–491.

Low, G.D. (1988). On teaching metaphor. *Applied Linguistics, 9,* 125–147.

MacWhinney, B. (1992). Competition and transfer in second language learning. In R.J. Harris (Ed.), *Cognitive processing in bilinguals* (pp. 371–390). Amsterdam: North-Holland.

(1997). Second language acquisition and the competition model. In A. M. B. de Groot & J.F. Kroll (Eds.), *Tutorials in bilingualism: Psycholinguistic perspectives* (pp. 113–142). Mahwah, NJ: Lawrence Erlbaum Associates.

(2002). The competition model: The input, the context, and the brain. In P. Robinson (Ed.), *Cognition and second language instruction* (pp. 69–90). Cambridge, UK: Cambridge University Press.

(2005). Extending the Competition Model. *International Journal of Bilingualism, 9,* 69–84.

(2008). A Unified Model. In P. Robinson & N. Ellis (Eds.), *Handbook of cognitive linguistics and second language acquisition* (pp. 341–371). Mahwah, NJ: Lawrence Erlbaum Associates.

Makkai, A. (1972). *Idiom structure in English.* The Hague, Netherlands: Mouton.

Mashal, N., Faust, M., & Hendler, T. (2005). The role of the right hemisphere in processing nonsalient metaphorical meanings: Application of Principle Components Analysis to fMRI data. *Neuropsychologia, 43,* 2084–2100.

Mashal, N., Faust, M., Hendler, T., & Jung-Beeman, M. (2008a). An fMRI investigation of the neural correlates underlying the processing of novel metaphoric expressions. *Brain and Language, 100,* 115–126.

(2008b). Hemispheric differences in processing the literal interpretation of idioms: Converging evidence from behavioral and fMRI studies. *Cortex, 44,* 848–860.

Matlock, T., & Heredia, R.R. (2002). Understanding phrasal verbs in monolinguals and bilinguals. In R.R. Heredia & J. Altarriba (Eds.), *Bilingual sentence processing* (pp. 251–274). Amsterdam: Elsevier.

McCarthy, M. (1990). *Vocabulary.* Oxford, UK: Oxford University Press.

Meara, P. (1978). Learners' word associations in French. *Interlanguage Studies Bulletin, 3,* 192–211.

(1980). Vocabulary acquisition: A neglected aspect of language learning. *Language Teaching and Linguistics Abstracts, 13,* 221–246.

(1993). The bilingual lexicon and the teaching of vocabulary. In R. Schreuder & B. Weltens (Eds.), *The bilingual lexicon* (pp. 279–298). Amsterdam: John Benjamins.

Meara, P., & Ingle, S. (1986). The formal representation of words in an L2 speaker's lexicon. *Second Language Research, 2,* 160–171.

Moon, R. (1997). Vocabulary connections: Multi-word items in English. In N. Schmitt & M. McCarthy (Eds.), *Vocabulary: Description, acquisition and pedagogy* (pp. 40–63). Cambridge, UK: Cambridge University Press.

Mueller, R. A. G., & Gibbs, R.W. (1987). Processing idioms with multiple meanings. *Journal of Psycholinguistic Research, 16,* 63–81.

Nation, P. (1993). Vocabulary size, growth, and use. In R. Schreuder & B. Weltens (Eds.), *The bilingual lexicon* (pp. 115–134). Amsterdam: John Benjamins.

Nation, I.S.P. (2001). *Learning vocabulary in another language.* Cambridge, UK: Cambridge University Press.

Nunberg, G. (1979). The non-uniqueness of semantic solutions: Polysemy. *Linguistics and Philosophy, 3,* 143–184.

Nunberg, G., Sag, I., & Wasow, T. (1994). Idioms. *Language, 70,* 491–538.

Odlin, T. (1989). *Language transfer. Cross-linguistic influence in language learning.* Cambridge, UK: Cambridge University Press.

Oliveri, M., Romero, L., & Papagno, C. (2004). Left but not right temporal involvement in opaque idiom comprehension: A repetitive transcranial magnetic stimulation study. *Jornal of Cognitive Neuroscience, 16,* 848–855.

Papagno, C., & Cacciari, C. (2010). The role of ambiguity in idiom comprehension: The case of a patient with a reversed concreteness effect. *Journal of Neurolinguistics, 23,* 631–643.

Pollio, H., Barlow, J., Fine, H., & Pollio, M. (1977). *Psychology and the poetics of growth: Figurative language in psychology, psychotherapy, and education.* Hillsdale, NJ: Lawrence Erlbaum Associates.

Pulman, S.G. (1993). The recognition and interpretation of idioms. In C. Cacciari & P. Tabossi (Eds.), *Idioms: Processing, structure, and interpretation* (pp. 249–270). Hillsdale, NJ: Lawrence Erlbaum Associates.

Rapp, A.M., Leube, D.T., Erb, M., Grodd, W., & Kircher, T.T.J. (2004). Neural correlates of metaphor processing. *Cognitive Brain Research, 20,* 395–402.

Rizzo, S., Sandrini, M., & Papagno, C. (2007). The dorsolateral prefrontal cortex in idiom interpretation: An rTMS study. *Brain Research Bulletin, 71,* 523–528.

Romero Lauro, L., Tettamanti, M., Cappa, S.F., & Papagno, C. (2008). Idiom comprehension: A prefrontal task? *Cerebral Cortex, 18,* 162–170.

Schmitt, N. (Ed.). (2004). *Formulaic sequences: Acquisition, processing, and use.* Amsterdam/Philadelphia: John Benjamins.

Searle, J.R. (1975). Indirect speech acts. In P. Cole & J.L. Morgan (Eds.), *Syntax and semantics. Speech acts* (pp. 59–82). New York: Academic.

Singleton, D. (1987). Mother tongue and other tongue influence on learner French. *Studies in Second Language Aquisition, 9,* 327–346.

  (1999). *Exploring the second language mental lexicon.* Cambridge, UK: Cambridge University Press.

Singleton, D., & Little, D. (1991). The second language lexicon: Some evidence from university-level learners of French and German. *Second Language Research, 7,* 61–81.

Siyanova-Chanturia, A., Conklin, K., & Schmitt, N. (2011). Adding more fuel to the fire: An eye-tracking study of idiom processing by native and non-native speakers. *Second Language Research, 27,* 251–272.

Skoufaki, S. (2008). Investigating the source of idiom transparency intuitions. *Metaphor and Symbol, 24,* 20–41.

Söderman, T. (1993). Word associations of foreign language learners and native speakers- the phenomenon of shift response type and its relevance for lexical development. In H. Ringbom (Ed.), *Near-native proficiency in English* (pp. 91–182). Abo, Finland: Abo Akademi, English Department Publications.

Sonaiya, R. (1991). Vocabulary acquisition as a process of continuous lexical disambiguation. *International Review of Applied Linguistics, 29,* 273–284.

Spötl, C., & McCarthy, M. (2003). Formulaic utterances in the multi-lingual context. In J. Cenoz, B. Hufeisen, & U. Jessner (Eds.), *The multilingual lexicon* (pp. 133–151). Dordrecht: Kluwer.

Sprenger, S.A., Levelt, W.J.M., & Kempen, G. (2006). Lexical access during the production of idiomatic phrases. *Journal of Memory and Language, 54,* 161–184.

Steinel, M.P., Hulstijn, J.H., & Steinel, W. (2007). Second language learning in a paired-associate paradigm: Effects of direction of learning, direction of testing, idiom imageability, and idiom transparency. *Studies in Second Language Acquisition, 29,* 449–484.

Stringaris, A.K., Medford, N., Giora, R., Giampietro, V.C., Brammer, M.J., & David, A.S. (2006). How metaphors influence semantic relatedness judgments: The role of the right frontal cortext. *NeuroImage, 33,* 784–793.

Stringaris, A.K., Medford, N.C., Giampietro, V., Brammer, M.J., & David, A.S. (2007). Deriving meaning: Distinct neural mechanisms for metaphoric, literal, and non-meaningful sentences. *Brain and Language, 100,* 150–162.

Swinney, D.A., & Cutler, A. (1979). The access and processing of idiomatic expressions. *Journal of Verbal Learning and Verbal Behavior, 18,* 523–534.

Tabossi, P., Fanari, R., & Wolf, K. (2008). Processing idiomatic expressions: Effects of semantic compositionality. *Journal of Experimental Psychology: Learning, Memory, and Cognition, 34,* 313–327.

Tabossi, P., Wolf, K., & Koterle, S. (2009). Idiom syntax: Idiosyncratic or principled? *Journal of Memory and Language, 61,* 77–96.

Tabossi, P., & Zardon, F. (1993). The activation of idiomatic meaning in spoken language comprehension. In C. Cacciari & P. Tabossi (Eds.), *Idioms: Processing, structure, and interpretation* (pp. 145–162). Hillsdale, NJ: Lawrence Erlbaum Associates.

(1995). The activation of idiomatic meaning. In M. Everaert, E.-J. v.d. Linden, A. Schenk, & R. Schreuder (Eds.), *Idioms: Structural and psychological perspectives* (pp. 273–282). Hillsdale, NJ: Lawrence Erlbaum Associates.

Titone, D. (1998). Hemispheric differences in context sensitivity during lexical ambiguity resolution. *Brain and Language, 65,* 361–394.

Titone, D.A., & Connine, C.M. (1994a). Comprehension of idiomatic expressions: Effects of predictability and literality. *Journal of Experimental Psychology: Learning, Memory, and Cognition, 20,* 1126–1138.

(1994b). Descriptive norms for 171 idiomatic expressions: Familiarity, compositionality, predictability, and literality. *Metaphor and Symbolic Activity, 9,* 247–270.

(1999). On the compositional and noncompositional nature of idiomatic expressions. *Journal of Pragmatics, 31,* 1655–1674.

Vega Moreno, R.E. (2005). Idioms, transparency, and pragmatic inference. *UCL Working Papers in Linguistics, 17,* 389–425.

(2007). *Creativity and convention: The pragmatics of everyday figurative s peech.* Amsterdam/Philadelphia: John Benjamins.

Vespignani, F., Canal, P., Molinaro, N., Fonda, S., & Cacciari, C. (2010). Predictive mechanisms of idiom comprehension. *Journal of Cognitive Neuroscience, 22,* 1682–1700.

Wasow, T., Sag, I., & Nunberg, G. (1983). Idioms: An interim report. In S. Hattori & K. Inoue (Eds.), *Proceedings of the XIIIth International Congress of Linguistics* (pp. 102–105). Tokyo: CIPL.

Wray, A. (2000). Formulaic sequences in second language teaching: Principle and practice. *Applied Linguistics, 21,* 463–489.

Yorio, C.A. (1989). Idiomaticity as an indicator of second language proficiency. In K. Hyltenstam & L.K. Obler (Eds.), *Bilingualism across the lifespan: Aspects of acquisition, maturity, and loss* (pp. 55–72). Cambridge, UK: Cambridge University Press.

Zempleni, M.-Z., Haverkort, M., Renken, R., & Stowe, L.A. (2007). Evidence for bilateral involvement in idiom comprehension: An fMRI study. *NeuroImage, 34,* 1280–1291.

Zughoul, M.R. (1991). Lexical choice: Towards writing problematic word lists. *International Review of Applied Linguistics, 29,* 45–60.

8   Neurophysiological Markers of Phrasal Verb Processing: Evidence from L1 and L2 Speakers

Silke Paulmann[1], Zainab Ghareeb-Ali[1], and Claudia Felser[2]

[1]University of Essex, UK; [2]University of Potsdam, Germany

ABSTRACT

Language is often ambiguous. For instance, verb-preposition strings such as *look up* can be interpreted either as a single verb + preposition combination leading to a literal interpretation (e.g., *to look up the chimney*), or can be interpreted as a so-called phrasal verb that requires a figurative interpretation (e.g., *to look up the number*). Past research has primarily used behavioral methodologies to investigate how first (L1) and second language (L2) learners deal with this phenomenon. However, *event-related potentials* (ERPs) are highly time sensitive and may shed additional light on this issue. In this chapter, we will first provide an overview of evidence on phrasal verb processing in L1 and L2 speakers. We will then present some of our own ERP data exploring phrasal verb processing in native speakers of English and native Arabic-speaking L2 learners of English. We will conclude with directions for future ERP research in this domain.

Keywords: bilingualism, event-related potentials (ERPs), figurative language, phrasal verbs, second language acquisition

Psycholinguistic research has a long tradition in exploring how native speakers successfully master the complexities encountered in everyday language. Lexical and structural ambiguities form a vital part of this complexity and are a frequent feature of language. For instance, multi-word expressions such as phrasal verbs (e.g., *run into*), which can have a figurative interpretation (e.g., *to meet*), have been estimated by some to form about one-third of the English verb vocabulary (Li, Zhang, Niu, Jiang, & Srihari, 2003). That is, these verbs are commonly used and language users will have to distinguish them from *prepositional verbs* (i.e., single verb + preposition combinations) that may contain the same words but require a literal interpretation (e.g., *take up a collection*).

The vast majority of research on this kind of multiword expression has concentrated on determining how native speakers of English (easily) distinguish between different meanings that can be generated from sentences such as *Peter ran into Zara on Oxford Street*, which can either be interpreted figuratively (*A man called Peter met his friend called Zara when walking along Oxford Street*) or literally (*A man called Peter went into the Zara store that is located on Oxford Street*). Underlying each of these two possible interpretations is a different syntactic structure. While *run into* in its figurative sense is often taken to be a single lexical unit or a compound verb (e.g., Di Sciullo & Williams, 1987), the preposition *into* functions as the head of a post-verbal prepositional phrase in the literal case.

Little is known to date about how non-native, or second language (L2), speakers deal with the fact that sometimes a lexical form such as *run into* has to be interpreted as a phrasal verb (i.e., figuratively) and sometimes as a single *verb + preposition combination* (i.e., literally). How do non-native speakers of English overcome the problem that it is often not sufficient to simply know each individual word alone to reach the correct interpretation of a sentence? In the first part of this chapter, we will review recent evidence on phrasal verb processing in first (L1) and L2 learners of English. This is followed by presenting data from our own laboratory in which we investigated the cognitive mechanisms underlying phrasal verb processing in native speakers of English and native Arabic-speaking L2 learners of English by means of *event-related potentials* (ERPs). ERPs possess the sensitivity to assess how meaning is processed (i.e., accessed) while words unfold in real time. Our discussion of the data will be followed by suggestions for future directions of research in this field.

Representation and Access of Phrasal Verbs in the Mental Lexicon

As mentioned above, investigations on how native speakers end up with the correct interpretation of ambiguous multiword strings such as *run into* or *kick the bucket* have played an important role in psycholinguistic research. Some of this research has focused on how idioms such as *kick the bucket* or phrasal verbs are stored and accessed in the mental lexicon. For instance, while some propose that these expressions are processed as whole lexical chunks (e.g., Estill & Kemper, 1982; Swinney & Cutler, 1979), others suggest that they may be processed compositionally, similarly to any other word string (e.g., Cacciari & Tabossi, 1988). Of related interest is the question of whether specific meanings or interpretations of multiword expressions are accessible and activated in the lexicon before others. That is, what happens when language users encounter phrases that cannot be interpreted by relying solely on the meaning of each single word of the phrase? For example, is there a temporal processing advantage for one specific interpretation?

Various hypotheses have been proposed to explain how we process figurative language. For instance, when initially introducing the *Idiom List Hypothesis*, Bobrow and Bell (1973) proposed that literal meanings are accessed first. A few years later, Gibbs (1980) in his *Direct Access Hypothesis*, proposed the opposite, namely that figurative interpretations of multiword expressions are accessed before literal interpretations (i.e., the figurative meaning of a phrase is preferentially processed). Around the same time, the *Lexical Representation Hypothesis* favored by Swinney and Cutler (1979) put forward the view that both meanings are processed in parallel (i.e., there is no processing advantage for one specific interpretation). In this case, when encountering expressions that can be interpreted literally or nonliterally, two different processing strategies are applied. On the one hand, activated words undergo a structural analysis necessary for a literal interpretation, while simultaneously whole units get activated in order to access the figurative interpretation. Similarly, the *Configuration Hypothesis* by Cacciari and Tabossi (1988) proposes that initially, both figurative and literal meaning interpretations are considered; however, once idiomatic expressions are recognized as units, only figurative interpretations receive further activation. Literal interpretations of these expressions are no longer pursued once this recognition point has been reached. It is worthwhile to note that the processing mechanisms can be influenced by biasing context. Specifically, if one interpretation is favored over another – for example, if the sentence context biases toward a figurative rather than a literal interpretation – then the processing mechanisms described by the Configuration Hypothesis are altered so that an expression can be recognized even before arriving at its uniqueness point. For example, in an appropriate context the expression *build castles in the air*, which lacks a literal reading, may be recognized as an idiom before the final noun *air* has been processed.

Phrasal Verb Processing in Native and Non-Native Speakers

The processing models mentioned above were built on evidence gathered from L1 speakers. Research investigating whether non-native speakers process multiword expressions in the same way as native speakers do is scarce. This is surprising given that difficulties of phrasal verb usage for L2 learners are well documented. For instance, one of the earlier studies conducted by Dagut and Laufer (1985) explored the avoidance of phrasal verbs using three different tasks in native Hebrew-speaking L2 learners of English. For instance, in one task, participants were required to fill in the blanks of sentences with one of four verb choices, one of them being a phrasal verb (e.g., *We didn't believe that John could ever _____ his friends [let down, solve, disappoint, carry on]*). In another task, the same blanks had to be completed, but instead of providing the learners with different verb options, a Hebrew translation was included (e.g., *We didn't believe that John could ever _____ his friends [leachzev]*). Their results showed that Hebrew speakers predominantly preferred single verbs over phrasal verbs. Hebrew does not have phrasal verbs, but the authors suggested that the avoidance of their use is linked to this absence. In other words, L2 learners prefer to use single verbs whose usage they fully comprehend. Other research has since replicated this avoidance phenomenon in native Dutch (Hulstijn & Marchena, 1989), as well as native Swedish and native Finnish-speaking (Sjöholm, 1995) learners of English. However, results from these studies suggest that both proficiency (Hulstijn & Marchena, 1989) and L1-L2 language distance (Sjöholm, 1995) can modulate phrasal verb avoidance. It should be noted that Laufer and Eliasson (1993) found no phrasal verb avoidance in advanced Swedish learners of English, which indirectly supports the assumption that proficiency alters phrasal verb usage. This is in contrast to more recent evidence from Siyanova and Schmitt (2007), who investigated usage of single (e.g., *to train*) and multiword verbs (e.g., *to work out*) in native English speakers and advanced learners of English. In a questionnaire study, the authors asked both participant groups to indicate their preferred usage of twenty-six selected single and multiword verbs on a six-point Likert scale. Results revealed that non-native speakers were less likely to use multiword verbs than native speakers. Thus, although they were advanced learners of English, the non-native speakers in Siyanova and Schmitt's study showed a higher tendency to use one-word verbs as opposed to multiword verbs.

One of the few studies that explored phrasal verb comprehension (rather than production) in native and non-native speakers of English utilized a cross-modal semantic priming paradigm (McPartland-Fairman, 1989). Phrasal verbs (*sign up, carry on*) as well as matched verb + preposition combinations were embedded in sentences that either biased toward the literal (1a) or figurative (1b) interpretation.

1a. *The soldier was writing to his girlfriend and he had a lot to tell her that day. When he finished, there wasn't enough space for his name at the bottom of the letter. He didn't have any choice, so he signed up*[position 1] *the side of the paper.*

2a. *The doctor told the patient he was working too hard and needed to do more exercise or he would get a heart attack. He didn't have any choice, so he signed up*[position 1] *the next day for an exercise class).*

Participants' task was to name visually presented target words that were either related to the figurative or literal interpretations or unrelated control words, which appeared during auditory sentence presentation at phrasal verb offset (at position 1 in the example above). In general, naming times were faster for related than for control targets. However, similar naming times were found for target words that were related to literal and figurative interpretations, suggesting that both meaning interpretations were activated during reading, as predicted by the Lexical Representation Hypothesis. This was the case for both language groups, suggesting that online comprehension of multiword expressions is comparable between native and non-native speakers of English (McPartland-Fairman, 1989).

More recently, Matlock and Heredia (2002) revisited phrasal verb processing in native and non-native speakers of English. Specifically, the authors sought to explore differences between native and non-native speakers in phrasal verb processing by means of a sentence completion and an online reading comprehension task. The sentence completion task examined whether non-native speakers of English preferentially produced phrasal verb (figurative) or single verb + preposition combinations (literal interpretation) of ambiguous lexical forms. Interestingly, the results from this task revealed that both native and non-native speakers of English produced *more* phrasal verbs than verb + preposition combinations, suggesting that both language groups were equally comfortable using phrasal verbs.

The online reading task investigated the time-course of computing literal versus figurative interpretations. Specifically, Matlock and Heredia (2002) explored whether readers from both language groups would activate the figurative meaning of phrasal verbs (e.g., *to go over the exam*) or the literal meaning (*to go over the street*) first. For the second experiment, the L2 learners were divided into participants who had started to learn English before the age of 12 (i.e., early bilinguals), or after 12 (i.e., late bilinguals). The results revealed that L1 speakers and early bilinguals read sentences with phrasal verbs more quickly than sentences that required single verb + preposition interpretations. This suggests that figurative meanings were processed more quickly than literal meanings. In contrast, late bilinguals showed no such effect. This seemed to suggest that late learners of English have difficulties interpreting sentences that do not allow for a one-to-one translation of words, supporting evidence from production studies that showed that non-native speakers suffer from difficulties using phrasal verbs and that avoidance behavior may be modulated by language proficiency (e.g., Dagut & Laufer, 1985; Hulstijn & Marchena, 1989; Liao & Fukuya, 2004; Siyanova & Schmitt, 2007). Liao and Fukuya, for example, report that intermediate but not advanced Chinese-speaking learners of English avoided using phrasal verbs in comparison to English native speakers.

Although the results from Matlock and Heredia's (2002) second experiment seem to complement findings from the production literature, they should be interpreted with some caution. For instance, both early and late bilinguals came from a variety of language backgrounds; while the early bilingual group was predominately native Spanish speakers (54% of participants) and closely followed by native Chinese speakers (22%), the late bilingual group comprised speakers from a larger pool of backgrounds, with Spanish (23%) and Chinese (30%) native speakers being less dominant. Although unlikely, the difference between early and late bilinguals might thus stem from differences in L1 background. More importantly, group sizes differed (22 early vs. 13 late bilinguals), and given that the late bilinguals showed a numerical difference in reading times for phrasal verbs and verb + preposition combinations that went in the same direction (a 171 ms advantage for reading phrasal verbs) as found in the early bilinguals and native monolinguals, the question arises as to whether the lack of an effect is actually a statistical power problem. This is supported by the observation that the authors' between-subjects analysis did not reveal a significant two-way interaction between group (early vs. late) and verb type (phrasal verb vs. verb phrase), pointing to the possibility that phrasal verb comprehension may not be fundamentally different between early and late bilinguals. Finally, as Matlock and Heredia (2002) point out themselves, sentence reading times lack the temporal resolution needed to assess the time-course underlying online phrasal verb processing. Taken together, we believe more research using time-sensitive methodologies is needed to explore differences and similarities between native and non-native speakers of English when processing phrasal verbs.

Electrophysiological Investigations of Figurative Language Processing

ERPs are highly time sensitive and are now frequently used in psycholinguistic research on bilingualism (see Mueller, 2005, for a review). Whereas behavioral methodologies always measure at discrete points of time (e.g., after a decision has been made), ERPs allow for psychological processes underlying language comprehension to be monitored while words or sentences unfold in real time. Briefly, ERPs are small voltage variations in the *electroencephalogram* (EEG) and result from the brain's response to an event (e.g., auditory/visual stimulus). The series of voltage peaks caused by an event (or stimulus) are called ERP components. Over the past 30 years, several language-related components have been identified (for a short review, see, Friederici, 2004). For instance, the so-called N400 component is a negative ERP peaking at around 400 ms after the onset of a critical event that has been linked to lexical-semantic processes. Specifically, the N400 is elicited in response to words that mismatch preceding sentence context (e.g., the word *socks* elicits a larger N400 than the word *butter* when preceded by sentence contexts such as *He spread the warm bread with...*; Kutas & Hillyard, 1980), making the N400 an ideal candidate when investigating lexical-semantic expectancies.

Several previous studies exploring figurative language processing have reported N400 effects. For instance, Laurent and colleagues investigated idiom processing in a lexical decision task to test Giora's (2003) *Graded Salience Hypothesis*, which claims that salient meanings enjoy a processing advantage over less salient ones. According to Giora (2003, p. 10), salient meanings are "coded meanings foremost on our mind due to conventionality, frequency, familiarity, or prototypicality." Briefly, in the lexical decision tasks, participants are asked to determine if a presented word (e.g., *house*) is a legal word in English (yes) or a non-legal word (no) in English (e.g., *houst*). Participants were presented with strongly (e.g., *rendre les armes* "to surrender weapons") and weakly (e.g., *enfoncer le clou* "to hammer it home") salient idiomatic expressions followed by targets that could be related to the figurative or literal interpretation. The strength of idiomatic saliency of stimuli was determined in a previous study by asking participants to read each expression and then to jot down the first word that struck them. N400 amplitudes measured at the last word of strongly salient idiomatic expression were smaller than amplitudes measured at the last word of weakly salient idiomatic expressions. This suggests that salience (or expectancy) is critical when processing idioms. That is, highly salient expressions are more easily processed than less salient expressions (Laurent, Denhieres, Passerieux, Iakimova, & Hardy-Bayle, 2006). An earlier study exploring idiomatic, literal, and nonsense language processing in schizophrenics and healthy controls also revealed N400 effects. Specifically, participants were presented with stimuli such as *vicious circle* (idiomatic expressions) or *vicious dog* (literal expressions). The authors report stronger N400 amplitudes in response to literal expressions than in response to idiomatic expressions for the healthy control group. This suggests that literal language can be harder to integrate and process than figurative language, especially if figurative language is high in cloze probability as was the case in this study (Strandburg, Marsh, Brown, Asarnow, Guthrie, Harper, Yee, & Nuechterlein, 1997). Other studies report N400 effects in response to metaphors (e.g., Coulson & Van Petten, 2002, 2007; Pynte, Besson, Robichon, & Poli, 1996) or irony (e.g., Cornejo, Simonetti, Aldunate, Ibáñez, López, & Melloni, 2007; Regel, Gunter, & Friederici, 2011).

The Present Study

Thus, it seems as if the N400 can be particularly useful when exploring *how* and *when* figurative and literal meanings are accessed during phrasal verb processing. In particular, we can look at ERPs elicited in response to disambiguating nouns when reading a phrasal verb embedded in neutral sentence contexts to assess whether one reading is preferred (that is, more expected) over another. The present study explores exactly this in both monolingual (native English) and bilingual (native Arabic) populations. We presented sentences such as (2a-b), which contain temporarily ambiguous verb-preposition strings and compared ERPs elicited in response to the disambiguating noun (e.g., *bridge* vs. *farmer*). Notice that in 2a, *ran over* means to *walk over something* and in 2b, it means to *kill someone by driving*.

2a. *I heard that Mr. Smith ran over the old bridge early this morning.*
2b. *I heard that Mr. Smith ran over the old farmer early this morning.*

If figurative meanings are preferred over literal meanings, we expect nouns that allow for such an interpretation to elicit a smaller N400 than nouns that require a literal sentence interpretation. Conversely, if literal meanings are easier to compute than figurative ones, we might expect nouns that disambiguate toward a literal reading to elicit a smaller N400 component. In short, in the present study, the N400 is used as an indicator of integration difficulty. Specifically, component amplitudes are used to infer which reading (literal/figurative) of a noun following neutral sentence requires enhanced cognitive effort.

Methods

Participants
Overall, 20 (10 women, $M = 25.6$ years of age) students from the University of Essex volunteered to participate in the experiment.

They received a small fee for participation. Ten participants (two women, $M = 23.2$ years of age, range $= 18$ to 43 years of age) were native speakers of British English and 10 participants (eight women, $M = 28$ years of age, range $= 24$ to 36 years of age) were native speakers of Arabic. Arabic speakers came from Syria ($n = 1$), Saudi Arabia ($n = 3$), Kuwait ($n = 3$), and Libya ($n = 3$). The L2 participants had started to learn English at school around the age of 8 years (range $= 4$ to 12 years of age) and, on average, had spent 3 years and 9 months in an English-speaking country (range $= 4$ to 84 months). L2 participants self-assessed their English proficiency on a four-point scale (4 = Excellent, 3 = Very good, 2 = Good, and 1 = Poor) for auditory comprehension ($M = 3.4$, $SD = 0.69$), reading comprehension ($M = 3.2$, $SD = 0.63$), speaking ($M = 3.2$, $SD = 0.63$), and writing skills ($M = 3.1$, $SD = 0.56$). The grammar part of the Oxford Placement Test (OPT; Allan, 2004) was also given to L2 learners prior to taking part in the experiment. Total scores ranged from 70–97 percent ($M = 81\%$, $SD = 9$), placing the L2 participants within the upper intermediate (competent user) to highly proficient (very advanced user) range according to the OPT language scale.

Stimuli

The experimental items were created using 18 different, temporarily ambiguous verb-preposition strings such as *run over*. These were embedded in neutral sentences and were semantically disambiguated either toward a literal (single verb + preposition combination) or a figurative interpretation (phrasal verb construction) by the following noun, as illustrated in (2a-b) above. Each experimental sentence consisted of 13 words in total and pairs of critical and disambiguating nouns were matched on frequency from the British National Corpus, $t(35) = .793$, $p = .433$, and were also approximately matched in length. To increase the number of trials in the ERP experiment, each critical verb-preposition string was used four times in total. Specifically, each verb-preposition string was embedded in two different sentence contexts, each of which came in two conditions (i.e., literal vs. figurative). Thus, 72 experimental sentences were presented to each participant. In addition, 144 filler sentences, of which some contained idioms (*My grandfather is as old as the hills*), binomials (*Lisa and her friend ate some fish and chips*), collocations (*Angelina likes to drink strong tea*), or compounds (*Last night my daughter did all of her homework*), were presented. We created four differently randomized presentation lists in which the 36 test items (18 for literal and 18 for figurative interpretation) were intermixed with 144 fillers. Using SuperLab Version 4.07b, sentences were presented using *Rapid Serial Visual Presentation* (RSVP) of one word at a time.

In order to encourage participants to read the sentences actively for meaning, a set of yes/no comprehension questions were constructed that were randomly included in the experiment. For each list, 18 comprehension questions followed critical experimental sentences and 36 questions followed filler sentences.

Procedure

All participants were tested in a quiet laboratory room. Before the start of the EEG experiment, participants were asked to fill out a short demographic and language questionnaire. For the EEG experiment, participants faced a computer monitor from a distance of approximately one meter. Before the start of the experiment, participants engaged in a practice session of four trials. Each trial started with an eye fixation cross displayed for 450 ms, followed by the sentences presented word by word (word presentation duration was set at 450 ms and words were separated by blank screens of 200 ms), followed by a 1000 ms inter-trial interval. All words were displayed in lower case Arial font (64 point) black letters against a white background in the center of the screen. Comprehension questions were presented randomly between trials to ensure that participants were paying attention to the sentences. Breaks were included after every 54 trials. At the end of the EEG session, participants were asked to complete a plausibility rating questionnaire that consisted of 86 sentences in total and included all 72 experimental sentences and additionally 14 fillers that were either perfectly plausible (e.g., *The researchers who are researching the causes of cancer are making progress*) or totally implausible sentences (e.g., *Diana met her whistle in a blue skirt full of beans*). Participants were asked to rate the sentences according to their plausibility on a scale from one to three (1 to indicate *low plausibility* and 3 to indicate *high plausibility*). The results from this questionnaire can be found in Table 1. The EEG experiment lasted approximately 40–45 minutes, while the plausibility rating questionnaire took approximately 10 minutes to fill out. One experimental session (including EEG set up) lasted no longer than two hours.

ERP Recording

Sixty-four EEG channels were recorded from the scalp by means of silver/silver chloride (Ag/AgCl) electrodes attached to an elastic Quikcap (Neuroscan) according to the international 10–20 system: FP1, FPZ, FP2, AF7, AF3, AFZ, AF4, AF8, F9, F7, F5, F3, FZ, F4, F6, F8, F10, FT9, FT7, FC5, FC3, FCZ, FC4, FC6, FT8, FT10, T9, T7, C5, C3, CZ, C4, C6, T8, T10, TP9, TP7, CP5, CP3, CPZ, CP4, CP6, TP8, TP10, P9, P7, P5, P3, PZ, P4, P6, P8, P10, PO7, PO3, POZ, PO4, PO8, O1, OZ, O2, M1, M2. Each EEG channel was amplified with

Table 1. *Mean Rating Scores (SDs in Parentheses) of the Plausibility Rating Split by Group and Condition*

	Verb Type	
Language Group	Literal	Figurative
Native English (n = 10)	2.15 (.585)	2.37 (.447)
Native Arabic (n = 10)	2.05 (.473)	2.25 (.349)

a band pass from DC to 100 Hz with a digitization rate of 500 Hz. AFz served as a ground electrode. All electrodes were online referenced to the left mastoid (M1). Horizontal and vertical electro-oculograms (EOG) were recorded to control for eye movement artifacts. Electrode impedances were kept below 7 kΩ.

ERP Data Analyses

EEG data were processed with EEGLab (Delorme & Makeig, 2004). For each participant, EEG recordings were first re-referenced to the average of both mastoids offline. Next, recordings were band pass filtered between 0.1 Hz and 40 Hz. The continuous EEG was then epoched and baseline corrected using a 200-ms pre-stimulus baseline. Epochs were extracted from 200 ms before the appearance of the disambiguating critical noun up to 800 ms after noun onset. Data for each participant were scanned for artifacts and epochs contaminated with eye blinks and/ or muscle/electrical artifacts were removed for each participant using the *find abnormal values* function in EEGLab. The threshold for this automatic rejection procedure was set at 75 μV. Data were also visually inspected for artifact rejection purposes. Following this procedure, 23 percent of trials had to be rejected for English speakers, whereas 31 percent of trials were rejected for Arabic speakers. Finally, separate ERPs for each condition at each electrode site were averaged for each participant. For graphical illustration purposes only, grand average ERPs were smoothed with a 7 Hz low-pass filter.

In all experiments, the critical group comparisons of the ERP data were quantified for correct responses by calculating amplitudes relative to a 200-ms pre-stimulus baseline. A 2 (Native vs. Non-native participants) × 2 (Literal vs. Figurative meaning) x 7 (Region of Interest, see below) repeated measurements analysis using the PROC GLM function in SAS 9.2 was conducted. The factor *Region of Interest* (ROI) defined a critical region of seven scalp sites: left frontal (LF): F7 F5 F3 FT7 FC5 FC3; right frontal (RF): F8 F6 F4 FT8 FC6 FC4; left central (LC): T7 C5 C3 TP7 CP5 CP3; right central (RC): T8 C6 C4 TP8 CP6 CP4; left posterior (LP): P7 P5 P3 PO7 PO3 O1; right posterior (RP): P8 P6 P4 PO8 PO4 O2 and the midline (ML): FZ FCZ CZ CPZ PZ POZ. The Geissser-Greenhouse correction (Geisser & Greenhouse, 1959) was applied to all repeated measures with greater than one degree of freedom. Main effects of topographical factors are not of interest for the present investigation and are thus not followed up.

Results

Plausibility Rating
A 2 (Language Group: Native vs. Non-native) × 2 (Verb Type: Literal vs. Figurative) ANOVA revealed a significant main effect of verb type, $F(1,18) = 19.6$, $p < .001$, reflecting the fact that participants' plausibility rating scores were higher for figurative than for literal sentences. There was no significant main effect of group, $F(1,18) = .679$, $p = .421$, suggesting that overall, plausibility rating scores did not significantly differ between native and non-native speakers ($M = 2.26$ vs. $M = 2.15$), and no significant interaction between group and verb type was revealed, $F(1,18) = .015$, $p = .904$. Means of the plausibility rating can be found in Table 1 above.

Visual inspection of ERPs
See Figure 1 for visualization of the ERP data. Visual inspection of the data shows an early negativity (N100) peaking at about 100 ms post-stimulus, followed by a positivity (P200) that peaks at around 200 ms, followed by a negative-going wave peaking at 400 ms (N400). Modulations dependent on Type are particularly pronounced in the last component. Thus, a classical N400 time window ranging from 300 to 500 ms after noun onset was chosen for analysis after visual inspection of the data. In addition to a mean *amplitude* analysis, a *peak time* analysis was also run as visual inspection of the data revealed slightly later component onsets for non-native speakers (bottom-half of the figure) when compared to native speakers (top half of the figure).

N400
The ERP analysis for mean amplitudes showed no significant group effect, $F(1,18) = 2.32$, $p = .15$. Crucially, the Verb Type effect was significant, $F(1,18) = 4.61$, $p < .05$, showing more negative ERP amplitudes in response to nouns requiring a literal interpretation than nouns

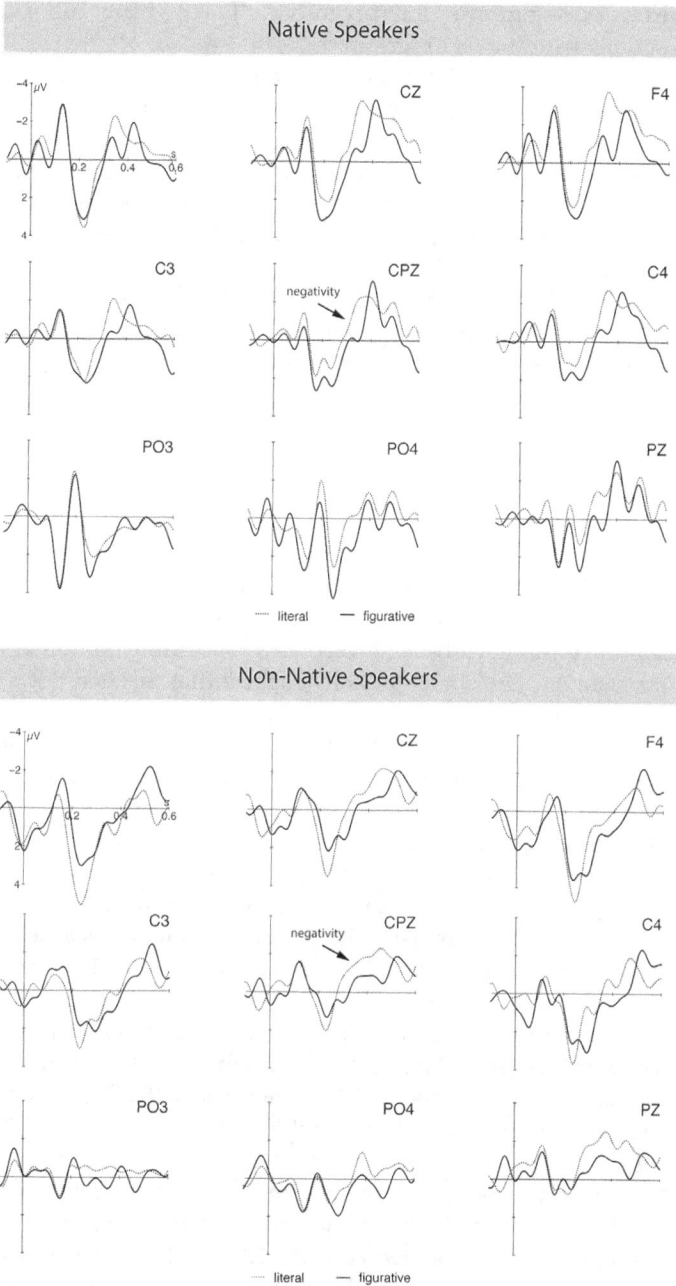

Figure 1. The Significant N400 Effect at Selected Electrode Sites for Native and Non-Native Speakers of English

requiring a figurative interpretation. There were no significant interactions with the factor group or Verb Type.

To assess whether N400 *peak amplitude times* differ between nouns requiring a literal and those requiring a figurative interpretation, we ran an additional ERP *peak time analysis*. This analysis helps to establish whether the two groups differed in processing time rather than in the way they processed the ambiguity. There were no significant main effects. The three-way interaction between ROI x Verb Type x Group reached significance, $F(4,72) = 2.81$, $p = .05$. However, follow-up analyses revealed no further significant effects. Taken together, these results revealed comparable processing mechanisms for native and non-native speakers of English when processing sentences containing phrasal verbs or verb + preposition combinations.

Discussion

The present study set out to explore the time-course underlying phrasal verb and verb + preposition processing in native and non-native speakers of English by means of ERPs. Specifically, we sought to establish whether native and non-native speakers process sentences containing phrasal verbs and verb + preposition combinations in a similar fashion. The current results suggest that this is indeed the case; we report larger N400 components in response to literal when compared to figurative interpretations for both native speakers of English and proficient L2 learners of English with native Arabic language background.

The present results challenge the view that phrasal verb processing is *per se* difficult for L2 learners. Rather, results emphasize once more that language production and language comprehension mechanisms do not always have to go hand in hand. While second language learners may well avoid using phrasal verbs in everyday speech (e.g., Dagut & Laufer, 1985; Hulstijn & Marchena, 1989; Siyanova & Schmitt, 2007), our results support previous findings from comprehension studies applying cross-modal priming (McPartland-Fairman, 1989) or online reading tasks (Matlock & Heredia, 2002), which show that comprehension of phrasal verbs is not necessarily problematic in proficient L2 learners of English.

Moreover, our results complement previous behavioral studies investigating phrasal verb and verb + preposition processing in monolinguals and bilinguals (Matlock & Heredia, 2002), which show *preferred* processing of figurative as opposed to literal meanings for native speakers and early, arguably highly proficient, bilingual speakers. The finding that nouns that require a sentence to be interpreted in a figurative way are more easily integrated into a sentence context than nouns that require the same preceding sentence to be interpreted in a literal way suggests that figurative sentence interpretations are anticipated (i.e., predicted) by readers. Specifically, enhanced N400 components in response to nouns leading to a literal sentence interpretation suggest that these nouns were less expected and hence require enhanced processing effort during sentence integration processes. Note that from an incremental sentence processing perspective, analyzing verb-preposition strings as phrasal verbs would also seem to be the easier option as the structural processor is thought to prefer integrating new upcoming words (here, a preposition immediately following a verb) into the current constituent over postulating a new phrase (Frazier, 1979).

As mentioned in the introduction, previous ERP studies investigating how idiomatic expressions are processed by native speakers have revealed similar N400 results. For instance, Strandburg et al. (1997) compared processing of two-word phrases that were either highly idiomatic (e.g., *pot luck, fat chance, vicious circle*), literal (e.g., *vicious dog*), or nonsensical phrases (e.g., *square wind*) in schizophrenics and healthy controls. Healthy controls showed reduced N400 amplitudes in response to idiomatic two-word phrases when compared to literal and nonsensical phrases, suggesting that the first word of the two-word phrase provides enough context for readers to expect the second word of the phrase (i.e., idiomatic expressions are highly conventionalized). This leads to ease of integration of the second part of the two-word phrase, suggesting preferred processing of figurative interpretations of two-word phrases as opposed to literal interpretations. Similarly, Vespignani, Canal, Molinaro, Fonda, and Cacciari (2010) report reduced N400 amplitudes in response to idioms when compared to literal control conditions, again suggesting that figurative analysis of phrases is highly expected. Finally, Laurent et al. (2006) tried to disentangle *figurativity* (i.e., whether an expression is literal or idiomatic) and saliency effects. Specifically, they presented weakly and strongly salient idiomatic expressions, that is, highly conventionalized idioms such as *rendre les armes* ("surrender the weapons") versus expressions whose idiomatic meaning is less salient such as *enfoncer le clou* ("to hammer it home"). These were followed by target words that were either related to a figurative or literal interpretation. The authors report smaller N400 amplitudes for highly conventionalized (i.e., familiar) idioms when compared to less salient idioms. They also report a reduced N400 in response to figurative targets (e.g., *abandonner* "to give up") that followed highly salient idioms such as *rendre les armes* when compared to (a) literal targets that followed highly salient idioms (e.g., *déposer* "to put down" following *rendre les arms*) as well as (b) literal (e.g., *fixer* "to fix") and (c) figurative targets (e.g., *insister* "to insist") that followed less salient idiomatic expressions such as *enfoncer le clou* "to hammer it home." Given that the authors do not report any diminished amplitudes to figurative targets following *less* conventionalized idioms when compared to literal targets following the same idioms, they argue that it may not be *figurativity per se* that drives the effects reported in previous studies, but that the saliency of idiomatic expressions is more crucial. This claim is partly supported by recent eye-tracking data. In their study, Siyanova-Chanturia, Conklin, and van Heuven (2011) investigated whether native and non-native speakers of English are sensitive to phrasal frequency of multiword sequences. Specifically, the authors compared processing of phrases such as *king and queen* or *right and wrong* with their reversed form *queen and king* or *wrong and right*. It was found that both native and proficient non-native speakers of English were sensitive to frequency information at the phrasal level. Interestingly, reading times of less proficient learners of English were not influenced by phrasal frequency. Taken together, this suggests that multiword sequences are subject to learning and that their saliency or frequency can influence readers' processing mechanisms.

Although the present material contained highly conventionalized expressions (e.g., *eat up the fish* versus *eat up the hill*), we also included less conventionalized items (e.g., *coloring in the picture* vs. *coloring in the garden*). Given that we nevertheless found N400 differences for nouns requiring a verb + preposition or phrasal verb interpretation, our results might suggest that saliency of expressions is not as crucial when processing phrasal verbs as it is when processing idiomatic expressions. Unfortunately, the numbers of items included in the present study do not allow further disentangling this effect (i.e., compare highly conventionalized forms with less conventionalized forms), but future studies of phrasal verb processing could try to control for this potential confound more closely.

Taken together, our results are thus in line with previous electrophysiological findings that support the view that figurative sentence interpretations are often strongly favored by readers. Our offline plausibility rating task also suggests that figurative sentence interpretations are preferred over literal sentence interpretations. When processing temporally ambiguous sentences, the *default* for both L1 and L2 learners might be to go for the figurative interpretation. Literal interpretations would only be considered if a figurative analysis is not successful. Further studies are needed to explore whether this preference is modulated by L2 proficiency or exposure by testing learners of English across a range of proficiencies and how it is affected by the frequency or salience of items.

The view that figurative interpretations of multiword expressions are preferentially processed is emphasized in different theoretical frameworks (e.g., Cacciari & Tabossi, 1988; Gibbs, 1980; Swinney & Cutler, 1979;). For instance, Gibbs (1980) suggests that the figurative meaning of a phrase is accessed before its literal counterpart. Thus, when reading a sentence containing a verb such as *look into*, readers automatically activate lexical-semantic meaning for the whole phrase (*investigate*, *dig*, *search*) rather than for its individual constituents *look* and *into* (literal interpretation). Gibbs (1980) based his Direct Access Hypothesis on the observation that participants were quicker to rate the meaningfulness of phrases that could be interpreted in an idiomatic way (e.g., *kick the bucket*) than those that could only be interpreted in a literal way (e.g., *lift the bucket*). However, judging the meaningfulness of a phrase is a metalinguistic task that is carried out *at the end* of an online reading process. Here, we applied an online sentence reading task and time-locked brain activity to the point in time when readers would first know whether the verb phrase had to be interpreted as a phrasal verb (figurative) or as a verb + preposition combination (literal). Given that we find no differences in the *latency* of the N400 peak amplitude between the two conditions, it can be hypothesized that both literal and figurative interpretations were activated simultaneously, but that phrasal verbs received stronger activation than verb-preposition strings given the processor's preference for late closure (Frazier, 1979).

Language processing is strongly determined by expectancies and context-based predictions (e.g., Federmeier, 2007); here, nouns that allowed for a figurative sentence interpretation elicited smaller N400 amplitudes than frequency- and length-matched nouns that enforced a literal sentence interpretation. Cacciari and Tabossi (1988) proposed that both figurative and literal meaning interpretations would be considered initially (i.e., no timing differences) by the reader but that readers would disregard one interpretation as soon as a recognition point has been reached. Given our neutral sentence context, the *recognition point* (i.e., the point in time at which the ambiguity was resolved) must have occurred at the same time for both tested conditions, meaning that at least initially both sentential interpretations were pursued to the *same* degree. However, after finishing reading the two-word phrase, participants anticipated a noun that allowed for a figurative interpretation of the verb phrase. Nouns that did not match this expectancy elicited larger N400 components in both groups. In conclusion, the current results provide support for models that allow for *simultaneous* activation of phrasal verb and verb + preposition interpretations of two-word phrases; however, processing mechanisms (e.g., timing or degree of activation) can be altered by predictability of (upcoming) constituents (c.f. Vespignani et al., 2010).

Summary and Conclusions

The present study set out to explore how native and non-native speakers of English process phrasal verbs and verb + preposition com-binations. Both language groups show an enhanced N400 component in response to nouns that require the two-word phrase to be interpreted in a literal as opposed to figurative way. This is in line with previous ERP studies exploring idiom processing in native speakers as well as behavioral studies testing phrasal verb processing in native and proficient learners of English (e.g., Matlock & Heredia, 2002). Our results suggest that non-native but proficient speakers of English use similar processing mechanisms when processing phrasal verbs. In particular, expectancy seems to favor figurative sentence interpretations over literal ones. Clearly, figurative meanings have to be learned over time and as mentioned previously cannot always be derived based on individual constituents alone. Future research should thus investigate when second language learners start to prefer figurative interpretations over literal ones. Matlock and Heredia (2002) suggest that age of acquisition can influence processing mechanisms; we suggest also testing language proficiency (irrespective of age of acquisition). Testing learners with the same native language background but who master English to a different degree could give rise as to *when* figurative meaning interpretation is considered to be the default interpretation. Moreover, testing learners with different first language backgrounds allows assessing how far language transfer can influence processing mechanisms.

In addition to exploring the influence of proficiency on phrasal verb processing mechanisms, future studies could also investigate the role of sentence context. In the present investigation, phrasal verbs and verb + preposition strings were embedded in neutral sentence context; however, one might ask whether the apparent preference for figurative interpretations is upheld when introducing biasing contextual informa-tion. In other words, will the figurative meaning of phrasal verbs be accessed when the sentence or discourse context is biased toward the literal interpretation?

Acknowledgments

The authors would like to thank Katharina Mursin for help with data collection, Chelsea Harmsworth for help with data analysis, and Roger Deeble for technical assistance.

List of Keywords

Age of acquisition, Ambiguity resolution, Amplitude, Avoidance, Configuration Hypothesis, Context-based predictions, Conventionalized idioms, Cross-modal semantic priming paradigm, Direct Access Hypothesis, Early bilinguals, Electroencephalogram (EEG), Event-related potentials (ERPs), Figurative language processing, Graded Salience Hypothesis, Idiom List Hypothesis, Incremental sentence processing perspective, Late bilinguals, Lexical decision task, Lexical Representation Hypothesis, Lexical semantic expectancies, Literal interpretation, Mental lexicon, N400, Non-native language processing, Online comprehension, Phrasal verbs, Rapid Serial Visual Presentation (RSVP), Recognition point, Region of interest (ROI), Saliency, Simultaneous activation, Time-locked brain activity, Uniqueness point, Voltage peaks

Thought Questions

1. If non-native speakers are native-like in their ability to access phrasal verb meanings during comprehension, then why do they tend to avoid using phrasal verbs in language production?
2. What are the advantages and possible disadvantages of using ERPs to investigate figurative language processing?
3. Does the similarity of native and non-native speakers' brain responses to figurative versus literal disambiguation in the study reported mean that the same neural mechanisms and pathways are involved in both populations?
4. Many linguists assume that phrasal verbs such as *look up* in *to look up a number* are mentally stored as lexical units, whereas other verb-preposition combinations (as in *to look up the chimney*) are not. How might this difference help account for comprehenders' apparent preference for the figurative (phrasal verb) interpretation of verb-preposition combinations?
5. What linguistic and nonlinguistic factors might influence L2 learners' ability to process phrasal verbs?

6. Should L2 learners of English whose native language also uses verb-particle combinations find phrasal verbs easier to acquire and process in the L2 compared to learners whose native language does not use phrasal verbs?

Suggested Student Research Projects

1. Design an experiment that investigates how native and non-native speakers' interpretation preferences for ambiguous verb-preposition combinations are affected by different types of biasing context. This could, for example, be an offline sentence completion task in which sentence fragments such as *Mary ate up ___* are preceded by a context sentence or paragraph that either biases toward the literal (prepositional verb) or toward the figurative (phrasal verb) interpretation. For examples of suitable sentence fragments, see the materials provided in Matlock and Heredia (2002, Experiment 1). Do the proportions of phrasal versus prepositional verb completions differ between the two context conditions, and are native and non-native speakers' completions affected in the same way by contextual biases?

2. One diagnostic for identifying phrasal verbs in English is the fact that these normally require definite object pronouns to appear between the verb and the preposition (e.g., *She looked it up* vs. *★She looked it into*). Design an acceptability judgment experiment to test whether L2 learners are aware of this grammatical difference between phrasal and prepositional verbs. You could ask participants to make binary (yes/no) judgments on grammatical and ungrammatical stimuli like those above. To help ensure that participants understand whether the figurative (i.e., phrasal verb) or literal (i.e., prepositional verb) reading is intended, the critical stimuli should be presented within appropriate contexts (e.g., *John could not remember Susan's number. Mary quickly looked it up*). To verify whether participants are familiar with the phrasal and prepositional verbs used in the acceptability judgment task, you could additionally carry out a brief vocabulary check or paraphrase task (e.g., asking participants to paraphrase sentences such as *Mary looked up the number*). Do learners who are aware of the meaning difference between (figurative) phrasal verbs and prepositional verbs also make the correct corresponding acceptability judgments? If not, then what does this tell us about the mental representation of phrasal verbs in the L2?

Related Internet Sites

Even Related Potentials: https://en.wikipedia.org/wiki/Event-related_potential

N400 and Meaning: www.youtube.com/watch?v=5d9DPhGS KVo&feature=relmfu

Phrasal Verbs: http://en.wikipedia.org/wiki/Phrasal_verb

Phrasal Verb Bibliography: http://mwe.stanford.edu/phrasalV. html

Phrasal Verb Dictionary: www.usingenglish.com/reference/phrasal-verbs

Suggested Further Readings

Dehé, N. (2002). *Particle verbs in English: Syntax, information structure, and intonation.* Amsterdam/Philadelphia: John Benjamins.

Moreno, E.M., Rodriguez-Fornells, A., & Laine, M. (2008). Event-related potentials (ERPs) in the study of bilingual language processing. *Journal of Neurolinguistics, 21,* 477–508.

Mueller, J.L. (2005). Electrophysiological correlates of second language processing. *Second Language Research, 21,* 152–174.

REFERENCES

Bobrow, S., & Bell, S. (1973). On catching on to idiomatic expressions. *Memory & Cognition, 1,* 343–346.

British National Corpus. (2007). BNC XML Edition (Version 3). [Distributed by Oxford University Computing Services on behalf of the BNC Consortium]. Retrieved from www.natcorp.ox.ac.uk

Cacciari, C., & Tabossi, P. (1988). The comprehension of idioms. *Journal of Memory and Language, 27,* 668–683.

Cornejo, C., Simonetti, F., Aldunate, N., Ibáñez, A., López, V., & Melloni, I. (2007). Electrophysiological evidence of different interpretative strategies in irony comprehension. *Journal of Psycholinguistic Research, 36,* 411–430.

Coulson, S., & Van Petten, C. (2002). Conceptual integration and metaphor: An event-related potential study. *Memory & Cognition, 30,* 958–968.

(2007). A special role for the right hemisphere in metaphor comprehension? ERP evidence from hemifield presentation. *Brain Research, 1146,* 128–145.

Dagut, M., & Laufer, B. (1985). Avoidance of phrasal verbs: A case for contrastive analysis. *Studies in Second Language Acquisition, 7,* 73–79.

Delorme, A., & Makeig, S. (2004). EEGLAB: An open source toolbox for analysis of single-trial EEG dynamics. *Journal of Neuroscience Methods, 134,* 9–21.

Di Sciullo, A.M., & Williams, E. (1987). *On the definition of word.* Cambridge, MA: MIT Press,

Estill, R.B., & Kemper, S. (1982). Interpreting idioms. *Journal of Psycholinguistic Research, 11,* 559–568.

Federmeier, K.D. (2007). Thinking ahead: The role and roots of prediction in language comprehension. *Psychophysiology, 44,* 491–505.

Frazier, L. (1979). *On comprehending sentences: Syntactic parsing strategies.* Bloomington: Indiana University Linguistics Club.

Friederici, A.D. (2004). Event-related brain potential studies in language. *Current Neurology and Neuroscience Reports, 4,* 466–470.

Geisser, S., & Greenhouse, S. (1959). On methods in the analysis of profile data. *Psychometrica, 24,* 95–112.

Gibbs, R.W. (1980). Spilling the beans on understanding and memory for idioms in conversation. *Memory & Cognition, 8,* 149–156.

Giora, R. (2003). *On our mind: Salience, context, and figurative language.* Oxford, UK: Oxford University Press.

Hulstijn, J.H., & Marchena, E. (1989). Avoidance: Grammatical or semantic causes? *Studies in Second Language Acquisition, 11,* 241–255.

Kutas, M., & Hillyard, S.A. (1980). Reading senseless sentences: Brain potentials reflect semantic incongruity. *Science, 207,* 203–208.

Laufer, B., & Eliasson, S. (1993). What causes avoidance in second language learning: L1-L2, difference, L1-L2 similarity, or L2 complexity? *Studies in Second Language Acquisition, 15,* 35–48.

Laurent, J.-P., Denhieres, G., Passerieux, C., Iakimova, G., & Hardy-Bayle, M.-C. (2006). On understanding idiomatic language: The salience hypothesis assessed by ERPs. *Brain Research, 1068,* 151–160.

Li, W., Zhang, X., Niu, C., Jiang, Y., & Srihari, R. (2003). An expert lexicon approach to identifying English phrasal verbs. In *Proceedings of the 41st Annual Meeting of the ACL* (pp. 513–520). Sapporo, Japan.

Liao, Y., & Fukuya, Y.J. (2004). Avoidance of phrasal verbs: The case of Chinese learners of English. *Language Learning, 54,* 193–226.

Matlock, T., & Heredia, R.R. (2002). Lexical access of phrasal verbs and verb-prepositions by monolinguals and bilinguals. In R.R. Heredia & J. Altarriba (Eds.), *Bilingual sentence processing* (pp. 251–274). Amsterdam: Elsevier.

McPartland-Fairman, P. (1989). *The processing of phrasal verbs by native and non-native speakers of English* (Unpublished doctoral dissertation). The City University of New York.

Mueller, J.L. (2005). Electrophysiological correlates of second language processing. *Second Language Research, 21,* 152–174.

Pynte, J.L., Besson, M., Robichon, F.H., & Poli, J. (1996). The time-course of metaphor comprehension: An event-related potential study. *Brain and Language, 55,* 293–316.

Regel, S., Gunter, T.C., & Friederici, A.D. (2011). Isn't it ironic? An electrophysiological exploration of figurative language processing. *Journal of Cognitive Neuroscience, 23,* 277–293.

Siyanova-Chantuira, A., Conklin K., & van Heuven, W. J. B. (2011). Seeing a phrase "time and again" matters: The role of phrasal frequency in the processing of multiword sequences. *Journal of Experimental Psychology: Learning, Memory, and Cognition, 37,* 776–784.

Siyanova, A., & Schmitt, N. (2007). Native and nonnative use of multi-word vs. one-word verbs. *International Review of Applied Linguistics, 45,* 109–139.

Sjöholm, K. (1995). *The influence of crosslinguistic, semantic and input factors on the acquisition of English phrasal verbs.* Turku, Finland: Abo Akademi University Press.

Strandburg, R.J., Marsh, J.T., Brown, W.S., Asarnow, R.F., Guthrie, D., Harper, R., Yee, C.M., & Nuechterlein, K.H. (1997). Event-related potential correlates of linguistic information processing in schizophrenics. *Biological Psychiatry, 42,* 596–608.

Swinney, D., & Cutler, A. (1979). The access and processing of idiomatic expressions. *Journal of Learning and Verbal Behavior, 18,* 523–534.

Vespignani, F., Canal, P., Molinaro, N., Fonda, S., & Cacciari, C. (2010). Predictive mechanisms in idiom comprehension. *Journal of Cognitive Neuroscience, 22,* 1682–1700.

9 Irony Processing in L1 and L2: Same or Different?

Katarzyna Bromberek-Dyzman
Adam Mickiewicz University, Poland

ABSTRACT

This chapter provides an overall review of irony processing research as well as evidence showing that it is not the literal/nonliteral language distinction that determines irony processing patterns, but its affective meaning. In everyday communication, next to saying what they think, speakers impart their attitudes (i.e., likes, dislikes) to express what they feel. Attitudinal content, whether explicit or implicit as in irony, is intended to shape the affective state of the hearer and prime the comprehension of the message. Implicit attitudinal meaning conveyed by ironic comments exploits this affect-driven mechanism. Recent behavioral and neuroimaging evidence shows that attitudinal content instantaneously impacts comprehension. New experimental evidence demonstrates the special role attitudinal content plays in irony processing and is consistent with behavioral and neuroimaging evidence, pointing to an affect-driven mechanism in irony processing. Based on the available experimental evidence exploring irony processing in bilingual population of Polish users of English, preliminary empirical insights point to the primary role of attitudinal content and secondary role of language in irony processing.

Keywords: affective load, bilingualism, contextual effects, implicit attitude, irony processing

Traditionally, verbal irony has been analyzed as a trope. Tropes are utterances with figurative meanings that relate to their literal meanings in one of several standard ways. In irony, figurative meaning is assumed to be the opposite of, or contrary to, the literal meaning and is based on *substitution*, in which the literal meaning is substituted with the figurative meaning. The major drawback of irony as a trope approach is that it neither differentiates between irony and other figures of speech nor explains how the figurative meaning is derived from linguistic evidence. The figurative meaning approach based on literal sense substitution with figurative sense does not explain how people saying one thing communicate something *instead* of what they say, nor why they choose to communicate *instead*.

Major proponents of the figurative approach to irony are Grice (1975, 1989) and Giora (1995, 1997, 2003). Grice refined the rhetorical approach to tropes by proposing an inferential approach (i.e., arriving at the intended communicative meaning by conversational inferencing, combining linguistic meaning with contextual information) to figurative meaning. While Grice was correct in claiming that figurative meaning is arrived at by inferencing, he failed to discriminate between various types of figurative meaning (i.e., irony, metaphor, hyperbole, litotes), assuming that all tropes are *cut to the same pattern* (cf. Wilson, 2010). Grice's account stirred a breakthrough in pragmatic analysis of implied meaning by centering research attention on the inferential processes involved in meaning comprehension. According to Grice, when hearers notice lack of fit between what is said and the context of an utterance, they strive to reconcile the misfit between *the said* and the communicative context at hand. They process the literal meaning and, only if it makes no sense, do they reinterpret it. Irony requires reinterpreting; therefore, it takes more time to process. The Gricean approach to tropes in general and irony in particular has been questioned on descriptive and theoretical grounds (e.g., Wilson, 2006). Grice's account was modified and revised by Giora (1995, 1997), who proposed the *indirect negation view* and the *Graded Salience Hypothesis* (GSH) to account for how people comprehend figurative meaning. The indirect negation view proposes that irony involves the presence of both literal and implied meanings and that the relationship between the two is of indirect (i.e., non-explicit) negation (Giora, 1995). While Grice postulated that the literal meaning is discarded as soon as the comprehender realizes that the literal meaning is not what the speaker means, Giora claims that the rejected literal meaning is retained, and its role in the comprehension process (i.e., *contrast effect*) is essential. According to the GSH, more salient meanings enjoy priority in interpretation (Giora, 1997), and nonsalient meanings are interpreted after the salient ones. Giora (1997) rejects the priority and primacy of literal meanings in favor of the primacy of salient sense (literal or figurative). The GSH makes clear empirical predictions for irony processing. Nonconventional irony is less salient than its literal reading; hence, it takes longer to process. Literal meanings remain available after nonliteral meanings have been activated. The GSH diverges from the Gricean approach in two main ways: (1) It claims salience over literal priority, and (2) literal meanings are retained, not rejected, when no longer assumed intended. Yet, they both agree that irony is processed longer than its literal equivalents.

Irony Processing

Processing-oriented irony research adheres to the literal/nonliteral meaning distinction as *the* variable accounting for the differential response time patterns, consistently varying for literal and ironic meaning processing. This line of research strives to investigate the stages taken to process irony. What is the sequence of comprehending irony? Is the literal meaning always activated first, followed by the figurative interpretation, or vice versa? Moreover, does the online processing of ironic statements take longer than equivalent literal language statements? It reflects a long-standing controversy over the role of literal meaning in nonliteral language processing. Two paradigms have dominated irony-processing research, the *two-* versus the *one-stage approach*. These two views adhere to the literal/nonliteral meaning distinction as the source and explanation of the differential irony/non-irony processing, yet they each harbor discrepant theoretical and processing assumptions and elicit incompatible empirical results. Two-stage models build on the assumption that figurative language processing proceeds in two subsequent stages. First, literal (*coded, salient*) interpretations are accessed and rejected as incompatible with context. Second, context-fitting, nonliteral/ironic interpretations are accessed. In terms of processing, irony comprehension requires an extra inferential step; therefore, it takes longer than literal language comprehension (e.g., Giora, 1995, 1997, 2002, 2003; Giora & Fein, 1999; Giora, Fein, & Schwartz, 1998; Giora, Fein, Laadan, et al., 2007; Filik & Moxey, 2010). In contrast, one-stage models predict that literal language has no processing advantage or priority over nonliteral language. In fact, literal and nonliteral language are governed by a common set of processing and comprehension principles. In relation to comprehension, no significant distinctions between literal and nonliteral meaning are postulated (e.g., Gibbs 1983, 1986b, 2002; Sperber & Wilson, 1986, 1995, 2002). A growing body of experimental evidence demonstrates that comprehending irony takes no longer than comprehending literal language (e.g., Gibbs, 1979, 1983, 1986a, 1986b, 1986c, 1994, 2000; Gibbs & O'Brien, 1991; Gibbs, O'Brien, & Doolittle 1995; Ivanko & Pexman, 2003). *Parallel processing* accounts challenge the assumption of sequentiality in literal and nonliteral meaning processing and emphasize the crucial role of context, especially its unconditional and immediate impact on the comprehension process (e.g., Gibbs, 1994, 2002; Sperber & Wilson, 1986, 1995). Provided sufficient and supportive context, with contextual effects appropriately manifested, nonliteral meanings are arrived at directly. Context primes the comprehension of contextually compatible meanings instantly and entirely. Ironic meanings can get a head start if contextually primed. Parallel-processing models posit that comprehension processes are equally sensitive to linguistic and extralinguistic information. According to Gibbs (1994), the ability to recognize and interpret incongruity between what people say and what they mean is a reflection of the ability to think ironically. Accordingly, understanding irony requires no special cognitive processes and does not need to be particularly effortful. When primed with ironic cues, people adopt an ironic frame of mind, which facilitates irony processing. In support of this claim, Gibbs (1986b) presented results of three experiments in which he examined irony reading and paraphrasing speed. The results show that irony (i.e., ironic praise and ironic criticism) may be processed faster than its literal equivalents, provided it is embedded in an irony-supportive context. According to Gibbs, irony processing speed depends on context supportiveness and degree of irony manifestness. There is no way of once and for all saying that literal comments are processed faster, or irony is processed faster. Comprehension speed is cued by and depends on the degree of context supportiveness. Both reading and paraphrase time patterns in Gibbs (1986b) consistently show that ironic reading is enhanced in irony-supportive contexts and impaired in nonsupportive contexts. In Gibb's study, participants consistently took less time to read and paraphrase critical irony (1767 ms) than literal criticism (1901 ms) embedded in supportive contexts. Critical irony (1503 ms) and literal praise (1525 ms) were processed more quickly than literal criticism (1643 ms). Subjects took less time to read critical irony (1716 ms) in irony-supportive contexts than they did in nonsupportive contexts (1987 ms). Participants were also faster at reading literal praise (1554 ms) than at reading literal criticism (1721 ms). The results overall show that ironic comments may be processed as fast as or faster than non-ironic comments and that the processing is facilitated or inhibited by the contextual features (supportive vs. nonsupportive context). Evidence showing that ironic remarks can be comprehended as fast as or faster than literal equivalents indicates that literal or nonliteral meaning of the comment is not the key factor in irony comprehension. Context is.

One- versus Two-Stage Models in Irony Processing

Both one-stage and two-stage accounts examine the comprehension of nonliteral language, yet focus on different aspects of the examined phenomena. While two-stage accounts (e.g., Giora, 1995, 1997, 2003; Giora, Fein, & Schwartz, 1998; Giora & Fein, 1999) assume that linguistic (coded) contents enjoy processing priority, one-stage accounts (e.g., Gibbs, 1986b, 2000; Gibbs et al., 1995; Gibbs & O'Brien, 1991; Ivanko & Pexman, 2003) posit that contextual effects instantaneously and unconditionally constrain comprehension. Also, different ranges of experimental variables were tested by the two models. Giora and associates (e.g., Giora, 1997; Giora et al., 1998, 2007; Giora & Fein, 1999) systematically employed one type of comment: literal praise, which in positive context conveys literal praise and in negative context conveys critical irony. When comparing critical irony (e.g., a comment *You are so punctual* when someone is in fact late) against literal praise (e.g., the same comment *You are so punctual* when someone is on time), literal praise is processed faster. This specific combination of variables produced the same results in Gibbs' (1986b) experiment three. This pattern has also been observed in other irony studies, consistently showing that when comparing congruity – literal praise versus incongruity – and critical irony, critical irony is processed longer than literal praise (e.g., Dews & Winner, 1999; Schwoebel et al., 2000; Filik & Moxey, 2010). Giora and colleagues provide consistent data showing that congruity (i.e., literal praise) is processed faster than incongruity (i.e., ironic criticism). Yet, this specific combination of variables (literal praise vs. critical irony) does not encompass a wide enough range of ironic and non-ironic conditions to make strong claims about irony processing. The range of context (e.g., supportive vs. nonsupportive) and comment combinations (e.g., literal praise versus ironic praise; literal criticism vs. ironic criticism) in Gibbs' designs allows for a more comprehensive analysis of literal and ironic meanings. The results obtained by Gibbs (1986b) show that, while critical irony takes longer to process than literal compliments, it is also processed faster than praising irony and literal criticism. The speed of irony processing is, as Gibbs' results show, context contingent. Therefore, contextual effects involved in irony communication must be explicitly factored out in irony research. Both strongly (explicitly) and weakly (implicitly) manifested contextual effects seem equally important for the comprehension of irony (cf. Sperber & Wilson, 1986).

The significance of context, and especially the role of weak communicative effects in irony comprehension, has recently been tested by Regel, Gunter, and Friederici (2010), who set out to test when and how listeners integrate implicit extralinguistic information to compute ironic meaning. Regel et al. wanted to find out whether or how the implicit knowledge about the speaker's communicative style (ironic vs. nonironic), activates predictions and processing expectations and how these reverberate in brainwave patterns. In two experimental sessions, they manipulated the speaker's use of irony to see how irony frequency implicitly cued anticipation for irony. The study showed that unexpected irony produced by a non-ironic speaker resulted in increased amplitudes of P600 brain waves associated with semantic and syntactic expectations, and both ironic and literal statements made by an ironic speaker elicited similar patterns of brain activity (P600 amplitudes). Session two, conducted one day later, featured balanced irony use, yet the *event-related potentials* (ERPs) showed increased brain activity for irony processing for the ironic speaker, but not for the non-ironic speaker. This finding indicates that implicit knowledge about the speaker's preference for explicit/implicit attitude communication does affect language comprehension in early processing (200 ms after the onset of a critical word), as well as in the later stages of comprehension (500–900 ms post-onset). Bits of pragmatic, extralinguistic information about the speaker's communicative preferences (explicit/implicit attitude display) have a direct bearing on the neurophysiology (brainwaves) of inferential processing. This study shows that explicit/implicit attitude display style triggers anticipated processing and determines brainwave patterns. The implicit extralinguistic cue manifested by the frequency of ironic comments plays a significant role in modulating brainwave patterns in message comprehension. The results attest to the importance of extralinguistic contextual cues in irony comprehension and show that implicit cues about a speaker's communicative style alter ironic message processing. This finding further shows that irony processing patterns differ as a function of expectations, implicitly triggered by the speaker's attitude-manifesting style, not the literality/nonliterality of the message.

Attitude in Irony Comprehension

How does attitude enter ironic meaning and shape its comprehension? Irony is used to serve a wide range of communicative functions conveyed by a repertoire of irony vehicles. For instance, Leggitt and Gibbs (2000) in a series of experiments showed that different irony vehicles (e.g., sarcasm, banter, metaphor, overstatement, understatement) might be employed to convey a range of ironic meanings (praise, criticism, jocularity, metaphorical irony, metonymic irony, hyperbole, litotes) and evoke different patterns of emotional reactions in hearers. Irony in communication may be a true chameleon, blending with a variety of other language forms to achieve varied communicative ends (e.g., Gibbs, 1994, 2000; Kreuz, Roberts, Johnson, & Bertus, 1996; Leggitt & Gibbs, 2000; Winner et al., 1987). Next to expressing politeness (e.g., Dews, Kaplan, & Winner, 1995; Jorgensen, 1996; Kumon-Nakamura, Glucksberg, & Brown, 1995), jocularity and humor (e.g., Martin, 2007; Gibbs, 2000; Dews et al., 1995; Roberts & Kreuz, 1994), and emotional bonding (e.g., Attardo, 2000; Dews & Winner, 1995; Dews, Kaplan, & Winner, 1995; Gibbs, 2000), irony commonly serves to express affective attitudes (cf. Kreuz, Long, & Church, 1991; Roberts & Kreuz, 1994; Sperber & Wilson, 1986, 1995). Irony is commonly employed whenever speakers want to implicitly *manifest* their unwelcome attitudes (i.e., dislikes, criticism) in a brief unchallengeable manner.

Feature-oriented irony research has singled out a range of markers that might accompany irony and facilitate its comprehension. While cues might facilitate irony interpretation, irony might as well be successfully communicated without extra cues. Markers commonly employed to highlight ironic meaning are not exclusive markers of irony. Research on an ironic tone of voice and ironic facial expression shows that there is no single pattern of ironic tone of voice or a specific facial expression to mark irony exclusively (e.g., Attardo, Eisterhold, Hay, & Poggi, 2003; Bryant & Fox Tree, 2002, 2005). Various prosodic and facial markers may be optionally used as contrastive markers cueing irony. They signal a contrast between what is said and how it is said to cue irony comprehension. They are not, however, irony exclusive or constitutive features (i.e., constituting the essence of ironicity). Barbe (1995) highlights that irony essentially boils down to the duality or dichotomy that implicitly binds some incongruity. It introduces ambiguity triggered by the concurrent availability of two or more interpretations. This dichotomous duality is *the* constitutive feature of irony. When the dichotomy is removed, irony is gone. Irony is inherently *two-faced*, humorous and hurtful, funny and stingy, criticizing and praising at the same time. Various types of ironic duality have been explored and described. According to Barbe (1995), the most commonly researched ones include (a) contrast between reality and an appearance, (b) incongruity between language and the context or behavior and the situation, and (c) blatant discord between what the speaker explicitly says and feels or nonverbally manifests (i.e., emotional load).

Various mechanisms have been postulated to trigger ironic duality and constrain its interpretation. Utsumi (2000) points to the ironic environment as a prerequisite for successful irony communication/comprehension. Ironic environment is hinged on failed expectations implicitly displayed. In order for an utterance to be ironic, the speaker must implicitly manifest her disappointment at failed expectations. Kihara (2005) claims that verbal irony refers to a mutually manifest expectation space, in which an expectation is implicitly held and it gets explicitly failed. Accordingly, the only necessary and sufficient condition for an utterance to be ironic is the mutually manifest expectation (e.g., we implicitly expect people to be punctual; when they are not, this expectation is thwarted). Ironical speakers say that something is the case in order to make it mutually manifest that it is not what they have expected. Colston (2002) endorses a view that verbal irony comprehension is correlated with the perceptual and cognitive effect of contrast. According to Colston, irony comprehension is a function of contrast effects produced by the discrepancy between semantic meaning of ironic comment and its referent situation (cf. Colston, 1997; Colston & Keller, 1998; Colston & O'Brien, 2000). Colston (2002) tested a broad family of biasing effects to conclude that irony comprehension is facilitated by contrast effects (cf. Colston & O'Brien, 2000).

Contrast effects in irony comprehension, conveyed by expressing positive comments when one intends to criticize, have also been studied by Ivanko and Pexman (2003). Their study shows that strongly negative situations stir expectation for literal criticism. Moderately negative situations preempt expectation for moderate criticism. Moderately negative context prompts facilitated processing of ironic criticism, which is the prototypical and most widespread type of irony. Strongly negative context thwarts irony processing. The degree of perceptual contrast between ironic comment and its referent situation works as a preemptive trigger preparing the hearer for the expected comment (e.g., a moderately critical comment: *You are so punctual* to someone who is slightly late). Strongly negative context prepares for strongly negative comment (e.g., a strongly critical comment: *You are never punctual* to someone who is very late). Moderately negative context preempts moderately negative comment (irony) processing. Shelley (2001) posits that a situation counts as ironic when it is conceived as having a bicoherent structure and activates concepts in a bicoherent pattern (i.e., two incoherent elements simultaneously as in complimenting someone who is late, *You are so punctual*). While coherence relations are based on a positive association between concepts (i.e., similarity, analogy, collocation), incoherence is hinged on negative association (i.e., dissimilarity, asymmetry, antonymy). For a situation to be ironic, it must be surprisingly and saliently bicoherent. Kotthoff (2003) proposes that the most conspicuous aspect of irony is the evaluative gap anchored between the said and the intended. Kotthoff posits that the said and the meant in irony communicate opposite (positive and negative) evaluations. In other words, irony is a form of evaluation. It communicates an evaluative gap. Specifically, irony conveys incongruous evaluative options through the *dictum* and the *implicatum*. This structure gives an addressee an option to respond either to the said (dictum) or to the meant (implicatum). Partington (2007) proposes that the principal mechanism driving irony is an implied reversal of evaluative meaning. The implied evaluative reversal is set between a favorable evaluation in the dictum and an unfavorable evaluation in the implicatum. According to Partington, neither picturing irony as the statement of the opposite of what is meant, nor as a defeated expectation, is sufficient in itself to explain irony. Rather than being set at the say/mean opposition, Partington views irony in a spectrum of *evaluative duality*. According to Partington, irony is driven by evaluation and should be understood in a dualistic, bi-dimensional sense of how speakers approve or disapprove and applaud or criticize the contents they verbally endorse.

Several theoretical accounts highlight attitude as the key factor in irony communication and comprehension (e.g., Barbe, 1995; Clark & Gerrig, 1984; Kreuz & Glucksberg, 1989; Kumon-Nakamura et al., 1995; Sperber & Wilson, 1981, 1986, 1995). One of the main accounts advocating the essential role of attitude in irony communication is the *Echoic Mention Theory* (Sperber & Wilson, 1981, 1986, 1995, 1998; Wilson, 2006, 2010; Wilson & Sperber, 1992, 2004). Sperber and Wilson developed the Echoic Mention Theory as a response to the traditional substitution approach to irony (Grice, 1975, 1978, 1989). They posit that irony is not arrived at by substitution of literal with figurative meaning, but by the echoic mention mechanism. Implicit attitude, conveyed against explicit verbal contents, *echoes* some failed expectation or social norm. Echoic utterances achieve relevance by informing the hearer that the speaker is entertaining a dissociative attitude toward the expressed opinion. A number of alternative accounts grew out of the echoic mention account to posit attitude as crucially involved in irony communication (e.g., Clark & Gerrig, 1984; Kreuz & Glucksberg, 1989; Kumon-Nakamura et al., 1995).

Irony and Neuroimaging

Irony is often considered a test case for exploring and explaining mind-reading infrastructure involved in implicit meaning comprehension (i.e., *Theory of Mind [ToM]*). To grasp irony, a hearer needs to access implicit attitude on top of what the speaker literally says. Recent ToM neuroimaging research has corroborated the importance of attitude in irony comprehension. Neuroimaging and lesion studies show that irony comprehension consistently activates mindreading circuits (i.e., medial prefrontal cortex, temporal poles, and superior temporal sulcus) on a regular basis (e.g., Regel, Coulson, & Gunter, 2010; Regel, Gunter, & Friederici, 2011; Shamay-Tsoory, Tomer, & Aharon-Peretz, 2005a; Shamay-Tsoory, Tomer, Berger, Goldsher, & Aharon-Peretz, 2005b; Shibata, Toyomura, Itoh, & Abe, 2010; Uchiyama et al.,

2006; Wang, Lee, Sigman, & Dapretto, 2006; Wakusawa et al., 2007). Shamay-Tsoory and associates explored a distinction between *cognitive* (attribution of thoughts) and *affective* (attribution of feelings) ToM and irony comprehension. They employed a number of mindreading tasks to assess differential ToM circuitry involvement in cognitive and affective processing. Basic cognitive mindreading capacity was tested by a *second-order false belief task* (belief about belief). An irony comprehension task was used to assess higher level affective and cognitive processing, because next to the ability to understand second-order false beliefs, irony comprehension also requires the ability to identify the affective attitude conveyed implicitly. Shamay-Tsoory et al.'s results revealed that patients with ventromedial prefrontal lesions were significantly impaired in irony, but not in second-order false belief, as compared to patients with posterior lesions and normal control subjects. This might be interpreted as an indication that the posterior brain regions are not so crucially involved in mindreading and irony comprehension. Shamay-Tsoory et al. posit that the deficits observed in patients with ventromedial lesions result from the impaired affect-related circuitry. Belief and attitude attribution, as Shamay-Tsoory et al. show, are performed by non-overlapping ToM circuitries (cf. Bechara, Tranel, Damasio, & Damasio, 1996; Damasio, 1994; Damasio, Tranel, & Damasio 1991). Their results show that inferences about mental states of others include not only assumptions about their thoughts and beliefs, but also assumptions about affective states and feelings. The study shows that ToM circuitry comprises cognitive and affective sub-circuitries, and the authors postulate that irony should be studied in paradigms that provide for the cognitive and affective aspects of processing respectively.

Affect and Attitude Comprehension

The conspicuous role of affect and especially its most basic attitude-expressing contents (i.e., likes, dislikes) in perception and communication/comprehension were highlighted by Zajonc (1980, 1984), who argued that affective reactions to stimuli are the very first reactions that occur automatically and guide further stimuli processing and judgment. According to Zajonc, both perception and inference are *affect-saturated* (i.e., neither perception nor comprehension are ever affect-free). Zajonc proposed the *Affective Primacy Hypothesis* in which he claimed that affective stimuli, as opposed to cognitive stimuli, require no inferencing and are independent and primary in social perception, comprehension, and interaction. According to Zajonc, affect is a component of the meaning system, pictured as *feeling tones* that accompany concepts and constitute part of their meaning. The Affective Primacy Hypothesis holds that affective, attitudinal contents are processed differently and separately from cognitive contents. Cognitive and affective processes vary and have different characteristics. Detection, recognition, discrimination, and categorization are cognitive processes, while evaluation is an affective process that differs from the cognitive processes on several grounds. Affective responses are body-based physiological patterns driven by fast, subconscious routines, independent from and primary to cognitive processes (cf. Cacioppo, Larsen, Smith, & Berntson, 2004; Damasio, 2010). Zajonc reasoned that because affective and cognitive processes differ, the difference must be triggered by features manifesting affective and cognitive contents.

There is growing evidence showing that *affective* and *non-affective* stimuli features differ and that the cues effective in retrieval of descriptive contents are not effective in retrieval of evaluative, attitudinal contents. Bargh, Litt, Pratto, and Spielman (1989) presented trait adjectives below the subjects' conscious awareness. Participants were asked to respond to either evaluative or descriptive features of the presented stimuli. As the presentation durations of the stimuli dropped below the consciousness threshold, participants retained the ability to respond correctly to the evaluative traits at better than chance levels, but were not able to respond to the semantic traits with a greater than chance probability. This shows, according to Bargh et al., that subjects have had access to the evaluative information about the target independently of conscious access to the semantic information about the target. The ability to respond to attitudinal content was independent of the ability to respond to semantic contents of the target. In the experiment with subliminal presentation of Chinese ideographs, Zajonc (1980) observed that the liking judgment (i.e., judgments about attitudes) response times were much shorter than the recognition judgments and that cognitive discrimination required longer access to stimulus information. Murphy and Zajonc (1993) primed participants with affective and cognitive stimuli presented under extremely brief (suboptimal) and longer (optimal) exposure durations. At suboptimal exposures only affective primes produced correct judgments. At optimal exposures, the pattern of results was reversed, showing that only cognitive primes produced correct judgments. These results show that affective qualities of stimuli (i.e., the ones referring to the attitudinal meaning, such as good/bad, positive/negative) can be processed faster than their non-affective attributes, are based on rudimentary information, and are processed subconsciously. Additionally, the study showed that affective stimuli elicit early affective reaction that can be sustained or diluted by subsequent cognitive operations. Lodge and Taber (2000) found that it took subjects less than 700 ms to make an affective response, about twice as fast as the time to verify a cognitive association in a true/false verification task. These findings support Zajonc's (1980, 1984) Affective Primacy Hypothesis showing that affect and cognition work independently. Affective judgments based on attitudinal meaning (e.g., good vs. bad) are made faster and with greater confidence than cognitive judgments.

Research by LeDoux, Iwata, Cicchetti, and Reis (1988) and LeDoux, Ruggiero, Forest, Stornetta, and Reis (1987) shows that affective associative connections bypass cognitive processing mechanism entirely. Affective pathways in the brain can be independent of cognitive pathways that operate on different principles. LeDoux (1995, 1996, 2000) provided experimental evidence showing that affective reactions need not depend on cognition. Affect and cognition are under control of separate and partially independent systems. Both constitute independent sources of information (cf. Damasio et al., 1991). In a series of experiments involving brain stimulation in rats, Shizgal (1999) provided evidence that neural circuitry involved in computing the affective significance of stimuli (evaluative processing) diverges from the circuitry involved in identification and discrimination (non-evaluative processing). Damasio and colleagues in numerous neurological studies provided compelling evidence that affective reactions are evolutionarily programmed, separate from cognitive reactions, and inescapable (e.g., Bechara 2003; Bechara, 2004; Bechara & Damasio, 2005; Bechara, Damasio, H., & Damasio, A. R. 2000; Bechara, Damasio, H., Tranel, & Damasio, A. R., 1997, 2005; Damasio, 1994; Damasio et al., 1991). Affective content processing patterns exhibit speed, quality, and accuracy advantages when compared to cognitive content processing.

Neurological research shows that affective stimuli are handled by phylogenetically more ancient, highly automatized brain circuitry. More ancient circuitries in the brain (i.e., reptilian brain) evolved to respond to life-threatening challenges and, because of their survival value, have enjoyed automatic processing advantages (e.g., Damasio, 2010; Panksepp, 1998). Damasio (1994) describes a *Somatic Marker Mechanism* (SOM) as an extension of the automatic affective system, which has evolved to mark the environmental stimuli with a value tag (i.e., good, beneficial vs. bad, harmful). Based on the survival-driven physiological *know-how* inscribed in neural circuitry, somatic markers are patterned dispositions to rapidly and unconsciously evaluate and respond to environmental challenges. From the evolutionary perspective, SOM is the oldest biological value-driven decision-making device. Damasio

(2010) argues that we continuously assign value to everything that surrounds us. Evaluation is incessant, and the notion of value is central to the brain activity. Whatever we perceive, it is never a mere collection of features. It is a collection of features that we like or do not like. Value marking, according to Damasio, is perceived as *gut feeling*, physiological response patterns that incessantly operate as markers of value (our likes and dislikes), a principal component of an attitude.

Barrett (2006) depicts evaluative processing as a mode of processing whereby an entity (stimulus) is assigned some degree of valent meaning, and it is interpreted along a good/bad evaluative spectrum. Affective stimuli initiate evaluative processes through which the stimuli are interpreted, and an evaluative tag is attached as a result. Valuation can be thought of as a simple form of meaning analysis in which the currently processed stimulus is being assessed as good or bad in a given instance. Humans (and animals too) constantly and instantly *read* the environment in terms of valence and sense it as a basic feature of their experience and a primary source of responding. The speed and apparent ubiquity of the automatic evaluative process render it one of the most fundamental and perhaps most immediate mind's reactions to the world (cf. Barrett & Bar, 2009; Van Berkum, 2010). Ito and Cacioppo (2000) emphasize that the implicit evaluation is the brain's spontaneous response that has adaptive utility, allowing the brain to perform its basic function (i.e., avoid harm), even when it is not explicitly involved in or sensitized to do any evaluative processing. The growing body of evidence demonstrates that people continually and automatically evaluate situations and objects for their value, that is, whether they signify something as good or bad (e.g., Bargh & Ferguson, 2000; Brendl & Higgins, 1996; Ferguson, 2007).

In their discussion of the linguistic features of evaluation, Thompson and Hunston (2000) stress that value (i.e., the attitudinal contents) could be embedded in lexical items, grammar, or at text level. Despite a considerable consensus concerning the evaluative power of words, it is by no means easy to establish criteria for distinguishing evaluative from non-evaluative lexemes (cf. Osgood, Suci, & Tannenbaum, 1957). Winter (1982, p. 191) emphasizes that evaluation is first and foremost in the situation and occurs at discourse boundaries (i.e., in *what* people say and *how* they say it). Cortazzi and Lixian (2000) make a distinction between how lexical items evaluate and how language users use linguistic items to evaluate. On the one hand, evaluation refers to a structural element; on the other, it is a functional element that is spread throughout and overlaps with other elements. In communicative context, primarily non-evaluative lexemes can be used evaluatively. The evaluative meaning a word carries is one thing; evaluative use is quite another. Some layers of evaluative meaning are in the message and others are in the telling, or in the context of the message. Evaluative and non-evaluative contents carried by words only partially depend on the explicitly coded evaluative contents. Evaluative attitude–expressing use is a function of context. Context may implicitly endow linguistic cues with evaluative value. Evaluative cues carrying attitudinal import are usually scattered throughout the message and may be merely weakly marked (cf. Sperber & Wilson, 1986; Thompson & Hunston, 2000). Hunston (2000, p. 176) observes that evaluation carried by attitudes is a highly complex linguistic function, because it can employ different types of evaluation at different levels of linguistic structure. It remains to tease out how different types and modes of evaluation work and how the evaluative contents shape attitudinal meaning comprehension.

Attitude and the Evaluative Load in Irony Processing

Because attitude and the evaluative load it carries seem so crucially important for irony comprehension, it may only be commendable to explicitly test the attitude/irony interface. In a set of six experiments Bromberek-Dyzman and colleagues (Bromberek-Dyzman, forthcoming; Bromberek-Dyzman & Rataj, 2008; Bromberek-Dyzman, Rataj, & Dylak 2010) ventured to tease out how attitudinal meanings shape irony comprehension, and specifically to explore (a) the role of attitudinal (evaluative) contents in irony processing, (b) first language (L1, Polish) versus second language (L2, English) attitude-processing patterns, (c) explicit (literal criticism vs. literal praise) and implicit (critical irony) attitude-processing patterns, and (d) attitude-processing patterns in explicit (evaluative) and implicit (lexical) tasks. Experiments were designed to test the role of affective valence in explicit (literal compliment vs. literal criticism) and implicit (critical irony) attitudinal meaning (valence) processing patterns and to compare the processing patterns obtained in L1 and L2. Moreover, these experiments explored whether affective valence processing produces convergent or divergent processing patterns in dominant (Polish) and nondominant (English) language. Online explicit and implicit attitudinal meaning processing in an emotive decision task, in which participants explicitly judged whether the target comment expressed a favorable or unfavorable comment (the explicit valence-processing condition), and a lexical decision task, in which participants judged whether the target was a word (i.e., the implicit valence processing condition), under monolingual task conditions with only one language involved at a time, were used. Participants in the studies were Polish proficient users of English. Diversified input pacing (e.g., self-paced speed of reading versus limited reading time) and responding conditions (e.g., self-paced, and interstimulus intervals [ISIs] 0 and 1000 ms) were employed.

In a self-paced emotive decision task study in which participants decided whether a comment such as *She is so nice* was meant to convey a favorable or unfavorable opinion to someone's unwillingness, or willingness to help, Bromberek-Dyzman et al. (2010) explored irony processing in the participants' dominant and nondominant language. They found no differences between the tested languages in the accuracy and response latency data. However, language analyses showed significant differences between irony and literal language, demonstrating longer response latencies and higher error rates for irony than for literal language, in both L1 and L2. Participants were significantly slower in irony ($M = 1540$ ms) than in literal ($M = 1239$ ms) processing. Moreover, Polish users of English did not require more time and did not make more errors when processing ironic sentences in English than in Polish. Bromberek-Dyzman and Rataj (2008) tested irony comprehension using a speeded forced choice, emotive decision task (participants were allowed only a 1000-ms response window to indicate their decisions) probing again the participants' native (Polish) and non-native (English) language. Response latency data showed L1 and L2 convergent processing patterns. That is, when language was analyzed within blocks, it took longer to process irony than literal statements; this pattern was similar for L1 and L2. Accuracy for irony processing in the 1000 ms response window condition dropped significantly. Additionally, the error rates for irony in English were significantly higher than in Polish. The results showed that participants made significantly more errors processing irony in the L2 than in the L1; yet they did not need more time to process irony in the L2 than in the L1. The accuracy drop in L2 may be due to a speed-accuracy tradeoff imposed by the limited response window, which affected the less dominant, less frequently used, and hence less quickly accessible language (English). This result seems in line with the *Revised Hierarchical Model* of bilingual language organization (e.g., Kroll & Stewart, 1994), which claims that L1 has the capacity to activate L1 word meanings faster and more reliably than L2, due to stronger and hence faster accessibility of links to the conceptual store in the L1 than in L2 lexical store. However, this effect dissipated in the self-paced condition, when participants were allowed as much time as they needed for the online emotive decision task (Bromberek-Dyzman et al., 2010). These two studies explored irony latency response patterns and accuracy rates in L1 and L2 in one congruity condition, literal praise condition, and one incongruity condition, ironic criticism. This set of experimental conditions juxtaposing literal praise against ironic criticism was adopted from Giora et al. (1998, 2007) and Giora and Fein (1999). The results obtained are consistent with Giora and colleagues, showing that within language blocks (i.e., Polish vs. English) irony produces longer response latencies than the literal condition.

To account for the extant contradictory results in irony processing, Bromberek-Dyzman (forthcoming) set to test the role of affective attitude (valence) in irony processing manipulating a wider set of experimental variables, such as explicit attitude (literal praise vs. literal criticism) and implicit attitude (critical irony) processing patterns. An evaluative decision task was employed to explore the role and impact of attitudinal evaluative load in explicit attitudinal meaning processing (Experiments 1 and 2). A lexical decision task was used to explore the role of affective attitude in implicit evaluative processing (Experiments 3 and 4). A message valence (positive vs. negative) X target valence (positive vs. negative) X language (Polish vs. English) factorial design was used. Two valence congruent (literal praise vs. literal criticism) and one valence incongruent (critical irony) conditions were tested within and between language blocks in explicit evaluative processing (evaluative decision task) condition and implicit evaluative condition (lexical decision task). Experiments varied also in temporal aspects of input pacing (self-paced vs. limited reading and responding time) to control for attitude priming effects in short and long prime display conditions. Both studies tested how message level attitude (two-sentence mini-stories) impacts the speed and accuracy of attitudinal meaning processing in a direct (explicit) and indirect (implicit) evaluative task. Two types of attitudes were examined, simple attitudes with explicit, unambiguous literal meaning (compliment vs. criticism), and complex attitude carrying implicit, ambivalent meaning (ironic criticism). While simple attitudes unambiguously and explicitly convey either positive or negative opinion, complex attitudes convey ambivalent evaluative load, explicitly positive and implicitly negative at the same time.

In Experiment 1 (the self-paced task) two strikingly different valence patterns were observed, showing strong divergence between positive and negative attitude processing in response latencies and accuracy rates. Congruent response latency patterns for ambivalence and positive valence conditions were observed, showing no significant differences for positive attitude (e.g., literal praise) and irony conditions, which together differed significantly from the negative attitude condition. These patterns were observed in both languages investigated. In the second experiment (with ISIs of 0 and 1000 ms), two divergent attitude patterns were observed, showing facilitated positive attitude processing and inhibited negative attitude processing. In this experimental timing condition, convergent response latencies were revealed for the negative valence and the ambivalence conditions, showing no significant differences for the negative attitude and the irony condition. These patterns were identical for both languages. Both accuracy rates and response latencies showed similar patterns. In Experiment 3 (0 ISI) that tested implicit attitude processing, three different valence patterns were observed, showing significant differences between positive attitude, negative attitude, and irony conditions. The divergent valence patterns were similar for both languages for response latency and accuracy rates. Response time and error rates showed three-gradient patterns revealing enhanced response for positive valence, significant delay for ambivalence response latency, and a pronounced hindrance for negative valence response latency. In Experiment 4 (1000 ISI), implicit valence processing patterns showed a two-gradient valence pattern, emulating the two-gradient pattern observed in Experiment 2 (the explicit evaluative study), with facilitated positive valence, inhibited negative valence and ambivalence processing. Positive and negative valence showed strikingly different latency patterns, and no significant differences were observed for ambivalence and negative valence processing, which generated convergent latency patterns for both languages. These studies show that the speed of irony processing varies. Irony shows to be processed faster than negative comments (i.e., literal criticism) and longer than positive comments (i.e., literal praise). More importantly, irony processing in L1 and L2 show strikingly similar processing patterns in relation to response latency and accuracy.

The Role of Attitude in Irony Processing

What are these results telling us about the role of attitude in irony processing? The studies show that attitudinal meaning (i.e., literal criticism, praise, critical irony) is crucial in attitudinal contents carrying message comprehension. The studies demonstrate (a) consistent facilitation for positive valence and inhibition for negative valence; (b) variable patterns for irony/ambivalence, approximating either positive or negative valence pattern, contingent on the input pacing conditions; (c) valence processing automaticity (i.e., convergent processing patterns for explicit and implicit evaluative processing conditions); and (d) L1 and L2 response latencies and accuracy patterns convergence for all tested valence conditions.

Both studies in response time latencies and error rate data, for both language blocks, show positive valence-facilitated processing and inhibited negative-valence processing. Positive valence facilitation and negative-valence-inhibited processing are consistent across the four experiments. Irrespective of time, task, and language, participants consistently processed positive valence much faster and with higher accuracy than they processed negative valence. This consistently observed valence processing asymmetry can be accounted for by the *positivity offset* and *negativity bias* neurophysiological mechanisms. Positive stimuli show swift and smooth processing patterns (positivity offset), while negative stimuli show intense and slow response patterns (negativity bias). These effects have been copiously corroborated by behavioral research results (e.g., Baumeister, Bratslavsky, Finkenauer, & Vohs, 2001; Peeters & Czapinski, 1990; Pratto & John, 1991; Rozin & Royzman, 2001; Taylor, 1991) and a range of neuroimaging studies (e.g., Berntson & Cacioppo, 2008; Cacioppo & Berntson, 1994; Cacioppo et al., 1994, 1997, 2004; Ito & Cacioppo, 2000; Ito, Larsen, Smith, & Cacioppo, 1998).

Overall, the obtained results described above contribute to the ongoing debate on the respective affective-cognitive faculties involvement in linguistic valence processing. Language-carried valence in the experiments presented shows convergent processing patterns for L1 and L2 of the Polish participants. Neither response time nor accuracy rates have shown any processing advantages for valence processing in the dominant language. Lack of L1 and L2 divergent patterns for attitudinal load processing might be taken as an indication that affective competence is language independent and overrides linguistic processing patterns in dominant and nondominant languages alike. This might be taken to support the hypothesis that affective valence is controlled by affective systems that are independent or non-overlapping with cognitive (language) systems. Yet, these results need to be corroborated by further research on valence processing in a wider multilanguage paradigm.

Moreover, the obtained processing results further contribute to the literal/nonliteral meaning ongoing debate by suggesting that the distinction between literal and nonliteral meaning is not consistently divergent. The present results fail to evidence any consistently divergent literal/nonliteral meaning distinction. To the contrary, literal condition (literal praise, literal criticism) shows the most pronounced divergence between positive and negative valence representing the *literal* meaning condition. These results attest to the importance of valence and the relative irrelevance of the literal versus nonliteral distinction in attitudinal meaning processing. Colston and Gibbs (2007) argue that findings of different online studies exploring the so-called *literal meaning* in figurative language understanding should be interpreted with caution as they might capture and demonstrate quite different linguistic processes lumped together under the category of *literal meaning*. There is a general tendency in experimental studies on irony comprehension to contrast irony against its equivalent literal meaning, the underlying assumption being that the literal meaning reflects the standard default mode of linguistic processing, while irony and other forms of indirect and nonliteral language require some special mechanisms to guide their interpretation. The present results argue against this widespread assumption and point to the relative insignificance of literal meaning as a reliable variable in attitudinal meaning processing. Specifically, the results reported here suggest that literalness as a processing variable has failed to show distinctive consistency in attitudinal meaning analysis. The literal condition showed sharply diverging processing patterns for positive and negative literal meaning. A category revealing such a pronounced internal inconsistency and variety should not serve as a benchmark for analyzing other *nonliteral* phenomena. These results challenge previous findings in irony research that consider literal meaning as a homogenous entity consistently demonstrating processing priority over nonliteral, ironic meaning (e.g., Giora et al., 1998, 2007; Giora & Fein, 1999).

In short, irony processing produced varying patterns. In self-paced timing conditions (Experiment 1), irony was processed faster than negatively valenced literal conditions and only nonsignificantly slower than positively valenced literal trials. These patterns emerged in both languages and are consistent with Gibbs' (1986a, 1986b, 1986c, 1994, 2002) and Ivanko and Pexman's (2003) results, which also demonstrated that irony may be processed as fast as literal equivalents, or even faster. Irony in the limited response time condition (Experiment 2) was processed nonsignificantly faster than negatively valenced literal conditions and significantly longer than positively valenced literal conditions. These patterns consistently present in both languages of the participants are partially compatible with Giora (1995, 1997; Giora et al., 1998; Giora & Fein, 1999), who showed that irony processing takes longer than literal meaning processing. The divergent irony processing results provide evidence (for both L1 and L2) that irony might be processed significantly slower than literal meaning, when compared to positive (literal) valence, but significantly faster than literal meaning, when compared to negative valence (literal) conditions. In the implicit evaluative processing study, participants were unaware that they were processing irony, yet the results obtained for the implicit ambivalence processing fully replicated the patterns obtained in the explicit evaluative study. Because ambivalence is ambiguous and ambiguity processing demands time, limiting processing and response time conditions were expected to show longer response latency patterns and higher error rates in the irony/ambivalence condition. Yet, neither explicit nor implicit irony nor ambivalence processing turned out to be more demanding. Ambivalence failed to elicit longer response latencies or lower accuracy rates as compared to literal conditions in both L1 and L2. Additionally, ambivalence processing patterns in the implicit processing conditions *replicate* the irony processing patterns in the explicit processing conditions, in L1 and L2 alike, and hence might be taken to indicate that explicit and implicit ambivalence processing also fall into the automatic processing range.

The primary aim of the explicit and implicit attitude processing study was to explore the role of attitude at the level of message processing in order to find out how attitudinal meaning impacts irony comprehension. Additionally, the study aimed to test explicit (literal criticism, praise) and implicit (irony) attitudinal contents processing in the participants' L1 and L2. Various time scales were used to determine valence processing patterns in short and long prime duration, as well as different ISI timing conditions. The present results show that both the explicit and implicit processing mode of the message level of evaluative meaning produce consistent valence processing patterns that do not differ for explicit or implicit processing mode, which might be interpreted as valence automaticity. Both studies also explored the role of language in attitudinal meaning processing. This was investigated by collecting and comparing valence response latency patterns in L1 and L2. Results show no differences for response latency and accuracy rate patterns for the examined languages, which indicates that valence is not a language dependent variable. The current results contribute to the debate on the nature of the cognitive architecture underlying the human verbal comprehension system, by demonstrating that valence (i.e., affective faculty) exerts stronger impact on attitudinal meaning processing patterns than does linguistic meaning (i.e., cognitive faculty).

Summary and Conclusion

What do these results tell us about irony processing? First, the results obtained in the present studies show consistent attitude processing patterns that are similar for both languages tested, which points to attitude as a language independent meaning ingredient. The data also argue against the literal versus nonliteral meaning distinction in attitudinal meaning research. These results show that valence in attitudinal meaning processing plays an *unexpectedly* significant role. These results are consistent with social cognitive research showing that perception of affect competent stimulus activates a vast array of semantic, affective, and social information that keeps influencing its representation and comprehension (e.g., Bargh, 1984, 1988, 1990; Bargh et al., 1988, 1989; Bargh & Pietromonaco, 1982; Ferguson & Bargh, 2004). Priming research has demonstrated that affective primes activate more contents than they carry (e.g., Bargh, Chaiken, Raymond, & Hymes, 1996; Bargh & Chartrand, 1999; Fazio et al., 1986), and do so in an automatic fashion (e.g., Bargh, 2007; Bargh & Ferguson, 2000; Bargh et al., 1996). In addition to linguistic meaning, verbal stimuli carry attitudinal contents, including sets of biases, preferences, emotional memories, and the associated bulk of mostly implicit knowledge. This bulk of emotional information *incidentally* activated implicitly guides the perception and comprehension of the processed contents (e.g., Bargh & Chartrand, 1999; Bargh & Ferguson, 2000). Research on affective priming has shown that people automatically evaluate words (e.g., Bargh et al., 1992, 1996; Fazio et al., 1986), faces (e.g., Baldwin et al., 1990; Murphy & Zajonc, 1993; Niedenthal & Cantor, 1986), pictures (e.g., Giner-Sorolla et al., 1999), and odors (Hermans et al., 1998) on their mere encounter. These results consistently show that affect-competent stimuli unconditionally trigger evaluative processing, irrespective of the stimulus domain and its modality (e.g., perception or cognition). Barrett and Bar (2009) proposed the *Affective Prediction Hypothesis* to account for the *privileged* processing of affective stimuli. They argued that people *see* with feeling, and that the brain's ability *to see* in the present incorporates a representation of the affective impact of the visual sensations in the past. According to Barrett and Bar, affective states have a top-down influence on perception and precede cognition. This is because the brain routinely makes affective predictions during visual recognition and uses special neural circuitry to handle affective contents. Barrett and Bar posit that affective salience, relevance, and value are not processed at separate steps, nor after the input has been identified, but run in parallel. According to the Affective Prediction Hypothesis, affect-competent content has a profound and instantaneous impact on how the brain does its processing job. Higgins (1998), in line with Barrett and Bar (2009), argues that individuals by default rely on feelings, experiences, memory, or any nonspecific bit of information that is evoked while specific contents are being processed. Higgins emphasizes that the influence of incidental, extralinguistic, and experiential information reflects the operation of a tacit *aboutness principle*. Accordingly, any feeling, experience, memory, or anything that comes to mind while we process information has a bearing on its processing. Research seems to belittle the role and impact of affective and other extralinguistic cues on linguistic contents processing. There is a widespread assumption that the mental contents (i.e., thoughts and feelings that appear while we process linguistic content of messages) are evoked by the verbal contents. The extralinguistic affective cues are usually taken for granted, and they remain *invisible* to experimental research. Yet, their impact on message processing is as much inestimable as unexplored.

List of Keywords

Affective Prediction Hypothesis, Affective Primacy Hypothesis, Affective processes, Attitude meaning, Automatic affective system, Contrast assimilation effects, Contrast effect, Echoic Mention Theory, Emotive decision task, Evaluative contents, Evaluative duality, Evaluative load, Graded Salience Hypothesis (GSH), Implicit attitude, Indirect negation view, Inferential approach, Message valence, Metaphor, Metonymic, Negativity bias, Normative context, One-stage models, P600, Parallel processing, Salient sense, Second-order false belief task, Somatic Marker Mechanism (SOM), Theory of Mind (ToM), Two-stage models, Valence, Verbal irony

Thought Questions

1. How can we account for propositional and nonpropositional effects in experimental research?
2. How do nonpropositional effects (i.e., affect related) impact communication and comprehension patterns?
3. How can we account for valence in communication? Do contemporary theories of language account for affective contents in verbal communication?
4. Can the concept of affective valence be accounted for by code-based language theories?
5. Are there any significant differences in valence processing patterns in the languages you know (L1, L2, L3)?

Suggested Student Research Projects

1. Investigate lexical valence congruence (e.g., good vs. nice), and lexical valence incongruity (e.g., good vs. bad) processing in the languages you know. You can use a lexical decision task for implicit valence processing and an evaluative decision task for explicit valence processing. Look for valence convergence or lack of convergence in the two tested languages. A good start is by replicating Pratto and John's (1991) study. The study uses an emotive Stroop task for testing

lexical valence. Carefully follow the instructions from the methods section. Were you able to replicate Pratt and John's results?

2. Use the attitude priming paradigm to assess how positive versus negative lexical priming impacts word processing. Start by replicating Bargh et al.'s (1996) study. The study uses a naming task for testing lexical valence processing patterns. Carefully follow the instructions from the methods section and report the findings of your experiment to your class. Were you able to replicated Bargh et al.'s results?

Related Internet Sites

Irony: https://en.wikipedia.org/wiki/Irony
Ironic Process Theory: https://en.wikipedia.org/wiki/Ironic_process_theory
Sarcasm Society: www.sarcasmsociety.com

Suggested Further Readings

Bargh, J.A. (Ed.). (2007). *Social psychology and the unconscious. The automaticity of higher mental processes.* New York: Psychology Press.
Gibbs, R., & Colston, H.L. (Eds.). (2007). *Irony in language and thought. A cognitive science reader.* New York: Lawrence Erlbaum Associates.

REFERENCES

Attardo, S. (2000). Irony as relevant inappropriateness. *Journal of Pragmatics, 32,* 793–826.
Attardo, S., Eisterhold J., Hay, J., & Poggi, I. (2003). Multimodal markers of irony and sarcasm. *Humor, 16,* 243–260.
Baldwin, M.W., Carrell, S.E., & Lopez, D.F. (1990). Priming relationship schemas: My advisor and the Pope are watching me from the back of my mind. *Journal of Experimental Social Psychology, 26,* 435–454.
Barbe, K. (1995). *Irony in context.* Amsterdam: John Benjamins.
Bargh, J.A. (1984). Automatic and conscious processing of social information. In R.S. Wyer & T.K. Srull (Eds.), *Handbook of social cognition 3* (pp. 1–43). Hillsdale, NJ: Lawrence Erlbaum Associates.
(1988). Automatic information processing: Implications for communication and affect. In L. Donohew & H.E. Sypher (Eds.), *Communication, social cognition and affect* (pp. 9–32). Hillsdale, NJ: Lawrence Erlbaum Associates.
(1990). Auto-motives: Preconscious determinants of social interaction. In E.T. Higgins & R.M. Sorrentino (Eds.), *Handbook of motivation and cognition 2* (pp. 93–130). New York: Guilford Press.
(Ed.). (2007). *Social psychology and the unconscious: The automaticity of higher mental processes.* New York: Psychology Press.

Bargh, J.A., & Pietromonaco, P. (1982). Automatic information processing and social perception: The influence of trait information presented outside of conscious awareness on impression formation. *Journal of Personality and Social Psychology, 43*, 437–449.

Bargh, J.A., Lombardi, W.J., & Higgins, E.T. (1988). Automaticity of person situation effects on impression formation: It's just a matter of time. *Journal of Personality and Social Psychology, 55*, 599–605.

Bargh, J.A., Litt, J., Pratto, F., & Spielman, L. (1989). On the preconscious evaluation of social stimuli. Paper presented at the XXIV International Congress of Psychology, Sydney.

Bargh, J.A., Chaiken, S., Raymond, P., & Hymes, C. (1996). The automatic evaluation effect: Unconditional automatic attitude activation with a pronunciation task. *Journal of Experimental Social Psychology, 32*, 104–128.

Bargh, J.A., & Chartrand, T.L. (1999). The unbearable automaticity of being. *American Psychologist, 54*, 462–479.

Bargh, J.A., & Ferguson, M. (2000). On the automaticity of higher mental processes. *Psychological Bulletin, 126*, 925–945.

Barrett, L.F. (2006). Valence is a basic building block of emotional life. *Journal of Research in Personality, 40*, 35–55.

Barrett, L.F., & Bar, M. (2009). See it with feeling: affective predictions during object perception. *Philosophical Transactions of Royal Society B, 364*, 1325–1334.

Baumeister, R.F., Bratslavsky, E., Finkenauer, C., & Vohs, K.D. (2001). Bad is stronger than good. *Review of General Psychology, 5*, 323–370.

Bechara, A. (2003). Risky business: Emotion, decision-making and addiction. *Journal of Gambling Studies, 19*, 23–51.

(2004). The role of emotion in decision-making: Evidence from neurological patients with orbitofrontal damage. *Brain and Cognition, 55*, 30–40.

Bechara, A., Tranel, D., Damasio, H., & Damasio, A.R. (1996). Failure to respond autonomically to anticipated future outcomes following damage to prefrontal cortex. *Cerebral Cortex, 6*, 215–25.

Bechara, A., Damasio, H., Tranel, D., & Damasio, A.R. (1997). Deciding advantageously before knowing the advantageous strategy. *Science, 275*, 1293–1295.

Bechara, A., Damasio, H., & Damasio, A.R. (2000). Emotion, decision-making, and the orbitofrontal cortex. *Cerebral Cortex, 10*, 295–307.

Bechara, A., & Damasio, A.R. (2005). The somatic marker hypothesis: A neural theory of economic decision. *Games and Economic Behavior, 52*, 336–372.

(2005). The Iowa gambling task and the somatic marker hypothesis: Some questions and answers. *Trends in Cognitive Sciences, 9*, 159–162.

Berntson, G., & Cacioppo, J.T. (2008). The functional neuroarchitecture of evaluative processes. In A. Elliot (Ed.), *Handbook of approach and avoidance motivation* (pp. 305–319). New York: Psychology Press.

Brendl, M.C., & Higgins, T.E. (1996). Principles of judging valence: What makes events positive or negative. In M.P. Zanna (Ed.), *Advances in experimental social psychology 28* (pp. 95–160). San Diego, CA: Academic Press.

Bromberek-Dyzman, K., & Rataj, K. (2008, May). Getting irony in L1 and L2. Paper presented at *New developments in linguistic pragmatics'*, 4th Łódź Symposium, Łódź.

Bromberek-Dyzman, K., Rataj, K., & Dylak, J. (2010). Mentalizing in the second language: Is irony online inferencing any different in L1 and L2? In I. Witczak-Plisiecka (Ed.), *Pragmatic perspectives on language and linguistics; Vol.1: Speech actions in theory and applied studies* (pp. 197–216). Newcastle: Cambridge Scholars Publishing.

Bromberek-Dyzman, K. (forthcoming). *On attitude and language: Explicit and implicit attitudinal meaning processing*. Poznań: Adam Mickiewicz University Press.

Bryant, G.A., & Fox Tree, J.E. (2002). Recognizing verbal irony in spontaneous speech. *Metaphor and Symbol, 17*, 99–117.

(2005). Is there an ironic tone of voice? *Language and Speech, 48*, 257–277.

Cacioppo, J.T., & Berntson, G.G. (1994). Relationship between attitudes and evaluative space: A critical review, with emphasis on the separability of positive and negative substrates. *Psychological Bulletin, 113*, 401–423.

Cacioppo, J.T., Crites, S.L., Gardner, W.L., & Berntson, G.G. (1994). Bioelectrical echoes from evaluative categorizations: A late positive brain potential that varies as a function of trait negativity and extremity. *Journal of Personality and Social Psychology, 67*, 115–125.

Cacioppo, J.T., Gardner, W.L., & Berntson, G.G. (1997). Beyond bipolar conceptualizations and measures: The case of attitudes and evaluative space. *Personality and Social Psychology Review, 1*, 3–25.

Cacioppo, J.T., Larsen, J.T., Smith, N.K., & Berntson, G.G. (2004). The affect system: What lurks below the surface of feelings? In A. S. R. Manstead, N.H. Frijda, & A.H. Fischer (Eds.), *Feelings and emotions: The Amsterdam conference* (pp. 223–242). New York: Cambridge University Press.

Clark, H.H., & Gerrig, R.J. (1984). On the pretense theory of irony. *Journal of Experimental Psychology: General, 113*, 121–126.

Colston, H.L. (1997). Salting a wound or sugaring a pill: The pragmatic functions of ironic criticism. *Discourse Processes, 23*, 25–45.

(2002). Contrast and assimilation in verbal irony. *Journal of Pragmatics, 34*, 111–142.

Colston, H.L., & Keller, S.B. (1998). You'll never believe this: Irony and hyperbole in expressing surprise. *Journal of Psycholinguistic Research, 27*, 499–513.

Colston, H.L., & O'Brien, J. (2000). Contrast and pragmatics in figurative language: Anything understatement can do, irony can do better. *Journal of Pragmatics, 32*, 1557–1583.

Colston, H.L., & Gibbs, R.W. (2007). A brief history of irony. In R. Gibbs & H. L. Colston (Eds.), *Irony in language and thought. A cognitive science reader* (pp. 3–21). New York: Lawrence Erlbaum Associates.

Cortazzi, M., & Lixian, J. (2000). Evaluating evaluation in narrative. In S. Hunston & G. Thompson (Eds.), *Evaluation in text* (pp. 102–120). Oxford, UK: Oxford University Press

Damasio, A.R. (1994). *Descartes' error: Emotion, reason, and the human brain.* New York: Penguin Books.

(2010). *Self comes to mind. Constructing the conscious brain.* New York: Pantheon Books.

Damasio, A.R., Tranel, D., & Damasio, H. (1991). Somatic markers and the guidance of behavior: Theory and preliminary testing. In H.S. Levin & H.M. Eisenberg (Eds.), *Frontal lobe function and dysfunction* (pp. 217–229). Oxford, UK: Oxford University Press.

Dews, S., & Winner, E. (1995). Muting the meaning: A social function of irony. *Metaphor and Symbolic Activity, 10,* 3–19.

Dews, S., Kaplan, J., & Winner, E. (1995). Why not say it directly? The social functions of irony. *Discourse Processes, 19,* 347–367.

(1999). Obligatory processing of literal and nonliteral meanings in verbal irony. *Journal of Pragmatics, 31,* 1579–1599.

Fazio, R.H., Sanbonmatsu, D.M., Powell, M.C., & Kardes, F.R. (1986). On the automatic activation of attitudes. *Journal of Personality and Social Psychology, 50,* 229–238.

Ferguson, M. (2007). The automaticity of evaluation. In J.A. Bargh (Ed.), *Social psychology and the unconscious. The automaticity of higher mental processes* (pp. 219–265). New York: Psychology Press.

Ferguson, M., & Bargh, J.A. (2004). How social perception can automatically influence behavior. *Trends in Cognitive Sciences, 8,* 33–39.

Filik, R. & Moxey, L.M. (2010). The on-line processing of written irony. *Cognition, 116,* 421–436.

Gibbs, R.W. (1979). Contextual effects in understanding indirect requests. *Discourse Processes, 2,* 1–10.

(1983). Do people always process the literal meanings of indirect requests? *Journal of Experimental Psychology: Learning, Memory, and Cognition, 9,* 524–533.

(1986a). Comprehension and memory for nonliteral utterances: The problem of sarcastic indirect requests. *Acta Psychologica, 62,* 41–57.

(1986b). On the psycholinguistics of sarcasm. *Journal of Experimental Psychology: General, 115,* 3–15.

(1986c). Skating on thin ice: Literal meaning and understanding idioms in conversation. *Discourse Processes, 9,* 17–30.

(1994). *The poetics of mind: Figurative thought, language and understanding.* Cambridge, UK: Cambridge University Press.

(2000). Irony in talk among friends. *Metaphor and Symbol, 15,* 5–27.

(2002). A new look at the literal meaning in understanding what is said and implicated. *Journal of Pragmatics, 34,* 457–486.

Gibbs, R.W., & O'Brien, J.E. (1991). Psychological aspects of irony understanding. *Journal of Pragmatics, 16,* 523–530.

Gibbs, R.W., O'Brien, J.E., & Doolittle, S. (1995). Inferring meanings that are not intended: Speakers' intentions and irony comprehension. *Discourse Processes, 20,* 187–203.

Giner-Sorolla, R., Garcia, M.T., & Bargh, J.A. (1999). The automatic evaluation of pictures. *Social Cognition, 17,* 76–96.

Giora, R. (1995). On irony and negation. *Discourse Processes*, 19, 239–264.

(1997). Understanding figurative and literal language: The graded salience hypothesis. *Cognitive Linguistics*, 8, 183–206.

(2002). Literal vs. figurative language: Different or equal? *Journal of Pragmatics*, 34, 487–506.

(2003). *On our mind: Salience, context and figurative language.* New York: Oxford University Press.

Giora, R., Fein, O., & Schwartz, T. (1998). Irony: Graded salience and indirect negation. *Metaphor and Symbol*, 13, 83–101.

Giora, R., & Fein, O. (1999). Irony: Context and salience. *Metaphor and Symbol*, 14, 241–257.

Giora, R., Fein, O., Laadan, D., Wolfson, J., Zeituny, M., Kidron, R., Kaufman, R., & Shaham, R. (2007). Expecting irony: Context versus salience-based effects. *Metaphor and Symbol*, 22, 119–146.

Grice, H.P. (1975). Logic and conversation. In P. Cole & J.L. Morgan (Eds.), *Syntax and semantics 3: Speech acts* (pp. 41–58). New York: Academic Press.

(1978). Further notes on logic and conversation. *Syntax and Semantics*, 9, 113–128.

(1989). *Studies in the way of words.* Cambridge, MA: Harvard University Press.

Hermans, D., Baeyens, F., & Eelen, P. (1998). Odours as affective-processing context for word evaluation: A case of cross-modal affective priming. *Cognition and Emotion* 12, 601–613.

Higgins, E.T. (1998). The aboutness principle: A pervasive influence on human inference. *Social Cognition*, 16, 173–198.

Hunston, S. (2000). Evaluation and the planes of discourse: Status and value in persuasive texts. In S. Hunston & G. Thompson (Eds.), *Evaluation in text* (pp. 176–207). Oxford, UK: Oxford University Press.

Ito, T.A., Larsen, J.T., Smith, N.K., & Cacioppo, J.T. (1998). Negative information weighs more heavily on the brain: The negativity bias in evaluative categorizations. *Journal of Personality and Social Psychology*, 75, 887–900.

Ito, T.A., & Cacioppo, J.T. (2000). Electrophysiological evidence of implicit and explicit categorization processes. *Journal of Experimental Social Psychology*, 36, 660–676.

Ivanko, S.L., & Pexman, P.M. (2003). Context incongruity and irony processing. *Discourse Processes*, 35, 241–279.

Jorgensen, J. (1996). The functions of sarcastic irony in speech. *Journal of Pragmatics*, 26, 613–634.

Kihara, Y. (2005). The mental space of verbal irony. *Cognitive Linguistics*, 16, 513–530.

Kotthoff, H. (2003). Responding to irony in different contexts: On cognition in conversation. *Journal of Pragmatics*, 35, 1387–1411.

Kreuz, R.J., & Glucksberg, S. (1989). How to be sarcastic: The echoic reminder theory of verbal irony. *Journal of Experimental Psychology*, 118, 374–386.

Kreuz, R.J., Long, D.L., & Church, M.B. (1991). On being ironic: Pragmatic and mnemonic implications. *Metaphor and Symbolic Activity*, 6, 149–162.

Kreuz, R.J., Roberts, R.M., Johnson, B.K., & Bertus, E.L. (1996). Figurative language occurrence and co-occurrence in contemporary literature. In R. Kreuz & M.S. MacNealy (Eds.), *Empirical approaches to literature and aesthetics* (pp. 83–97). Norwood, NJ: Ablex.

Kroll, J.F., & Steward, E. (1994). Category interference in translation and picture naming: Evidence for asymmetric connections between bilingual memory representations. *Journal of Memory and Language, 33,* 149–174.

Kumon-Nakamura, S., Glucksberg, S., & Brown, M. (1995). How about another piece of pie: The allusional pretense theory of discourse irony. *Journal of Experimental Pragmatics: General, 124,* 3–21.

LeDoux, J. (1995). Emotion: Clues from the brain. *Annual Review of Psychology, 46,* 209–235.

(1996). *The emotional brain: The mysterious underpinnings of emotional life.* New York: Simon and Schuster Paperbacks.

(2000). Emotion circuits in the brain. *Annual Review of Neuroscience, 23,* 155–184.

LeDoux, J., Ruggiero, D.A., Forest, R., Stornetta, R., & Reis, D.J. (1987). Topographic organization of convergent projections to the thalamus from the inferior colliculus and spinal cord in the rat. *The Journal of Comparative Neurology, 264,* 123–46.

LeDoux, J., Iwata, J., Cicchetti, P., & Reis, D.J. (1988). Different projections of the central amygdaloid nucleus mediate autonomic and behavioral correlates of conditioned fear. *Journal of Neuroscience, 8,* 2517–2529.

Leggitt, J.S., & Gibbs, R.W. (2000). Emotional reactions to verbal irony. *Discourse Processes, 29,* 1–24.

Lewin, K. (1935). *A dynamic theory of personality.* New York: McGraw Hill.

Lodge, M., & Taber, C. (2000).Three steps toward a theory of motivated political reasoning. In A. Lupia, M. McCubbins, & S. Popkin (Eds.), *Elements of reason: Cognition, choice, and the bounds of rationality* (pp. 183–213). Cambridge, UK: Cambridge University Press.

Martin, R.A. (2007). *The psychology of humor: An integrative approach.* Burlington, MA: Elsevier Academic Press.

Murphy, S.T., & Zajonc, R.B. (1993). Affect, cognition and awareness: Affective priming with optimal and suboptimal stimulus exposures. *Journal of Personality and Social Psychology, 64,* 723–739.

Niedenthal, P.M., & Cantor, N. (1986). Affective responses as guides to category-based inferences. *Motivation and Emotion, 10,* 271–232.

Osgood, C.E., Suci, G.J., & Tannenbaum, P.H. (1957). *The measurement of meaning.* Urbana: University of Illinois Press.

Panksepp, J. (1998). *Affective neuroscience. The foundations of human and animal emotions.* Oxford, UK: Oxford University Press.

Partington, A. (2007). Irony and reversal of evaluation. *Journal of Pragmatics, 39,* 1547–1569.

Peeters, G., & Czapinski, J. (1990). Positive-negative asymmetry in evaluations: The distinction between affective and informational effects. In W. Stroebe & M. Hewstone (Ed.), *European review of social psychology* (pp. 33–60). New York: John Wiley & Sons.

Pratto, F., & John, O.P. (1991). Automatic vigilance: The attention-grabbing power of negative social information. *Journal of Personality and Social Psychology, 61,* 380–391.

Regel, S., Coulson, S., & Gunter, T.C. (2010). The communicative style of a speaker can affect language comprehension? ERP evidence from the comprehension of irony. *Brain Research, 1311,* 121–135.

Regel, S., Gunter, T.C., & Friederici, A.D. (2011). Isn't it ironic? An electrophysiological exploration of figurative language processing. *Journal of Cognitive Neuroscience, 23,* 77–293.

Roberts, R., & Kreuz, R. (1994). Why do people use figurative language? *Psychological Science, 5,* 159–163.

Rozin, P., & Royzman, E.B. (2001). Negativity bias, negativity dominance and contagion. *Personality and Social Psychology Review, 5,* 296–320.

Schwoebel, J., Dews, S., Winner, E., & Srinivas, K. (2000). Obligatory processing of the literal meaning of ironic utterances: Further evidence. *Metaphor and Symbol, 15,* 47–61.

Shamay-Tsoory, S.G., Tomer, R. & Aharon-Peretz, J. (2005a). The neuroanatomical basis of understanding sarcasm and its relationship to social cognition. *Neuropsychology, 19,* 288–300.

Shamay-Tsoory, S.G., Tomer, R., Berger, B.D., Goldsher, D., & Aharon-Peretz, J. (2005b). Impaired "affective theory of mind" is associated with right ventromedial prefrontal damage. *Cognitive and Behavioral Neurology, 18,* 55–67.

Shelley, C. (2001). The bicoherence theory of situational irony. In R.W. Gibbs & H.L. Colston (Eds.), *Irony in language and thought* (pp. 531–580). New York: Lawrence Erlbaum Associates.

Shibata, M., Toyomura, A., Itoh, H., & Abe, J-I. (2010). Neural substrates of irony comprehension: A functional MRI study. *Brain Research, 1308,* 114–123.

Shizgal, P. (1999). On the neural computation of utility: Implications from studies of brain stimulation reward. In D. Kahneman, E. Diener, & N. Schwarz (Eds.), *Wellbeing: The foundations of hedonic psychology* (pp. 502–526). New York: Russell Sage Foundation.

Sperber, D., & Wilson, D. (1981). Irony and the use-mention distinction. In P. Cole (Ed.), *Radical pragmatics* (pp. 295–318). New York: Academic Press.

(1986). *Relevance: Communication and cognition.* Oxford, UK: Basil Blackwell.

(1995). *Relevance: Communication and cognition* (2nd ed.). Oxford, UK: Blackwell.

(1998). Irony and relevance: A reply to Seto, Hamamoto and Yamanashi. In R. Carston & S. Uchida (Eds.), *Relevance theory: Applications and implications* (pp. 283–293). Amsterdam: John Benjamins.

(2002). Pragmatics, modularity and mind-reading. *Mind and Language, 17,* 3–23.

Taylor, S.E. (1991). Asymmetrical effects of positive and negative events: The mobilization-minimization hypothesis. *Psychological Bulletin, 110,* 67–85.

Thompson, G., & Hunston, S. (2000). Evaluation: An introduction. In S. Hunston & G. Thompson (Eds.), *Evaluation in text* (pp. 1–27). Oxford, UK: Oxford University Press.

Thurstone, L.L. (1931). Measurement of social attitudes. *Journal of Abnormal and Social Psychology*, 26, 249–269.

Uchiyama, H., Seki, A., Kageyama, H., Saito, D.N., Koeda, T., Ohno, K., & Sadato, N. (2006). Neural substrates of sarcasm: A functional magnetic-resonance imaging study. *Brain Research, 1124*, 100–110.

Utsumi, A. (2000). Verbal irony as implicit display of ironic environment: Distinguishing ironic utterances from nonirony. *Journal of Pragmatics, 32*, 1777–1806.

Van Berkum, J.J.A. (2010). The brain is a prediction machine that cares about good and bad – Any implications for neuropragmatics? *Italian Journal of Linguistics, 22*, 181–208.

Wang, T.A., Lee, S.S., Sigman, M., & Dapretto, M. (2006). Developmental changes in the neural basis of interpreting communicative intent. *Social Cognitive and Affective Neuroscience, 1*, 107–121.

Wakusawa, K., Sugiura, M., Sassa, Y., Jeong, H., Horie, K., Sato, S., Yokoyama, H., Tsuchiya, S., Inuma, K., & Kawashima, R. (2007). Comprehension of implicit meanings in social situations involving irony: A functional MRI study. *NeuroImage, 37*, 1417–1426.

Wilson, D. (2006). The pragmatics of verbal irony: Echo or pretence? *Lingua, 116*, 1722–1743.

(2010). Irony and metarepresentation. *UCL Working Papers in Linguistics, 21*, 183–226.

Wilson, D., & Sperber, D. (1992). On verbal irony. *Lingua, 87*, 53–76.

(2004). Relevance theory. In L.R. Horn & G. Ward (Eds.), *The handbook of pragmatics* (pp. 607–632). Oxford, UK: Blackwell Publishing.

Winner, E., Windmueller, G., Rosenblatt, E., Bosco, L., Best, E., & Gardner, H. (1987). Making sense of literal and nonliteral falsehood. *Metaphor and Symbolic Activity, 2*, 13–32.

Winter, E.O. (1982). *Towards a contextual grammar of English: The clause and its place in the definition of sentence.* London: Allen and Unwin.

Zajonc, R.B. (1980). Feeling and thinking. Preferences need no inferences. *American Psychologist, 35*, 51–175.

(1984). On the primacy of affect. *American Psychologist, 39*, 117–123.

Cross-Linguistic Approaches and Applied Issues

10 Straight from the Horse's Mouth: Idiomaticity Revisited

John I. Liontas
University of South Florida

ABSTRACT

Idiomaticity has long been an area of intense research around the world. To date, many empirical findings have been disclosed and even more definitions and experimental tasks proposed. Yet little research accounts for the effect idiomatic tasks have on participants' overall performance. The present qualitative study asserts that different experimental tasks and idiom sub-types have different effects on the comprehension/ production of second language idioms and, furthermore, that qualitative data, combined with quantitative data, can supplement and complete more fully a researcher's understanding of a particular issue under investigation than quantitative data alone. Pedagogical implications are discussed and future research directions explored.

Keywords: figurative language, idiomatic competence, metacognitive strategies, second language idioms, vivid phrasal idioms

Using the answers to two questionnaires given to 60 third-year adult learners of Spanish, French, and German, Liontas (2002a) has provided convincing evidence that

(1) learners do want idioms to be an integral part of their language and culture training; (2) they can predict their performances on idiomatic tasks and, finally, (3) they have very specific beliefs about the importance of learning idioms, the nature of idiomatic learning, and the strategies that are most likely to facilitate such learning (p. 289).

From the ensuing analysis of data, Liontas concluded that second language (L2) "instructors should introduce idioms more regularly and systematically to their students, regardless of the specific approaches they take to idiomatic learning" (pp. 306–307).

While the insights provided in this study are valuable indeed, it is nonetheless less clear what effect the *idiomatic tasks* themselves had on the learner's overall performance. More specifically, what new insights may be gleaned from an analysis of the learners' post-study comments

301

regarding the three experimental tasks (i.e., *idiom detection task, zero context task*, and *full context task*) and sub-types of vivid phrasal idioms (i.e., lexical level idioms, semi-lexical level idioms, and post-lexical level idioms) employed? To what extent can the idiosyncratic nature of these individual participants be ascertained, described, and explained for the benefit of an informed idiom pedagogy? Will the insights gleaned from these evaluations add to the understanding of the issues surrounding the processing, comprehension, and interpretation of L2 idioms in and out-of context?

The answers to these questions form the purpose of this chapter. To ensure the reader's understanding of the idiom sub-types and experimental tasks referred to and discussed in this chapter, a brief overview of terms will be given first, followed by a discussion of the insights revealed. Pedagogical implications and areas of further research will conclude the discussion of the effects of different tasks and idiom sub-types on the comprehension and production of L2 idioms in third-year adult learners of Spanish, French, and German.

The Problem with L2 Idiomaticity

Idiomaticity has long been an area of research commanding the attention of lexicographers, linguists, researchers, teachers, and publishers around the world. While the literature in first language (L1) studies abounds, the same cannot be said about L2 or foreign languages. L2 idiomaticity remains an ill-defined subfield of the larger field now known as *Second Language Acquisition* (SLA). This is particularly true for those of us working in U.S. or Canadian universities and colleges. Fortunately, the picture in Europe and Asia is less grim. Part of the problem, stems from our inability to define the terrain of L2 idiomaticity as a field of research in its own right. Closely connected to that issue is the question of how to define the term *idiom*. Not surprisingly, consensus on both these issues is yet to be reached (Arnaud & Savignon, 1997; Barkema, 1996; Boers, 2000; Bortfeld, 2002, 2003; Fernando, 1996; Hockett, 1958; Hoffman, 1984; Katsarou, 2011; Liu, 2003; Moon, 1997; Pollio, Barlow, Fine, & Pollio, 1977; Strässler, 1982). Even less consensus exists among L2 idiomatologists as to what it is that we ought to be investigating.

Given these realities, it is not surprising that the field of L2 idiomaticity, while emerging as a viable SLA subfield in Europe and Asia, is still in its infancy in the United States and Canada. To this researcher's knowledge, L2 idiomaticity has yet to become the focal point of a conference, a book, or even an edited volume in one of the many journals making their home on this side of the Atlantic. As a result, L2 idiomaticity as a subfield of SLA or even applied linguistics remains undefined and unfalsifiable. Hence, few researchers can be said to be experts in L2 idiomaticity. And while I am not trying to ascribe blame here, the point remains: Unless we develop a common language and a vision that permeates all matters of L2 idiomaticity, how can we possibly develop a research agenda that benefits from discoveries made in psycholinguistics, sociolinguistics, artificial intelligence, pragmatics, and applied linguistics? How can we continue to shed light on a particular issue of L2 idiomaticity if we have not yet defined the finer parameters of our own research inquiry? How can we learn from one another if we lack a common voice or a well-defined platform from which to make our collective voice heard?

These and other questions take central stage within a subfield that still struggles to find its own voice and recognition. Not surprisingly, some SLA researchers working on matters of L2 idiomaticity seek theoretical and empirical support in L1 studies (Cooper, 1998, 1999), while others build their own theoretical models to describe and explain L2 idiomaticity (Abel, 2003; Cieślicka, 2006a, 2006b; Giora, 1997, 1999; Giora & Fein, 1999; Kecskes, 2006; Malt & Eiter, 2004). The *Idiom Diffusion Model of Second Languages* is one such recent model proposed by Liontas (1999, 2002b). It emerged from a series of studies with adult L2 learners of Modern Greek, *English as a Second Language* (ESL), Spanish, French, and German over a number of years. For the purposes of this discussion the model is described below:

[T]here are two broad stages in [vivid phrasal] VP idiom understanding: an initial "prediction phase" and a "confirmation or replacement, reconstructive phase." In the prediction phase, the learner, in the absence of context, uses the lexical items comprising the idiom in a variety of situations and contexts. This systematic free variation depends on *how close or distant the semantic/image opacity of the target idiom is from the domain idiom*, leading to the construction of a number of hypotheses and predictions. Learners are also limited by how much information they are able to process, based on the *nature of a given task* and their own information-processing abilities. In the confirmation or replacement, reconstructive phase, interpretation of VP idioms is restricted to its own context through the gradual elimination of possible interpretations. Even in context, learners are often not capable of attending to all the information available in the input. Some of it becomes the object of focused or selective attention, while other parts are attended to only peripherally. This leads to either the confirmation of earlier hypotheses/predictions, or to the replacement and reconstruction of new hypotheses/predictions in light of the constraints made by the context, suggesting that idiom variability and interpretation is context-induced. Any inference an L2 reader is found to make depends on what kind of inference it is (i.e., graphophonic, semantic, pragmatic, cultural) and on the condition of encoding (in context or out of context) (Liontas, 2002b, p. 182, emphasis added).

To add further clarity to the Idiom Diffusion Model of Second Languages, some of the terms and tasks first used in the Liontas (1999) study are discussed next.

Idiom Sub-Types and Experimental Tasks

The Liontas (1999) study employed for the very first time a new terminology for *idiom* called vivid phrasal (VP) idiom, thus differentiating VP idioms from other types of idioms. For Liontas, a VP idiom is "an inseparable phrasal unit whose lexicalized, holistic meaning is not deducible from the individual meanings of its separate words" (Liontas, 2002c, p. 77). The following distinct characteristics exemplify a VP idiom:

1. It is not a monomorphemic or polymorphemic expression such as *a pad, a flop, to splurge, to freeload, to rely on, to object to*, just as it must not be an ungrammatical expression, connective prepositional phrase, an incorporating verb idiom, or a social formula expression.
2. It does not readily correlate with a given grammatical part of speech, and more often than not requires a paraphrase longer than a word.
3. It is not decomposable; that is, its conventionalized figurative meaning cannot be readily derived from a linear compositional analysis of the familiar meanings of its separate words.
4. It is easily visualized in the mind of the learner by evoking a powerful mental image; due to its concrete, imageable meaning, it is thus *vivid*.
5. It is a conventionalized complex multilexemic phrasal expression occurring above word level and usually of sentence length; hence it is *phrasal*.
6. It is polysemous and has both a common/literal, referential meaning, as well as an institutionalized/figurative, metaphorical meaning – the latter of which is usually not predictable nor logically deducible from the grammatical, syntactic, structural, and semantic character of its individual constituent elements (Liontas, 2002c, pp. 77–78).

Accordingly, the nonliteral, metaphoric utterance meaning of such multiword utterances (e.g., *to let the cat out of the bag, to pull teeth, to pull someone's leg*) is not easily discernible from an analysis of the literal, referential/semantic meaning of its individual constituent elements (e.g., *die Katze aus dem Sack lassen: to let the cat out of the bag* = *to reveal a secret*; *die Würmer aus der Nase ziehen: to pull the worms out of one's nose* = *it's like pulling teeth from a mule*). The interplay of these two meanings – the abstract, figurative one and the literal, concrete one – becomes less or more transparent depending on how close or distant the semantic/image opacity of the target idiom is from the domain idiom.

To illustrate this, Liontas (1999, 2002c) plots his VP idioms on a *lexical-image continuum* referred to as the *conceptual-semantic image* (CSI) *distance* in an effort to denote how close or how distant a target-language idiom is from its equivalent native-language domain idiom (see Table 1 for examples). Those target VP idioms that exhibit a one-to-one lexical/pictorial match with corresponding native-language domain idioms are called *lexical-level* (LL) *idioms* and are plotted at one end of this Lexical-Image Continuum. In contrast, those target VP idioms that do not match native-language domain idioms either lexically or pictorially are called *post-lexical-level* (PLL) *idioms* and are plotted at the other end of this continuum. The middle of this continuum is reserved for partially matching idioms between target- and native-language domain idioms called *semi-lexical-level* (SLL) *idioms*. This sub-type of VP idioms exhibits in many ways the one-to-one lexical/image correspondence of LL idioms, yet differs from its equivalent native-language domain idiom by only a few or even just one lexeme.

Table 1. *Examples of Idiom Type as a Function of Language*

Language	Idioms	Type	Literal Translation	Idiomatic Meaning
Spanish	*Colgando de un hilo*	LL	To hang by a thread	To hang by a thread
French	*Joindre les deux bouts*	LL	To make ends meet	To make ends meet
German	*Das Kriegsbeil begraben*	LL	To bury the hatchet	To bury the hatchet
Spanish	*Al que le quede el guante que se lo plante*	SLL	If the glove fits, wear it!	If the shoe fits, wear it!
French	*Être au bout du rouleau*	SLL	To be at the end of the roll	To be at the end of one's rope
German	*In den sauren Apfel beißen*	SLL	To bite into the sour apple	To bite the bullet
Spanish	*Echar toda la carne al asador*	PLL	To put all the meat on the spit	To put all the eggs in one basket
French	*Mettre quelqu'un en boîte*	PLL	To put someone in a box	To pull someone's leg
German	*Die Würmer aus der Nase ziehen*	PLL	To pull the worms out of the nose	To pull teeth from a mule

Note. LL = Lexical level; SLL = Semi-lexical level; PLL = Post-lexical level.

This trilateral taxonomy of VP idioms became the basis of the Liontas (1999) study that emerged from an earlier two-year pilot study with 35 third-, fourth-, and fifth-semester students of Modern Greek at two U.S. universities (Liontas, 1997, 2001). Three hundred students at a U.S. university who were enrolled in 35 sections of third-year Spanish, French, and German courses served as the target population. Of those students, 70 volunteer students (randomly selected) formed the first sample of Liontas' study. An additional sample of 10 volunteer students, randomly selected from 600 students, who were enrolled in 20 sections of third-year Spanish, French, and German courses during the same semester at another U.S. university formed the study's second sample. The total student sample was, in turn, subdivided into two experimental groups in an effort to obtain multiple sources of information: a *computer-mediated interactional* group (70 participants), and a *computer-mediated interactional video* group (10 participants). The only difference between these two groups was the presence (vs. the absence) of a think-aloud oral reading and text retelling procedure.

A total of 303 VP idioms (101 per language) comprised the sample corpus of this study. Using the selection criteria established earlier in the sub-categorization of VP idioms into LL, SLL, and PLL idioms, each one of the 303 VP idioms was given a designation accordingly. Within each category, the LL, SLL, and PLL idioms for each of the three languages were tabulated and counted. Only those idioms that met the strict sub-categorization criteria of VP idioms were entered into the final sample corpus. In the end, a random sample of 10 idioms within each idiom sub-category was chosen for the purposes of this study for a total of 30 idioms for each of the three language groups. Within each language, 15 idioms were once again randomly chosen for the *idiom detection task*, while the remaining 15 idioms were used in the *zero context task*; first without context and then with the accompanying texts from which they were previously extracted in the *full context task* (see below for descriptions of tasks).

All 90 idioms and texts, accompanied by several illustrative examples, were then entered into a specially designed Macintosh computer application referred to as the *That's All Greek to Me!* program. All participants within a language group were exposed to the same number of idioms and idiomatic texts and the same number of times, including the schedule of trial practice and testing. The order of presentation was pseudo randomly distributed in such a way as to have all three VP idiom types— LL, SLL, and PLL idioms—intermixed throughout the time of the experiment. Participants took part in the three experimental tasks, two questionnaires (a pre- and a post-study questionnaire), and one post-task summative evaluation in two sessions at 1-week intervals:

Session I consisted of the administration of Questionnaire I (Pre-Study Questionnaire) and participants' participation in the idiom detection task.

Session II consisted of participants' participation in the zero context task, full context task, and the post-task summative evaluation for each of the aforementioned tasks. The session concluded with the administration of Questionnaire II (Post-Study Questionnaire).

For ease of presentation, Table 2, below, presents a summary of the six research questions and experimental tasks used in this study. The methodological procedures are discussed next.

Computer-Mediated Group's Use of Materials

Participants in the computer-mediated interactional task group were introduced to the materials via the use of the *That's All Greek to Me!* computer program. The design of the program is presented graphically in Figure 1. Within each session, an individual trial consisted of the following steps:

1. First, the task instructions appeared in the center of an Apple Macintosh computer screen in order to familiarize participants with the particular task, the demands of the task, and the procedures of the task. A button at the bottom of the card allowed participants to proceed forward to the next card. In the idiom detection task, participants were told that they would see a series of 15 texts containing only one idiomatic expression per text. Conversely, in the zero context task, they were told that they would see only one idiomatic expression (15 total) at a time without any contextual support, and last, in the full context task, that the same idioms from the zero context task would be presented to them along with the text from which they were previously extracted. In addition, in the zero context task, participants were encouraged to respond as quickly and as accurately as possible. Timed latency responses (in seconds) were recorded and measured for each idiom in the zero context task.
2. Each one of the three tasks above was preceded by an illustrative practice trial.
3. After the *instruction* card disappeared, the screen showed an illustrative *example* card to better reinforce participants the demands of the individual tasks. This card was followed by a preselected narrative or dialogue text containing either an LL, SLL, or PLL idiom. The bottom of the card made use of fields into which participants could

Table 2. *Overview of Research Questions and Methodology*

RESEARCH QUESTIONS	EXPERIMENTAL TASKS	
	CMI GROUP	CMIV GROUP
1. How do adult L2 learners locate VP idioms in reading of texts containing them? On what text "cues" are their decisions based?	• Idiom detection task • Self-reports • Post-task evaluation	• Idiom detection task • Think-aloud reading • Self-reports • Post-task evaluation
2. How do adult L2 learners decode and comprehend VP idioms once they have been located in a text?	• Idiom detection task • Full context task • Self-reports • Post-task evaluation	• Idiom detection task • Full context task • Think-aloud reading • Self-reports • Post-task evaluation
3. What reading strategies do adult L2 learners employ in the comprehension and interpretation of VP idioms?	• Idiom detection task • Full context task • Self-reports • Post-task evaluation	• Idiom detection task • Full context task • Think-aloud reading • Self-reports • Post-task evaluation
4. What are the processing constraints that adult L2 learners are likely to exhibit during VP idiom comprehension and interpretation?	• Idiom detection task • Full context task • Self-reports • Post-task evaluation	• Idiom detection task • Full context task • Think-aloud reading • Self-reports • Post-task evaluation
5. Which sub-types of VP idioms (LL, SLL, or PLL idioms) are easier to comprehend and interpret and why?	• Idiom detection task • Zero context task • Full context task • Self-reports • Post-task evaluation	• Idiom detection task • Zero context task • Full context task • Think-aloud reading • Self-reports • Post-task evaluation
6. Does context significantly affect the comprehension and interpretation of VP idioms?	• Full context task • Self-reports • Post-task evaluation	• Full context task • Self-reports • Post-task evaluation

Note. CMI = Computer-mediated interactional; CMIV = Computer-mediated interactional video.

type their responses. In the idiom detection task participants were also able to select the words they believed made up the idiom in each text using the highlighting feature of the computer mouse. This built-in self-selection feature assured reliability and accuracy of data across all 15 texts in the idiom detection task and across language groups. In addition to the available button that triggers the next card, each card containing an idiomatic text or an idiom in the three tasks, respectively, also had a button that participants could

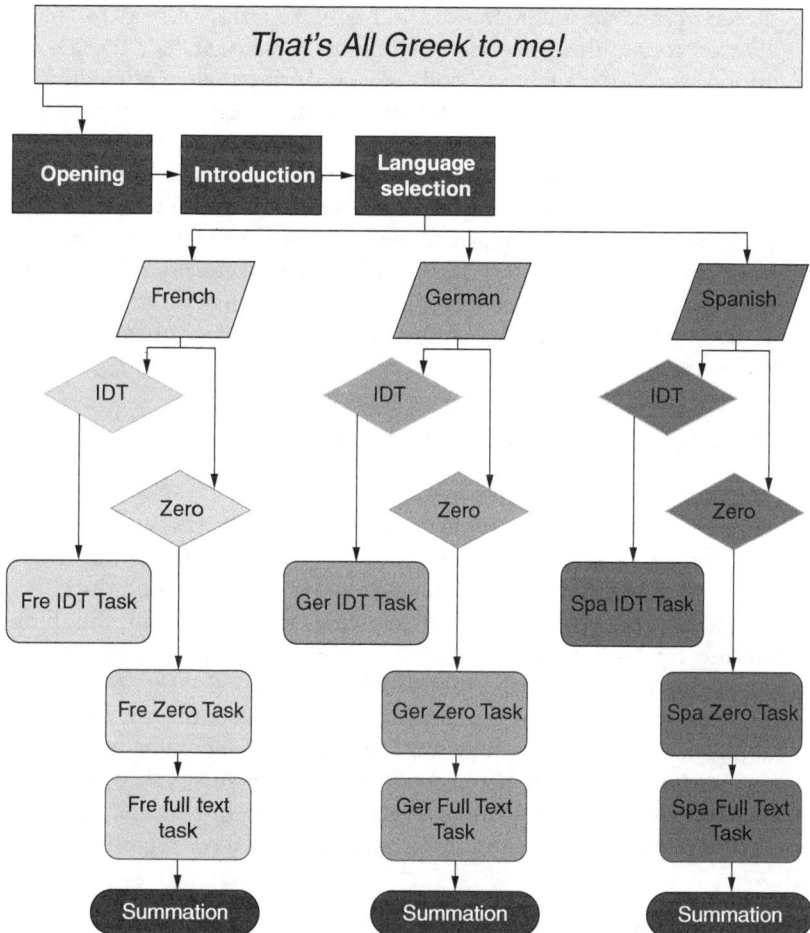

Figure 1. *That's All Greek to Me!* Computer Program
Note. Ger = German; Fre = French; Spa = Spanish; IDT = Idiom
detection task; Zero = Zero context task; Full text task = Full context task.

click in order to obtain the correct answer. This built-in *answer documentation* feature was purposefully integrated into *That's All Greek to Me!* in order to promote an interactive learning environment between the program and those individuals who had agreed to participate in this study, all the while motivating them to continue with the program. At no point, however, did the program allow participants to go back to their previous response to make corrections or changes. Only after the completion of the idiom detection task, and the combined zero context and full context tasks, were participants allowed to see the answers. For reasons already stated, the answer option was not available to both groups during their participation in the zero context task. From the early design stages of the program, affording participants the opportunity to learn the idioms used in *That's All Greek to Me!* was one of the study's principal aims.

4. During the transition from the zero context to the full context task, participants were encouraged to take a 5-minute break, although they were allowed to take more frequent breaks if necessary. Throughout the entire experimental session, participants were allowed to proceed at their own pace and to control the rate of program and answer presentation.

Computer-Mediated Interactional Video Group's Use of Materials

Participants in the computer-mediated interactional video task group were subjected to the exact same number of sessions, tasks, procedures, and materials as were those in the computer-mediated interactional group. The only difference between the two groups was the presence of a think-aloud oral reading and text retelling procedure. Both the think-aloud and retelling procedure were included for this group because, in fulfilling the demands of the individual experimental tasks, the participants' resulting protocols became immediate accounts of the idiom meaning-making processes they went through while actually using them. Thus, they provided an opportunity for participants to describe the characteristics of each individual experimental idiom text and task as it was carried out, while informing the researcher of their usefulness.

Post-Task Summative Evaluation

Following the completion of the preceding tasks, participants were asked to respond to specific queries about various aspects of their total experience with the range of VP idioms. To control the content of the feedback and to explore in more depth the idiosyncratic nature of the individual participants (i.e., the affective state of individuals), a set of five guiding questions was included in the instructions. For the benefit of this discussion, the task instructions are cited below:

Task Instructions: Report on your total experience with the idioms and the texts containing them. I would like you to reflect back on all the tasks — idiom detection task, zero context task, and full context task — and summarize your successes and failures during each of the procedures. Here are some questions that can guide your summary:

- What was the greatest challenge you faced?
- Did you overcome this challenge? How?
- What helped you and what did not?
- How do you feel about your total performance?
- Have you learned anything new about yourself as a language learner and reader?

Insights gleaned from these evaluations will add to the understanding of issues surrounding the processing, comprehension, and interpretation of idioms in and out of context (Liontas, 1999, pp. 153–154).

Following the end of the administration of Questionnaire II (Post-Study Questionnaire), a debriefing was conducted with a few of the participants in order to obtain feedback on specific kinds of information. While the interviews were relatively unstructured, nonetheless, they provided new insights into the usefulness of employing different experimental tasks, idiom-based computer software, observations, self-reports, question-naires, and debriefing sessions as a means of collecting more precise feedback before, during, and after the operational use of an instrument or task. Combined, the insights gleaned might provide the information needed for establishing an informed theoretical model of L2 idiomaticity that is amenable to both empirical and scientific scrutiny, leading to SLA theory development and idiom pedagogy.

The nature and analysis of data of the pre- and post-study question-naires has already been reported in Liontas (2002a) and will not be explicated here further. Overall, the data revealed that L2 learners do indeed want idioms to be an integral part of their language and culture training, that they can predict their performances on idiomatic tasks, and finally, that they have very specific beliefs about the importance of learning idioms, the nature of idiomatic learning, and the strategies that are most likely to facilitate such learning. Multimedia computer software investigating the process of idiom understanding positively influences their idiom-learning attitudes.

Similarly, the descriptive and quantitative analyses of data of the three experimental tasks – idiom detection task, zero context task, and full context task – have also been reported in Liontas (2002b, 2002c, 2002d, 2002e, 2003). The only two sets of data not yet reported are post-task summative evaluation data and *That's All Greek to Me!* data. These two sets of data and their analyses are presented next.

Analysis of Post-Task Summative Evaluation Data

The aim of this final summation was to ascertain participants' general experience with the range of VP idioms across the experimental tasks employed in this study. While each task had an aim in its own right, all experimental tasks, converged on the same affective issues: the feelings and difficulties participants had experienced during each task and whether they felt they were successful within each task.

All audio recordings made during the computer-mediated interactional video sessions were coded accordingly for future identification and transcribed into a text document for subsequent data analysis. Video recordings, on the other hand, were analyzed for body language. For instance, changes of posture, exclamations, facial expressions, and wandering eyes, among others, were identified and noted as significant in the analysis of video data. This type of data was considered to be indicative of the active thought processes as participants attempted to transact meaning of the texts containing VP idioms (see Liontas, 2007, for a more detailed account). Further, data obtained from the post-task summative evaluations were analyzed inductively for recurring thematic units, in addition to the units already identified during the participants' retrospective accounts. The data were then classified on the basis of a number of conceptual categories that emerged from the subsequent analysis. Whenever insights provided in the evaluations were ambiguous, follow-up interviews were conducted with those individual participants to triangulate and supplement understanding of the issues at hand. According to Fetterman (1989), "triangulation works with any topic, in any setting, and on any level ... The trick is to compare comparable items and levels during analysis" (p. 90).

The insights obtained as a result of the five open-ended questions posed in this summative evaluation serve primarily two functions. First, they further support the experimental data produced by the elicitation tasks discussed earlier by helping to account for successful or less-than-successful idiom recognition and production. Second, they serve as primary language data themselves, helping to delineate even further the issues surrounding the processing, comprehension, and interpretation of VP idioms in and out of context. Accordingly, the comments that have most relevance to this study fall into two categories: those that offer insight into the meaning-making process of VP idioms and those that reflect on the enhancement of reading comprehension and idiom pedagogy. Tables 3–5 (see Appendix A) present the most representative comments that add further validity to the observations here made. Specifically, Table 3 presents evidence regarding the challenges encountered during the completion of the three experimental tasks. In turn, Table 4 presents evidence regarding the participants' sense of accomplishment. Specifically, it shows the writing output that students produced in completing the experimental tasks. It shows how much they wrote when responding to the tasks. Table 5 reveals new insights regarding the lessons participants learned from this idiom-testing experience. Finally, Table 6 (see Appendix A) presents a descriptive summary of all student-produced data that were analyzed in this study according to task.

Analysis of That's All Greek to Me! Computer Program Data

As already reported in the Liontas (2002a) study, Questionnaire II, comprised of three parts, asked participants to offer value judgments about their affective needs when learning idioms in the second and foreign language classroom. One set of data not reported in that study was Part Three. Part Three of Questionnaire II, containing 24 items and using the same 5-point Likert scale employed in the other two parts of the questionnaire, solicited participants' opinions regarding the design and perceived effectiveness of That's All Greek to Me! (see Appendix B for Part Three of Questionnaire II). Specifically, participants were asked to rate their agreement or disagreement with statements reflecting their total experience with the multimedia program. Rating scales of 1–5 (with 1 = least important and 5 = most important) were used to obtain feedback from participants on the strength and direction of their feelings about specific program-related issues. Presentation, content, instructional quality, learner interaction, idiomatic tasks, and finally, learners' perceptions of and attitudes toward the program itself comprised the six parts of Part Three of Questionnaire II. Table 7 in Appendix A presents the weighted mean scores for the twenty-four statements included in this part of the questionnaire.

Findings and Discussion

The final summation task was employed in the Liontas (1999) study in an effort to obtain new insights regarding the effects the individual experimental tasks had on the learners' overall idiom performance, leading to a new understanding of the idiosyncratic nature of these participants and the issues closely associated with processing, comprehending, and interpreting L2 idioms in contextualized and uncontextualized reading of Spanish, French, and German texts. Not surprisingly, this final summation task did allow participants to reflect critically on the readings and the specific pieces of language that caught their attention, speculate on their idiom processing at work, and consider specific processing challenges they encountered in the processing, comprehension, and interpretation of VP idioms in and out of context. While the commentaries made reaffirmed and strengthened previous findings already reported, they also raised a number of larger language-learning issues. These issues will be discussed next.

Regarding Challenges Encountered

Several observations deserve comment here. To begin, many of the participants expressed their frustration with the vocabulary and the idiomatic texts, while others pointed to the positive challenge of the total experience. Their responses ranged from a sense of accomplishment to complete frustration. Specifically, when juxtaposing the full context task comments with those regarding the idiom detection or zero context tasks, a host of new insights becomes available. As discussed previously, the specific aim of the zero context task was to ascertain whether participants could assign meaning to an idiom independently of its context. The rationale behind this experimental task is perhaps best captured in the "I think that the zero content activity was necessary because you must look at how much can be understood without any more information than the idiom itself."

From the summative accounts given by the participants, it was revealed that this task was the most difficult one to complete successfully. Reasons offered ranged from being misled by the meaning of the target idiom to deciphering the *feel* of the idiom. A number of recurring thematic units in Table 3 in Appendix A deserve further explanation:

1. *Seeing an idiom without its supporting context.* Of all the comments made, (con)text (or lack thereof) appears to be the most central variable that permeates all other recurring themes. From the range of opinions offered, it is clear that the presence or absence of context *does* influence the idiom comprehension and interpretation process. Many participants found context to be extremely useful in their attempts to ascertain both the literal and figurative meaning of an idiom precisely because it helped them to think of an analogous situation and draw their attention to the meaning each idiom had in each particular context (or story): "Once I understood the situation, it was easier to understand the idiom," one participant exclaimed. Another participant put it even more laconically: "I used the story to give me a hint." Conversely, misinterpretation of an idiom may follow if no text is available to correlate with it. In fact, lack of supporting context forced many participants to resort to guessing the meaning of unfamiliar idioms at random: "[I] guessed the best I could," said one. Some of them even felt that high levels of

frustration develop when relying solely on guessing the meaning of individual lexical items for the correct interpretation of an idiom, especially if they are convinced of the existence of an equivalent English domain idiom. As one participant put it: "I was frustrated in knowing that there was an English equivalent that I couldn't come up with!" It is not surprising then to see their feelings ranging from uneasiness to frustration and a sense of struggling. Considering the many difficulties encountered during the completion of the zero context task, it is important to bear in mind that the success rate was nevertheless high (43%), but notably less than in the full context task (71%). This result is an important one, for it lends strong support to the LL/PLL distinction even in the absence of supporting context. Conversely, when context was introduced, the success rate increased by 28 percent. Based on obtained quantitative and qualitative data, context did influence the further creation of the idiomatic image and interpretation of LL and SLL idioms, and, in particular, that of PLL idioms.

2. *Knowing the vocabulary of the idiom.* Equally important to context is the issue of vocabulary, which has been characterized by this study's participants as the "main stumbling block." For the greater majority of participants, trying to understand and determine what an idiom meant without a supporting context was difficult, especially when participants had difficulties deciphering some or all of the individual words of the idiom. It is, therefore, not surprising to see participants repeatedly commenting on the importance of vocabulary. If most of the individual words were unknown, there were no other clues to allow one to hazard a guess. Even when all the lexical items were known to participants, certain VP idioms, in particular idioms of the PLL sub-type, were still difficult to interpret correctly. As one participant put it: "I had a hard time understanding the idiom even if I understood all the words." At other times, even the lack of one key word in the idiomatic phrase was enough to present difficulties for some participants: "If I didn't know even one word, then they [idioms] were almost impossible to understand," wrote one participant. Others, in trying to connect a target language idiom to an English domain idiom, engaged in conscious lexical associations and guessing. Representative comments include, but are not limited to, "I just used the surrounding words to help as much as possible, I overcame this by just thinking hard about the words I did know and what other words would make the idiom make sense, and guessed the best I could."

3. *Translating an idiomatic expression.* Closely tied to the issue of vocabulary is the issue of idiom translatability. Because most target language idioms did not translate directly into English, it was nearly impossible to literally translate an idiom phrase and expect to directly ascertain its figurative meaning. Not surprisingly, lack of vocabulary knowledge inhibited many participants from being able to translate an idiomatic string, which in turn barred them from possibly finding an acceptable English-domain idiom equivalent. According to participants, unless a target language idiom translated directly or closely to something in English, it was difficult to discover its true figurative meaning. This is particularly true for LL and SLL VP idioms, but not so true for PLL idioms. For some participants, it was extremely difficult to simply try to translate the idiom phrase *per se* and get an English idiom from it precisely because the target *vocabulary and structure used are so much different from English ones* and because the *words change slightly* even if they have the same meaning. As one participant succinctly put it: "Many of the idioms had the same feel as English idioms but with a different twist." For others, the process of meaning making was less of a challenge but no less arduous. In deciphering the *feel* of a Spanish, French, or German VP idiom, participants employed a host of metacognitive strategies before reaching a definitive interpretation. *Putting things together bit by bit, pulling the idiom apart* based on words recognized, *assigning figurative values* to words recognized, *scanning one's own idiom database to find an English idiom match,* and *thinking about an idiom's meaning* and *what other words would make the idiom make sense* are but a small sample of the most often used metacognitive strategies that had a direct impact on participants' overall rate of success.

4. *Non-familiarity with an idiom.* Depending on the VP idiom sub-type, idiom interpretation without context was strenuous to varying degrees, but primarily because no inferences could be drawn to arrive at the figurative meaning of an idiom. As one participant phrased it: "With the zero context task, I had an extremely difficult time. Some of the idioms were very obvious, but most of them weren't and I felt that I struggled with this part... I had to read the idiom over and over again, and very often that didn't help." In extracting the idioms from their supporting context, participants were challenged to assign meaning to an idiom by engaging in image creation and idiom *bridging* between the given L2 VP idiom and its equivalent L1 English domain idiom. Similarly, being unaware of one's own idiomatic knowledge hampered the success rate achieved by some participants. In the words of one participant, "Of my challenges, the one that I found to

be the most cumbersome is the realization that I, as a speaker, am not fully aware of idioms used in my own language." Idiom interpretation was less laborious, of course, if participants were familiar with the idiom *per se*, the individual words comprising the idiom were known to them, the idiom was of the LL or SLL VP idiom sub-type, or the VP idiom was presented within a context (situation, story) supporting its figurative interpretation. Without a doubt, the paragraphs and dialogues helped greatly to interpret correctly most of the idioms given to them even without knowing initially some of the individual words comprising them. In short, the context was very helpful in determining the figurative meaning of the idioms that participants did not immediately get.

Participants' Performance

Aside from the important revelations just discussed, participants also commented on their overall performance with the experimental tasks. Presented in Table 4 (see Appendix A), the attitudes expressed in the entries regarding their overall performance were indicative of stages of success. Positive entries, ranging from "I feel I did very well" to "I am confident," indicated a sense of accomplishment; negative entries, ranging from "I feel my performance could have been better" to "I feel awful about my performance," indicated areas being worked on, such as learning more focused vocabulary and idiomatic expressions, paying more attention to detail and the context surrounding idioms, and becoming even more aware of idiomatic knowledge. There were also some intermediate neutral statements such as "I feel okay," "I feel I did alright," and "I feel adequate."

While the emotional state of participants is indeed important, the insights they provide are valuable and relevant to the purposes of this study. It is only through their metalinguistic comments that we obtain a better glimpse at the reasons behind their self-imposed ratings. Thus, we now know that they linked their success to the presence of context; that some of the idioms were hard to figure out, especially because some of them *did not translate word for word*; that vocabulary is a crucial factor in the comprehension and interpretation of idioms and texts; that the connection between target and domain idiom is not as easy as one might imagine, especially when presented without contextual support; and, perhaps even more importantly, that instructors need to teach idioms more often in academic settings because learners appreciate so very much the learning of idioms in the second and foreign language classroom. This finding is not surprising, given all the previous comments already discussed. Nor is it surprising to find out that, for the most part, participants found the idiom exercises helpful and useful and were even satisfied with their total performance, as well as with the kinds and numbers of text exercises used.

Regarding Lessons Learned

Participants' comments also revealed the many lessons they had learned from having taken part in this study. Among the recurring lessons cited in Table 5, Appendix A, the most common ones fall under the realization that context exerts a profound positive influence on idiom understanding, that literal translation of an idiom does not lead one to the idiomatic meaning, and finally, that learning idioms helps with vocabulary building and enhances one's knowledge of culture. Some participants commented directly on the importance of teaching idioms to learners of second and foreign languages. Still others commented on their limitations of target-language knowledge and on the need to learn idioms and more vocabulary in the target language. Many of them even had altered their attitude toward idiom learning as a result of this study. They stressed the importance of becoming more aware of the ways in which they make sense of idioms and texts, while still others stressed the need to read target-language texts more closely in order to ascertain the meaning of an idiom. A smaller subset of participants emphasized the point that all skills need to be learned in orchestration if one is to be considered fluent enough in an L2, including idioms, and, finally, that transfer of idiomatic knowledge and strategies from one language to another is not an automatic process; rather, it is one that needs to be acquired and made concrete through repeated practice and systematic exposure.

Concluding the discussion of the summative insights, it is worthwhile noting that the many new insights obtained here are the direct result of the research design employed in this study. As presented in Table 6, the sheer volume of information obtained and put to analysis is laborious, indeed. Nevertheless, such data is imperative for painting an accurate picture of L2 idiomaticity – a picture that, by all accounts to the contrary, remains incomplete and misunderstood to this day.

This reality aside, all this data was obtained as a direct result of the extensive learner introspective and retrospective reports produced during and at the end of each idiom or idiomatic text in the experimental tasks and the final summative evaluation. A study based solely on idiom comprehension or production data by definition could not have revealed such telling insights. In particular, the richness of the insights made available in the summations as a source of information on idiomatic language, text processing, and idiom pedagogy reaffirms the task's usefulness as a viable source of data in its own right for qualitative study research. The fact that many insights would not have been available to this researcher had he not included this end task in the design of the *That's All Greek to Me!* multimedia computer program confirms the usefulness of this task in contributing to both SLA theory development and idiom pedagogy.

As seen in Table 7 (Appendix A), of the 24 total statements, only two statements (1 and 13) received mean scores of less than 4.00, while the mean scores of the remaining 22 statements ranged from a low of 4.05 (Statement 21) to a high of 4.59 (Statement 6). When participants were asked at the end of the study the reasons for scoring Statement 1 below a 4 or a 5, the majority said that they were unsure if the program was indeed free of technical problems or programming errors, hence their tendency to score this question lower. With respect to Statement 13, many of them felt that the idiom detection task, albeit at times challenging, was not nearly as difficult as the other two tasks—the zero context task and the full context task. This is clearly evident in the higher mean scores given for these tasks; in turn, these scores validate the actual performance task data reported in Liontas (2001, 2002a, 2002b, 2002c, 2002d, 2002e, 2003).

Perhaps the biggest compliment to the program is the high marks it received in the sub-section *Attitude* (Statements 18–24, see Table 7, Appendix A). Such high marks indicate that a multimedia computer program combining sound technology (in terms of Presentation, Content, and Instructional Quality) with language learning tasks that clearly challenge learners' knowledge of idiomaticity can potentially be highly satisfying to those who are asked to use it. Participants' great degree of satisfaction with the program was equally echoed in post-study discussions and semi-structured interviews with several respondents. The mutual satisfaction found in all language groups helps to validate the use of this program for investigating more systematically the process of L2 idiom understanding (i.e., the combined idiom comprehension and interpretation process; for a more detailed account of the *That's All Greek to Me!* multimedia computer program within Artificial Intelligence technologies and idiomaticity, in particular the future of these technologies and knowledge systems for idiom learning, see Liontas, 2009).

Beyond that, the findings of this summative evaluation, coupled with the many valuable insights gained from the previous individual tasks reaffirmed the correctness of *Assumption 1* (comprehension of L2 VP idioms will require a special processing mode, yielding two alternative interpretations), *Assumption 2* (lexical access is obligatory for individual words even when they are part of a VP idiom), and *Assumption 3* (syntactic, semantic, and pragmatic analysis is obligatory in L2 VP idiom comprehension, regardless of whether the idiom is embedded in its full context) of the *Process of L2 Idiom Comprehension and Interpretation of VP Idioms During Reading* given at the outset of this study: L2 learners do compute literal and idiomatic meanings separately, yielding two alternative interpretations. The *idiomatic* sense becomes available *only* after the literal interpretation has been considered and rejected, as posed by the Idiom Diffusion Model of Second Languages (Liontas, 1999, 2002b).

Limitations and Future Research

The richness of the insights made available in the participants' summations as a source of information on idiomatic language and text processing reaffirms the task's usefulness as a complementary source of data for qualitative study research. The fact that many insights would not have been available to the researcher had he not included this end task confirms the usefulness of this task in contributing to theory development and pedagogy. Nonetheless, there are some limitations to the claims made in this study that need to be addressed.

Because this study only investigated how learners understand VP idioms in reading dialogs and narratives of similar communicative nature, it would be informative to see how their performance is affected when learners are presented with different genres of reading, different media discourses (i.e., multimedia presentations), or different receptive sources of input. Results obtained from such research foci would expand upon our understanding of the factors (i.e., type, length, and source) and the role that each factor plays in the comprehension and interpretation of VP idioms in second and foreign languages. Equally informative would be to find out whether the results are consistent over various texts and across language groups or whether they show significant variance. Some such results are already beginning to emerge (see, for example, Cieślicka & Singleton, 2004; Deignan, Gabrys, & Solska, 2001; Grant, 2007; Laufer, 2000; Lennon, 1998; Olejniczak, 2006; Palmer, Shackelford, Miller, & Leclere, 2007; Piasecka, 2006; Vanlacker-Sidtis, 2003; Verspoor, & Lowie, 2003; Zimmermann, 2006).

As L2 idiomatologists around the world labor to develop a common language and a vision that permeates matters of L2 idiomaticity, it will become increasingly imperative to find out the precise combination of comprehension factors and the nature of instructional interventions that positively affect how well and how fluently learners of second and foreign languages develop figurative language in general and idiomatic competence (i.e., the ability to understand and use idioms appropriately and accurately in a variety of sociocultural contexts with the least amount of mental effort and to use them in a cultural manner similar to that of a native speaker; Liontas, 2002e, p. 212) in particular. For example, how are the findings reported here and elsewhere changed if a variety of multimedia presentations were used instead of a single computer program? How are the findings changed if a variety of receptive sources of input were used? Such insights would also make possible the discovery of stages of idiomatic competence development and, even more importantly, whether such development occurs in serial or in parallel with the more general psycholinguistic and cognitive mechanisms underlying the internalization of SLA processes and sequences. Indeed, should such insights be attainable, and there is no reason why it should not be so, not only will this new body of knowledge lead to future research projects in the L2 idiom arena and, consequently, to new linguistic rounds of focused discussions among researchers and language practitioners, but increasingly, it will also lead to a serious need for the reexamination and modification of current performance assessment, curriculum articulation, and materials development practices. In turn, the linguistic rounds of discussion may force the jury of idiom researchers and language practitioners alike to begin to contemplate the answers to the more profound research questions and crucial pedagogical issues in the L2 idiom research domain, the most important of which are given below in no particular order. They are surveyed here for the classroom implications they hold for future research and pedagogy precisely because their conception yields a powerful framework through which the development of idiomatic competence can be predicted, described, analyzed, and explained. This is necessary to present a coherent view of the whole of the research in the L2 idiom arena and pedagogy. Where possible, pertinent research questions and issues related to idiom instruction are grouped together in thematic units in an effort to delineate the parameters of the related issues at hand.

1. How are idioms learned over time? What particular stages in the development of idiom competence can be identified? What are the developmental patterns or stages of idiom acquisition? Does learners' performance change over time? If yes, how and why does it change?
2. Is the process of idiom acquisition the same or different in naturalistic or classroom settings? Does successful idiom learning result from comprehensible input? Do learners need explicit learning and contrived encounters in order to achieve significant fluency in idioms?

What is a reasonable number of encounters with idioms in the target language that results in idiomatic proficiency?

3. Does idiom acquisition require direct instruction and strategy training, as well as extensive exposure to idioms (through reading and listening)? Is contextualized idiom learning, plus systematic instruction, superior to contextualized learning of idioms alone?

4. Can idiom acquisition be enhanced through instructional intervention in the context of meaningful language use? How is this process best supported and made more direct and efficient?

5. Does input shaped through interaction contribute to idiom acquisition? Are there certain activities and tasks that increase the effectiveness of idiom learning through listening and reading practice more convincingly than others?

6. Does the nature of a task have a marked influence on learners' choice of cognitive and metacognitive strategies? That is, does it predispose learners to use a particular strategy or a combination of strategies? What combination of idiom learning and studying strategies is the most useful in ferreting out and learning the figurative meaning of an idiom?

7. What instructional practices encourage a low-anxiety learning atmosphere conducive to idiom learning and acquisition? How can idiom reception and production be made more successful? To what can successful, productive idiom use be attributed to?

8. Is the lack of figurative language control in L2 learners a *problem* of linguistic complexity or one of cognitive processing? What are the linguistic and cognitive mechanisms that are at work in understanding and acquiring various forms of figurative language such as metaphors, idioms, proverbs, similes, and so forth?

9. Can we presume that L2 learners can comprehend figurative language by way of demonstration, practice, and feedback? What types of interaction and stimuli affect the idiom processing mechanisms that impede or enhance the development of idiomatic competence?

10. What are the optimal interactional conditions that aid the development of idiomatic competence? Does the production of idiomatic output enhance the development of idiomatic competence? Does idiom automaticity result from multiple exposures to an idiom, repeated practice, and attempts at production?

These are only some of the most important research questions that the research community will need to address in the near future. In the meantime, however, it is still far from clear how L2 learners acquire idioms and, even more importantly, the question still remains as to whether instructional intervention could support the process and make it more direct and efficient. In the absence of empirical evidence to the contrary, it should be noted here that there are no theoretical reasons to suspect that instructional intervention would play an inhibiting role in the development of idiomatic competence. On the contrary, its role is believed to be a facilitating one. Above all, the development of idiomatic competence cannot proceed in isolation nor apart from the greater process of learning and acquiring language and culture in context. Neither can the development of idiomatic competence succeed without taking into serious consideration individual differences among learners, such as prior knowledge, abilities, motivation, aptitude, learning style preferences, metacognitive strategies, and affective/social factors. When such considerations are merged with the many other insights revealed in this study and filtered carefully through knowledge of language development, cognitive language acquisition processes, awareness of learners' linguistic and sociocultural capabilities, and, finally, student appeal, then such considerations have the potential to influence greatly how effectively and how efficiently L2 learners will develop idiomatic competence in a target language ultimately.

Summary and Conclusions

This study began with the assertion that different experimental tasks and idiom sub-types can have different effects on the comprehension and production of L2 idioms in third-year adult learners of Spanish, French, and German. Quantitative data alone, no matter how high the reliability, construct validity, authenticity, interactiveness, impact, and practicality of a given research design, cannot be used as the sole source of data to validate the robustness of the results achieved or justify a particular set of intended interpretations. Equally important is rich qualitative data, which, in more ways than one, can and often do supplement and complete the researcher's understanding of a particular issue under investigation. Such data were presented in this study in an effort to paint a more accurate and complete picture of the issues surrounding the processing, comprehension, and interpretation of L2 idioms in contextualized and noncontextualized contexts. The ensuing discussion revealed that (1) certain experimental tasks had more of a negative/positive effect than others on the learners' overall idiom performance; (2) VP idiom sub-type and lack of context affects performance in notable ways; (3) L2 learners can derive specific lessons from having taken part in a study and, even more importantly, that they are more than willing and able to make those lessons known to the researcher if only given the chance to articulate their concerns; and, finally, (4) an interactive, multimedia computer program specifically geared toward L2 idioms can address many of the issues surrounding idiom understanding and learning.

Mediated by the metacognitive strategies and facilitated by positive affect, participants were capable of using their topical knowledge and affective schemata for coping with the demands of the individual experimental tasks as well as their organizational (i.e., grammatical and textual knowledge) and pragmatic knowledge (i.e., functional and sociolinguistic knowledge), both of which form their language knowledge (for a discussion of these concepts, see Bachman & Palmer, 1996, pp. 67–70.) Specifically, they were found to (1) use and relate concepts, words, utterances, texts, structures, and functions directly linked to knowledge of idiomaticity; (2) set different goals in completing the tasks; and (3) take stock of their own inventory of knowledge of idiomaticity, performance, and positive/negative affective responses both to the characteristics of the VP idiom types and experimental tasks. In short, the participants of this study were capable of formulating and utilizing one or more plans for implementation as a direct response to a particular experimental VP idiom type or task. This sense of empowerment and satisfaction was particularly prevalent in this study.

When combined with the findings obtained in the other studies already reported, the insights revealed in this study become ever more powerful as a viable source of information on idiomatic language and text processing in their own right deserving equitable consideration in future theory development and idiom pedagogy. To help jumpstart this process, a series of related but thematically linked research questions were offered in an effort to delineate some of the parameters directly linked to the development of idiomatic competence in a target language.

In closing, it must be said that L2 idiomaticity, as a field of research in its own right, will remain undefined and unfalsifiable as long as those of us working on matters of L2 idiomaticity fail to come together as a community of concerted scholars in a conjoined effort to develop a common language and a vision equal to those so easily discernible in other well-established sub-fields of SLA, not to mention those enjoying a high profile in present psycholinguistics, sociolinguistics, artificial intelligence, pragmatics, applied linguistics, and cognitive science, in general. Above all, having a common research agenda can only hasten the emergence and viability of L2 idiomaticity around the world in general and in the United States and Canada in particular. Without exception, lexicographers, linguists, researchers, teachers, and publishers around the world can help shape the field's research agenda in the years ahead. Exploring L2 learners' notions of idiomaticity may well be the first step toward achieving this goal, especially if we find ourselves willing to take our cues *straight from the horse's mouth*—our learners, that is!

List of Key Words

Affective state, Computer-mediated interaction (CMI), Computer-mediated interactional video (CMIV), Conceptual-semantic image (CSI), Contextualized, Decomposable, Domain idiom, Elicitation tasks, Figurative meaning, Full context task, Idiom detection task, Idiomatic competence, Idiomaticity, Lexical access, Lexical-image continuum, Lexical-level (LL), Literal, Metacognitive strategies, Metaphoric, Native-language, Nonliteral, Opacity, Polysemous, Post-lexical level (PLL), Pragmatic knowledge, Qualitative research, Reconstructive phase, Referential, Second language acquisition (SLA), Semi-lexical level (SLL), Semi-structured interviews, Summative evaluation, Target idiom, Target-language, Textual knowledge, Vivid phrasal idiom (VP), Zero context task

Thought Questions

1. Consider one class of English learners. Identify the conceptual-semantic image (CSI) distance (also referred to as the lexical-image continuum) to denote how close or how distant a target-language idiom is from the students' equivalent native-language domain idiom. In what ways might instruction using the lexical-image continuum help them?
2. What are some advantages to learning and/or acquiring idioms in naturalistic or classroom settings? Does successful idiom learning result from comprehensible input? Do learners need explicit learning and contrived encounters in order to achieve significant fluency in idioms? What is a reasonable number of encounters with idioms in the target language that results in idiomatic proficiency?
3. Think of a lesson you have recently taught or one you might teach in the near future. Does input shaped through interaction contribute to idiom acquisition? Are there certain activities and tasks that increase the effectiveness of idiom learning through listening and reading practice more convincingly than others? What types of interaction

and stimuli affect the idiom-processing mechanisms that impede or enhance the development of idiomatic competence? Please provide examples.

4. Think of an idiom that was difficult for you to understand, learn, or acquire. Why was it difficult? What information would you have needed for it to make sense? What are the pedagogical implications for teaching idioms to all learners, including English learners?

5. Reflect on the difficulties you had in understanding and acquiring various forms of L2 figurative language such as metaphors, idioms, proverbs, and similes. Were your difficulties a *problem* of linguistic complexity or one of cognitive processing? What are some techniques you used to overcome these difficulties? What are some techniques you can use in your own classroom?

6. Determine with your classmates which type of instruction should be adopted for the development of idiomatic competence. Will learners with different learning styles benefit from different types of instruction (i.e., implicit instruction, explicit instruction, or combined instruction)? Will the individual learner factors (e.g., age, sex, social class, ethnic background, and motivation) and psychological factors (e.g., language aptitude, learning style and personality, and learners' attitudes and beliefs) influence the learning outcomes and the level of idiomatic competence achieved? Please be as specific as you can.

7. It is generally believed that context allows the integration of multiple sources of information and therefore the comprehension of an idiom. Does strong development in reading or listening comprehension assist the development of idiom comprehension and interpretation? What adjustments and techniques should a teacher use to promote the accurate production of idioms in speech and in writing? Describe the techniques you would implement to achieve maximum student output.

8. In reflecting on the content of this chapter, how would you respond to a teacher who says, "Idioms are difficult to comprehend and acquire for native language learners, and they are especially problematic for bilingual and second language learners. Besides, it takes too much valuable time from the other content areas that I need to teach, so why even bother?"

   a. Do you agree with this statement? Why or why not? What research presented in this chapter (book) supports your position?

   b. What "other" evidence is there that idioms (and figurative language in general) are not difficult to learn? Share with your colleague your ideas for maximizing idiom learning across the content areas.

Suggested Student Research Projects

1. Your school is interested in investigating how English learners learn idioms over time. They are particularly interested in knowing what the particular stages are, if any, in the development of idiom competence; how those stages can be best identified; and what are the developmental patterns of idiom acquisition over time. Write a study plan that aims to answer these questions. Delineate a sequence of experimental tasks and procedures involved in the study process to ensure the study's success and, even more importantly, the pedagogical implications derived from this study.

2. Your school is interested in developing research-based curricula for idiom learning. They are particularly interested in knowing the kind of idiomatic knowledge outcomes that are being envisioned; the most important functions idioms fulfill in communication; the nature, types, and range of idioms to be learned in the classroom; the opportunities learners will have to engage in interactive input (both type and amount of exposure to idioms) to produce idiomatic output; the nature of the tasks (or projects) learners will be asked to perform; the modalities to be involved in the learning process; the kind of idiom materials to be used (type, length, and source); and, finally, the learning environment in which idiom learning is to take place (implicit instruction vs. explicit instruction). Make a list and organize the elements that should be taken into account when *planning* curricula for idiom learning before addressing systematically the elements that should be emphasized when *executing* such curricula for idiom learning in the classroom and beyond.

3. You are being considered by a leading educational software company for the position of *Chief Software Engineer* to design and develop user-friendly, interactive multimedia software introducing English learners to the digital world of idioms. Your software is to encompass a variety of multimedia digital elements allowing learners to access animated images, texts, sounds, and video sequences (from movies, songs, native-speaker conversations, and the like) and play and replay them as necessary, using a variety of user interface and navigation controls. You are free to include in your software any language modality or combination of modalities you wish. Equally, you are given complete freedom over the design features, practice choices, and application/assessment learning formats. In short, you are free to set up both the conditions and the parameters under which idiomatic learning is to take place within the confined architectural structure of the software. Based on best practices of current theoretical and pedagogical

constructs to date, describe in detail the overall design and architecture of your idiom-learning software from A to Z and prepare a succinct prospectus for dissemination and discussion.

Related Internet Sites

English Club: www.englishclub.com/webguide/Vocabulary/ Idioms

Idiom Worksheets: www.superteacherworksheets.com/idioms. html

Lesson Planet: www.lessonplanet.com

Learning for Kids: www.learninggamesforkids.com/vocabulary_games/idioms.html

Suggested Readings

Boers, F., & Lindstromberg, S. (Eds.) (2008). *Cognitive linguistic approaches to teaching vocabulary and phraseology.* Berlin: Mouton de Gruyter.

Liu, D. (2008). *Idioms: Description, comprehension, acquisition, and pedagogy.* New York: Routledge.

McMarthy, M., & O'Dell, F. (2008). *English idioms in use.* Cambridge, UK: Cambridge University Press.

REFERENCES

Abel, B. (2003). English idioms in the first language and second language lexicon: A dual representation approach. *Second Language Research, 30,* 329–358.

Arnaud, P.J., & Savignon, S.J. (1997). Rare words, complex lexical units and the advanced learner. In J. Coady & T. Huckin (Eds.), *Second language vocabulary acquisition* (pp. 157–173). Cambridge, UK: Cambridge University Press.

Bachman, L.F., & Palmer, A.S. (1996). *Language testing in practice.* Oxford, UK: Oxford University Press.

Barkema, H. (1996). Idiomaticity and terminology: A multi-dimensional descriptive model. *Studia Linguistica, 50,* 125–160.

Boers, F. (2000). Metaphor awareness and vocabulary retention. *Applied Linguistics, 21,* 553–571.

Bortfeld, H. (2002). What native and non-native speakers images for idioms tell us about figurative language. In R.R. Heredia & J. Altarriba (Eds.), *Bilingual sentence processing* (275–295). Amsterdam: Elsevier.

(2003). Comprehending idioms cross-linguistically. *Experimental Psychology, 50,* 217–230.

Cieślicka, A. (2006a). Literal salience in on-line processing of idiomatic expressions by second language learners. *Second Language Research, 22,* 115–144.

(2006b). On building castles on the sand, or exploring the issue of transfer in interpretation and production of L2 fixed expressions. In J. Arabski (Ed.), *Cross-linguistic influences in the second language lexicon* (pp. 226–245). Clevedon, UK: Multilingual Matters Ltd.

Cieślicka, A., & Singleton, D. (2004). Metaphorical competence and the L2 learner. *Angles on the English-Speaking World, 4,* 69–84.

Cooper, T.C. (1998). Teaching idioms. *Foreign Language Annals, 31,* 255–266.

(1999). Processing of idioms in L2 learners of English. *TESOL Quarterly, 33,* 233–262.

Deignan, A., Gabrys, D., & Solska, A. (2001). Teaching English metaphors using cross linguistic awareness-raising activities. *ELT Journal, 51,* 352–360.

Fernando, C. (1996). *Idioms and idiomaticity.* Oxford, UK: Oxford University Press.

Fetterman, D.M. (1989). *Ethnography: Step by step.* Newbury Park and London: Sage Publications.

Giora, R. (1997). Understanding figurative and literal language: The graded salience hypothesis. *Cognitive Linguistics, 7,* 183–206.

(1999). On the priority of salient meanings: Studies of literal and figurative language. *Journal of Pragmatics, 31,* 919–929.

Giora, R., & Fein, O. (1999). On understanding familiar and less-familiar figurative language. *Journal of Pragmatics Special Issue: Literal and Figurative Language, 31,* 1601–1618.

Grant, L.E. (2007). In a manner of speaking: Assessing frequent spoken figurative idioms to assist ESL/EFL teachers. *System, 35,* 169–181.

Hockett, C.F. (1958). *A course in modern linguistics.* New York: Macmillan.

Hoffman, R.R. (1984). Recent psycholinguistic research on figurative language. *Annals of the New York Academy of Science, 433,* 137–166.

Katsarou, E. (2011). *The identification and comprehension of L2 idioms during reading: Implications for vocabulary teaching in the foreign language classroom.* Saarbrücken, Germany: Lambert Academic Publishing.

Kecskes, I. (2006). On my mind: Thoughts about salience, context and figurative language from a second language perspective. *Second Language Research, 22,* 219–237.

Laufer, B. (2000). Avoidance of idioms in a second language: The effect of L1-L2 degree of similarity. *Studia Linguistica, 54,* 186–196.

Lennon, P. (1998). Approaches to the teaching of idiomatic language. *International Review of Applied Linguistics, 36,* 11–30.

Liontas, J.I. (1997, November). *Building castles in the air: The comprehension processes of Modern Greek idioms.* Paper presented at the 15th International Symposium on Modern Greece, Kent State University, Kent, OH.

(1999). *Developing a pragmatic methodology of idiomaticity: The comprehension and interpretation of SL vivid phrasal idioms during reading.* Unpublished doctoral dissertation, The University of Arizona, Tucson, AZ.

(2001). That's all Greek to me! The comprehension and interpretation of modern Greek phrasal idioms. *The Reading Matrix: An International Online Journal, 1*, 1–32. Available: http://www.readingmatrix.com/articles/ john_liontas/article.pdf

(2002a). Exploring second language learners' notions of idiomaticity. *System: An International Journal of Educational Technology and Applied Linguistics, 30*, 289–313.

(2002b). Context and idiom understanding in second languages. In S.H. Foster-Cohen, T. Ruthenberg, & M-L. Poschen (Eds.), *EUROSLA Yearbook: Annual conference of the European second language association. Vol. 2* (pp. 155–185). Proceedings of the 2002 Annual Conference of the European Second Language Association. Amsterdam/Philadelphia: John Benjamin Publishing Company.

(2002c). Vivid phrasal idioms and the lexical-image continuum. *Issues in Applied Linguistics, 13*, 71–109.

(2002d). Transactional idiom analysis: Theory and practice. *Journal of Language and Linguistics, 1*, 17–53.

(2002e). Reading between the lines: Detecting, decoding, and understanding idioms in second languages. In J.H Sullivan (Ed.), *Literacy and the second language learner: Vol. 1. Research in second language learning* (pp. 177–216). Greenwich, CT: Information Age Publishing Inc.

(2003). Killing two birds with one stone: Understanding Spanish VP idioms in and out of context. *Hispania, 86*, 289–301.

(2007). The eye never sees what the brain understands: Making sense of idioms in second languages, *Lingua et Linguistica, 1*, 25–44.

(2009). Artificial intelligence and idiomaticity. *The APAMALL Higher Education Journal, Language Learning Technologies, 1*, 1–33.

Liu, D. (2003). The most frequently used spoken American English idioms: A corpus analysis and its implications. *TESOL Quarterly, 37*, 671–700.

Malt, B.C., & Eiter, B. (2004). Even with a green card, you can be put out to pasture and still have to work: Non-native intuitions of the transparency of common English idioms. *Memory & Cognition, 32*, 896–904.

Moon, R. (1997). Vocabulary connections: Multi-word items in English. In N. Schmitt & M. McCarthy (Eds.), *Vocabulary: Description, acquisition and pedagogy* (pp. 40–63). Cambridge, UK: Cambridge University Press.

Olejniczak, P. (2006). Phrasal verb idioms and the normative concept of the interlanguage hypothesis. In J. Arabski (Ed.), *Cross-linguistic influences in the second language lexicon* (pp. 259–272). Clevedon: Multilingual Matters Ltd.

Palmer, B.C., Shackelford, V.S., Miller, S.C., & Leclere, J.T. (2007). Bridging two worlds: Reading comprehension, figurative language instruction, and the English-language learner. *Journal of Adolescent & Adult Literacy, 50*, 258–267.

Piasecka, L. (2006). "Don't lose your head" or how Polish learners of English cope with L2 idiomatic expressions. In J. Arabski (Ed.), *Cross-linguistic influences in the second language lexicon* (pp. 126–258). Clevedon, UK: Multilingual Matters Ltd.

Pollio, H., Barlow, J.M., Fine, H.J., & Pollio, M.R. (1977). *Psychology and the poetics of growth*. Hillsdale, NJ: Lawrence Erlbaum Associates.

Strässler, J. (1982). *Idioms in English: A pragmatic analysis*. Tübingen, Germany: Gunter Narr Verlag.

Vanlacker-Sidtis, D. (2003). Auditory recognition of idioms by native and nonnative speakers of English: It takes one to know one. *Applied Linguistics*, *24*, 45–57.

Verspoor, M., & Lowie, W. (2003). Making sense of polysemous words. *Language Learning*, *53*, 547–587.

Zimmermann, R. (2006). Metaphorical transferability. In J. Arabski (Ed.), *Cross-linguistic influences in the second language lexicon* (pp. 193–209). Clevedon, UK: Multilingual Matters Ltd.

Appendix A: Tables 3–7

Table 3. *Summative Overview of Challenges*

Regarding Challenges Encountered	
Recognition of individual lexemes, laborious paragraphs, and dialogues helpful	The challenge was knowing the vocabulary of the idiom itself. It also helps if you are familiar with the idiom. I tried to put things together bit by bit, when I could by pulling the idiom apart with the words I DID KNOW, and then seeing if I was familiar with an English idiom that would match. The paragraphs and dialogue helped on most of them.
Recognition of individual lexemes; context helpful	The greatest challenge was not knowing the words in the idiom. To overcome ignorance of the words, I used the context. Seeing the idioms out of context was the most difficult part of the task because if the words were unknown, there were no other clues to allow one to hazard a guess.
Recognition of individual lexemes; context helpful	Most of the time when I misrepresented an idiom it was because I didn't have any text to correlate with it. There were a few instances where I didn't know a word within the idiom, but had I recognized the word, I believe I would have understood them. The text was very helpful in determining any of the idioms that I didn't immediately get.
Recognition of individual lexemes; context helpful	The greatest challenge was trying to understand the idioms without the context when I didn't understand some of the words. I had difficulty trying to translate the expressions in this case and just guessed the best I could. Context helped greatly!
Recognition of individual lexemes; context helpful	The greatest challenge I faced was not knowing certain vocabulary words. If I had a dictionary to look up the words in context, I would probably be able to figure out the idiom. Once I saw the passage in context, however, it became easier to interpret the idiom even without knowing the words.

Table 3. (*cont.*)

Regarding Challenges Encountered	
Recognition of individual lexemes, pragmatic knowledge, cultural background knowledge	The greatest challenge was the zero text exercises. It wasn't hard, of course, if I was familiar with the idiom. However, if I needed an inference to derive the meaning, no text existed to assist. This made it difficult. Also, the wording on some made finding the meaning difficult (if I wasn't used to hearing or seeing sentences structured in such way). Some I was able to overcome when the text was given later or if I really thought about it for a great deal of time. Obviously, the text helped me, but also thinking about their meaning helped.
Lexical association, connecting target language with native language idiom	The greatest challenge was not knowing the vocabulary to be able to translate and not being able to put the Spanish into English equivalents. I overcame this challenge by seeing the full context of the text.
Distinguishing between literal and figurative meaning; context useful	The greatest challenge was trying to find an interpretation for the Spanish version in English. The context helped a lot. The context was useful; the idioms without context were not. I had no idea what they meant unless they translated closely to something in English.
Distinguishing between literal and figurative meaning	The hardest part was trying to determine what an idiom meant without context. For some, it was very hard to simply try to translate the phrase and get an English idiom from it. For others, it was relatively simple.
Literal translations not helpful; context very important	I realize that in many cases, it is impossible to literally translate a phrase and understand what it really means. Context is very important.
Connecting the target language with the native language idiom; context helpful	The greatest challenge I faced was my non-familiarity with the idiomatic expressions of the Spanish language. I have never learned such phrases, and most of them don't translate directly into English. I partially overcame this challenge by using context clues, which was next to impossible in the zero-context section. I definitely need context clues to aid me in understanding the meaning of the phrases.
Unawareness of one's own idiomatic knowledge	Of my challenges, the one that I found to be the most cumbersome is the realization that I, as a speaker, am not fully aware of idioms used in my own language.
Regarding the Idiom Detection Task	
Detecting idioms easy, interpreting idiom difficult	The idiom detection task was easier for me than the full context task. It was easier for me to pinpoint which phrase was an idiom, but it was more difficult to know what it said.
Illogical literal meaning, key idiomatic lexemes,	I looked for phrases in the first part that did not make sense if taken literally and assumed that they were idioms. In figuring them out, I looked for key words that I knew from

Table 3. (*cont.*)

Regarding Challenges Encountered	
lack of vocabulary, compare/contrast	idioms. My biggest challenge was lack of vocabulary. Many of the idioms had the same feel as English idioms but with a different twist.

Regarding the Zero Context Task

Interpreting idioms without context difficult (frustrating at times), connecting the target language with the native language idiom strenuous, empowerment	Spanish idioms are difficult to decipher, because the vocabulary and structure used are so much different from English ones. It is much easier to figure them out when the examples show them in context. It is a little frustrating for me because I know what they are trying to say, but I can't think of the equivalent idiom. I think I got a little better at figuring things out towards the end, although I still don't think I answered too many questions correctly.
Idiom association hard, compare/contrast, interpreting idioms without context difficult	The hardest thing for me was to convert from Spanish to English because oftentimes the words change slightly. They have the same meaning but there is one word that is changed sometimes. When asked to give the meaning of the idiom without the text, it also became difficult to understand what the meaning was.
Frustrating and difficult, lexical manipulation of idiom not helpful	With the zero context task, I had an extremely difficult time. Some of the idioms were very obvious, but most of them weren't and I felt that I struggled with this part. I think it was because I wasn't able to find out what the answer is. I had to read the idiom over and over again, and very often that didn't help.
Interpreting idioms without context difficult	The most challenging of the tasks was the zero context task. I found this task the most difficult because of the lack of text and context. It is difficult to interpret other language and culture idioms without the use of context.
Interpreting idioms without context difficult, deciphering the feel of an idiom difficult	I have studied idioms and contextual analysis in several of my English classes as well as on my own time, but I did find it a little difficult to try and decipher the "feel" of an idiom in Spanish. I just tried to think of how the words would be perceived literally in Spanish and then assigned figurative values to them. My background as an English major and my current classes as a Spanish major were very helpful during the exercise: Some of the vocabulary was a little beyond me.
Connecting to English idioms hard	I was frustrated in knowing that there was an English equivalent that I couldn't come up with!

Table 3. (*cont.*)

Regarding Challenges Encountered	
Connecting to English idioms hard	I had a hard time understanding the idiom even if I understood all the words.
Connecting to English idioms hard, lexical association	The greatest challenge I faced was trying to figure out what words I did not know meant, and then putting them into the context of the idiom. I overcame this by just thinking hard about the words I did know and what other words would make the idiom make sense.
Connecting to English idioms hard, lack of vocabulary	I think the greatest challenges were first not being familiar with the vocabulary, and next simply not being able to come up with the appropriate idiom in English. Again, vocabulary was my main stumbling block. If I knew all of the words in the individual phrases they were easy to figure out. If I didn't know even one word then they were almost impossible to understand.
Guessing, translation, lexical association	The greatest challenge was when I had no context to support the idiom... that is how I find meaning for things I don't understand in another language. The only way I could overcome this challenge is if I started to directly translate and see if anything was similar in English... if I don't know all the words, I just used the surrounding words to help as much as possible. A few times I was completely off, but I think I did decently.
Regarding the Full Context Task	
Interpreting idioms in context easy, lack of practicing idioms	The contextual portion was much more helpful than trying to guess them without context, but even so, some were difficult, and I didn't know some of them at all. I guess as a reader, I get the gist of the idiom, even if I don't know the correlation to an English saying. However, I have not encountered many idioms in the Spanish that I have read, so I don't get too much practice identifying them.
Interpreting idioms in context easy	In the full context task, I was not familiar with these [idioms] so the text did help to interpret the text. The context also enabled a better understanding of these idioms, which was for my own benefit.
Interpreting idioms in context easy	The in-context part was very helpful. Once I understood the situation, it was easier to understand the idiom.
Interpreting idioms in context easy	I did not know all the vocabulary in the idioms; the context helped me to figure out what the idiom meant.
Interpreting idioms in context easy	They are fairly easy when they are in the Full Context because I used the story to give me a hint.

Table 4. *Overview of Participants' Performance*

	Regarding Participants' Performance
I feel I did very well	I feel I did very well on these exercises and I surprised myself a few times when I was able to come up with a meaning in English even without supporting context. This has given me a confidence in my Spanish abilities. Thank you!
I feel my performance was very good	I feel my performance was very good. I know that I understand the feeling of the meaning of the sentence even though I can't translate it.
I think I did well	Overall, I think I did well, considering that I am not familiar with the expressions.
I think I did fairly well	All in all, I think I did fairly well, barring a few mistakes.
I am confident	I am confident with my overall performance.
I feel ok	I feel ok about my performance. I feel I should have known some of the idioms, but some of them were hard to figure out.
I feel that I did ok	Overall, I feel that I did o.k.
I feel like I did okay	I feel like I did okay and that I actually have a lot more to learn in terms of idiomatic expressions.
I feel I did alright	I feel I did alright when there was text, but it was much harder to just read the idiom itself.
I think that I did OK	For the most part I think that I did OK. I was reminded that I need to spend more time learning vocabulary. I began thinking that the idioms would be hard to recognize, but the majority was rather easy to understand.
I think I did okay	I think I did okay. I could have done better.
I think I did okay	I think I did okay. I didn't know any of these idioms when I started. I was happy about figuring out some of these that did not translate word for word.
I think that I probably did about average	I think that I probably did about average given my small experience with idioms in Spanish.
I feel adequate	I feel adequate about my performance.
I feel my performance could have been better	I feel my performance could have been better and I realized that I need to work on learning more idioms.
I feel like I should have done better	I feel like I should have done better because aspects such as idioms and the role they play in language fascinate me.
I feel disappointed about my performance	I feel disappointed about my performance, but I think that idioms are something that I need to be taught and learn more.
I feel awful about my performance	I feel awful about my performance. I believe that I am a pretty good speaker, but I obviously have a lot more to learn. Hopefully, I am able to learn from my mistakes and I think I might find some exercises for idioms.

Table 5. *Overview of Lessons Learned*

Regarding Lessons Learned	
Need to learn more idioms, helpful in vocabulary	I was a little disappointed that I didn't know most of those after having had studied Spanish for so long. If I learned the idioms, I would learn new words and be able to say them in context as well.
Becoming more aware of idiomatic meaning	I think I have learned to be more aware and try to figure out the meaning behind the words.
All skills are necessary for fluency, idioms more than just language	I feel I have learned that there are really four parts to complete fluency and that they are really essential when one considers himself or herself fluent. And one other thing that I believe [is] that idioms are also a part of culture, not just language.
Macro context aids idiomatic understanding	I have learned that reading the entire passage can aid in understanding individual phrases. All of the tasks were challenging and thought-provoking. I think the test was very well written.
Context helpful, need for more vocabulary build-up	I have learned that context really can help you discover the meaning. Teachers should always teach vocabulary words in the same manner. We would learn the sense of the word and remember that more than a translation. That would make speaking the language easier instead of always spending time trying to translate everything in our head.
Comprehension transfer from the target language to the native language not always guaranteed	I have to rationalize that experience in one language does not necessarily role over to immediate comprehension in another.
Context helpful, discourse analysis	This was a great learning experience. The only difficulty was the zero context task. When the idioms are in context, one can make out what the point is by following what they are reading.
Context helpful	I learned that I need context clues to really understand the meaning. I also found out that while the expressions themselves do not directly translate from Spanish to English, the frustration being expressed is the same. Idioms actually reflect the feelings of the speaker in a way that using normal language (without the idiom) does not. I enjoy idioms as they help one express emotions and feelings about what is being said.
Context helpful	I learned the importance of learning the meaning of a word or phrase in context.
Context helpful	I have learned that I can decipher most things I don't know from the context it is in.
Context helpful	I found that you can read the paragraph and get a general meaning of the idiom, but when you know the idiom the paragraph is much more understandable.
Idioms need to be learned in context,	Teachers rarely teach idioms in class. I would love to learn an idiom (in context of the lesson) everyday in class. It would help when conversing with native speakers.

Table 5. (cont.)

Regarding Lessons Learned

---

improves communication **Teaching of idioms necessary and desired, more curriculum emphasis**	These [Idioms] really are not taught to Spanish students very much and are probably used a great deal. It's part of the conversational aspect of Spanish which this university's program is terrible at teaching or doesn't teach at all.
Teaching of idioms necessary and desired	I learned how much more I would like to learn about idioms and their varying uses. This would enrich my Spanish and make it more cultured. I think all would benefit from such instruction.
Teaching of idioms necessary and desired	I would like to see idioms taught in class. They are so much a part of the Spanish language.
Teaching of idioms necessary and desired	Idioms can easily be memorized and if we taught them more in the schools, like in high school and lower levels of Spanish, it would make listening and speaking to foreigners easier and people would feel more confident.
Teaching of idioms necessary and desired, vocabulary can be tricky	I also think that idioms may be overlooked in curricula because it is not an aspect of writing that is stressed as a positive aspect of good writing. While idioms are used in everyday speech, they are rarely found in good examples of writing. I felt like the ones I had trouble with were idioms that I hadn't been exposed to in English, or just don't use on a normal basis. Also, the vocabulary can be tricky at times.
Need to learn more idioms	I learned that I need to pay more attention to idiomatic expressions and I need to work on knowing them in Spanish, too. This was a positive experience overall.
Need to learn more idioms	I have learned that I have what I thought was excellent reading comprehension skills, but maybe after all I do not!
Becoming more aware	I realize I sometimes have to read things a second time to really take it in.
Becoming more aware, deducing/inferencing	I learned that I do not understand the exact processes in my brain, but I am aware that I am going through a process of linguistic deduction and inference.

Table 6. Summary Analysis of All *That's All Greek to Me!* Output Data

DATA	IDT	ZCT	FCT	TOTALS
Lines	912	1106	2108	4126
Summary Lines	N/A	N/A	378	378
Pages	76.75	58.75	120	255.5
Answers	668 (84.65%)	N/A	730 (90.42%)	1398 (87.53%)

Note. IDT = Idiom detection task; ZCT = Zero detection task; FCT = Full context task.

Table 7. *Questionnaire II, Part III*

It's All Greek to Me !

Questionnaire II (Part III)	Statements	Spanish	French	German	Mean
Presentation	1	3.9	4.1	4.1	**3.99**
	2	4.3	4.3	4.8	**4.43**
	3	4.2	4.6	4.9	**4.48**
	4	4.4	4.4	4.6	**4.43**
Content	5	4.3	4.4	4.5	**4.38**
	6	4.5	4.6	4.9	**4.59**
Instructional	7	4.4	4.4	4.9	**4.49**
Quality	8	4.4	4.4	4.7	**4.50**
	9	4.4	4.4	4.8	**4.46**
	10	4.4	4.2	4.6	**4.42**
Learner	11	4.1	3.9	4.4	**4.15**
Interaction	12	3.9	4.1	4.6	**4.12**
Idiomatic	13	4.0	3.8	3.9	**3.92**
Tasks	14	4.3	4.4	4.7	**4.44**
	15	4.4	4.6	4.8	**4.52**
	16	4.4	4.6	4.9	**4.57**
	17	4.3	4.4	4.8	**4.42**
Attitude	18	4.4	4.4	4.8	**4.46**
	19	4.2	4.1	4.4	**4.27**
	20	4.3	4.1	4.6	**4.33**
	21	3.9	4.2	4.3	**4.05**
	22	4.1	3.9	4.6	**4.19**
	23	3.9	4.1	4.6	**4.12**
	24	4.2	4.4	4.6	**4.37**

Appendix B: Questionnaire II — Part III (Post-Study Questionnaire)

Part III. Regarding *That's All Greek to Me!* Computer Program

DIRECTIONS
Follow the directions below. Please,
Use only a black lead pencil (No. 2 is ideal) Make heavy black marks that fill the oval. Erase cleanly any answer you wish to change. Make no stray markings of any kind.
Example: Will marks be made with a No. 2 pencil?
○ Yes ○ No

1 = Strongly Disagree
2 = Disagree
3 = Neutral/Unsure
4 = Agree
5 = Strongly Agree
(Mark one for each item)

Instructions: The following statements deal with your That's All Greek to Me! computer program experience. Read each statement carefully, think about it for a few seconds and, using the scale range of 1–5, mark the number that best indicates the extent to which you agree or disagree with each of the following statements.

Presentation

1. ①②③④⑤ The program *That's All Greek to Me!* is free of technical problems or programming errors.
2. ①②③④⑤ Screen displays are clear and easy to read.
3. ①②③④⑤ The color, print size, and spacing of text is appropriate.
4. ①②③④⑤ The program *That's All Greek to Me!* contains appropriate linking from text to text and from idiom to idiom.

Content

5. ①②③④⑤ The content of the program *That's All Greek to Me!* is appropriate for my level of learning.
6. ①②③④⑤ The content is presented clearly and logically.

Instructional Quality

7. ①②③④⑤ The program *That's All Greek to Me!* can be operated easily.
8. ①②③④⑤ The program *That's All Greek to Me!* is organized in a clear way.
9. ①②③④⑤ Directions on the screen are easy to follow.
10. ①②③④⑤ The examples are helpful to understanding the instructions for each task.

Learner Interaction

11. ①②③④⑤ I am motivated to finish the program *That's All Greek to Me!*
12. ①②③④⑤ I could control the rate of presentation.

Idiomatic Tasks

13. ①②③④⑤ The *Idiom Detection Task* challenged my reading skills.
14. ①②③④⑤ The *Zero Context Task* challenged my knowledge of equivalent expressions in English.
15. ①②③④⑤ The *Zero Context Task* made me want to read the accompanying supporting texts.
16. ①②③④⑤ The *Full Context Task* made a difference in my understanding of the idiomatic meaning.
17. ①②③④⑤ The *Full Context Task* gave me the contextual support I needed to understand the idioms.

Attitude

18. ①②③④⑤ The program *That's All Greek to Me!* challenged my knowledge of idioms.
19. ①②③④⑤ The program *That's All Greek to Me!* used my time efficiently.
20. ①②③④⑤ The program *That's All Greek to Me!* is easy to navigate.
21. ①②③④⑤ I am given the opportunity to learn the idioms used in the *That's All Greek to Me!* program.
22. ①②③④⑤ I am satisfied with what I learned.
23. ①②③④⑤ Answers to specific idioms is satisfactory.
24. ①②③④⑤ I could work at my own pace.

Additional Comments: *If you feel that this questionnaire has failed to address certain issues of importance to your idiom learning experience, please take some time to write comments or suggestions you may have. Any additional input is greatly appreciated!* **(Please use reverse side for further comments)**

11 Anger Metaphors across Languages: A Cognitive Linguistic Perspective

Zoltán Kövecses[1], Veronika Szelid[2], Eszter Nucz[3], Olga Blanco-Carrión[4], Elif Arica Akkök[5], and Réka Szabó[6]

[1]Eötvös Loránd University, Hungary; [2]Szent Margit Gimnázium, Hungary; [3]Corvinus University of Budapest, Hungary; [4]Universidad de Córdoba, Spain; [5]Ankara University, Turkey; and [6]Research Institute for Linguistics, Hungarian Academy of Sciences

ABSTRACT

This chapter studies metaphors for anger in four languages, American English, Spanish, Turkish, and Hungarian from a cognitive linguistic perspective. Our database includes large corpora and standard newspapers and magazines in the four languages for the past 10 years. First, we intend to uncover the most common conceptual metaphors in the respective languages. Second, we discuss the main systematic similarities and differences between the languages regarding the way anger is talked about and conceptualized in the languages under investigation. Given our results, we assess some of the implications of our work for the cross-cultural corpus-based study of metaphor. In particular, we propose a new complex measure of *metaphorical salience* as a tool to determine the cultural importance of conceptual metaphors.

Keywords: anger metaphor, conceptual metaphor, corpus analysis, metaphorical mappings, metaphorical salience

In the *cognitive linguistic view*, metaphor is conceptualizing one domain of experience in terms of another (Lakoff & Johnson, 1980; Kövecses, 2010). The domain of experience that is used to comprehend another domain is typically more physical, more directly experienced, and better known than the domain we wish to comprehend, which is typically more abstract, less directly experienced, and less known. The more concrete domain is called the *source domain* and the more abstract one is called the *target domain*. Domains of experience are represented in the mind as concepts given as mental frames. This is why we talk about *conceptual metaphors*. More specifically, in this view, metaphor is a set of correspondences, or mappings, between the elements of two mental frames. For example, a set of correspondences between a traveler and an ordinary person, how the traveler is going and the manner in which the person lives, the destination the traveler wants to reach and the life goals of the person, the physical obstacles along the way and the life difficulties of the person all comprise the set of mappings that make up the conceptual metaphor LIFE IS A JOURNEY.

A conceptual metaphor typically has a number of linguistic manifestations (i.e., metaphorically used words and more complex expressions) to talk about the target domain. In the example of the conceptual metaphor LIFE IS A JOURNEY, the sentences *I hit a roadblock*, *She wanders aimlessly in life*, *This is not the right way to live*, for example, make manifest, or simply express, correspondences between the elements of obstacle and difficulty, destination and purpose, and path and manner, respectively. Taken together, they indicate that the highly abstract concept of LIFE is understood in terms of the more concrete concept of JOURNEY.

Our general goal in this chapter is to show how the emotion of *anger* is talked about and conceptualized in four different languages/cultures. The languages/cultures under study are American English, Spanish, Turkish, and Hungarian. We focus on the issue of which metaphors play a major role in the conceptualization of anger in the four cultures and how a combined quantitative and qualitative analysis of these metaphors can help us identify the prototypical scenario of anger. In other words, a large part of our study is concerned with which conceptual metaphors are most frequently used and which ones are the most extensively elaborated in the four languages/cultures.

The chapter is divided into several sections. In the next section we describe the methodology that was used in our project. Then, we present the results of the corpus analysis of anger metaphors in the four languages/cultures. This section is followed by a discussion of some of the issues that emerge as a result of the analysis. Finally, we summarize the main findings and draw some conclusions in the last section.

Methodology

Corpus Analysis

In our study, we made an attempt to combine qualitative and quantitative methods. We investigated the national corpora and/or texts taken from leading newspapers and magazines of the cultures whose concept of anger we were interested in and examined 2000 random linguistic expressions of anger in each. An obvious limitation of our study was that the national corpora available for investigation were of different sizes, and in Turkish no national corpus was available.

Metaphorical linguistic expressions of anger in American English were collected from the *Corpus of Contemporary American English* (876 expressions in total). The Spanish metaphors relating to *ira* ("anger" in Spanish, 1518 expressions in total) come from *CREA* corpus (*Corpus from the Real Academia Española*) and the Internet archives of two leading Spanish newspapers, *El País* and *ABC*. Hungarian metaphorical linguistic expressions of *düh* ("anger" in Hungarian, 1074 expressions in total) were collected from the *Hungarian Historical Corpus* (1990–1997) and the more recent material from the newspapers and magazines *Magyar Hírlap* (1994–2002), *Magyar Rádió Krónika* (2000–2001), *Századok* (1994–2000), and *Figyelő* (1995–2000). As for the Turkish data, five current newspapers were selected: *Hürriyet, Milliyet, Cumhuriyet, Zaman*, and *Sabah*. These are national mainstream newspapers with a large circulation and different political and cultural biases: Whereas *Hürriyet, Milliyet*, and *Sabah* can be considered liberal/central right, *Cumhuriyet* is secular, and *Zaman* is conservative. The Turkish metaphorical material (1879 in total) was based on the lexeme *öfke* ("anger" in Turkish).

A corpus-linguistic approach has several advantages, as suggested by Heylen, Tummers, and Geeraerts (2008). First, data are analyzed as they occur naturally in real life, and the method avoids biased choices of texts and unnatural examples. They call this the "complexity of spontaneous usage." Second, corpora contain a *representative* sample of language use by socioculturally diverse speakers of a language.

A disadvantage of corpus analysis, however, is that the researcher is left alone with the text without knowing the circumstances in which it was created and the background of the producer of the text. This is called *offline usage* by Heylen et al. (2008). In addition, we believe that this approach is very time-consuming and therefore only a limited number of keywords can be examined at one time to study a concept.

Because of this, we decided to restrict our investigation to a single keyword only (corresponding to the emotion of anger in four languages), and consequently, all the other expressions referring to anger were left out of the study. Finding the most suitable word denoting a concept is not always easy. In American English, for example, there are four common basic expressions for the concept of anger: *anger, rage, fury*, and *wrath*. Before choosing our key lexeme for the analysis, we investigated how many times these words appear in the *Corpus of Contemporary American English*. Our results indicated that the frequency of the word *anger* (6145) is much higher than that of the others (*rage* = 2656, *fury* = 975, *wrath* = 672), so we simply chose the most frequently appearing word. But how can we be sure that the lexemes we use as key words for the analysis of the three other languages describe the concept that is closest to anger in the respective cultures? This is where we certainly had to rely on our intuitions. For instance, even if we know that *harag* has been the most frequent lexeme of the near-synonyms expressing anger in Hungarian, we have chosen the word *düh*, because *harag* denotes an emotion that lasts for a long time and is not intense, while *düh* describes its opposite in this respect. We did not have such difficulties in the case of Spanish and Turkish, because in both languages the most frequent and the intuitively closest word for the emotion was the same, *ira* in Spanish and *öfke* in Turkish.

Salience-Based Metaphor Analysis

Corpus linguistic studies usually calculate word frequencies in an effort to identify the most important conceptual metaphors that apply to a particular target concept. However, this is not always a reliable method to see which conceptual metaphors contribute most to the conceptualization of a particular target concept. Therefore, we developed a more complex view of how the conceptual significance of a conceptual metaphor can be established. Our method is based on the notion of *metaphorical salience*. We measure metaphorical salience in terms of three factors:

1. The number of mappings, or correspondences, in a conceptual metaphor.
2. The type frequency of linguistic expressions belonging to a conceptual metaphor.
3. The token frequency of linguistic expressions belonging to a conceptual metaphor.

For our purposes, a *type* is a lexeme or a phrase, and a *token* is one of the various forms of a lexeme or phrase, as these occur in real texts. Thus, tokens are actual occurrences of types.

The number of mappings in a conceptual metaphor

We calculated the number of correspondences, or mappings, a conceptual metaphor makes use of in the corpora. Here we did not make a distinction between basic, systematic correspondences and entailments, or inferences. For instance, the ANGER IS A SUBSTANCE IN A PRESSURIZED CONTAINER conceptual metaphor can have the following basic, systematic correspondences: THE HUMAN BODY IS A CONTAINER, THE

INTENSITY OF THE EMOTION IS THE RISING OF THE SUBSTANCE, CON-
TROL OVER THE EMOTION IS PUTTING A LID ON THE TOP OF THE
CONTAINER, LOSING CONTROL OVER THE EMOTION IS SUBSTANCE
COMING OUT OF THE CONTAINER, LOSING CONTROL OVER THE EMO-
TION IS PART OF THE CONTAINER GOING UP IN THE AIR, for example.

The type frequency of linguistic expressions belonging to a conceptual metaphor

Relying on the type-token distinction, we calculated how many different types of linguistic expressions are motivated by the same conceptual metaphor. To illustrate using a made-up example, if we detect the ANGER IS A SUBSTANCE IN A PRESSURIZED CONTAINER conceptual metaphor in only three American English expressions (*explode*, *try to hold in anger*, and *force the lid off*), the type frequency is three, regardless of how many times the three expressions occur in the American English corpus.

The token frequency of linguistic expressions belonging to a conceptual metaphor

We counted all the occurrences of linguistic expressions that belong to a particular conceptual metaphor. In other words, we did a token frequency analysis of all the metaphorical expressions relating to anger in the corpora.

We performed the three calculations for all the conceptual metaphors we identified in the corpora separately, then we calculated percentages. The percentage of the number of tokens belonging to a metaphor is calculated from the total number of metaphorical tokens. In a similar fashion, the percentage of the number of types is calculated from the total number of metaphorical expression types, and the percentage of metaphorical mapping types is calculated from the total number of metaphorical mapping types. It is important to note that we found metaphorical linguistic expressions whose meaning is not motivated by one conceptual metaphor only. Metaphorical linguistic expressions of this type were grouped in all the conceptual metaphors that underlie their meaning (this was taken as 100%).

Given the three percentage values, we calculated an aggregate value for each conceptual metaphor by adding the percentage of the following: (1) the mapping types within a conceptual metaphor, (2) the type frequency of linguistic expressions belonging to a conceptual metaphor, and (3) the token frequency of linguistic expressions belonging to a conceptual metaphor. *We take this aggregate value to be an indicator of the metaphorical salience of a conceptual metaphor.* This type of analysis was used by Szelid and Geeraerts (2008) in their study of the Csángó dialect of Hungarian. The analysis makes the different corpora comparable.

Results of the Corpus Analysis

In the present section, we discuss our results concerning the metaphorical conceptualization of anger in American English, Spanish, Turkish, and Hungarian.

Anger in American English

The American English corpus yielded 876 linguistic expressions that illustrate the metaphorical conceptualization of anger. Table 1 in the Appendix lists all the conceptual metaphors we identified in the American English corpus. The top three conceptual metaphors (or more precisely in the present context, source domains) of anger ranked according to metaphorical salience are the CONTAINER, the POSSESSED OBJECT, and the OPPONENT metaphors.

The first is the CONTAINER source domain (aggregate value = 45.92%). In this case we have two conceptual metaphors: ANGER IS A SUBSTANCE IN A CONTAINER and ANGER IS A FORCEFUL ENTITY IN A PRESSURIZED CONTAINER.

The conceptual correspondences, or mappings, of ANGER IS A SUBSTANCE IN THE CONTAINER conceptual metaphor are as follows:

- THE LEVEL OF INTENSITY IS THE DEPTH OF THE CONTAINER (e.g., *a deep vein of anger*)
- THE LEVEL OF INTENSITY IS THE LEVEL OF THE LIQUID IN THE CONTAINER (e.g., *level of anger*)
- GROWING INTENSITY IS THE RISING OF THE LIQUID (e.g., *fill somebody with anger*)
- DECREASING INTENSITY IS THE LEVEL OF THE LIQUID GOING DOWN (e.g., *anger subsides*)
- LOSING CONTROL IS THE LIQUID GOING OUT OF THE CONTAINER (e.g., *anger spills out*)
- COMPLETE LOSS OF CONTROL IS THE LIQUID BEING OUT OF THE CONTAINER (e.g., *to soak up the anger of the street*)

The conceptual correspondences of the ANGER IS A FORCEFUL ENTITY IN A PRESSURIZED CONTAINER conceptual metaphor are as follows:

- CONTROLLING ANGER IS TRYING TO KEEP THE LIQUID INSIDE THE CONTAINER (e.g., *to suppress anger*)

- LOSING CONTROL IS A SUBSTANCE GOING OUT OF THE CONTAINER (e.g., *outbursts of anger*)
- LOSING CONTROL OVER ANGER IS THE SUBSTANCE CAUSING THE LID TO GO UP IN THE AIR (e.g., *anger forces the lid off*)

The second is the POSSESSED OBJECT conceptual metaphor (aggregate value = 32.21%). The corpus provides metaphorical linguistic expressions like *X's anger, the anger of X,* or *to have anger,* which depict anger as an entity possessed by a person who is affected by the emotion.

The third is the OPPONENT conceptual metaphor (aggregate value = 31.9%). This way of conceptualizing anger in American English has two subtypes. In the first case, the emotion appears as the opponent that the person (i.e., the rational self) struggles with for the purpose of keeping control. The outcome of the fight is that the person either keeps control (e.g., *to push anger down* or *to get anger under control*) or loses it (e.g., *anger takes over* or *to be erased by anger*). In the second case, the emotion appears as a weapon in the struggle of the two opponents (e.g., *to hold anger at somebody* or *to turn anger on somebody*). The conceptual correspondences of the ANGER IS AN OPPONENT IN A STRUGGLE conceptual metaphor are as follows:

- STRUGGLE WITH THE OPPONENT IS TRYING TO KEEP CONTROL OVER ANGER (e.g., *huffing with anger*)
- KEEPING THE OPPONENT DOWN IS MAINTAINING CONTROL (e.g., *to push anger down*)
- LOSING THE STRUGGLE IS LOSING CONTROL (e.g., *to be overcome by anger*)
- OPPONENT 1 BEING AFRAID OF OPPONENT 2 IS THE RATIONAL SELF BEING AFRAID OF ANGER (e.g., *to be afraid of anger*)
- WINNING THE STRUGGLE IS MAINTAINING CONTROL (e.g., *to fight off anger*)
- OPPONENT 2 BECOMING MORE INTENSE DUE TO A CAUSE IS THE EMOTION BECOMING MORE INTENSE DUE TO A CAUSE (e.g., *widespread anger*)
- OPPONENT 2 FIGHTING AGAINST CONTROL IS THE EMOTION FIGHTING AGAINST CONTROL (e.g., *anger struggles*)

The conceptual correspondences of the ANGER IS A WEAPON conceptual metaphor are as follows:

- ANGER USED IS A WEAPON USED (e.g., *to hold anger at somebody*)
- THE AMOUNT OF ANGER USED IS THE AMOUNT OF WEAPON USED (e.g., *to have a lot of anger against somebody*)

As can be observed, two of the top three conceptual metaphors of anger in American English highlight *intensity* and *control* in the conceptualization of anger. Highlighting these aspects of the concept is achieved by the CONTAINER and OPPONENT source domains. This is what Kövecses calls the *main meaning focus* of a metaphor (see Kövecses, 2000a). *Intensity* and *control* (*keeping control* or *losing control*) seem to be the most important aspects of conceptualizing the emotion, and, importantly, they appear together in a coherent fashion in the mappings of the CONTAINER and the OPPONENT metaphors. These aspects can also be found in the mappings of several other metaphors of anger, but in those cases they do not appear together. For instance, in the case of the CAPTIVE ANIMAL metaphor, *control* is emphasized but *intensity* is not.

In sum, in the American English data the two versions of the CONTAINER metaphor turned out to be the most salient, given our metaphorical-salience-based corpus analysis. This was followed by the POSSESSED OBJECT and OPPONENT metaphors that were salient to a similar degree.

Anger in Spanish

The Spanish corpus yields 1518 linguistic expressions that illustrate the metaphorical conceptualization of anger. Table 2 in the Appendix lists all the conceptual metaphors we identified in the Spanish corpus. Given these corpus results, the three most salient conceptual metaphors of *anger* in Spanish are the POSSESSED OBJECT (aggregate value = 57%), the OPPONENT (aggregate value = 53.29%), and the SUBSTANCE IN A CONTAINER (aggregate value = 35.17%) metaphors.

With regard to ANGER IS A POSSESSED OBJECT, the corpus yielded 774 instances, which is equivalent to 46.45 percent of all metaphor instances in the corpus. Here the emotion is depicted as an OBJECT POSSESSED by a person who is affected by the emotion. It is based only on a single mapping: "having anger –> an object possessed by the person," which may be linguistically expressed in three ways: "X's anger, "the anger of X," and "X has anger." The most profiled aspect of the concept of anger in this metaphor is *existence*.

The second most salient conceptual metaphor is ANGER IS AN OPPONENT. It is also the second most frequent conceptual metaphor with 127 tokens, representing 7.62 percent of the examples in the corpus. In Spanish, the ANGER IS AN OPPONENT takes the form of the WEAPON metaphor in the majority of the examples. It is a highly elaborated metaphor with 27 different types of linguistic expressions.

However, only three conceptual correspondences of this metaphor can be identified in the corpus:

1. EMOTION IS THE WEAPON IN THE FIGHT BETWEEN TWO OPPONENTS (e.g., *Un enemigo sobre el que desviar las iras* "An enemy over whom to divert one's anger"; *Esgrimir contra ella su ira* "Brandish his anger against her"; *Le espetaron con cierta ira* "They skewered him with anger"; *Carga su ira con Adrián* "She loaded her anger against Adrián"; *Desplegué mi ira* "I displayed/deployed my anger").
2. THE CAUSE OF ANGER IS THE TARGET OF THE FIRING (e.g., *Arrojó su ira sobre ella* "He threw his anger on/over her"; *La ira de los puristas le alcanzó* "He was hit by the purists' anger"; *Le escupía en la cara su ira* "She spit her anger on his face").
3. SHOOTING MORE IS INCREASING INTENSITY (e.g., *Ha disparado las iras aún más* "It has shot anger up even more").

The most frequently used mapping is the second one: THE CAUSE OF ANGER IS THE TARGET OF THE FIRING. The most commonly occurring linguistic expression types for this mapping (and this metaphor) are the following: [anger's target] with 23 tokens and other synonymous expressions in Spanish, which make up a total of 86 tokens; other frequent expression types such as [direct anger to/toward] (15 tokens) and [show anger against somebody] (15 tokens) belong to the first mapping. Although the most frequent mapping is THE CAUSE OF ANGER IS THE TARGET OF THE FIRING, the most profiled aspect of the concept of anger in this metaphor is "losing control," present in the first two mappings and in 26 out of the 27 different expression types.

The third most salient conceptual metaphor is ANGER IS A SUBSTANCE IN A CONTAINER. In addition to its 63 tokens, it has 28 linguistic expression types and 9 different mappings. These mapping are the following:

1. ANGER IS A SUBSTANCE IN A CONTAINER
2. LEVEL OF INTENSITY IS THE DEPTH OF THE CONTAINER/INTENSITY IS AMOUNT
3. GROWING INTENSITY IS THE RISING OF THE LIQUID
4. LEVEL OF INTENSITY IS THE LEVEL OF PRESSURE IN THE CONTAINER
5. KEEPING CONTROL IS KEEPING THE LIQUID IN A CONTAINER
6. LOSING CONTROL IS THE SUBSTANCE GOING OUT
7. LOSING CONTROL CAUSES THE CONTAINER TO EXPLODE
8. LOSING CONTROL CAUSES THE CONTAINER TO BREAK
9. LOSING THE ENERGY TO FEEL ANGRY IS RUNNING OUT OF LIQUID

In sum, the two most salient conceptual metaphors in the Spanish data are POSSESSED OBJECT and OPPONENT, followed by the CONTAINER metaphor. In the Spanish data, a large portion of the generic OPPONENT metaphor is expressed by the more specific WEAPON source domain.

Anger in Turkish

The Turkish corpus yielded 2572 linguistic expressions revealing the metaphorical conceptualization of anger. Table 3 in the Appendix lists all the conceptual metaphors we identified in the Turkish corpus.

The most salient conceptual metaphor in Turkish is the CONTAINER metaphor, with an aggregate value of 72.32 percent. Here *anger* is conceptualized as an entity in a container. The container is the human body, and anger is conceptualized as a substance, which can be either a fluid or a solid, in this container. In some examples in the data, there are different sub-containers that are related to body parts such as the *eyes*, *face*, *heart*, or *look* (the last one being a metaphorically viewed container). Most examples indicate the quality of the substance as fluid. As the intensity of the substance in the container increases, the substance produces pressure. The self attempts to control the force by either suppressing it and manages to control or lose control and the substance comes out of the container. In some cases, intense anger produces pressure on the container, and the angry person approaches the limit of exploding. In some cases the pressure is related to being tense. One can become tense with the pressure of container. The tense person has two choices, either suppressing anger or exploding (i.e., when a person explodes, what was inside comes out), or sometimes the self suppresses anger, which then subsides.

When we analyze the mappings of this conceptual metaphor, we can observe that it focuses on the intensity and control aspects. Its metaphorical mappings and entailments can be summarized as follows:

- INTENSITY IS AMOUNT
  - o DEGREE OF INTENSITY IS THE DEPTH OF THE CONTAINER (e.g., *derin öfke* "deep anger")
  - o DEGREE OF INTENSITY IS THE LEVEL OF FLUID IN THE CONTAINER (e.g., *öfkenin düzeyi* "the level of anger")
  - o INCREASE IN INTENSITY OF ANGER IS THE LEVEL GOING UP (e.g., *öfke yükseliyor* "rising anger")
  - o DECREASE IN INTENSITY OF ANGER IS THE LEVEL GOING DOWN (e.g., *öfkenin azalması* "decrease of anger")

- INTENSITY IS HEAT
  - DECREASE IN INTENSITY IS THE COOLING OF THE FLUID (e.g., *öfkemi soğuttum* "anger cools down")
  - ANGER INTENSIFIES IN THE CONTAINER (e.g., *öfke yoğunlaşıyor* "anger getting intense"; *öfke demleniyor* "brewing anger")
- KEEPING CONTROL IS KEEPING THE LIQUID IN THE CONTAINER
  - INTENSITY OF ANGER PRODUCES PRESSURE ON THE CONTAINER (e.g., *öfkeyle gerilmek* "to be tensed with anger"
  - CONTROLLING ANGER IS TRYING TO SUPPRESS THE ENTITY IN A CONTAINER (e.g., *öfkesini tutmak* "suppress anger"
- LOSING CONTROL OF ANGER IS THE SUBSTANCE GOING OUT OF THE CONTAINER
  - LOSING CONTROL CAUSES THE CONTAINER TO EXPLODE (e.g., *öfkesi patlamak* "anger explodes")
  - LOSING CONTROL IS SUBSTANCE GOING UP IN THE AIR (e.g., *öfke kafasının tasını attırdı* "anger flipped X's head lid")
  - LOSING CONTROL IS THE SUBSTANCE ⁻OWING OUT OF THE CONTAINER (e.g., *öfke akmak* "anger flows")
  - LOSING CONTROL IS EMPTYING THE CONTAINER (e.g., *öfkeyi atmak* "throw out X's anger"; *öfkeyi boşaltmak* "empty X's anger")

NATURAL FORCE is the second most salient source domain in the corpus. In the data we find numerous examples of a natural event. It accounts for 14.19 percent of all metaphorical expressions. This metaphor has three mapping types. The types of linguistic expressions make up 10.13 percent of all expressions in the database. Its aggregate salience value is 30.09 percent. Here, anger is understood as an event and the self undergoes its effects. So, the person responds in a passive way and undergoes the effects of the natural force.

The NATURAL FORCE metaphor is closely followed in salience by the OPPONENT metaphor (aggregate value = 27.55%). It has five metaphorical mappings. Anger here is mostly conceptualized as an opponent in a struggle. In this conceptualization, the opponent causes the person to respond. The person tries to control his or her anger and either loses or maintains control over the opponent. Thus, this metaphor focuses on the keeping and losing control stages of the anger scenario. The data also provides many examples of this metaphor, where the expressions map on various parts of a struggle scene.

Finally, we note that the POSSESSED OBJECT conceptual metaphor in Turkish appears in 26.94 percent of all metaphorical linguistic expressions, but it scores very low on types of expressions (1.98% of all types) and the number of metaphorical mappings (1.72% of all conceptual correspondences), yielding altogether the aggregate value of 30.64 percent.

In sum, in Turkish the CONTAINER metaphor is clearly the most dominant one in terms of metaphorical salience. It is followed by the NATURAL FORCE, OPPONENT, and POSSESSED OBJECT metaphors, all three scoring roughly the same on metaphorical salience.

Anger in Hungarian

The Hungarian corpus yielded 1074 metaphorical linguistic expressions for *düh*. Table 4 lists all the conceptual metaphors that we identified for the metaphorical expressions. The top three conceptual metaphors ranked according to metaphorical salience are ANGER IS A SUBSTANCE/FLUID IN A CONTAINER (aggregate value = 53.4%), ANGER IS AN OPPONENT (aggregate value = 32.5%), and ANGER IS A POSSESSED OBJECT (aggregate value = 32.17%) metaphors.

The first is the ANGER IS A SUBSTANCE/(HOT/BOILING) FLUID IN A CONTAINER conceptual metaphor. The systematic correspondences of this metaphor are as follows.

- CAUSES ARE SOURCES (e.g., *a düh forrása (anger-OF-source)*, *vmiből fakadó düh* "sg-FROM-coming-anger")
- INTENSITY IS AMOUNT
  - o DEGREE OF INTENSITY IS THE DEPTH OF THE CONTAINER (e.g., *feneketlen düh* "bottomless anger")
  - o DEGREE OF INTENSITY IS THE LEVEL OF THE FLUID IN THE CONTAINER (e.g., *fuldoklik a dühtől* "suffocate-the anger-FROM;" *rengeteg a düh X-ben* "lot of-the anger-X-IN")
  - o DEGREE OF INTENSITY IS THE LEVEL OF PRESSURE IN THE CONTAINER (*mennyi düh szorult belé* "how much-anger-clogged up-INTO")
  - o INCREASE IN INTENSITY IS THE RISING OF THE LIQUID/SUBSTANCE (e.g., *betölti a düh* "fills-the-anger-(HIM)")
  - o DECREASE IN INTENSITY OF ANGER IS A DECREASE IN THE AMOUNT OF THE SUBSTANCE/FLUID (e.g., *elpárolog a dühe (evaporates-the-anger-HIS/HER)*, *nincs benne düh* "no-in-HIM/HER-anger")
- INTENSITY IS HEAT
  - o INCREASE IN INTENSITY IS GROWING HEAT OF THE FLUID (e.g., *forr benne a düh* "boil-in-HER/HIM-the-anger"; *fortyogó düh* "bubbling anger")
- KEEPING CONTROL IS KEEPING THE SUBSTANCE/LIQUID IN THE CONTAINER
  - o CONTROLLING ANGER IS TRYING TO SUPPRESS THE SUBSTANCE/LIQUID IN A CONTAINER (e.g., *elfojtott/visszafojtott düh* "repressed

anger"; *a dühöt lenyelni* "the-anger-to swallow"; *visszatartja a dühét* "keeps back-the-anger-HIS/HER")

- LOSING CONTROL OF ANGER IS THE SUBSTANCE GOING OUT OF THE CONTAINER
  - LOSING CONTROL CAUSES THE CONTAINER TO EXPLODE (e.g., *fel/szét/kirobban* a *dühtől* "up/apart/out-bursts-the-anger-FROM"; *robban a düh* "blows-the-anger")
  - LOSING CONTROL IS THE SUBSTANCE COMING OUT OF THE CONTAINER (e.g., *feltör a düh* "up-burst-the-anger"; *kitör a düh* "out-burst-the-anger"; *X-ből dől a düh* "X-out of-comes-the-anger"; *ömlik ki a düh* "streams-OUT-the-anger")
  - LOSING CONTROL IS EMPTYING THE CONTAINER (e.g., *kitölti a dühét* "vent-the-anger-HIS/HER"; *kiereszti a gőzt dühében* "let out-the-anger-in-anger-HIS/HER")

The second is the ANGER IS AN OPPONENT conceptual metaphor. There are two types of struggle represented in the corpus. One is about the struggle where the rational self and anger are metaphorically in struggle. For example, *X-et elfogja a düh* ("X is taken/captured by anger"), *X-et elkapja a düh* ("X is caught by anger"), *X-en erőt vesz a düh* ("X is overpowered by anger"), *X-et elnémítja a düh* ("X is muted by anger"), *X-re rátör a düh* ("X is attacked by anger"), *X-et támadásra ingerli a düh* ("X is provoked to attack by anger"). A third person or thing can also get involved: *Y áldozatul esik X dühének* ("Y can become the victim of X's anger"), *Z áldozatul veti Y-t X dühének* ("Z makes Y victim of X's anger"), *Z megmenti Y-t X dühétől* ("Z saves Y from X's anger").

The other type of the struggle is the struggle of the angry self with another self. In this relationship the self uses his/her anger as a weapon. For example, in expressions *X dühe kiirtja Y-t* ("X's anger exterminates Y"), *X dühe fenyegeti Y-t* ("X's anger threatens Y"), *Y megmenekül X dühe elől* ("Y escapes from X's anger"), *X Y ellen fordítja dühét* ("X turns his/her anger against Y"), *Y a düh célpontja* ("Y is the target of anger"), *X ráirányítja Y-ra dühét* ("X directs his/her anger to Y").

The third is the ANGER IS A POSSESSED OBJECT conceptual metaphor. This metaphor is expressed with one type of linguistic expression. The possessive form in Hungarian is expressed with suffixes like *-e*, *-(ü)nk*, *-(ö)m*; as a result, we have linguistic expressions of anger in the POSSESSED OBJECT conceptual metaphor such as *dühe* ("anger-HIS/HER"), *dühünk* ("anger-OUR"), *dühöm* ("anger-MINE"). It is important to notice that the POSSESSED OBJECT source domain is closely related to the LOCATION source domain, which is another frequently used source domain we identified in the database.

In sum, the Hungarian data show the CONTAINER metaphor as the strongest as regards metaphorical salience. This is followed by the OPPONENT and POSSESSED OBJECT metaphors sharing roughly the same aggregate value.

Summary and Discussion

In this section, we discuss some issues that emerge from the results of the corpus linguistic analyses above.

The Top Conceptual Metaphors Ranked According to Metaphorical Salience

We can summarize our main findings as follows. Given our corpus-linguistic analysis of anger metaphors, we found that the top three conceptual metaphors ranked according to their metaphorical salience in the four languages/cultures are (note that only the source domains are given):

> American English: (1) CONTAINER, (2) POSSESSED OBJECT, (3) OPPONENT
> Spanish: (1) POSSESSED OBJECT, (2) OPPONENT, (3) CONTAINER
> Turkish: (1) CONTAINER, (2) NATURAL FORCE, (3) OPPONENT AND POSSESSED OBJECT
> Hungarian: (1) CONTAINER, (2) OPPONENT, (3) POSSESSED OBJECT

Given that in all four languages we identified dozens of conceptual metaphors and in light of the large linguistic-cultural differences between American English, Spanish, Turkish, and Hungarian, this is a remarkable result. The top three salient metaphors in a set of fairly diverse languages are essentially the same. On a scale of metaphorical salience, CONTAINER, OPPONENT, and POSSESSED OBJECT came out on top, in different order, in American English, Spanish, Turkish, and Hungarian. The only conceptual metaphor other than the above in the top three is NATURAL FORCE in Turkish.

The Concept of Anger in the Four Languages: The Cultural Model

The goal of the corpus-linguistic study of conceptual metaphors cannot simply be identifying the most frequent metaphors for a target concept (e.g., Stefanowitch, 2006a, b). The ultimate goal should be the characterization of the target concept, which is partially defined by means of such metaphors (Kövecses, 2008, 2011). In other words, we should attempt to characterize the prototypical case of anger, given the metaphors identified above – that is, the prototypical cultural model of anger.

An early attempt to this end was Lakoff and Kövecses' (1987) paper on anger. Based on an intuitive collection of anger-related metaphors and metonymies in American English, they set up a five-stage model of anger consisting of (1) cause of anger, (2) existence of anger, (3) attempt to control anger, (4) loss of control over anger, and (5) retribution. The model of anger they identified is characterized by especially two aspects: *intensity* and *control*. Intensity primarily applies to the existence stage of anger, where anger is portrayed as a highly intense emotional state. The aspect of control is clearly present in stages (3) and (4). Intensity and control are "naturally" connected: The issue of control often emerges as a result of some highly intense state or action that becomes difficult to control.

What does our corpus-driven study say about this issue? Strikingly, as the results of our metaphorical salience analysis indicate, the two most important aspects of the concept of anger in the four cultures are intensity and control. Intensity is manifested by the CONTAINER metaphor, whereas control is expressed by means of both the OPPONENT and CONTAINER metaphors in all four languages and cultures. The co-presence of the CONTAINER and OPPONENT metaphors in the different cultures indicates that these cultures share a great deal in their conceptualization of anger. Moreover, this result also suggests that Lakoff and Kövecses' characterization of anger in American English was on the right track despite the intuitively collected data in their work.

This finding does not mean, however, that the specific cultural model, that is, the prototype, of anger should be or is the same cross-culturally. What is shared by the four languages analyzed here seems to be on a fairly schematic level. At a more specific level, the concept of anger varies considerably (see Kövecses, 2000a, 2005). However, to point out such differences in an explicit manner was not a goal of our project. For example, we do not know how the high salience of the NATURAL FORCE metaphor influences the prototypical cultural model of anger in Turkish.

Metaphorical Salience and the Possessed Object Metaphor

The POSSESSED OBJECT metaphor is tied to the existence stage of anger. In all four languages, when people attribute the state of anger to someone, they resort to this conceptual metaphor. In general, attributed states are conceptualized as possessed objects; hence the metaphor ATTRIBUTED STATES ARE POSSESSED OBJECTS, of which ANGER IS A POSSESSED OBJECT is a more specific version. Because any attributed state can be a possessed object, it is not surprising that anger is also commonly conceptualized as such.

We suggest, for this reason, that the POSSESSED OBJECT source domain has a very *wide scope* (see for example, Kövecses, 2000b). This means that it applies to a wide spectrum of different target domains. As a matter of fact, its application to different target domains is so wide that it does not really feel like a metaphor specific to anger. The CONTAINER and OPPONENT metaphors are more limited in their scope, and because of this, our intuitions tell us that they are more characteristic of anger than the POSSESSED OBJECT metaphor. However, the difference in scope between CONTAINER and OPPONENT, on the one hand, and POSSESSED OBJECT, on the other, is just a matter of degree, because neither CONTAINER nor OPPONENT is *unique* to anger.

At the same time, ideally, it would be good to have measures of metaphorical salience that are capable of capturing such intuitively felt differences in the scope of source domains. Clearly, the three factors we have used are not sensitive enough to show this. The POSSESSED OBJECT metaphor scores very high on token frequency, but very low on type frequency and number of mappings. It appears that a very high score on one measure can offset very low scores on other measures. A solution to this methodological problem might be to include the *scope of metaphorical source* in the set of measures for metaphorical salience, together with adding differential weights to the three (in the future, four) measures. Thus, a more reliable aggregate value of metaphorical salience would be one that would work with token frequency, type frequency, number of mappings, and scope of metaphor. This aggregate would probably provide a more faithful representation of our intuitions concerning concept-specificity as well.

Summary and Conclusions

We examined the metaphorical conceptualization of anger and its closest counterparts in four languages/cultures, American English, Spanish, Turkish, and Hungarian. We used a corpus-linguistic methodology to see which conceptual metaphors of anger and its counterparts are most salient in the respective languages/cultures. We defined metaphorical salience as the aggregate value of percentages of occurrence obtained for token frequency, type frequency, and the number of mappings of a given conceptual metaphor.

Somewhat surprisingly, we found that out of the more than a dozen conceptual metaphors identified in each of the four languages/cultures, the same three metaphors came out on top of our lists of metaphors ranked according to metaphorical salience: CONTAINER, OPPONENT, and POSSESSED OBJECT. The reason for this, we suggested, is that in all four languages, two aspects of the concept of anger dominate: intensity and control. Intensity is expressed primarily by the CONTAINER metaphor, while control is chiefly conceptualized as both CONTAINER and OPPONENT. The POSSESSED OBJECT metaphor is highly frequent in all four languages, due to the fact that it is the main way of capturing the existence aspect of anger, that is, the fact that the state of anger actually exists in a given situation.

These results suggest that in all four languages/cultures under study, people must have remarkably similar cultural models of anger: Anger as an emotional state exists in fairly intense forms, and because of its high intensity, it needs to be controlled in some way. This is a rather schematic characterization of the core of the concept of anger that leaves ample room for more specific elaborations in different languages (see for example, Kövecses, 2000a). But, we feel, the surprising similarities in metaphorical conceptualization at the schematic level may be just as instructive for the study of metaphorical concepts in general as the finding of divergences would be.

Finally, we proposed (but actually did not work out in any detail in the chapter) an improved complex measure of metaphorical salience. This would include token frequency, type frequency, the number of mappings, and the scope of the source domain. We can regard these four factors as capturing different aspects of how we use conceptual metaphors to comprehend various target domains. Token frequency can be seen as the *frequency of occurrence* of metaphorical expressions relating to a target. Type frequency involves the *lexical productivity* of a conceptual metaphor. The number of mappings that characterize a conceptual metaphor indicate the *conceptual depth* to which a source domain is used. The scope of the source can be taken to indicate the *extent of the applicability of the source*, that is, the extent to which a source domain applies to various target domains. By applying these four factors (in place of the raw measures of frequency), we could probably eliminate the difficulties posed by such source domains as POSSESSED OBJECT, which is highly frequent but intuitively not very revealing given a target domain involving attributed states. The new complex measure of metaphorical salience could bring us closer to a realistic characterization of target domains that are metaphorically constituted and to determining the relative cultural importance of their metaphors.

List of Key Words

Anger, Conceptual depth, Conceptual metaphors, Container metaphor, Corpus analysis, Cultural model, Emotion, Extent of applicability of the source, Frequency, Frequency of occurrence, Intensity, Lexical productivity, Mappings, Metaphor, Metaphorical salience, Opponent metaphor, Possessed object metaphor, Prototype, Qualitative analysis, Quantitative analysis, Salience, Scope of the source, Source domain, Target concept/domain, Token, Token frequency, Type frequency

Thought Questions

1. What is the relationship between our understanding of the concept *marriage* and the conceptual metaphor LIFE IS A JOURNEY?
2. Have you ever wondered about why almost everything we do relates to *time*? Sometimes we get paid by the hour, we don't like *to waste time*, and tests of all kinds involve some sort of *time*. The metaphorical concepts TIME IS MONEY, TIME IS A RESOURCE, and TIME IS A COMMODITY capture the overall importance of our conceptualization of *time*. Can you think about some other cultures/languages that might have a different conceptualization of *time*?
3. What can conceptual metaphors tell us about how we understand language?

Suggested Student Research Projects

1. Given the database you are working with, analyze which aspects of another emotion concept (such as *causality, intensity, control, existence*) are highlighted by the various metaphors for that emotion and how they are profiled.
2. Do the same kind of analysis as in the chapter concerning a concept corresponding to anger in a language not investigated here (e.g., German, French, or Polish). Given the results, what would be your conclusions?
3. Take the various *synonyms* of anger in English (such as *rage, fury, wrath, indignation*) and perform the same kind of analysis as the one described in this chapter. What do your results show about the relationship between the metaphors for anger and those for its synonyms?

Related Internet Sites

Conceptual Metaphor: https://en.wikipedia.org/wiki/Conceptual_metaphor

Metaphor Analysis Project: http://creet.open.ac.uk/projects/metaphor-analysis/index.cfm

Multilingual Metaphor: www.icsi.berkeley.edu/icsi/gazette/ 2012/ 05/metanet-project

Suggested Readings

Barcelona, A. (1989). Análisis contrastivo del léxico figurado de la ira en inglés y en español. *Actas del VI Congreso Nacional de Lingüística Aplicada*. AESLA. Santander: Universidad de Cantabria, Spain.

Blanco, O. (2012). Conceptualization of anger in English pop fiction stories. *Praxis, 3*. Retrieved from http://praxisjp.org/index.php.

Oster, U. (2010). Pride-Stolz-orgullo: A corpus-based approach to the expression of emotion concepts in a foreign language. In F. García & M. Sandino (Eds.), *Language windowing through corpora* (pp. 593–610). Universidade da Coruña, Coruña.

Sánchez, J., & Blanco-Carrión, O. (2007). Frames and critical discourse analysis in violence-related emotive event analysis. In C. Hart & D. Lukeš (Eds.), *Cognitive linguistics in critical discourse analysis: Application and theory* (pp. 232–254). Newcastle: Cambridge Scholars Publishing.

Soriano, C. (2004). *The conceptualization of anger in English and Spanish: A cognitive approach* (Unpublished doctoral dissertation). Universidad de Murcia, Spain.

REFERENCES

Heylen, K., Tummers, J., & Geeraerts, D. (2008). Methodological issues in corpus-based cognitive linguistics. In G. Kristiansen & R. Dirven (Eds.), *Cognitive sociolinguistics: Language variation, cultural models, social systems* (pp. 91–128). Berlin: Mouton de Gruyter.

Hungarian Academy of Sciences. (1999). *Historical dictionary corpus*. Retrieved from http://www.nytud.hu/hhc

Kövecses, Z. (2000a). *Metaphor and emotion: Language, culture, and body in human feeling*. Cambridge, UK: Cambridge University Press.

(2000b). The scope of metaphor. In A. Barcelona (Ed.), *Metaphor and metonymy at the crossroads* (pp. 79–92). Berlin: Mouton de Gruyter.

(2005). *Metaphor in culture: Universality and variation*. Cambridge, UK: Cambridge University Press.

(2008). Metaphor and emotion. In R. Gibbs (Ed.), *The Cambridge handbook of metaphor and thought* (pp. 380–396). Cambridge, UK: Cambridge University Press.

(2011). Methodological issues in conceptual metaphor theory. In S. Handl & H-J. Schmid (Eds.), *Windows to the mind: Metaphor, metonymy and conceptual blending* (pp. 23–39). Berlin/New York: Mouton de Gruyter.

Lakoff, G., & Johnson, M. (1980). *Metaphors we live by*. Chicago, IL: The University of Chicago Press.

Lakoff, G., & Kövecses, Z. (1987). The cognitive model of anger inherent in American English. In D. Holland & N. Quinn (Eds.), *Cultural models in language and thought* (pp. 195–221). Cambridge, UK: Cambridge University Press.

Real Academia Española. (n.d). *Corpus de la Referencia del Español Actual* (CREA). Retrieved from http://corpus.rae.es/creanet.html

Stefanowitsch, A. (2006a). Corpus-based approaches to metaphor and metonymy. In A. Stefanowitsch & S.T. Gries (Eds.), *Corpus-based approaches to metaphor and metonymy* (pp. 1–16). Berlin: Mouton de Gruyter.

(2006b). Words and their metaphors. In A. Stefanowitsch & S.T. Gries (Eds.), *Corpus-based approaches to metaphor and metonymy* (pp. 64–105). Berlin: Mouton de Gruyter.

Szelid, V., &, Geeraerts, D. (2008). Usage-based dialectology: Emotion, concepts, in the southern Csango dialect. *Annual Review of Cognitive Linguistics, 6*, 23–49.

Appendix

Table 1. *ANGER in American English*

Metaphorical Source Domain	Token of Linguistic Expressions	% of All Tokens	Type of Linguistic Expression	% of All Types (Conceptual Metaphor)	Type of Metaphorical Mappings	% of All Types (Metaphorical Mappings)	Aggregate
OPPONENT	69	7.87	34	11.53	9	12.5	31.9
OPPONENT 1 – ANGER IS AN OPPONENT IN A STRUGGLE	27	3.08	22	7.46	7	9.72	20.26
OPPONENT 2 – ANGER IS A WEAPON	42	4.79	12	4.07	2	2.78	11.64
CAPTIVE ANIMAL	28	3.19	8	2.71	2	2.78	8.68
FORCE	48	5.48	15	5.08	5	6.94	17.5
NATURAL FORCE	13	1.48	8	2.71	1	1.38	5.57
VICIOUS ANIMAL	8	0.91	5	1.69	2	2.78	5.38
SOCIAL SUPERIOR	24	2.74	3	1.01	1	1.38	5.13
HEAT	15	1.71	6	2.03	2	2.78	6.52
FIRE	4	0.46	2	0.68	1	1.38	2.52
LIGHT	19	2.17	8	2.71	1	1.38	6.26
INTENSITY IS AMOUNT	74	8.45	28	9.49	3	4.16	22.1
POSSESSED OBJECT	222	25.34	8	2.71	3	4.16	32.21
OBJECT	27	3.08	20	6.77	7	9.72	19.57
PERSON	30	3.42	24	8.13	5	6.94	18.49
PLANT	2	0.23	2	0.67	2	2.78	3.68
POSITIVE ENERGY	19	2.17	15	5.08	1	1.38	8.63

Table 1. (*cont.*)

Metaphorical Source Domain	Token of Linguistic Expressions	% of All Tokens	Type of Linguistic Expression	% of All Types (Conceptual Metaphor)	Type of Metaphorical Mappings	% of All Types (Metaphorical Mappings)	Aggregate
NEGATIVE ENERGY	7	0.79	3	1.01	1	1.38	3.18
BURDEN	5	0.57	3	1.01	1	1.38	2.96
DISEASE	12	1.37	11	3.72	4	5.55	10.64
PROBLEM	39	4.45	15	5.08	4	5.55	15.08
STATE OF ANGER IS LOCATION	23	2.63	8	2.71	3	4.16	9.5
INTENSITY OF ANGER IS DARKNESS OF ANGER (INTENSITY IS COLOR)	2	0.23	2	0.68	1	1.38	2.29
FORCEFUL ENTITY	41	4.68	18	4.75	4	5.55	14.98
CONTAINER	145	16.55	49	16.88	9	12.49	45.92
FORCEFUL ENTITY IN A PRESSURIZED CONTAINER	82	9.36	24	8.14	3	4.16	21.66
ENTITY IN A CONTAINER	63	7.19	25	8.74	6	8.33	24.26
Total	**876**		**295**		**72**		

Table 2. *ANGER in Spanish*

Metaphorical Source Domain	Token of Linguistic Expressions	% of All Tokens	Type of Linguistic Expression	% Of All Types (Conceptual Metaphor)	Type of Metaphorical Mappings	% of All Types (Metaphorical Mappings)	Aggregate
POSSESSED OBJECT	774	50.99	8	4.19	1	1.82	57
OPPONENT	207	13.64	41	21.47	10	18.18	53.29
OPPONENT I (IN A STRUGGLE)	75	4.94	14	7.33	7	12.73	25
OPPONENT 2 (WEAPON)	132	8.7	27	14.14	3	5.45	28.29
CAPTIVE ANIMAL	125	8.23	4	2.09	2	3.64	13.96
OBJECT	90	5.93	26	13.61	11	0.2	19.74
PERSON	84	5.53	17	8.90	6	10.91	25.34
FORCE (INCLUDES NATURAL FORCE AND DESTRUCTIVE FORCE)	66	4.35	20	10.47	6	10.91	25.73
SUBSTANCE IN A CONTAINER	63	4.15	28	14.66	9	16.36	35.17
VICIOUS ANIMAL	48	3.16	8	4.19	5	9.1	16.45
SOCIAL SUPERIOR	33	2.17	20	10.47	1	1.82	14.46
FIRE/HEAT	28	1.84	19	9.95	4	7.27	19.06
Total	1518		191		55		

Table 3. *ANGER in Turkish*

Metaphorical Source Domain	Token of Linguistic Expressions	% of All Tokens	Type of Linguistic Expression	% of All Types (Conceptual Metaphor)	Type of Metaphorical Mappings	% of All Types (Metaphorical Mappings)	Aggregate
POSSESSED OBJECT	693	26.94	7	1.98	1	1.72	30.64
ENTITY IN A CONTAINER	674	26.21	90	25.42	12	20.69	72.32
NATURAL FORCE	365	14.19	38	10.73	3	5.17	30.09
OPPONENT	232	9.02	29	8.19	6	10.34	27.55
OPPONENT (1)	182	7.08	22	6.21	5	8.62	21.91
OPPONENT (2) THE TARGET OF ANGER IS A PHYSICAL TARGET	50	1.94	7	1.98	1	1.72	5.64
SOCIAL SUPERIOR	34	1.32	9	2.54	1	1.72	5.58
WAR	17	0.66	5	1.41	3	5.17	7.24
BURDEN	14	0.54	10	2.82	2	3.45	6.81
CAPTIVE ANIMAL	18	0.70	11	3.11	3	5.17	8.98
WILD ANIMAL	27	1.05	10	2.82	2	3.45	7.32
FIRE	66	2.57	45	12.71	3	5.17	20.45
INSANITY	62	2.41	15	4.24	2	3.45	10.1
COLD	2	0.08	2	0.56	1	1.72	2.36
INTENSITY IS AMOUNT/QUANTITY	99	3.85	19	5.37	1	1.72	10.94

MORE IS UP	22	0.86	11	3.11	1	1.72	5.69
SPEED	20	0.78	2	0.56	1	1.72	3.06
STRENGTH	7	0.27	6	1.69	1	1.72	3.68
PERSON	35	1.36	8	2.26	1	1.72	5.34
PLANT	12	0.47	5	1.41	1	1.72	3.6
NUTRIENT	16	0.62	8	2.26	2	3.45	6.33
SHARP OBJECT	8	0.31	6	1.69	2	3.45	5.45
STATES ARE LOCATIONS	90	3.50	1	0.28	1	1.72	5.5
DISEASE	48	1.87	9	2.54	4	6.90	11.31
MOVING ENGINE	8	0.31	6	1.69	2	3.45	5.45
MOTIVATING FORCE	1	0.04	1	0.28	1	1.72	2.04
DEMON	2	0.08	1	0.28	1	1.72	2.08
Total	2572		354		58		

Table 4. ANGER in Hungarian

Metaphorical Source Domain	Token of Linguistic Expressions	% of All Tokens	Type of Linguistic Expression	% of All Types (Conceptual Metaphor)	Type of Metaphorical Mappings	% of All Types (Metaphorical Mappings)	Aggregate
POSSESSED OBJECT	324	30.28	1	0.42	1	1.47	32.17
(HOT/BOILING) FLUID IN A CONTAINER	174	16.26	46	19.49	12	17.65	53.4
STATES ARE LOCATIONS	125	11.68	4	1.69	2	0.29	13.66
CHANGES ARE MOVEMENTS	73	6.82	8	3.39	3	4.41	14.62
DISEASE	71	6.64	14	5.93	2	2.94	15.51
THING COMING INTO BEING	61	5.7	11	4.66	3	4.41	14.77
OPPONENT	59	5.51	29	12.29	10	14.7	32.5
OPPONENT I (ENEMY IN A STRUGGLE)	52	4.86	23	9.75	7	10.29	24.9
OPPONENT (2) WEAPON	7	0.65	6	2.54	3	4.41	7.6
INTENSITY IS AN AMOUNT/QUANTITY	34	3.18	13	5.51	2	2.94	11.63
SUBSTANCE/MATTER	27	2.52	23	9.75	4	5.88	18.15
CAPTIVE ANIMAL	25	2.34	13	5.51	5	7.35	15.2

INSTRUMENT	20	1.87	18	7.63	2	12.44
NATURAL FORCE	16	1.5	10	4.24	2	8.68
FIRE/HEAT	14	1.3	12	5.08	3	10.79
PHYSICAL ANNOYANCE	12	1.12	5	2.12	2	6.18
INTENSITY IS STRENGTH	11	1.03	7	2.97	2	9.88
SOCIAL SUPERIOR	10	0.93	7	2.97	2	6.84
OBJECT TO BE HIDDEN	9	0.84	6	2.54	2	6.32
LIVING BEING	3	0.28	3	1.27	3	5.96
DARKNESS (OR LIGHT)	2	0.19	2	0.85	2	3.98
DRIVING FORCE	2	0.19	2	0.85	1	2.51
BURDEN	1	0.09	1	0.42	1	1.98
INTENSITY IS SPEED	1	0.09	1	0.42	2	3.45
Total	1074		236		68	

12 Gauging the Semantic Transparency of Idioms: Do Natives and Learners See Eye to Eye?

Frank Boers and Stuart Webb
Victoria University of Wellington

ABSTRACT

The semantic opacity of idioms poses challenges to second language (L2) learners. L2 learners are known to be more inclined than first language users to activate literal readings of the constituent words of idioms. While this inclination can be put to good use in instructional methods that stimulate multimodal learning, it is also a double-edged sword when learners use lexical cues to work out idiomatic meanings independently. Pedagogy-minded applied linguists have in recent years proposed collections of high-utility lexical phrases for prioritized learning and teaching, and one of the recurring criteria used for selection has been the relative non-transparency of the expressions. We report a study in which we compare native speaker teachers' ratings of the relative semantic transparency of multiword units to those of advanced learners. The results reveal poor inter-rater agreement among the teachers and marked divergence between the teachers' and the learners' transparency ratings.

Keywords: cognitive linguistics, cognitive semantics, compositionality, idioms, second language learning

Idioms are traditionally characterized as institutionalized (semi-)fixed expressions whose overall meaning does not follow straightforwardly from adding up the meanings of their constituents. A classic example is *to kick the bucket*, the idiomatic meaning of which (*to die*) does not follow from combining the separate meanings of *kick* and *bucket*. Put technically, the meaning of idioms is noncompositional. In other words, the meaning of an idiom transcends the combined meanings of its components, and this renders the form-meaning connection of the expression non-transparent to various degrees (Cacciari & Glucksberg, 1991; Gibbs, Nayak, & Cutting, 1989). In this chapter we will argue that this phenomenon in fact extends beyond the class of expressions that are typically included in idiom dictionaries and in linguistic studies of idioms. Many more multiword expressions have a meaning that does not follow directly from the primary meanings of their constituent words (Hoey, 2005; Taylor, 2006) and can therefore be expected to cause comprehension problems for second language (L2) learners, even though the individual words look (deceptively) familiar to them. *To run a tight ship* is included in idiom dictionaries because its idiomatic meaning (to keep firm control of an organization) is obviously different from the meanings of *run, tight,* and *ship* that come to mind most readily if one encounters these words in isolation. On the other hand, *to run a bath, run a business,* and *to run the risk,* for instance, are absent from well-known English idiom dictionaries such as *Collins Cobuild Dictionary of Idioms* (2002) and *Oxford Idioms Dictionary for Learners of English* (2001), although *run* is not used in its primary literal sense in these expressions either. Idiom dictionaries represent just the tip of the iceberg of semantically challenging expressions, so to speak.

Semantic transparency is evidently a matter of degree. While, by definition, the meaning of idioms cannot be derived directly from their lexical composition, this does not mean that the form-meaning connection of all idioms is utterly opaque or unexplainable. Indeed, the school of thought known as *Cognitive Linguistics,* and its branch of *Cognitive Semantics* in particular, has generated a stream of studies to show that the meaning and use of idioms is often far less arbitrary than it used to be assumed. Impetus for this research came from Lakoff and Johnson's seminal book *Metaphors We Live By* (1980) and subsequent books that helped shape *Cognitive Semantics* (e.g., Lakoff, 1987). According to *cognitive semanticists,* people try to comprehend intangible domains of experience by seeking correspondences with concrete domains of experience. These systematic mappings of the structure of concrete domains onto abstract ones, called *Conceptual Metaphors,* are believed to be manifested in language, most notably in conventionalized figurative expressions (i.e., idioms). For example, expressions such as *being hot under the collar, being hot-tempered, losing one's cool,* and *blowing off steam* all refer to anger in terms of heat, and thus suggest the existence of an overarching metaphor, ANGER IS HEAT. It is a metaphor that is grounded in physical experience (e.g., a rising body temperature is symptomatic of agitation). According to Cognitive Semantics, the existence of such a set of idioms in the language is therefore *motivated.* A combination of metaphor recognition and world knowledge can render idioms such as these relatively transparent. For example, *add fuel to the fire* (i.e., *inciting anger*) becomes transparent once you realize that *fire* is used metaphorically for *anger* and if you know what happens when you add fuel to a fire.

In a similar vein, the idioms *lend someone a hand, have your hands full, sit on your hands,* and several more *hand* expressions are motivated by our shared understanding that we typically use our hands (rather than other body parts) to *mani*pulate or *handle* things. In other words, the use of *hand* as a metonym for doing an activity is again underpinned (i.e., motivated) by physical experience. The meanings of phrasal and prepositional verbs, which are also sometimes subsumed under idioms, are often motivatable as well. For example, *cheer up, feeling up to a task,* and *living up to high expectations* can all be related to a GOOD IS UP metaphor (see also Kövecses et al., this volume).

Motivating the meaning of an idiom thus involves an appreciation of the correspondence between a literal reading of the expression and the idiomatic, figurative meaning, which has over time become institutionalized as the principal meaning. If the literal reading is congruent with the idiomatic meaning of the expression, then the scene evoked by the literal reading can render the expression semantically transparent. For instance, recognizing that *take a back seat* literally means taking the role of passenger in a car can help one implicitly relate the idiom to a conceptual metaphor such as A PROJECT IS A JOURNEY and subsequently add the inference that comes with not being in the driver's seat. It is when the link with the literal scene is ruptured that idioms become truly opaque for language users in the sense that the meaning of the idiom appears unrelated to the meaning of the words it is composed of. That is the case with idioms such as *by and large, a red herring,* and *through thick and thin,* whose literal origins are unknown to most contemporary language users. However, etymological information about these can reveal the literal meaning, and if the latter is still congruent with the contemporary meaning, then the opacity of the idiom can be reduced. An explanation that *through thick and thin* is elliptic (the noun *wood* at the end was dropped) and originally referred to arduously making one's way through forest and bushes helps to see why the expression means what it means (i.e., *persevere despite difficult circumstances*). According to Grant and Bauer (2004), only a very small proportion of the idiom repertoire of English ultimately defies the motivation of their figurative meaning.

This does not mean, of course, that native speakers are usually aware of the literal underpinnings of the idioms they encounter and use. For one thing, most native speakers have no knowledge of the origin of idioms such as *kick the bucket* or *a red herring*. They acquired the idiomatic meaning of expressions such as these directly from encounters in usage, without any need to ponder their lexical makeup. This is generally believed to be the default way of multiword unit acquisition in the first language (L1; Wray, 2002). For another, under the exigencies of real-time, message-focused communication, native speakers will immediately activate the meaning of an expression that is most salient to them (Giora, 1997; Laurent, Denhières, Passerieux, Iakimova, & Hardy-Baylé, 2005; Siyanova, Conklin, & Schmitt, 2011; Tabossi, Fanari, & Wolf, 2009), and in the case of L1 idioms, it is the idiomatic meaning that is the most frequent and thus most readily activated one. For example, one does not often encounter *spill the beans* with reference to a scene where someone has physically spilled beans. The native speaker will be much more familiar with its idiomatic use and meaning (i.e., *tell a secret*). It stands to reason that the likelihood of a language user being conscious that a literal reading of an idiom is also available will depend on the nature of the idiom (transparent vs. utterly opaque) and on the circumstances in which it is used (planned vs. online speech; signs of wordplay) (Sprenger, Levelt, & Kempen, 2006; Titone & Connine, 1999).

Importantly for the purposes of the present chapter, L2 learners have been found to be much more inclined than native speakers to activate a literal reading of idioms in their additional language (e.g., Cieślicka, 2006; 2010). More generally, while most multiword expressions are acquired holistically in one's native tongue during childhood (Peters, 1983; Wray, 2002, p. 131), adult learners of an additional language are more inclined to process multiword expressions *analytically*, breaking up the expressions into words (Fitzpatrick & Wray, 2006; Wray, 2002, pp. 206–210). As we shall argue in this chapter, this analytic mode of processing expressions such as idioms is likely to be *a double-edged sword*. On the one hand, as we shall see further below, it is an inclination that in the case of idioms is exploitable for pedagogical purposes, because a literal reading makes an idiom imageable – a property that is positively associated with memorability (e.g., Steinel, Hulstijn, & Steinel, 2007). On the other hand, it is an inclination that may lead learners to independently try to make sense of unfamiliar idioms via their lexical constituents. As we shall demonstrate further below, there are grounds for believing such learner-autonomous strategy risks engendering misguided interpretations. First, however, it is necessary to address the fundamental question of whether idioms are worthy of language learners' (and teachers') attention in the first place.

The Relevance of Acquiring L2 Idioms

Idioms have long had an *icing-on-the-cake* reputation in circles of instructed L2 acquisition. Idioms were considered to be a marginal phenomenon, unworthy of much attention, because their communicative function was merely to embellish discourse that could be just as effective without them. Language was viewed as a dual system made up of a grammar and a lexicon (Taylor, 2010, for an insightful critique of this view), where grammar rules were thought to provide sentence templates and the lexicon the meaning-bearing elements to fill the slots in those templates. Recent, usage-based linguistic theories, such as *Cognitive Linguistics* (Langacker, 1990) and *Construction Grammar* (Goldberg, 2006), reject this lexis-grammar dichotomy and view language as an inventory of meaningful units on a cline from small to large. This naturally brings to the fore what lies between single words and syntactic patterns on that cline, namely a plethora of multiword units, such as idioms. Support for such a view of language comes from psycholinguistics (e.g., Ellis, 2008; Tomasello, 2003; Wray, 2002) and corpus linguistics (e.g., Sinclair, 1991). Multiword units (including idioms) afford important processing advantages, because they need not be assembled word by word during language production nor parsed word by word during language reception. Instead, they can be retrieved from the mental lexicon as prefabricated chunks, which fosters fluency, and hearing or reading part of a multiword unit is often sufficient to predict the rest, so that attention can be allocated to the less predictable segments of incoming messages. For example, a native speaker of English will be able to guess the ending of *I'll help you through thick and __ (thin)* and *Please stop beating about the __ (bush)*.

This processing advantage afforded by procedural or automatized knowledge of idioms would be of scant relevance if idiomatic expressions were rare in discourse. However, corpus evidence shows that, while many idioms are of low frequency when taken individually (e.g., Moon, 1998), taken as a class, idioms are in fact quite common. Based on idiom counts by Stengers (2007) in the online *Word Banks* corpus (e.g., *Collins Cobuild* series), it can be estimated that on average 2,400 instances of idioms occur per million words of English discourse. Replication of the exercise in Spanish and German yields eerily similar estimates (Stengers, 2007; Stengers, Boers, Housen, & Eyckmans, 2011), which debunks the myth that English might be an exceptionally idiomatic language. It is worth mentioning that these idiom frequencies are in fact bound to be underestimations. For one thing, the searches were confined to idioms listed in idiom dictionaries compiled for learners, and these are unlikely to be exhaustive compilations of a language's stock of institutionalized (semi-)fixed expressions. For another, many idioms display far greater variability than what dictionary entries lead one to assume (e.g., Herrera & White, 2010), and given the different guises in which an idiom can be instantiated, a considerable number of instances may escape the kind of automatic searches for idioms in electronic corpora that were resorted to in the aforementioned counts. Finally, there are reasons to believe that idioms are particularly frequent in conversation (McCarthy, 1998), and the corpora used in the afore-mentioned studies underrepresent spoken language.

It is now also recognized that, far from being the *icing on the cake,* idioms fulfill vital functions in discourse, including conveying an evaluative stance and signaling topic changes (O'Keeffe, McCarthy, & Carter, 2007, pp. 80–99). *Idioms are never just neutral alternatives* (McCarthy, 1998, p. 145) to a more literal way of conveying a message. Given their important pragmatic functions, the relative abundance of idioms in natural discourse (especially in conversation) is not surprising, and it is clear that L2 learners stand to gain a lot from a broad knowledge of the idiom repertoire of their interlocutors, if only for comprehension purposes. We turn next to the challenges faced by the learner who wishes to build such knowledge.

In the Learner's Shoes

Given the ubiquity of idiomatic language, one might be hopeful that many idioms in an L2 will be picked up as a by-product of message-focused activities, such as extensive reading and listening, and – in the case of immersion contexts – conversing with native (or otherwise expert) speakers. L2 vocabulary research on such *incidental* acquisition has tended to focus on extensive reading and on the uptake of single words rather than multiword units. The body of evidence shows that incidental acquisition from extensive reading occurs, but typically at a slow pace (e.g., Laufer, 2005, for a review, and a plea for more deliberate vocabu-lary instruction). One of the reasons why incidental acquisition of vocabulary tends to be slow is that it is contingent upon multiple exposures to the same lexical item in a relatively short time span (e.g., Waring & Takaki, 2003). This holds true for multiword vocabulary also. Webb, Newton, and Chang (2013) have measured learners' retention of multiword units such as *face the fact* and *run the risk* after encountering these in a short story. The researchers manipulated the text so that learners met each target expression between one and 15 times in the course of reading a graded reader. As predicted, the more often an expression was met, the better the chances of retention (although even as many as 15 encounters did not warrant full scores in the posttests). Encountering an expression just once had no measurable effect. While it may be feasible to adapt texts for pedagogic purposes such that learners are repeatedly exposed to certain vocabulary items, un-adapted texts

374 Bilingual Figurative Language Processing

are very unlikely to afford this enhanced opportunity for incidental uptake. As said, idioms may be quite common as a class, but individual idioms are unlikely to be repeatedly encountered in a short time span. For example, Boers and Lindstromberg (2009, p. 67) found over 90 instances of idioms (where *idiom* was operationalized as an expression listed in the *Collins Cobuild Dictionary of Idioms*) in 120 pages of a popular novel (which they estimated to be worth about four hours of reading for an advanced learner). While this confirms that idiom use as a phenomenon is common, at least in certain genres, almost all of the attested idioms occurred just once in this stretch of text, and thus the chances of uptake of idioms from leisurely reading appear very small indeed.

One might wish to argue that the findings concerning the slow uptake of single words may not be transferrable to idioms. For example, owing to their multiword nature and to their enigmatic nature, idioms might attract more attention – and attention is known to be positively associated with learning (Schmidt, 2001). However, learners cannot be expected to recognize the idiomatic status of the word strings they encounter, especially if those strings are made up of familiar words. Martinez and Murphy (2011), for example, report how English as a foreign language (EFL) learners in a study on reading comprehension failed to appreciate the idiomaticity of expressions such as *he's over the hill* (which they interpreted as *he lives on the other side of the hill*). But even if learners do recognize that a given word string must have an overall meaning that differs from that of the constituent words, this recognition *per se* hardly guarantees an adequate interpretation. Littlemore, Chen, Koester, and Barnden (2011) report disconcerting evidence on the extent to which international students at a British university misinterpret the idioms used by their university lecturers. One may be hopeful that the context in which an idiom is used will steer a learner toward an adequate interpretation, but an experiment reported by Boers, Eyckmans, and Stengers (2007) suggests that learners usually fail to comprehend idioms even when these are embedded in contexts that are rich in contextual cues. In this experiment, participants tended to become successful at inferring the meaning of the idioms only when they were informed of the original, literal use of the expressions (e.g., that *putting someone through their paces* is derived from the context of training horses) in addition to the contextual cues.

It is not surprising, of course, that idioms in an L2 are hard to figure out without any guidance. As mentioned in the introduction, the form-meaning connection of an idiom may be motivatable, but this involves retrospective explanation: When you know the idiomatic meaning of the expression and when you recognize how this meaning is congruent with the image evoked by a literal reading of the expression, then the idiom *makes sense* (i.e., it is motivated). This does not mean, however, that a literal reading of the expression is necessarily a reliable clue for learners to autonomously work out the idiomatic meaning of the idiom. Idioms may simply contain words that are unknown to the learner, either because they are low-frequency words (e.g., *tether* in *at the end of your tether; trumps* in *turn up trumps; rein* in *keep a tight rein on someone*) or because they are obsolete outside the idiom in which they have been preserved (e.g., *doldrums* in *be in/out of the doldrums*). Another obstacle to interpretation is the elliptic nature of many idioms. For instance, how can a learner be expected to guess what object is cut in the expression *to cut and run?* Moreover, the lexical makeup of idioms such as *cut and run* is often in part motivated by considerations of euphony, with sound repetitive (most notably assonant and alliterative) word strings being privileged at the expense of word strings that would probably be better semantic clues (Boers & Lindstromberg, 2009, pp. 106–125). Examples may include the alliterative *chop and change, the gift of the gab, not pull one's punches,* and the *cream of the crop,* each of which consists of word combinations that may be phonologically catchy but offer little help to the language learner who does not know what is meant by *chop* or by the *gab,* and who is mystified by the proposition that a punch can be pulled and that a crop can be creamy.

But the lexical composition of an idiom can also be deceptively transparent, which can all too easily put learners on the wrong foot if they wish to make guesses at the idiomatic meaning. For example, a learner may attach the wrong meaning to homonyms (i.e., different words that happen to share the same form). When encountering *to follow suit,* for instance, the learner is more likely to activate the more frequent meaning of *suit* as an article of clothing than its less frequent meaning of a type of card in card games, a meaning the learner may also be unfamiliar with (Boers, Demecheleer, & Eyckmans, 2004a). The learner may then wrongly infer that the idiom means something like *obeying authority* given her world knowledge that people in positions of status tend to wear suits.

Polysemy (i.e., having different, related meanings) or vagueness of word meaning is also bound to lead learners astray. On encountering *to show someone the ropes* the learner may think of the ropes used by a hangman or perhaps the ropes of a boxing ring instead of the ropes on a sailing vessel. The incorrect interpretation could then have a rather threatening ring instead of sounding like an offer to explain things. Similarly, the *gun* in (the assonant word string) *to jump the gun* can easily be mistaken for the kind that kills rather than the pistol used to signal the start of a racing contest. This idiom may then perhaps be misinterpreted as referring to an act of bravery, because it may evoke the scene of someone trying to disarm a man holding a gun. In a similar vein, the *shot* in *a shot in the arm* may be mistaken for a shot from a weapon instead of an injection. Another example is the *plank* in *to walk the plank*, which may activate a scene of fashion models parading on a wooden board instead of the scene of someone being forced to jump into the ocean from the deck of a ship. Moreover, even if the learner has managed to guess the source of origin correctly, there is usually plenty of room left for misinterpretation. For example, a learner who correctly guesses that *the gloves are off* is an idiom derived from boxing may nevertheless get the wrong end of the stick if she assumes it is meant to evoke a scene where the boxers take off their gloves because the fight is over – instead of the scene where they want to use their bare fists to cause more serious injury.

Interference from L1 may be an additional obstacle to L2 idiom interpretation (Boers, 2003). The meaning of a given idiom in L2 need not coincide with that of a similar sounding expression in L1, after all. Cross-cultural differences can also play a part (Kövecses, 2005). An example is the way different communities may construe the domains of reason and emotion. In Western culture, the Cartesian division between the mind and the body still reigns and so does the Jamesian view of emotion: The mind (associated with the head) is the seat of reason, while the emotions reside in the body, especially the heart. This is reflected in the high number of *heart* expressions used to talk about emotions in the idiom repertoire of a language such as English (e.g., *a bleeding heart, a broken heart, to lose heart, to wear your heart on your sleeve,* and *to eat your heart out*). In other cultures, a division between reason and emotion need not correspond to a mind/head versus body division. In Mandarin Chinese, the concept of mind actually coincides with the concept of heart (*xin*), and so Mandarin Chinese idioms with *xin* (*heart*) do not instantiate the same metaphor as English idioms with *heart* (Hu, 2002). Unsurprisingly, Chinese EFL learners find it relatively hard to make sense of English idioms containing the words *heart, mind,* and *head* (Hu & Fong, 2010). Conversely, Westerners learning Chinese can be expected to be puzzled by Chinese idioms containing *xin*. Other organs associated with emotions in non-Western cultures include the stomach (in Japanese; Matsuki, 1995) and the liver (in Malay; Charteris-Black, 2002), which undoubtedly render idioms referring to these organs relatively hard to grasp for Western-background learners of these languages. But cultural variation may hamper L2 idiom comprehension even in the case of closely related languages. Obvious examples are idioms derived from sports that do not share the same popularity across cultures. For example, the Spanish stock of idioms contains many more expressions derived from bull fighting than the English repertoire. Conversely, the English idiom repertoire contains more expressions derived from ball games such as cricket in British English (e.g., *off your own bat* and *hit someone for six*) and baseball in American English (e.g., *go in to bat for someone* and *touch all the bases*), which are quite foreign to speakers of language communities where these sports are virtually unknown (Boers & Stengers, 2008), and which appear particularly hard to acquire (Boers, Demecheleer, & Eyckmans, 2004b).

In sum, there are grounds for skepticism about the pace at which L2 learners can be expected to pick up idioms from exposure when they are left to their own devices. There may therefore be justification for investing time and effort in more deliberate instruction of L2 idioms. To our knowledge, the most systematic approach to teaching idioms to date is that informed by *Cognitive Linguistics*. What follows is a brief sketch of that approach.

Cognitive Linguistics (CL)-informed proposals for idiom teaching exploit the motivated nature of idioms to help learners comprehend and remember these expressions (Boers & Lindstromberg, 2009, 79–102, for a review). Learners are shown that the meaning of a given idiom *makes sense* once one recognizes how it instantiates a common conceptual metaphor or how it is derived through figuration from a context in which the expression was originally used with a literal meaning. Resuscitating that literal meaning as part of motivating the idiomatic usage of the expression evokes a fair amount of mental imagery, which not only capitalizes on the attested inclination of L2 learners to try and process idioms through analysis and literal reading of the constituent words (see above), but which also, according to models of multimodal processing (e.g., Paivio, 1986) fosters retention and facilitates retrieval. Crucially, the learner is guided toward an understanding of the literal usage of the expression that is congruent with its idiomatic meaning – something that cannot be taken for granted if the learner is left unaided, as we demonstrated above.

In addition, it has been suggested that CL-style instruction can help learners appreciate that the stock of idioms in the target language may reflect the degrees to which certain domains of life have preoccupied (past) users of the language. For example, given the history of Britain as a seafaring nation, it is not surprising that its stock of idioms abounds with expressions from that domain, such as *to clear the decks, to be on an even keel, all hands on deck, to give someone a wide berth, to take something on board, plain sailing, to run a tight ship, when your ship comes in, be out of your depth,* and *a leading light.* Likewise, students can be made aware of the recreational importance of horses in British culture (e.g., horse racing) and of the affinity the British have traditionally felt toward this animal by pointing out the abundance of horse-related idioms: for example, *to win hands down, be neck and neck, too close to call, off the rails, in the running, a dark horse, from the horse's mouth, across the board, give someone free rein,* and *ride high.*

As part of language-focused classroom activities students, can be asked to group idioms under the headings of conceptual metaphors or to identify their common source domains themselves. For instance, *to set the stage for something, be waiting in the wings, to take center stage, in the limelight, to play to the gallery, behind the scenes,* and *the curtain comes down* should suffice for learners to recognize the theater as a source domain. *To flex your muscles, to lower your guard, to take it on the chin, to be on the ropes, be down for the count,* and *to throw in the towel* can all neatly be grouped under a boxing theme. Alternatively, one may prefer to avoid the potential risk of between-idiom interference that is carried by a presentation of several idioms in one go and instead point out the motivation behind an idiom as the opportunity presents itself, for example, as an idiom happens to be encountered in a reading or listening text. The meaning of an idiom can in addition be made more memorable by means of visuals, such as pictures, drawings, and mime (e.g., Szczepaniak & Lew 2011) = provided these are congruent with the figurative meaning, of course.

There is a growing body of evidence from effect-of-instruction studies to support the kind of CL-informed proposals for pedagogy that we have briefly sketched here. A review of over twenty published studies reveals an almost univocal advantage of CL-style instruction over comparison treatments (Boers, 2011). However, it needs to be acknowledged that not all of these studies display optimal rigor in their design and/or data analysis and that replication studies would be most useful. It is certainly encouraging to see that efforts at validation are being made and that effective pedagogical means of tackling L2 idioms are becoming available. It must also be conceded, though, that these CL-informed techniques may not be straightforwardly applicable to idiomatic expressions at large. For one thing, some idioms defy motivation. For another, as we mentioned in the introduction, many more multiword items than those included in idiom dictionaries may to some extent be semantically non-transparent to L2 learners.

Beyond Idioms

Idiomaticity can be taken to refer to a broader phenomenon than the use of the kind of expressions one finds in idiom dictionaries (Grant & Bauer, 2004). Corpus linguists have shown the prevalence of what Sinclair

(1991) called the *Idiom Principle* in natural discourse. Discourse abounds with word partnerships, or collocations, such as *commit suicide, give someone a warm welcome,* and *utterly disgusting,* and with other fixed phrases (e.g., *nice to meet you* and *last but not least*) that characterize discourse as native-like (Erman & Warren, 2001; Pawley & Syder, 1983). In the literature, a distinction is sometimes made between idioms and collocations because the latter are believed to be semantically transparent (Fernando, 1996; Moon, 1998; Nesselhauf, 2003). Indeed, collocations such as *make a mistake* have a meaning that appears to follow straightforwardly from the meaning of the constituent words. It is a distinction that has also been applied to the development of study materials. For example, in the series of books for independent study of English vocabulary authored by McCarthy and O'Dell, books are devoted separately to idioms (2002, 2003) and to collocations (2005, 2008). Yet, in the introduction to their first book on collocations (pp. 4–5), the authors explain that they selected collocations that were deemed *not immediately obvious*, which hints at a certain degree of non-transparency in collocations also. The distinction between idioms and collocations is thus not clear-cut.

Thanks to corpus linguistics it has become possible to develop inventories of phrasal expressions that are especially frequent in a particular genre (e.g., Biber, Conrad, & Cortes, 2004; Liu, 2011; Shin & Nation, 2008; Simpson-Vlach & Ellis, 2010) or across genres (Martinez & Schmitt, 2012). Such inventories are intended to help L2 learners and pedagogues decide which L2 expressions merit prioritization in learning and instruction. Some inventories are based on raw frequencies of word strings (e.g., Biber et al., 2004), while others complement the criterion of raw frequency with statistical measures to extract particularly strong word partnerships (e.g., Simpson-Vlach & Ellis, 2010). Some of the criteria for inclusion in the phrase list proposed by Martinez and Schmitt (2012) are reminiscent of McCarthy and O'Dell's criteria for selecting collocations (2005): "[T]he general idea regarding the items to be included in the PHRASE list is that they should be ones that are identified as potentially causing difficulty for learners of English, particularly on a receptive level" (p. 308), and "When selecting phrasal expressions, an item was also often judged to potentially fit into this category when the most common and familiar meaning of at least one of the words in the expression was likely to pose confusion" (p. 309).

The question this raises is who does the judging of which expressions and which words are likely to cause confusion, and for which learners (e.g. Japanese, Spanish, Italian; beginner, intermediate, advanced levels) are the expressions confusing? How reliably can researchers, materials writers, and teachers gauge the likelihood that a given expression (be it an idiom or a collocation) will be hard or easy to comprehend for a particular language learner, in the absence of experimental evidence? Bortfeld (2003, p. 219) argues that it must be hard for native speakers to empathize with learners trying to make sense of idioms in the L2. The native speakers' knowledge of the idiomatic meaning will lead them – if so required – to analyze the word string in a way that is congruent with that idiomatic meaning. For example, native speakers are highly unlikely to associate the *shot* in *a shot in the arm* with a shot from a gun, for the simple reason that such imagery would be incompatible with the idiomatic meaning (*give a boost*), and so will not spring to mind. It must then be difficult for the native speaker to imagine that, in their attempt at figuring out the meaning of the idiom, language learners may actually misinterpret a clue such as *shot*. In addition, the native speaker may be unaware that a particular language learner may not share the same culturally grounded associations with particular concepts or may lack knowledge of culture-specific customs that have left a mark on the idiom repertoire (see above).

As recognized by Martinez and Schmitt (2012), the learner's misreading of lexical components of multiword units is a potential risk that is not confined to idioms in a narrow sense. Also, expressions that for many would qualify as collocations rather than idioms may invite (partial) misinterpretations, even if at first glance all the lexical constituents are familiar. This is because those constituents are likely to be polysemous, and the sense of a word that is most readily activated in the learner's mind need not be the sense that contributes to the actual meaning of the collocation. For example, activation of the financial transaction sense of *pay* in *pay attention, pay tribute,* and *pay one's last respects* may not aid comprehension of these expressions much. Activating the primary meaning of *catch* (which suggests an intentional act) is probably unhelpful for adequate interpretation of *catch a cold*. In a similar vein, activating the public display sense of *perform* may lead to an inadequate interpretation of (the contemporary use of) *perform surgery*. The literal sense of *break* combined with the homonymy of *record* may conceivably lead to a misinterpretation of *break a record* as destroying an album or a file. Activating the sense of *take* as the intentional act of taking possession of something may lead to attaching a negative connotation to *take turns*. The core sense of *make* involves intentionality, too, but surely few people *make mistakes* intentionally. Conventionalized metonymies may be an additional barrier to cross-linguistic comprehension. For instance, *word* in *have a word* is used metonymically for *conversation*. *Tea* in *have tea* is a metonym for more than just the hot drink in British culture.

One may argue that potential misinterpretations of the above kind would quickly be resolved thanks to repeated encounters with the same collocations, accompanied by contextual cues that will help the learners fine-tune their comprehension of the expressions. But, again, it appears that repeated encounters with one and the same collocation in authentic text tend to be few and far between. For example, Boers and Lindstromberg (2009, p. 42) counted about fifty instances of strong verb-noun collocations (e.g., *see the point, lose your mind, crack a joke, climb stairs, make a point, give pause*) in 120 pages of a popular novel (see above for a comparison with counts of idioms), but the vast majority of the collocations occurred just once in this text sample. It would thus appear that second language learners' comprehension of phrasal expressions at large could benefit from more deliberate guidance as well (see, e.g., Laufer & Girsai, 2008; Laufer & Waldman, 2011, for arguments in favor of deliberate instruction about collocations). The development of the aforementioned study materials devoted to high-utility phrasal expressions is a welcome step toward meeting this need. Questions remain, of course, about the relative efficacy of proposed instructional procedures (e.g., Boers & Lindstromberg, 2012; Boers, Demecheleer, Coxhead, & Webb, 2013). The question we address in the following section concerns issues of targeting. In order for pedagogy-minded applied linguists to be able to anticipate cases where learners are likely to misconstrue the meaning of a phrasal expression, they *need to put themselves into those learners' shoes.* As a first step in evaluating how much empathy we can expect native teachers and materials writers to have with L2 learners when it comes to anticipating misinterpretations, we will gauge how well teachers of English to speakers of other languages (TESOL) practitioners' ratings of the semantic transparency of multi-word expression (in particular verb-noun expressions) match those of a group of language learners.

Intuitions about Transparency

In what follows, we report a study set up to investigate the extent to which native speaker teachers' intuitions about the relative transparency of multiword expressions correspond to learners', and the extent to which teachers' intuitions can help predict which expressions the learners will find relatively easy to infer the meaning of.

We presented a group of EFL teachers and a group of advanced language learners with 45 verb-noun expressions, which to us varied in degrees of transparency. At the one extreme were collocations that we considered totally transparent, such as *read a book*. At the other extreme were idioms whose form-meaning connection is deemed quite opaque even to native speakers, such as *shoot the breeze*. In between these extremes were expressions taken from McCarthy and O'Dell's independent study books on idioms (2002, 2003) and collocations (2005, 2008). Each expression was accompanied by a seven-point transparency scale on which the respondents were required to locate the expression. The questionnaire, which was administered on paper, was introduced by the following instructions:

Please look at each of the phrases below and consider their meanings. Does the meaning of the phrase as a whole follow from adding up the meanings of the words? For example, the meaning of the phrase *kick the bucket* is *to die*. If you didn't know that the phrase had this meaning, you would probably be unable to guess it, even if you understand the words *kick* and *bucket*. So, the meaning of the phrase *kick the bucket* is not clear from the words it consists of. In comparison, the meaning of *kick the ball* (i.e., *use your foot to make the ball move*) follows directly from combining the meaning of the words *kick* and *ball*. Understanding the meanings of those words is sufficient for you to understand the phrase as a whole.

Please mark the degree to which the meaning of the phrase as a whole is clear if you understand the words it consists of. Put a cross in the appropriate box on the scale of 1 (the meaning is not at all clear) to 7 (the meaning is very clear). For example, I wouldn't be able to guess the meaning of *kick the bucket* (*to die*) at all from the combined meaning of *kick* and *bucket*. So I give it a rating of 1.

	The meaning of the phrase is not at all clear from the words					The meaning of the phrase is very clear from the words
	1	2	3	4	5	6	7
Kick the bucket	X						

On the other hand, the meaning of *kick the ball* (*to use your foot to move the ball*) seems to follow directly from combining the meanings of *kick* and *ball*. My rating for this phrase is 7.

	The meaning of the phrase is not at all clear from the words					The meaning of the phrase is very clear from the words
	1	2	3	4	5	6	7
Kick the ball							X

Now it's your turn. Thank you for your help!

The 45 verb-noun phrases for the respondents to rate for transparency are listed in the Appendix. We collected questionnaire responses from two groups: 7 native-speakers and 33 non-native speakers. The native speakers were teachers of English who were on the verge of completing an MA program in applied linguistics or TESOL. They all had over three years of experience teaching English, including overseas experience in countries such as Korea, Thailand, China, Laos, and Japan. The non-native speakers were either EFL teachers or studying to be EFL teachers in a Master of Arts degree program in Japan. They all had experienced many years of formal language instruction and were considered to have a high level of English language proficiency in that context.

Because we could not assume that the non-native speakers were familiar with all of the expressions, we gave them a version of the questionnaire where each expression was accompanied by a Japanese translation. All respondents made use of the whole seven-point scale. Each of the respondents' ratings of the expressions was transposed into a ranking order of the expressions from judged least to most transparent. We then calculated Pearson correlation coefficients (r) between these rankings. We also calculated the mean ratings per group of respondents for each expression and calculated the correlation between the two groups' rankings.

The correlation coefficients between the transparency rankings by the native speaker TESOL practitioners ranged from a meager .29 to .71. The average was .54 ($SD = .13$). This suggests only a moderate level of agreement among the native speaker teachers about which expressions are comparatively transparent or opaque. The level of agreement among the Japanese EFL learners was higher: Pearson's r ranged from .51 to .85 and averaged .69 ($SD = .072$).

If we take each of the seven teachers' transparency rankings and correlate those separately with the mean ranking of the learners, we obtain correlations of .28, .49, .51, .53, .64, .73, and .85. The lower end of these figures signals that native speaker teachers' evaluations of the degree of compositionality of multiword units can differ quite markedly from the learners. It follows that relying on just one or two raters to estimate the degree of semantic transparency of multiword units is unlikely to be reliable. Reliability is enhanced when the estimates of several raters are pooled: The mean ranking by the teachers and the mean ranking by the learners correlated at .79. While this is much more reassuring, it is doubtful whether teachers and study material writers customarily resort to such inter-rater agreement checks. Moreover, this pooled correlation is still indicative of discrepancies between teachers' and learners' intuitions. Expressions that were deemed much more opaque by the learners than the teachers included *jump ship, cut corners, make the grade, walk the plank, hit the roof, kick the habit, raise a family, perform surgery,* and *close a meeting* (see Appendix). The latter four expressions are absent from the idiom dictionaries we have consulted, and thus illustrate our point that noncompositionality from a learner's perspective extends beyond idioms in a narrow sense. When it comes to selecting multiword units for pedagogic targeting, it seems the motto should be: *When in doubt, leave it in.*

Summary and Conclusions

Figurative idioms have been a rewarding showcase for pedagogic interventions inspired by *Cognitive Linguistics* (or, more specifically, *Cognitive Semantics*). These are interventions that capitalize on adult L2 learners' inclination to look for *rhyme and reason* in idioms, and their inclination to break up multiword units more generally (in contrast with the way such multiword units tend to be acquired and processed in the mother tongue). This inclination may well be a *double-edged sword*, however, when the learner is left without guidance. Idioms being idioms, their lexical composition is wide open to misinterpretation. Anticipating a particular learner's risk of misinterpretation requires insight into the multi-interpretability of the lexical constituents of the expression, a reliable estimate of the learner's knowledge of the diverse form-meaning mappings of these lexical constituents, and the potential interference from the learner's L1 and cultural background.

With the advent of corpus linguistics and psycholinguistic ventures into formulaic language, it has become abundantly clear that *idiomaticity* extends far beyond the class of expressions one finds explained in idiom dictionaries. Although at first sight other multiword expressions, such as collocations, seem less susceptible to learners' misinterpretations, we hope to have demonstrated that this cannot be taken for granted. We are not alone in that assertion, of course. Recent proposals for the development of phrasal expressions lists and for study materials that target multiword units such as collocations recognize that lack of semantic transparency must be one of the criteria for selection. What our small-scale study has shown, however, is that it is not self-evident for native speaker teachers or materials writers to predict which multiword phrases are likely to be experienced as semantically transparent or as non-transparent by learners. *Seeing eye to eye* on this with a particular learner requires good knowledge of that learner's L1 and cultural background, insight into polysemy, and a reliable estimation of which word meaning is likely to spring to the language learner's mind most readily. Given the unique perspective that every L2 learner brings to bear on the challenge of making sense of L2 multiword expressions, this is a combination of prerequisites that is not easily met, either by teachers or by pedagogy-minded lexicographers and phrase-list compilers.

List of Keywords

Cognitive linguistics (CL), Cognitive semantics, Collocations, Compositionality, Conceptual metaphor, Construction grammar, Corpus linguistics, English as a Foreign Language (EFL), English as a Second Language (ESL), Idiom Principle, Idiomaticity, L1 Interference, Metaphor, Metonymy, Noncompositional, Non-transparent, Online processing, Opaque, Polysemy, Semantic transparency, Source domain, Teachers of English to speakers of other languages (TESOL)

Thought Questions

1. It is a laudable effort to include potential confusability among the criteria for compiling inventories of phrases for pedagogic targeting. Given the likelihood that confusability will to some extent depend on the learner's L1, however, should such inventories not be adapted to the particular target population, and should they not be compiled in consultation with members of that population? Why or why not?

2. Studies of figurative language have so far tended to focus on semantics. Yet, a conspicuous number of standardized figurative expressions (idioms, proverbs, and similes) display phonological repetition such as alliteration (e.g., *bite the bullet, that's the way the cookie crumbles, fit as a fiddle*) and/or (near) rhyme (e.g., *an eager beaver, the early bird, drunk as a skunk*). This suggests that phonology plays a non-negligible part in the coinage and the memorability of phrases, too, and may help explain lexical selection where synonyms are available (e.g., *time will tell* rather than *time will say* and *it takes two to tango* rather than *it takes two to waltz*) (e.g., Boers & Lindstromberg, 2005). Can you think of examples of phrases in your native language or any other foreign language you know that use alliteration and rhyme? Are there many such phonologically based phrases in the language you have chosen?

Suggested Student Research Projects

1. Do native speaker teachers become better over time at gauging the degree of semantic opacity of phrases from the learner's vantage

point? Do training sessions that raise teachers' awareness of the noncompositionality of many phrases help teachers make more reliable predictions about their students' (mis)interpretation of phrasal lexis? Address these questions by conducting a repeated measures study. In this study, you need to conduct a pre-test with a group of teachers and another pre-test with a group of learners. In the pre-test, the teachers and learners will be provided with the same list of around 50 idiomatic expressions and asked to rate their transparency on a scale from 1 = not transparent/opaque to 7 = transparent. After you have collected the ratings from both the teachers and the learners, compare their ratings and see if there is a high or low correlation between them. In the next stage of the project, you will prepare a short training session for the group of teachers who participated in your study. In this session, you will discuss such phenomena such as polysemy, homonymy, and cross-cultural variation in metaphor and how these may impede learners' ability to work out the meaning of L2 phrasal expressions. To check the effectiveness of this training, you will ask the teacher participants in a post-test to rate the original list of expressions for transparency again. You will then calculate whether their new estimates are closer to the learners.

2. The majority of effect-of-instruction studies informed by *Cognitive Linguistic Theory* have measured only short-term effects. The evidence suggests that activating a literal reading renders the idioms more memorable – probably owing to *concreteness effects*. Longitudinal studies would be useful to find out if the effect is durable, and whether it is attested not only in learners' recall in discrete-item tests but also in their communicative use of idiomatic expressions. To address this question, prepare a research project in which your experimental group will receive vocabulary instruction emphasizing the concreteness effect (activating literal meanings of newly learned idiomatic expressions), whereas the control group will be taught in a traditional manner, with no emphasis on the literal meaning of the newly learned idioms. Give both groups an immediate recall test after the learning session is over. Which group remembered more idiomatic expressions? As a delayed test, ask both groups to write a composition at home. Analyze compositions from both groups and see which group used more idiomatic phrases in its writing. Did students whose awareness of metaphor was raised through training incorporate more figurative phrases in their essay writing than students who did not receive this training?

Related Internet Sites

International Cognitive Linguistics Association: www.cogling. org

Conceptual Metaphor: www.conceptualmetaphor.net

Suggested Further Readings

Boers, F. (2011). Cognitive Semantic ways of teaching figurative phrases: An assessment. *Review of Cognitive Linguistics, 9,* 227–261.

Boers, F., & Lindstromberg, S. (2012). Experimental and intervention studies on formulaic sequences in a second language. *Annual Review of Applied Linguistics, 32,* 83–110.

REFERENCES

Biber, D., Conrad, S., & Cortes, V. (2004). "If you look at...": Lexical bundles in university teaching and textbooks. *Applied Linguistics, 25,* 371–405.

Boers, F. (2003). Applied linguistics perspectives on cross-cultural variation in conceptual metaphor. *Metaphor and Symbol, 18,* 231–238.

(2011). Cognitive semantic ways of teaching figurative phrases: An assessment. *Review of Cognitive Linguistics, 9,* 227–261.

Boers, F., Demecheleer, M., & Eyckmans, J. (2004a). Etymological elaboration as a strategy for learning figurative idioms. In P. Bogaards & B. Laufer (Eds.), *Vocabulary in a second language: Selection, acquisition and testing* (pp. 53–78). Amsterdam: John Benjamins.

(2004b). Cultural variation as a variable in comprehending and remembering figurative idioms. *European Journal of English Studies, 8,* 375–388.

Boers, F., Demecheleer, M., Coxhead, A., & Webb, S. (2013). Gauging the effects of exercises on verb-noun collocations. *Language Teaching Research.* DOI: 10.1177/1362168813505389

Boers, F., Eyckmans, J., & Stengers, H. (2007). Presenting figurative idioms with a touch of etymology: More than mere mnemonics? *Language Teaching Research, 11,* 43–62.

Boers, F., & Lindstromberg, S. (2005) Finding ways to make phrase-learning feasible: The mnemonic effect of alliteration. *System, 33,* 225–238.

(2009). *Optimizing a lexical approach to instructed second language acquisition.* Basingstoke, UK: Palgrave Macmillan.

(2012). Experimental and intervention studies on formulaic sequences in a second language. *Annual Review of Applied Linguistics, 32,* 83–110.

Boers, F., & Stengers, H. (2008). A quantitative comparison of the English and Spanish repertoires of figurative idioms. In F. Boers & S. Lindstromberg (Eds.), *Cognitive linguistic approaches to teaching vocabulary and phraseology* (pp. 355–374). Berlin: Mouton Degruyter.

Bortfeld, H. (2003). Comprehending idioms cross-linguistically. *Experimental Psychology*, *50*, 217–230.

Cacciari, C., & Glucksberg, S. (1991). Understanding idiomatic expressions: The contribution of word meanings. In G.B. Simpson (Ed.), *Understanding word and sentence* (pp. 217–240). Amsterdam: Elsevier.

Charteris-Black, J. (2002). Second language figurative proficiency: A comparative study of Malay and English. *Applied Linguistics*, *23*, 104–133.

Cieślicka, A. (2006). Literal salience in on-line processing of idiomatic expressions by second language learners. *Second Language Research*, *22*, 115–144.

(2010). Formulaic language in L2: Storage, retrieval and production of idioms by second language learners. In M. Pütz & L. Sicola (Eds.), *Cognitive processing in second language acquisition* (pp. 149–168). Amsterdam: John Benjamins.

Collins Cobuild Dictionary of Idioms (2nd ed.). (2002). Glasgow: Harper Collins Publishers.

Ellis, N.C. (2008). Phraseology: The periphery and the heart of language. In F. Meunier & S. Granger (Eds.), *Phraseology in foreign language learning and teaching* (pp. 1–13). Amsterdam: John Benjamins.

Erman, B., & Warren, B. (2001). The idiom principle and the open choice principle. *Text*, *20*, 87–120.

Fernando, C. (1996). *Idioms and idiomaticity*. Oxford, UK: Oxford University Press.

Fitzpatrick, T., & Wray, A. (2006). Breaking up is not so hard to do: Individual differences in L2 memorization. *Canadian Modern Language Review*, *63*, 35–57.

Gibbs, R.W., Nayak, N.P., & Cutting, C. (1989). How to kick the bucket and not decompose: Analyzability and idiom processing. *Journal of Memory and Language*, *28*, 576–593.

Giora, R. (1997). Understanding figurative and literal language: The graded salience hypothesis. *Cognitive Linguistics*, *7*, 183–206.

Goldberg, A. (2006). *Constructions at work: The nature of generalization in language*. Oxford, UK: Oxford University Press.

Grant, L., & Bauer, L. (2004). Criteria for redefining idioms: Are we barking up the wrong tree? *Applied Linguistics*, *25*, 38–61.

Herrera, H., & White, M. (2010). Canonicity and variation in idiomatic expressions: Evidence from business press headlines. In S. De Knop, F. Boers, & A. De Rycker (Eds.), *Fostering language teaching efficiency through cognitive linguistics* (pp. 167–187). Berlin: Mouton de Gruyter.

Hoey, M. (2005). *Lexical priming: A new theory of words and language*. London: Routledge.

Hu, Y-H. (2002). *A cross-cultural investigation of Mandarin Chinese conceptual metaphors of anger, happiness and romantic love* (Unpublished doctoral dissertation. University of Edinburgh, Edinburgh, UK.

Hu, Y.-H., & Fong, Y.-Y. (2010). Obstacles to conceptual-metaphor guided L2 idiom interpretation. In S. De Knop, F. Boers, & T. De Rycker (Eds.), *Fostering language teaching efficiency through cognitive linguistics* (pp. 293–317). Berlin: Mouton de Gruyter.

Kövecses, Z. (2005). *Metaphor in culture: Universality and variation.* Cambridge, UK: Cambridge University Press.

Lakoff, G., & Johnson, M. (1980). *Metaphors we live by.* Chicago: University of Chicago Press.

Lakoff, G. (1987). *Women, fire and dangerous things: What categories reveal about the mind.* Chicago: University of Chicago Press.

Langacker, R.W. (1990). *Foundations of cognitive grammar, volume 2: Descriptive applications.* Stanford, CA: Stanford University Press.

Laufer, B. (2005). Focus on form in second language vocabulary acquisition. In S. Foster-Cohen (Ed.), *EUROSLA Yearbook 5* (pp. 223–250). Amsterdam: John Benjamins.

Laufer, B., & Girsai, N. (2008). Form-focused instruction in second language vocabulary learning: A case for contrastive analysis and translation. *Applied Linguistics, 29,* 694–716.

Laufer, B., & Waldman, T. (2011). Verb-noun collocations in second language writing: A corpus analysis of learners' English. *Language Learning, 61,* 647–672.

Littlemore, J., Chen, P.T., Koester, A., & Barnden, J. (2011). Difficulties in metaphor comprehension faced by international students whose first language is not English. *Applied Linguistics, 32,* 408–429.

Laurent, J-P., Denhières, G., Passerieux, C., Iakimova, G., & Hardy-Baylé, M-C. (2005). On understanding idiomatic language: The salience hypothesis assessed by ERPs. *Brain Research, 1068,* 151–160.

Liu, D. (2011). The most frequently-used multiword constructions in academic written English: A multi-corpus study. *English for Specific Purposes, 31,* 25–35.

Martinez, R., & Murphy, V.A. (2011). Effect of frequency and idiomaticity on second language reading comprehension. *TESOL Quarterly, 45,* 267–290.

Martinez, R., & Schmitt, N. (2012). A phrasal expressions list. *Applied Linguistics, 33,* 299–320.

Matsuki, K. (1995). Metaphors of anger in Japanese. In J. Taylor & R. MacLaury (Eds.), *Language and the cognitive construal of the world* (pp. 153–179). Berlin: Mouton de Gruyter.

McCarthy, M. (1998). *Spoken language and applied linguistics.* Cambridge, UK: Cambridge University Press.

McCarthy, M., & O'Dell, F. (2002). *English idioms in use.* Cambridge, UK: Cambridge University Press.

(2003). *English idioms in use: Advanced.* Cambridge, UK: Cambridge University Press.

(2005). *English collocations in use.* Cambridge, UK: Cambridge University Press.

(2008). *English collocations in use: Advanced.* Cambridge, UK: Cambridge University Press.

Moon, R. (1998). *Fixed expressions and idioms in English: A corpus-based approach.* Oxford, UK: Clarendon Press.

Nesselhauf, N. (2003). The use of collocations by advanced learners of English and some implications for teaching. *Applied Linguistics, 24,* 223–242.

O'Keeffe, A.M., McCarthy, M., & Carter, R. (2007). *From corpus to classroom: Language use and language teaching.* Cambridge, UK: Cambridge University Press.

Oxford idioms dictionary for learners of English. (2001). New York: Oxford University Press.

Paivio, A. (1986). *Mental representations: A dual coding approach.* New York: Oxford University Press.

Pawley, A., & Syder, F. (1983). Two puzzles for linguistic theory: Nativelike selection and nativelike fluency. In J. Richards & R. Schmidt (Eds.), *Language and communication* (pp. 191–226). London: Longman.

Peters, A.M. (1983). *Units of language acquisition.* Cambridge, UK: Cambridge University Press.

Schmidt, R. (2001). Attention. In P. Obinson (Ed.), *Cognition and second language instruction* (pp. 3–32). Cambridge, UK: Cambridge University Press.

Shin, D., & Nation, P. (2008). Beyond single words: The most frequent collocations in spoken English. *ELTj, 62,* 339–48.

Simpson-Vlach, R., & Ellis, N.C. (2010). An academic formulas list: New methods in phraseology research. *Applied Linguistics, 31,* 487–512.

Sinclair, J. (1991). *Corpus, concordance, collocation.* Oxford, UK: Oxford University Press.

Siyanova, A., Conklin, K., & Schmitt, N. (2011). Adding more fuel to the fire: An eye-tracking study of idiom processing by native and non-native speakers. *Second Language Research, 27,* 251–272.

Sprenger, S.A., Levelt, W.J.M., & Kempen, G. (2006). Lexical access during the production of idiomatic phrases. *Journal of Memory and Language, 54,* 161–184.

Steinel, M.P., Hulstijn, J.H., & Steinel, W. (2007). Second language idiom learning in a paired-associate paradigm: Effects of direction of learning, direction of testing, idiom imageability, and idiom transparency. *Studies in Second Language Acquisition, 29,* 449–484.

Stengers, H. (2007). Is English exceptionally idiomatic? Testing the waters for a lexical approach to Spanish. In F. Boers, J. Darquennes, & R. Temmerman (Eds.), *Multilingualism and applied comparative linguistics: Pedagogical perspectives* (pp. 107–125). Newcastle: Cambridge Scholars Publishing.

Stengers, H., Boers, F., Housen, A., & Eyckmans, J. (2011). Formulaic sequences and L2 oral proficiency: Does the type of target language influence the association? *International Review of Applied Linguistics, 49,* 321–343.

Szczepaniak, R., & Lew, R. (2011). The role of imagery in dictionaries of idioms. *Applied Linguistics 32,* 323–347.

Tabossi, P., Fanari, R., & Wolf, K. (2009). Why are idioms recognized fast? *Memory & Cognition, 37,* 529–540.

Taylor, J. (2006). Polysemy and the lexicon. In G. Kristiansen, M. Achard, R. Dirven, & J. Ruiz de Mendoza Ibañez (Eds.), *Cognitive linguistics: Current applications and future perspectives* (pp. 51–80). Berlin: Mouton de Gruyter.

(2010). Language in the mind. In S. De Knop, F. Boers, & A. De Rycker (Eds.), *Fostering language teaching efficiency through cognitive linguistics* (pp. 29–57). Berlin: Mouton de Gruyter.

Titone, D.A., & Connine, C.M. (1999). On the compositional and noncompositional nature of idiomatic expressions. *Journal of Pragmatics, 31,* 1655–1674

Tomasello, M. (2003). *Constructing a language: A usage-based theory of language acquisition.* Cambridge, MA: Harvard University Press.

Waring, R., & Takaki, M. (2003). At what rate do learners learn and retain new vocabulary from reading a graded reader? *Reading in a Foreign Language, 15,* 130–163.

Webb, S., Newton, J., & Chang, A.C.S. (2013). Incidental learning of collocation. *Language Learning, 63,* 91–120.

Wray, A. (2002). *Formulaic language and the lexicon.* Cambridge, UK: Cambridge University Press.

Appendix: Expressions Used in the Questionnaire (From Least to Most Transparent)

According to the Teachers	According to the Learners
Shoot the breeze	Chew the fat
Chew the fat	Bite the dust
Touch wood	Touch wood
Jump the gun	Jump ship
Bite the dust	Walk the plank
Follow suit	Shoot the breeze
Have a ball	Jump the gun
Pull strings	Hit the roof
Clear the air	Follow suit
Run a bath	Have a ball
Turn the tables	Cut corners
Take root	Pull strings
Lose face	Clear the air
Hit the roof	Stay the course
Have a word	Turn the tables
Run the risk	Make the grade
Draw the line	Run a bath
Stay the course	Kick the habit
Kill time	Take root
Buy time	Have a word
Lose touch	Lose touch
Make the grade	Change the bed
Raise questions	Buy time
Kick the habit	Run the risk
Get the point	Draw the line

(cont.)

According to the Teachers	According to the Learners
Change the bed	Spread the word
Play a part	Lose face
Cut corners	Raise a family
Pay attention	Kill time
Jump ship	Raise questions
Spread the word	Meet a demand
Face facts	Get the point
Meet a demand	Face facts
Run a business	Take turns
Take turns	Play a part
Break a record	Perform surgery
Break the silence	Run a business
Take a photo	Break a record
Raise a family	Close a meeting
Reach a decision	Break the silence
Perform surgery	Turn the page
Catch a cold	Pay attention
Turn the page	Reach a decision
Take a break	Catch a cold
Close a meeting	Take a photo

Author Index

Abe, J-I., 276
Abel, B., 120, 172–173, 177–178, 182, 213, 219–220, 226, 303
Abutalebi, J., 11
Aharon-Peretz, J., 276
Aiello, D., 74
Aine, C.J., 147
Aldunate, N., 252
Alexander, R.J., 209
Almor, A., 90, 93–94, 107
Altamira, W.A., 134
Altarriba, J., 17, 69, 103, 107–108, 130, 133, 143, 147, 181
Altenberg, B., 32
Alvarez, R.P., 150
Anderson, J.R., 90, 94, 108
Andreou, E., 180
Andreou, G., 180
Anes, M.D., 129
Arabski, J., 214
Ariel, M., 231
Arnaud, P.J., 302
Arnell, K.M., 134
Arnon, I., 172, 194
Arunachalam, S., 90
Arzouan, Y., 147
Asarnow, R.F., 252
Athanasopoulus, P., 17
Athanatou, E., 125
Attardo, S., 274
Atwood, M., 171, 177

Baayen, R.H., 172, 194
Bachman, L.F., 324
Bachoud-Levy, A.C., 150
Baker, J., 178
Baldwin, M.W., 288
Bannard, C., 172
Bar, M., 280, 288
Barbe, K., 274, 276
Barber, H.A., 150
Bargh, J.A., 278, 280, 288, 290

Barkema, H., 302
Barlow, J., 209
Barlow, J.M., 302
Barnden, J., 374
Barr, D., 185
Barrett, L.F., 280, 288
Basnight-Brown, D.M., 143
Bates, D.M., 185
Batori, G., 222
Bauer, L., 224, 370, 378
Baumeister, R.F., 285
Beaton, A., 214
Bechara, A., 277, 279
Beeman, M., 132, 224, 227
Bell, S.M., 174, 210, 247
Belnap, R., 214
Ben-Artzi, E., 11
Ben-Zeev, S., 69
Berens, M., 11
Berger, B.D., 276
Berntson, G.G., 278, 285
Bertus, E.L., 273
Besson, M., 252
Bever, T.G., 93
Bialystok, E., 9, 58, 73
Bianco, M., 94
Biber, D., 33, 379
Bickerton, D., 4–5
Binkofski, F., 20
Blair, D., 120–121
Blais, M.J., 120, 140, 157
Blasko, D.G., 57, 91–92, 94, 108, 143,
Blom, S., 17
Blumentritt, T.L., 90, 94, 103, 143, 146
Bobrow, S.A., 174, 210, 247
Bock, K., 174, 211, 227
Boers, F., 172, 209, 217, 223, 233, 302, 372, 374, 376, 378, 381, 385
Bolander, M., 45
Bolger, P.A., 122–123, 128, 130, 134, 137, 150
Bolinger, D., 32

393

Subject Index